Lecture Notes in Computer Science 11279

Commenced Publication in 1973
Founding and Former Series Editors:
Gerhard Goos, Juris Hartmanis, and Jan van Leeuwen

More information about this series at http://www.springer.com/series/7409

Milena Dobreva · Annika Hinze
Maja Žumer (Eds.)

Maturity and Innovation in Digital Libraries

20th International Conference
on Asia-Pacific Digital Libraries, ICADL 2018
Hamilton, New Zealand, November 19–22, 2018
Proceedings

 Springer

Editors
Milena Dobreva 🆔
University College London Qatar
Doha, Qatar

Maja Žumer 🆔
University of Ljubljana
Ljubljana, Slovenia

Annika Hinze 🆔
University of Waikato
Hamilton, New Zealand

ISSN 0302-9743   ISSN 1611-3349   (electronic)
Lecture Notes in Computer Science
ISBN 978-3-030-04256-1   ISBN 978-3-030-04257-8   (eBook)
https://doi.org/10.1007/978-3-030-04257-8

Library of Congress Control Number: 2018960913

LNCS Sublibrary: SL3 – Information Systems and Applications, incl. Internet/Web, and HCI

This Springer imprint is published by the registered company Springer Nature Switzerland AG
The registered company address is: Gewerbestrasse 11, 6330 Cham, Switzerland

Preface by Program Chairs

This volume contains the papers presented at the 20th International Conference on Asia-Pacific Digital Libraries (ICADL 2018), held during November 19–22, 2018, in Hamilton New Zealand. Since its beginnings in Hong Kong in 1998, ICADL has become one of the premier international conferences for digital library research. The conference series explores digital libraries as a broad foundation for interaction with information and information management in the networked information society. Bringing together the achievements in digital libraries research and development from Asia and Oceania with work from around the globe, ICADL serves as a unique forum where the regional drive for exposure of the rich digital collections often requiring out-of-the box solutions meets global excellence.

ICADL 2018 at the University of Waikato in New Zealand offered a further valuable opportunity for researchers, educators, and practitioners to share their experiences and innovative developments. The conference was held at Waikato University in Hamilton, New Zealand, a city of 140,000 people centered on the Waikato River in the heart of New Zealand's rolling pastures. The main theme of ICADL 2018 was "Maturity and Innovation in Digital Libraries." We invited high-quality, original research papers as well as practitioner papers identifying research problems and future directions. Submissions that resonate with the conference's theme were especially welcome, but all topics in digital libraries were given equal consideration.

After 20 years, digital libraries have certainly reached maturity. At first glance, research of digital libraries on the general level is no longer needed and the focus has moved to more specialized areas – but in fact many new challenges have arisen. The proliferation of social media, a renewed interest in cultural heritage, digital humanities, research data management, new privacy legislation, changing user information behavior are only some of the topics that require a thorough discussion and an interdisciplinary approach. ICADL remains an excellent opportunity to bring together expertise from the region and beyond to explore the challenges and foster innovation.

The 2018 ICADL conference was co-located with the annual meeting of the Asia-Pacific iSchools Consortium and brought together a diverse group of academic and professional community members from all parts of the world to exchange their knowledge, experience, and practices in digital libraries and other related fields.

ICADL 2018 received 77 submissions from over 20 countries, attracting also this year some submissions from the Middle East, a region that does not have its own designated digital library forum. Each paper was carefully reviewed by the Program Committee members. Finally, 20 full papers and six short papers were selected to be presented, and 11 submissions were invited as work-in-progress papers. The submissions to ICADL 2018 covered a wide spectrum of topics from various areas, including semantic modeling, social media, Web and news archiving, heritage and localization, user experience, digital library technology, digital library use cases, research data management, librarianship, and education.

On behalf of the Organizing and Program Committees of ICADL 2018, we would like to express our appreciation to all the authors and attendees for participating in the conference. We also thank the sponsors, Program Committee members, external reviewers, supporting organizations, and volunteers for making the conference a success. Without their efforts, the conference would not have been possible.

We also acknowledge the University of Waikato for hosting the conference and hope the following years of this forum bring further maturity and innovation drive to the global digital library community.

November 2018   Milena Dobreva
                                                                Annika Hinze
                                                                Maja Žumer

Preface by Steering Committee Chair

The International Conference on Asia-Pacific Digital Libraries (ICADL) started in 1998 in Hong Kong. ICADL is widely recognized as a top-level international conference similar to conferences such as JCDL and TPDL (formerly ECDL), although geographically based in the Asia-Pacific region. The conference has been successful in not only collecting novel research results, but also connecting people across global and regional communities. The Asia-Pacific region has significant diversity in many aspects such as culture, language, and development levels, and ICADL has been successful in bringing novel technologies and ideas to the regional communities and connecting their members.

In its 20-year history, ICADL has been held in 12 countries across the Asia-Pacific region. The 20th conference was hosted by the University of Waikato in New Zealand – a country that ICADL has never visited. The University of Waikato is well known in the digital library community as a leading institution from the early days of digital libraries research, e.g., Greenstone Digital Library.

As the chair of the Steering Committee of ICADL, I would like to thank the organizers of ICADL 2018 for their tremendous efforts. I would also like to thank all the organizers of the past conferences who have contributed not only in keeping the quality of ICADL high but also in helping establish and expand the Asia-Pacific digital library research community. Last but not least, I would like to thank all the people who have contributed to ICADL as an author, a reviewer, a tutor, a workshop organizer, or audience member.

Shigeo Sugimoto

Organization

Program Committee Co-chairs

Annika Hinze · · · · · · University of Waikato, New Zealand
Maja Žumer · · · · · · · University of Ljubljana, Slovenia
Milena Dobreva · · · · · UCL Qatar, Qatar

General Conference Chairs

Sally Jo Cunningham · · · University of Waikato, New Zealand
David Bainbridge · · · · University of Waikato, New Zealand

Workshop and Tutorial Chair

Trond Aalberg · · · · · · Norwegian University of Science and Technology,
Norway

Poster and Work-in-Progress Chair

Fernando Loizides · · · · Cardiff University, UK

Doctoral Consortium Chairs

Sally Jo Cunningham · · · University of Waikato, New Zealand
Nicholas Vanderschantz · · University of Waikato, New Zealand

Treasurer

David Nichols · · · · · · University of Waikato, New Zealand

Local Organization

Renee Hoad
Tania Robinson
Bronwyn Webster

Program Committee and Reviewers

Trond Aalberg · · · · · · Norwegian University of Science and Technology,
Norway
Sultan Al-Daihani · · · · University of Kuwait, Kuwait
Mohammad Aliannejadi · · University of Lugano (USI), Switzerland

Contents

Heritage and Localization

User Experience

Digital Library Technology

Use Cases and Digital Librarianship

Topic Modelling and Semantic Analysis

Evaluating the Impact of OCR Errors
on Topic Modeling

Stephen Mutuvi[1], Antoine Doucet[2(✉)], Moses Odeo[1], and Adam Jatowt[3]

[1] Multimedia University Kenya, Nairobi, Kenya
smutuvi@mmu.ac.ke
[2] La Rochelle University, La Rochelle, France
antoine.doucet@univ-lr.fr
[3] Kyoto University, Kyoto, Japan

Abstract. Historical documents pose a challenge for character recognition due to various reasons such as font disparities across different materials, lack of orthographic standards where same words are spelled differently, material quality and unavailability of lexicons of known historical spelling variants. As a result, optical character recognition (OCR) of those documents often yield unsatisfactory OCR accuracy and render digital material only partially discoverable and the data they hold difficult to process. In this paper, we explore the impact of OCR errors on the identification of topics from a corpus comprising text from historical OCRed documents. Based on experiments performed on OCR text corpora, we observe that OCR noise negatively impacts the stability and coherence of topics generated by topic modeling algorithms and we quantify the strength of this impact.

Keywords: Topic modeling · Topic coherence · Text mining
Topic stability

1 Introduction

Recently, there has been rapid increase in digitization of historical documents such as books and newspapers. The digitization aims at preserving the documents in a digital form that can enhance access, allow full text search and support efficient sophisticated processing using natural language processing (NLP) techniques. An important step in the digitization process is the application of optical character recognition (OCR) techniques, which involve translating the documents into machine processable text.

OCR produces its best results from well-printed, modern documents. However, historical documents still pose a challenge for character recognition and therefore OCR of such documents still does not yield satisfying results. Some of

This work has been supported by the European Union's Horizon 2020 research and innovation programme under grant 770299 (NewsEye).

© Springer Nature Switzerland AG 2018
M. Dobreva et al. (Eds.): ICADL 2018, LNCS 11279, pp. 3–14, 2018.
https://doi.org/10.1007/978-3-030-04257-8_1

the reasons why historical documents still pose a challenge include font variation across different materials, same words spelled differently, material quality where some documents can have deformations and unavailability of a lexicon of known historical spelling variants [1]. These factors reduce the accuracy of recognition which affects the processing of the documents and, overall, the use of digital libraries.

Among the NLP tasks that can be performed on digitized data is the extraction of topics, a process known as topic modeling. Topic modeling has become a common topic analysis tool for text exploration. The approach attempts to obtain thematic patterns from large unstructured collections of text by grouping documents into coherent topics. Among the common topic modeling techniques are the Latent Dirichlet Allocation (LDA) [3] and the Non-negative Matrix factorization (NMF) [11]. The basic idea of LDA is that the documents are represented as random mixtures over latent topics, where a topic is characterized by a distribution over words [30]. The standard implementation of both the LDA and NMF rely on stochastic elements in their initialization phase which can potentially lead to instability of the topics generated and the terms that describe those topics [14]. This phenomena where different runs of the same algorithm on the same data produce different outcomes manifests itself in two aspects. First, when examining the top terms representing each topic (i.e. topic descriptors) over multiple runs, certain terms may appear or disappear completely between runs. Secondly, instability can be observed when examining the degree to which documents have been associated with topics across different runs of the same algorithm on the same corpus. In both cases, such inconsistencies can potentially affect the performance of topic models. Measuring the stability and coherence of topics generated over the different runs is critical to ascertain the model's performance, as any individual run cannot decisively determine the underlying topics in a given text corpus [14].

This study examines the effect of noise on unsupervised topic modeling algorithms, through comparison of performance of both the LDA and NMF topic models in the presence of OCR errors. Using a dataset comprising corpus of OCRed documents described in Sect. 4, both the topic stability and coherence scores are obtained and comparison of models' performance on noisy and the corrected OCR text is conducted. To the best of our knowledge, no other study has attempted to evaluate both the stability and coherence of the two models on noisy OCR text corpora.

The remainder of the paper is structured as follows. In Sect. 2 we discuss related work on topic modeling on OCR data. In Sect. 3 we describe the metrics for evaluating the performance of topic models, namely topic stability and coherence, before evaluating LDA and NMF topic models in the presence of noisy OCR in Sect. 4. We discuss the experiment results and conclusion of the paper with ideas for future work in Sects. 5 and 6, respectively.

2   Related Work

2.1   OCR Errors and Topic Modeling

Optical Character Recognition (OCR) enables translation of scanned graphical text into editable computer text. This can substantially improve the usability of the digitized documents allowing for efficient searching and other NLP applications. OCR produces its best results from well-printed, modern documents. Historical documents, however pose a challenge for character recognition and their character recognition does not yield satisfying results. Common OCR errors include punctuation errors, case sensitivity, character format, word meaning and segmentation error where spacings in different line, word or character lead to mis-recognitions of white-spaces [22]. OCR errors may also stem from other sources such as font variation across different materials, historical spelling variations, material quality or language specific to different media texts [1].

While OCR errors remain part of a wider problem of dealing with "noise" in text mining [23], their impact varies depending on the task performed [24]. NLP tasks such as machine translation, sentence boundary detection, tokenization, and part-of-speech tagging on text among others can all be compromised by OCR errors [25]. Studies have evaluated effect of OCR errors on supervised document classification [28,29], information retrieval [26,27], and a more general set of natural language processing tasks [25]. The effect of OCR errors on document clustering and topic modeling has also been studied [9]. The results indicated that the errors had little impact on performance for the clustering task, but had a greater impact on performance for the topic modeling task. Another study explored supervised topic models in the presence of OCR errors and revealed that OCR errors had insignificant impact [31].

While results suggest that OCR errors have small impact on performance of supervised NLP tasks, the errors should be considered thoroughly for the case of unsupervised topic modeling as the models are known to degrade in the presence of OCR errors [9,31]. We thus focus in this work on OCR impacts for unsupervised topics models and in particular on their coherence and stability, and our studies are conducted on large document collection.

2.2   Topic Modeling Algorithms

Topic models aim to discover the underlying semantic structure within large corpus of documents. Several methods such as probabilistic topic models and techniques based on matrix factorization have been proposed in the literature. Much of the prior research on topic modeling has focused on the use of probabilistic methods, where a topic is viewed as a probability distribution over words, with documents being mixtures of topics [2]. One of the most commonly used probabilistic algorithms for topic modeling is the Latent Dirichlet Allocation (LDA) [3]. This is due to its simplicity and capability to uncover hidden thematic patterns in text with little human supervision. LDA represents topics by word probabilities, where words with highest probabilities in each topic determine the topic. Each latent topic in the LDA model is also represented as a probabilistic distribution over words and the word distributions of topics share a common Dirichlet prior. The generative process of LDA is illustrated as follows [3]:

 (i) Choose a multinomial topic distribution θ for the document (according to a Dirichlet distribution $\text{Dir}(\alpha)$ over a fixed set of k topics)?
 (ii) Choose a multinomial term distribution φ for the topic (according to a Dirichlet distribution $\text{Dir}(\beta)$ over a fixed set of N terms)
(iii) For each word position
   (a) Choose a topic Z according to multinomial topic distribution θ.
   (b) Choose a word W according to multinomial term distribution φ.

Various studies have applied probabilistic latent semantic analysis (pLSA) model [4] and LDA model [5] on newspaper corpora to discover topics and trends over time. Similarly, LDA has been used to find research topic trends on a dataset comprising abstracts of scientific papers [2]. Both pLSA and LDA models are probabilistic models that look at each document as a mixture of topics [6]. The models decompose the document collection into groups of words representing the main topics. Several topic models were compared, including LDA, correlated topic model (CTM), and probabilistic latent semantic indexing (pLSI), and it has been found that LDA generally worked comparably well or better than the other two at predicting topics that match topics picked by human annotators [7]. MAchine Learning for LanguagE Toolkit (MALLET) [8] was used to test the effects of noisy optical character recognition (OCR) data using LDA [9]. The toolkit has also been used to mine topics from the Civil War era newspaper dispatch [5], and in another study to examine general topics and to identify emotional moments from Martha Ballards diary [10].

Non-negative Matrix Factorization (NMF) [11] has also been effective in discovering topics in text corpora [12,13]. NMF factors high-dimensional vectors into a low-dimensionality representation. The goal of NMF is to approximate a document-term matrix $\mathbf{A}$ as the product of two non-negative factors $\mathbf{W}$ and $\mathbf{H}$, each with k dimensions that can be interpreted as k topics. Like LDA, the number of topics k to generate is chosen beforehand. The values of $\mathbf{H}$ and $\mathbf{W}$ provide term weights which can be used to generate topic descriptions and topic memberships for documents respectively. The rows of the factor $\mathbf{H}$ can be interpreted as k topics, defined by non-negative weights for each [14].

3 Topic Model Stability

The output of topic modeling procedures is often presented in the form of lists of top-ranked terms suitable for human interpretation. A general way to represent the output of a topic modeling algorithm is in the form of a ranking set containing k ranked lists, denoted $S = R_1, ..., R_k$. The ith topic produced by the algorithm is represented by the list R_i, containing the top t terms which are most characteristic of that topic according to some criterion [15].

The stability of a clustering algorithm refers to its ability to consistently produce similar results on data originating from the same source [16]. Standard implementations of topic modeling approaches, such as LDA and NMF, commonly employ stochastic initialization prior to optimization. As a result, the algorithms can achieve different results on the same data or data drawn from the same source, between different runs [14]. The variation manifests itself either in relation to term-topic associations or document-topic associations. In the former, the ranking of the top terms that describe a topic can change significantly between runs. In the latter, documents may be strongly associated with a given topic in one run, but may be more closely associated with an alternative topic in another run [14].

To quantify the level of stability or instability present in a collection of topic models $\{M_1, ..., M_r\}$ generated over r runs on the same corpus, the Average Term Stability (ATS) and Pairwise Normalized Mutual Information (PNMI) measures have been proposed [14].

We begin by determining the Term Stability (TS) score, which involves comparison of the similarity between two topic models based on a pairwise matching process. The measuring of the similarity between a pair of individual topics represented by their top t terms is based on the Jaccard Index:

$$Jac(R_i, R_j) = \frac{|R_i \cap R_j|}{|R_i \cup R_j|} \tag{1}$$

where R_i denotes the top t ranked terms for the i-th topic (topic descriptor). We can use Eq. 1 to build a measure of the agreement between two complete topic models (i.e., Term Stability).

$$TS(M_i, M_j) = \frac{1}{k} \sum_{x=1}^{k} Jac(R_{ix}, \pi(R_{ix})) \tag{2}$$

where $\pi(R_{ix})$ denotes the topic in model M_j matched to R_{ix} in model M_i by the permutation π. Values for TS take the range $[0, 1]$, where similarity between two topic models will result in a score of 1 if identical.

For a collection of topic models M_r, we can calculate the Average Term Stability (ATS):

$$ATS = \frac{1}{r \times (r-1)} \sum_{i,j:i \neq j}^{r} TS(M_i, M_j) \tag{3}$$

where a score of 1 indicates that all pairs of topic descriptors matched together across the r runs contain the same top t terms [14].

Topic model stability can also be established from document-topic associations. PNMI determines the extent to which the dominant topic for each document varies between multiple runs. The overall level of agreement between a set of partitions generated by r runs of an algorithm on the same corpus can be computed as the mean Pairwise Normalized Mutual Information (PNMI) for all pairs:

$$PNMI = \frac{1}{r \times (r-1)} \sum_{i,j:i\neq j}^{r} NMI(P_i, P_j) \tag{4}$$

where P_i is the partition produced from the document-topic associations in model M_i. If the partitions across all models are identical, PNMI will yield a value of 1.

3.1 Quality of Topics

While topic model stability is important, it is unlikely to be useful without meaningful and coherent topics [14]. Measuring topic coherence is critical in assessing the performance of topic modeling approaches in extracting comprehensible and coherent topics from corpora [17]. The intuition behind measuring coherence is that more coherent topics will have their top terms co-occurring more often together across the corpus. A number of approaches for evaluating coherence exist, although many of these are specific to LDA. A more general approach is the Topic Coherence via Word2Vec (TC-W2V), which evaluates the relatedness of a set of top terms describing a topic [18]. TC-W2V uses the increasingly popular word2vec tool [21] to compute a set of vector representations for all of the terms in a large corpus. The extent to which the two corresponding terms share a common meaning or context (e.g. are related to the same topic) is assessed by measuring the similarity between pairs of term vectors. Topics with descriptors consisting of highly-similar terms, as defined by the similarity between their vectors, should be more semantically coherent [19].

TC-W2V operates as follows. The coherence of a single topic t_h represented by its t top ranked terms is given by the mean pairwise cosine similarity between the t corresponding term vectors generated by the *word2vec* model [18].

$$\text{coh}(t_h) = \frac{1}{\binom{t}{2}} \sum_{j=2}^{t} \sum_{i=1}^{j-1} cosine(wv_i, wv_j) \tag{5}$$

An overall score for the coherence of a topic model T consisting of k topics is given by the mean of the individual topic coherence scores:

$$\text{coh}(T) = \frac{1}{k} \sum_{h=1}^{k} \text{coh}(t_h) \tag{6}$$

In the next section, we use the theory described in this section to determine the stability and coherence scores of topics generated by LDA and NMF topic models, from the data described in Sect. 4.1.

4   Experiments

In this section, we seek to apply topic modeling techniques, LDA and NMF, on the OCR text corpus described below, in an attempt to answer the following two questions:

(i) To what extent do OCR errors affect the stability of topic models?
(ii) How do the topic models compare in terms of topic coherence, in the presence of OCR errors?

4.1   Data Source

A large corpus of historical documents [20], comprising twelve million OCRed characters along with the corresponding Gold Standard (GS) was used to model topics. This dataset comprising monographs and periodical has an equal share of English- and French-written documents ranging over four centuries. The documents are sourced from different digital collections available, among others, at the National Library of France (BnF) and the British Library (BL). The corresponding GS comes both from BnF's internal projects and external initiatives such as Europeana Newspapers, IMPACT, Project Gutenberg, Perseus, Wikisource and Bank of Wisdom [20].

4.2   Experimental Setup

The experiment process involved applying LDA and NMF topic models to the noisy OCRed_toInput, aligned OCRed and Gold Standard (GS) text data. Only the english language documents from the dataset was considered in the experiment. The OCRed_toInput is the raw OCRed text while the aligned OCR and GS represent the corrected version of the text corpus provided for training and testing purposes. The alignment was made at the character level using "@" symbols with "#" symbols corresponding to the absence of GS either related to alignment uncertainties or related to unreadable characters in the source document [20].

The three categories of text were extracted from the corpus, separately preprocessed and the models were applied on each one of them to obtain topics. Fifty topic models (M_{50}) for each value of k, where k is the number of topics ranging from 2 to 8, were generated for both the NMF and LDA. The selection of this number of topic k was based on a previous study which proposed an approach for choosing this parameter using a term-centric stability analysis strategy [15]. The LDA algorithm was implemented using the popular Mallet implementation with Gibbs sampling [8].

The stability measures for the two topic modeling techniques were obtained and evaluated to determine their performance on the noisy and corrected OCR text. A high level of agreement between the term rankings generated over multiple runs of the same model is an indication of high topic stability [15]. The assumption in this study was that noisy OCRed text would register a lower topic stability value compared to the corrected text, an indication that OCR errors have a negative impact on topic models.

4.3   Evaluation of Stability

To assess the stability of topics generated by each model, the term-based measure (ATS) for each topic's top 10 terms and the document-level (PNMI) measure were computed using Eqs. 3 and 4, respectively. The results of the average topic stability and the average partition stability are shown in Tables 1 and 2, respectively. Figure 1 provides a graphical representation of LDA and NMF stability scores on the different dataset categories.

Table 1. Average topic stability.

Model	Dataset	Mean stability
LDA	GS_aligned	0.265*
LDA	OCR_aligned	0.256
LDA	OCR_toInput	0.252*
NMF	GS_aligned	0.414*
NMF	OCR_aligned	0.384
NMF	OCR_toInput	0.383*

Asterisk (*) indicates p-value was less than 0.05 for independent samples t-test

Both models recorded higher average topic stability on the aligned text compared to the raw OCR text. The mean stability on the Gold Standard text was 0.265 and 0.414 while for the noisy OCR text was 0.252 and 0.383 for LDA and NMF topic models, respectively.

Table 2. Average partition stability.

Model	Dataset	Mean stability
LDA	GS_aligned	0.115
LDA	OCR_aligned	0.115
LDA	OCR_toInput	0.114
NMF	GS_aligned	0.117*
NMF	OCR_aligned	0.115
NMF	OCR_toInput	0.114*

Asterisk (*) indicates p-value was less than 0.05 for independent samples t-test

The average partition stability for LDA remained unchanged for both aligned and raw OCR text. However, NMF recorded a mean partition stability score of 0.117 and 0.114 for the Gold Standard and raw OCR text, respectively.

4.4 Topic Coherence Evaluation

The quality of the topics generated by the models was evaluated by computing the coherence of the topic descriptors using the approach described in Sect. 3.1.

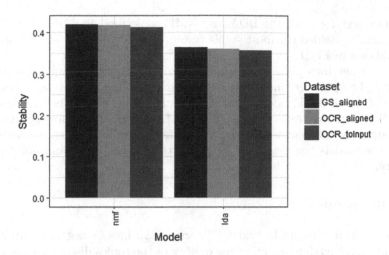

Fig. 1. Model stability on noisy and corrected OCR texts.

The results of the average coherence score for LDA and NMF algorithms, on the noisy and corrected data are presented in Table 3.

Table 3. Mean topic coherence.

Model	Dataset	Mean coherence
LDA	GS_aligned	0.3622
LDA	OCR_aligned	0.3585
LDA	OCR_toInput	0.3529
NMF	GS_aligned	0.4748
NMF	OCR_aligned	0.4737
NMF	OCR_toInput	0.4720

The mean coherence score on the aligned OCR text was 0.4737 and 0.3585 for NMF and LDA algorithms respectively. On the other hand, the mean coherence using the raw OCR text was marginally lower recording 0.4720 for NMF and 0.3529 for LDA topic model.

5 Discussions

Topic modeling algorithms have been evaluated based on model quality and stability criteria. The quality and stability of the algorithms was determined by examining topic coherence and term and document stability respectively. Overall, the aligned corpus text had higher stability score compared to the noisy

OCR input text for both the LDA and NMF topic modeling techniques. The NMF algorithm yielded the most stable results both at the term and document-level, as shown in Fig. 1.

On the other hand, the evaluation of topic coherence showed topics from the corrected corpus were more coherent compared to the original noisy text for both the LDA and NMF models. As expected, LDA had a lower coherence score than NMF, which may reflect the tendency of LDA to produce more generic and less semantically-coherent terms [18]. The difference in average coherence score between the models was relatively small for the aligned OCR and noisy OCR text corpus.

6 Conclusions

It is evident from this study that OCR errors can have a negative impact on topic modeling, therefore affecting the quality of the topics discovered from text datasets. Overall, this can impede the exploration and exploitation of valuable historical documents which require use of OCR techniques to enable their digitization. Advanced OCR post correction techniques are required to address the impact of OCR errors on topic models.

Future research can explore the impact of OCR errors on the accuracy of other text mining tasks such sentiment analysis, document summarization and named entity extraction. In addition, multi-modal text mining approaches that put into consideration textual and visual elements can be explored to determine their suitability in processing and mining of historical texts. Evaluating the stability and coherence for different number of topic models can also be examined further.

References

1. Silfverberg, M., Rueter, J.: Can morphological analyzers improve the quality of optical character recognition? In: Septentrio Conference Series, vol. 2, pp. 45–56 (2015)
2. Rosen-Zvi, M., Griffiths, T., Steyvers, M., Smyth, P.: The author-topic model for authors and documents. In: Proceedings of the 20th Conference on Uncertainty in Artificial Intelligence, pp. 487–494. AUAI Press (2004)
3. Blei, D.M., Ng, A.Y., Jordan, M.I.: Latent dirichlet allocation. J. Mach. Learn. Res. **3**, 993–1022 (2003)
4. Newman, D.J., Block, S.: Probabilistic topic decomposition of an eighteenth-century American newspaper. J. Assoc. Inf. Sci. Technol. **57**(6), 753–767 (2006)
5. Nelson, R.K.: Mining the dispatch (2010)
6. Yang, T.I., Torget, A.J., Mihalcea, R.: Topic modeling on historical newspapers. In: Proceedings of the 5th ACL-HLT Workshop on Language Technology for Cultural Heritage, Social Sciences and Humanities, pp. 96–104. Association for Computational Linguistics (2011)
7. Chang, J., Gerrish, S., Wang, C., Boyd-Graber, J.L., Blei, D.M.: Reading tea leaves: how humans interpret topic models. In: Advances in Neural Information Processing Systems, pp. 288–296 (2009)

8. McCallum, A.K.: Mallet: a machine learning for language toolkit (2002)
9. Walker, D.D., Lund, W.B., Ringger, E.K.: Evaluating models of latent document semantics in the presence of OCR errors. In: Proceedings of the 2010 Conference on Empirical Methods in Natural Language Processing, pp. 240–250. Association for Computational Linguistics (2010)
10. Blevins, C.: Topic modeling Martha Ballard's diary. http://historying.org/2010/04/01/topic-modeling-martha-ballards-diary. Accessed 23 Feb 2018
11. Lee, D.D., Seung, H.S.: Learning the parts of objects by non-negative matrix factorization. Nature **401**, 788–91 (1999)
12. Arora, S., Ge, R., Moitra, A.: Learning topic models - going beyond SVD. In: Proceedings of 53rd Symposium on Foundations of Computer Science, pp. 1–10. IEEE (2012)
13. Kuang, D., Choo, J., Park, H.: Nonnegative matrix factorization for interactive topic modeling and document clustering. In: Celebi, M.E. (ed.) Partitional Clustering Algorithms, pp. 215–243. Springer, Cham (2015). https://doi.org/10.1007/978-3-319-09259-1_7
14. Belford, M., Mac Namee, B., Greene, D.: Stability of topic modeling via matrix factorization. Expert Syst. Appl. **91**, 159–169 (2018)
15. Greene, D., O'Callaghan, D., Cunningham, P.: How many topics? Stability analysis for topic models. In: Calders, T., Esposito, F., Hüllermeier, E., Meo, R. (eds.) ECML PKDD 2014. LNCS (LNAI), vol. 8724, pp. 498–513. Springer, Heidelberg (2014). https://doi.org/10.1007/978-3-662-44848-9_32
16. Lange, T., Roth, V., Braun, M.L., Buhmann, J.M.: Stability-based validation of clustering solutions. Neural Comput. **16**(6), 1299–1323 (2004)
17. Fang, A., Macdonald, C., Ounis, I., Habel, P.: Using word embedding to evaluate the coherence of topics from Twitter data. In: Proceedings of the 39th International ACM SIGIR Conference on Research and Development in Information Retrieval - SIGIR 2016, pp. 1057–1060 (2016)
18. O'Callaghan, D., Greene, D., Carthy, J., Cunningham, P.: An analysis of the coherence of descriptors in topic modeling. Expert Syst. Appl. **42**(13), 5645–5657 (2015)
19. Greene, D., Cross, J.P.: Exploring the political agenda of the European parliament using a dynamic topic modeling approach. Polit. Anal. **25**, 77–94 (2017)
20. Chiron, G., Doucet, A., Coustaty, M., Visani, M., Moreux, J.P.: Impact of OCR errors on the use of digital libraries: towards a better access to information. In: Proceedings of the ACM/IEEE Joint Conference on Digital Libraries (2017)
21. Mikolov, T., Chen, K., Corrado, G., Dean, J.: Efficient estimation of word representations in vector space (2013)
22. Afli, H., Barrault, L., Schwenk, H.: OCR error correction using statistical machine translation. In: 16th International Conference Intelligent Text Processing Computational Linguistics (CICLing 2015), vol. 7, pp. 175–191 (2015)
23. Knoblock, C., Lopresti, D., Roy, S., Subramaniam, V.: Special issue on noisy text analytics. Int. J. Doc. Anal. Recogn. **10**(3–4), 127–128 (2007)
24. Eder, M.: Mind your corpus: systematic errors in authorship attribution. Literary Linguist. Comput. **10**, 1093 (2013)
25. Lopresti, D.: Optical character recognition errors and their effects on natural language processing. Presented at The Second Workshop on Analytics for Noisy Unstructured Text Data, Sponsored by ACM (2008)
26. Taghva, K., Borsack, J., Condit, A.: Results of applying probabilistic IR to OCR text. In: Croft, B.W., van Rijsbergen, C.J. (eds.) SIGIR 1994, pp. 202–211. Springer, New York (1994)

27. Beitzel, S., Jensen, E.C., Grossman, D.A.: A survey of retrieval strategies for OCR text collections. In: Proceedings of 2003 Symposium on Document Image Understanding Technology (2003)
28. Taghva, K., Nartker, T., Borsack, J., Lumos, S., Condit, A., Young, R.: Evaluating text categorization in the presence of OCR errors. In: Document Recognition and Retrieval VIII. International Society for Optics and Photonics, vol. 4307, pp. 68–75 (2000)
29. Agarwal, S., Godbole, S., Punjani, D., Roy, S.: How much noise is too much: a study in automatic text classification. In: Proceedings of the Seventh IEEE International Conference on Data Mining, ICDM 2007, pp. 3–12 (2007)
30. Steyvers, M., Griffiths, T.: Probabilistic topic models. In: Handbook of Latent Semantic Analysis, vol. 427, no. 7, pp. 424–440 (2007)
31. Walker, D., Ringger, E., Seppi, K.: Evaluating supervised topic models in the presence of OCR errors. In: Document Recognition and Retrieval XX, vol. 8658, p. 865812. International Society for Optics and Photonics (2013)

Measuring the Semantic World – How to Map Meaning to High-Dimensional Entity Clusters in PubMed?

Janus Wawrzinek[(✉)] and Wolf-Tilo Balke

IFIS TU-Braunschweig, Mühlenpfordstrasse 23, 38106 Brunswick, Germany
{wawrzinek, balke}@ifis.cs.tu-bs.de

Abstract. The exponential increase of scientific publications in the medical field urgently calls for innovative access paths beyond the limits of a term-based search. As an example, the search term "diabetes" leads to a result of over 600,000 publications in the medical digital library PubMed. In such cases, the automatic extraction of semantic relations between important entities like active substances, diseases, and genes can help to reveal entity-relationships and thus allow simplified access to the knowledge embedded in digital libraries. On the other hand, for semantic-relation tasks distributional embedding models based on neural networks promise considerable progress in terms of accuracy, performance and scalability. Yet, despite the recent successes of neural networks in this field, questions arise related to their non-deterministic nature: Are the semantic relations meaningful, and perhaps even new and unknown entity-relationships? In this paper, we address this question by measuring the associations between important pharmaceutical entities such as *active substances (drugs)* and *diseases* in high-dimensional embedded space. In our investigation, we show that while on one hand only few of the contextualized associations directly correlate with spatial distance, on the other hand we have discovered their potential for predicting new associations, which makes the method suitable as a new, literature-based technique for important practical tasks like e.g., drug repurposing.

Keywords: Digital libraries · Information extraction · Neural embeddings

1 Introduction

In digital libraries the increasing information flood requires new and innovative access paths that go beyond simple term-based searches. This is of particular interest in the scientific field where the number of publications is growing exponentially [17] and access to knowledge is getting increasingly difficult, such as to (a) *medical entities* like active substances, diseases, or genes and (b) *their relations*. However, these entities and their relations play a central role in the exploration and understanding of entity relationships [2]. Extracting entity relations automatically is therefore of particular interest, because it bears the potential for new insights and numerous innovative applications in important medical research areas such as the discovery of new drug-disease associations (DDAs) needed, e.g., for drug repurposing [14]. Previous work has recognized

© Springer Nature Switzerland AG 2018
M. Dobreva et al. (Eds.): ICADL 2018, LNCS 11279, pp. 15–27, 2018.
https://doi.org/10.1007/978-3-030-04257-8_2

this trend and focuses on the recognition of these pharmaceutical entities and their relationships [3, 6, 9]. *What is a DDA?* A DDA is in general an effect of drug x on disease y [3], which means (a) an active substance helps (cures, prevents, alleviates) a certain disease or (b) an active substance causes/triggers a disease in the sense of a side effect. *Why are DDAs of interest?* DDAs are considered as potential candidates for drug repurposing. Pharmaceutical research attempts to use well-known and well-proven active substances against other diseases. This generally leads to a lower risk (in the sense of well-known side effects [4]) and significantly lower costs [4, 6]. Based on the interests mentioned above, numerous computer-based methods were developed to derive DDAs from text corpora as well as from specialized databases [9]. The similarity between active substances and diseases forms the basis here, and numerous popular methods exists for calculating a similarity between these pharmaceutical entities such as chemical (sub) structure similarity [8] or network-based similarity [4].

Newer approaches attempt to derive an intrinsic connection between pharmaceutical entities with a linguistic, context-based similarity [7, 10, 11]. The basic idea is the distributional hypothesis: a similar linguistic word-context indicates a similar meaning (or properties) of the entities contained in texts. In this kind of entity-contextualization the currently popular distributional semantic models (also embedding models or neural language models) play a major role because they enable an efficient way for learning semantic word-similarities in huge corpora. However, non-deterministic word-embedding models like Word2Vec are on one hand popular models for semantic, as well as analogy tasks, but on the other hand their properties are not fully investigated [15].

In this context, we address the following research questions: (Q1) Is a meaningful DDA also represented in the word embedding space and can we measure it in terms of a linguistic distance? (Q2) How can this be measured, evaluated, and what are meaningful baselines and datasets? (Q3) Since a word-context is learned on the basis of millions of publications, is new knowledge discovered with this kind of contextualization? (Q4) Are even DDA predictions possible with such models, and if so, how high is the respective *predictive factor*?

In this paper we answer all these questions and follow our use case of pharmaceutical entities drug/disease and their relations (DDAs). We evaluate the embedded entities both with manually curated data from specialized pharmaceutical databases as well as text-mining approaches. In addition, we carry out a retrospective analysis, which shows that low-distance relations (which previously did not explicitly occur in documents) will actually occur in future publications with a high probability. This indicates that a future relation already exists at an early stage in embedded space which can also help us to reveal a future drug-disease relation. The paper is organized as follows: Sect. 2 revisits related work accompanied by our extensive investigation of embedded drug-disease associations in Sect. 3. We close with conclusions in Sect. 4.

2   Related Work

Research in the field of digital libraries has long been concerned with semantically meaningful similarities for entities and their relations. With a high degree of *manual curation* numerous existing systems guarantee a reliable basis for value-adding services and research planning. On the one hand, automation can help to handle the *explosion* of scientific publications in this field, but on the other hand automation should not have a negative impact on quality, i.e. a high degree of precision has to be guaranteed. Arguably, the Comparative Toxogenomics Database (CTD[1]) is one of the best databases for curated relations between drugs and diseases. CTD contains both curated and derived drug-disease relationships. Because of the high quality, we use the curated relationships from CTD as ground-truth. Although manual curation achieves the highest quality it also comes with high expenses and tends to be incomplete [20]. In the past this led to the development of methods for automatic extraction of DDAs: *Drug-centric:* These approaches try to infer new and unknown properties (e.g. new application/side effect) of drugs from a drug-to-drug-similarity by means of chemical (sub-) structure (chemical similarity) [8]. *Disease-Centric:* This approach calculates a similarity based on diseases and their characteristics. The hypothesis is: The same active substances can also be used for similar diseases (guilt-by-association rule, [14]). For example, phenotype information is compared to determine disease-similarity, whereby similar phenotypes indicate similar diseases. *Drug Disease Mutual:* This approach is also known as the network-based approach and uses both, drug-centric and disease-centric approaches to derive/predict DDAs (see [4] for a good overview of different approaches). **Co-occurrence/mentioning:** Here, two entities are seen as similar and are thus related, if they co-occur within the same document. Moreover, co-occurrences in more documents of a collection speak for stronger entity relations [5]. The co-occurrence approach consists of two simple steps: (1) recognition of medical entities (through Named Entity Recognition) in documents (usually restricted to abstracts or even the same sentence) and (2) counting their common occurrences. Afterwards, counts can be used to infer DDAs. In our investigation, we also use the co-occurrence approach as a baseline for DDAs.

For the investigation of semantic relations between words, distributional semantic models are currently the state-of-the-art approaches [12]. The basic hypothesis is that words with a similar surrounding word context also have a similar meaning [18]. According to Baroni et al. [1] distributional semantic models (DSMs) can be divided into count-based models and predict models. Count-based models are generally characterized by (word) co-occurrence matrices being generated from text corpora. In contrast to count-based models, predict models try to predict the surrounding word-context of a word [1]. Compared to classical count-based models (e.g. LSA [16]), current, predict models such as Word2Vec presented by Mikolov et al. [13] lead to better results for predicting analogies as well as for other semantic tasks [1, 12]. Therefore, in our investigation we will rely on predict models as the state-of-the-art method for entity contextualization. In particular, we use the Word2Vec Skip-Gram model implementation from the open source Deep-Learning-for-Java[2] library.

With the increasing popularity of predict models, interest in the study of the semantic meaning of distance in high-dimensional spaces is growing. This is because of the non-deterministic character of these models. State-of-the-art models such as

---

[1] http://ctdbase.org/.
[2] https://deeplearning4j.org/.

Word2Vec use neural networks to predict contexts. To do this efficiently on large text corpora, random parameters are used, which however means that these methods are generally not deterministic. Therefore, it is rather difficult to decide whether a distance between entities always reflects a meaningful relation [15]. Elekes et al. [15] investigated the influence of hyperparameters and document corpus size to the similarity of word pairs. In their investigation they compare word pair distances in the embedding space with a WordNet Similarity [19] in order to determine for which distance a measured word pair reflects relatedness or associatedness. They also point out that similarity of words in natural language is blurred and therefore problematic to measure. In contrast to natural language, the word pairs we are investigating feature rather a binary, than a blurred relation to each other (a drug x has an effect on disease y or not [3]). In our investigation we measure the quality of this binary relation in the word embedding space.

3 Investigation of Embedded Drug-Disease Associations

We will first describe our pharmaceutical text corpus and basic experimental set-up decisions. Furthermore, we perform a ground-truth comparison and first show that DDAs are reflected in the embedding space. Here, we initially perform a comparison with the CDT data set followed by a text-mining co-occurrence comparison and we give the answers to our scientific questions Q1 and Q2 from Sect. 1. Then, we examine the predictive properties of the model with a retrospective analysis and show that DDA predictions are indeed possible and thus embedded DDAs can point to a future relation between drugs and diseases (Q3 and Q4).

Experimental Setup

Evaluation Corpus. PubMed[3] is with more than 27 million document citations the largest and most comprehensive digital library in the biomedical field. Since a full text access is not available for the most publications we used only abstracts for our evaluation corpus. With more training data, more accurate contexts can be learned. Thus, we decided to use a minimum of the 1000 most relevant abstracts for each entity (active substance). Whereby we relied on the relevance weighting of PubMed's search engine. Diseases as well as drugs often consist of several words (e.g. diabetes mellitus). This is a problem, because word embedding algorithms usually train on single words, resulting in one vector per word and not per entity. A solution to this problem is (1) recognize the entities in documents and (2) place a unique identifier at the entity's position in the text. For the recognition of the entities we used PubTator[4], a tool which is able to recognize pharmaceutical entities and returns a MeSH-Id for each of them.

Query Entities. As query entities for the evaluation, we randomly selected 350 drugs from the *DrugBank*[5] collection, which is a 10% sample of all approved drugs. Thus,

---

[3] https://www.ncbi.nlm.nih.gov/pubmed/.

[4] https://www.ncbi.nlm.nih.gov/CBBresearch/Lu/Demo/PubTator/.

[5] https://www.drugbank.ca/.

our final document set for evaluation contains ~ 2.5 million abstracts for 350 drugs. As ground truth, we selected for each drug all manually curated drug-disease associations from CTD. Moreover, we ensured that each selected drug has at least one manually curated drug-disease association in CTD.

Experiment Implementation and Parameter Settings

1. Text Preprocessing: Stop-word removal and stemming was performed using a *Lucene*[6] index. For stemming we used Lucene's *Porter Stemmer* implementation. We considered all words contained in more than half of the indexed abstracts as stop-words. Here we made sure that the drug and disease identifiers were not affected.

2. Word Embeddings: After preprocessing, word embeddings were created with DeepLearning4 J's *Word2Vec*[7] implementation. To train the neural network, we set the word window size to 20, the layer size to 200 features per word and we used a minimum word frequency of 5 occurrences. Training iterations were set to 4. We tested several parameter settings but the above-mentioned turned out best.

3. Similarity-Measure: As the similarity measure between the drug/disease embeddings we choose cosine similarity in all experiments. A value of 1 between two vectors means a perfect similarity (vectors match perfectly) and the value 0 means a maximum dissimilarity (vectors are orthogonal to each other).

3.1 Experimental Investigation

First, we need to clarify how a relationship between drugs and diseases in embedding space can be qualitatively evaluated. We verify in the following tests that a DDA can be inferred on the basis of a linguistic distance and whether an unknown DDA is actually either an error or points to a future drug-disease association (DDA). In this context, the following quality criteria should be fulfilled:

- *Semantic Relationship Accuracy:* First, as the distance between a drug and a disease decreases, the likelihood for establishing a true DDA should increase. Furthermore, the distances of all true DDAs and the distances of all false ones should differ statistically significantly, so that the two sets are generally distinguishable. In addition, a sufficiently good quantitative result (i.e. high precision) should be achieved.

- *Prediction Accuracy:* Do embedded DDAs provide *more* or simply *different* information compared to text-mining co-occurrence approaches? Embedded DDAs should help to reveal a hidden context which is not expressed exclusively via co-occurrence in documents but via word-contexts. This hidden context should be meaningful which means *false* DDAs in time period t should become *true* DDAs in future publications (time period $t + E$).

---

[6] https://lucene.apache.org/.
[7] https://deeplearning4j.org/word2vec.

3.2 Semantic Relationship Accuracy

In our first experiment we initially investigate whether a meaningful (true) DDA can be measured and in what degree of quality (precision). We also verify how a DDA-probability changes with a decreasing distance. For a measurement of DDAs, we first had to choose between a distance-threshold and a k-nearest-neighbors (k-NN) approach. Since distance-thresholds are difficult to determine in context-predicting models [15], we choose the k-NN approach. In our experiments we select the closest k-nearest disease neighbors (k-NDN) for each drug and measure the average precision for the following k's = 1, 3, 5, 10, 20.

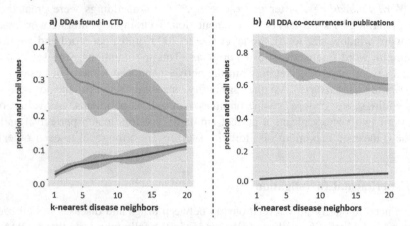

Fig. 1. Comparison of AVG-precision (red line) and AVG-recall (blue line) for different k-nearest disease neighbors using (a) CTD and (b) publications co-occurrence count and variance area in dark grey. (Color figure online)

Figure 1(a) shows the results of our first experiment based on the CTD dataset. At k = 1 the precision is 0.38 and drops to a value of 0.18 at k = 20. The result confirms the hypothesis: With increasing distance the probability of a true DDA actually decreases. The CTD has a high quality due to the high manual effort but this is often accompanied by the disadvantage that a manually curated source is not complete and usually the most popular or most important DDAs are curated first [20]. Therefore we carry out an additional experiment (Fig. 1(b), with scientific publications as another comparison source which contains on the one hand (theoretically) all DDAs but is correct only under a co-occurrence assumption [5]: A DDA exists if an active substance *dr* and a disease *di* co-occur together within at least *x* publications. In addition, with a higher *x* the probability for a true DDA increases. For our experiments we set *x* on "at least 3" publications. Therefore, for a DDA embedding there must be at least 3 publications containing this pair. Only then do we count this co-occurrence as a true DDA. We repeated our first experiment with the new source and present the results for the k-nearest disease-neighbors of each drug in Fig. 1b. At k = 1 the precision is at ∼0.80 and drops to ∼0.60 at k = 20. We achieve an AVG precision of ∼0.7 for the different k's. Like in the previous experiment this experiment supports the hypothesis that the probability for a true DDA decreases with an increasing distance. And secondly, we can assume accurate precision-values within the first 20 k-nearest disease neighbors (k-NDN).

With our next experiment we would like to answer the following questions: Which AVG cosine-similarity values have true DDAs compared to false DDAs? Is there a general and meaningful threshold that can help us to distinguish between true and false DDAs? Are there statistically significant differences in these quantities? To test this we first measure all diseases for each of the 350 drugs up to a minimum cosine-similarity of 0.001. In total, we obtain 184,553 DDAs in this way. To analyze the DDA pairs and to answer the questions we use a histogram, density, boxplot, and a Welch two sample t-test.

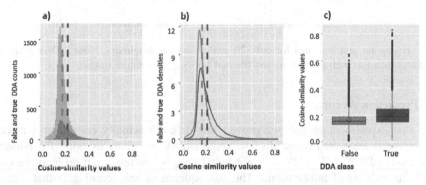

Fig. 2. Histogram, density and boxplot for all nearest-disease neighbors. False DDAs (red) and true DDAs (blue) as well as their means (dotted lines). (Color figure online)

Can we find meaningful similarity-based thresholds? As can be seen in Figs. 2a–c (diamond represents the means), the amounts of true (blue) and false (red) DDAs overlap strongly. The majority of all true DDAs share a large amount of similar similarity values with the set of false DDAs. The result suggests the assumption that (1) the DDAs are generally difficult to separate by a *cut-off* value and (2) in general DDAs are surprisingly poorly represented by the word embedding model. *Are the two sets significantly different?* To prove this we performed a Welch two sample t-test with a confidence interval of 99%. With a p-value $< 2.2e{-}16$ we are significantly below the threshold of 0.05 and thus there is a significant difference between the two sets.

Our previous experiment suggests that both sets of true and false DDAs cannot be meaningfully separated (e.g. many false positives) with a similarity threshold, even though the sets differ significantly. On the other hand, our co-occurrence experiment (see Fig. 1b) promises an adequate precision (between 60% and 80%) with a maximum of 20 disease neighbors. For this purpose we limit the k-NDN in our next experiment again and investigate whether the sets can be better separated using a smaller k. The Figs. 3a and b show the results for the k = 20 next disease neighbors. Compared to the results shown in Fig. 2, the figures in 3 exhibit that the distributions of true and false DDAs can be separated better. We have a larger proportion of true DDAs ($\sim$60%)

compared with the portion of true DDAs from our second experiment (~ 0.35, using density curve intersection cut-off point). Experiment 1–3 indicate that a (adequate) meaningful result can only be achieved with smaller k's.

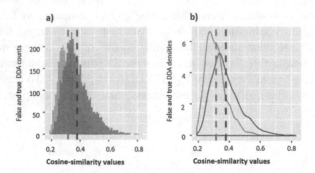

Fig. 3. Histogram and densities for only 20 nearest disease neighbors. False DDAs (red) and true DDAs (blue) as well as their means (dashed lines). (Color figure online)

3.3 Prediction Accuracy

In the first experiment section we proved that distance actually correlates with correctness for at least 20 nearest disease neighbors. What gives us hope for possible predictions of DDAs? Word2Vec is not based on co-occurrence but on learning contexts from millions of publications. The consequence of this learning is that entities with a similar context are probably closer together in vector space. This property can be used and transferred on DDAs. Which means: A similar context points to an intrinsic relation between drugs and diseases. *Can new relationships (DDAs) be predicted with this property and how can we measure it?* A possible approach to verify this is a retrospective analysis and the determination of the proportion of all false DDAs at time t (don't co-occur in publications) that become *true* at time $t + E$ (co-occur in publications). Here, we refer to this type of entities as *future* DDAs. This experiment requires adjustments to the evaluation corpus and to the evaluation implementation:

> *Evaluation corpus:* In order to calculate the change in different time periods we divide our previous corpus into four corpuses: 1900–1987, 1900–1997, 1900–2007, 1900–2017. Each corpus contains only the documents for the respective time period.
> *Evaluation implementation:* Now we train our model with each time period using the same parameters as described in the previous experiments. Afterwards, we first check the proportion of DDAs that are true in time period t. Then we check how the precision changes when we measure in time $t + E$ (next time period). *How fast grows the prediction of DDAs compared to the general increase of DDAs found in literature?* To enable a comparison of increase we generate the two control groups *R2* and *R3*. For *R3*, we identify all *future* DDAs in time period t and replace the disease with a random selected disease. Then we measure the proportion of *true*

DDAs at $t + E$. With *R3* we investigate how big the difference to a randomly *coming true* of a DDA really is. For control group *R2* we replace the future DDAs with randomly selected disease neighbors (at a range between 21- and 40-NDNs) and compare the difference to *R1* (20-NDSs). With R2 we want to investigate if with increasing distance the probability for a DDA-prediction decreases. We calculate AVG precision for the following k = 1, 3, 5, 10, 20 again. Using this approach we compare all time periods:

Table 1. Avg. precision values for the different time periods. Results of 20-NDNs *(R1)*, *(R2)* results of control group with replaced future DDAs with nearest disease neighbors (range 21 to 40-NDNs), *(R3)* results of control group with replaced future DDAs with randomly selected diseases. Best predictive results in bold.

Time periods	1900—1987	1900—1997	1900—2007	1900—2017
1900—1987	R1: 0.566 R2: 0.566 R3: 0.566	**R1: 0.573** R2: 0.568 R3: 0.566	**R1: 0.589** R2: 0.573 R3: 0.567	**R1: 0.661** R2: 0.610 R3: 0.570
1900—1997	x	R1: 0.623 R2: 0.623 R3: 0.623	**R1: 0.628** R2: 0.626 R3: 0.623	**R1: 0.680** R2: 0.644 R3: 0.625
1900—2007	x	x	R1: 0.671 R2: 0.671 R3: 0.671	**R1: 0.685** R2: 0.677 R3: 0.671
1900—2017	x	x	x	R1: 0.700 R2: 0.700 R3: 0.700

Table 1 shows the results of our retrospective analysis. As we can see, AVG precision increases measurably for all subsequent time periods. In fact, each time period actually contains DDAs that will appear in future publications. The largest percentage increase of future DDAs can be observed for the time period 1900–1987 (increased from 0.566 to 0.661). Whereby in this case future DDAs denote DDAs contained in the period 1900–2017 (contains all known/true DDAs) minus all DDAs contained in the period 1900–1987. Taking these future DDAs into account, the AVG precision increases for the time period 1900–1987 by 17% from 0.566 to 0.661. Thus, the best results are achieved for the longest time period (30 years). Compared to control group *R3* (random disease swap) there is a remarkable difference (total increase till 2017 is less than 1%) between a randomly coming true of a future DDA. R2 (swap with 21–40 NDNs) has a slower prediction increase compared to *R1*, which means: With increasing distance the probability for a DDA prediction decreases. It can be seen that for *R1* there is always growth and therefore predictions can always be made using the context-based method. In short, the procedure is able to predict DDAs. Surprisingly, there is also a pattern in the columns: The column values in column 1900–2017 hardly differ. For example the standard deviation in the column is only ~0.016. *Is there a certain similarity-distance area where future DDAs concentrate?* After showing that DDA predictions are possible in general, our next step is to investigate the distance range of DDAs that are currently false but will become true in future time periods. Knowing in which area these future DDAs are located can help us to find more useful cut-offs for later applications (e.g. DDA prediction). For this purpose we analyze the position of median, mean, and also the distribution density of the 20 nearest disease neighbors in detail. As time periods we choose 1900–1987, 1900–1997, 1900–2007, and analyze the proportion of *false* DDAs that will become *true* by the end of 2017. Figure 4 shows the results of our last experiment. Row 1 shows the results of the distribution and row 2 the density of true DDAs (green), false DDAs (red), and future true DDAs (blue). Each column in Fig. 4 represents the results of the different time periods 1900–1987, 1900–1997, and 1900–2007. In all figures, the mean values are shown as dotted lines. The median values for the different periods and DDA types are listed in Table 2.

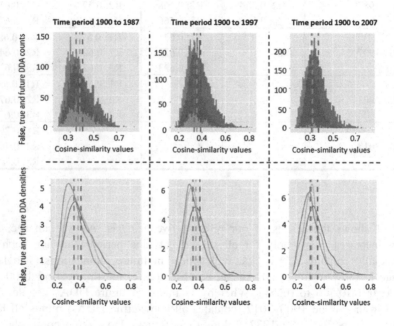

Fig. 4. False DDAs (red), true DDAs (green) and future DDAs that will co-occur in publications by the end of 2017 (blue). Dashed lines represent the mean values of the respective sets. (Color figure online)

As can be seen in the distributions of Fig. 4, the proportion of future- as well as false DDAs decreases over time and the proportion of true DDAs increases. Surprisingly, both mean (Fig. 4) and median (Table 2) values remain relatively stable, although for example the corpus of time period 1900–1987 is more than twice as large as the corpus of 1900–2007 and the proportion of true and false DDAs changes remarkably.

Table 2. Median values for different time periods and DDA types.

Time period	True DDA	Future DDA	False DDA
1900–1987	0.39	0.37	0.34
1900–1997	0.38	0.34	0.32
1900–2007	0.36	0.33	0.31

In addition, mean and median values of the future DDAs always lie between the false and the true DDAs. Furthermore, there is always a stable ∼5% distance between false and true DDAs. Thus, the corpus size as well as the proportion of true and false DDAs seem to have less effect on the distance between these two groups.

4 Conclusion and Future Work

We investigated in this paper if relations between embedded pharmaceutical entities are reflected in high-dimensional space and if their distance to each other correlates with the probability of their (binary) relationship. This is currently an important research question because non deterministic Word-Embedding models, like Word2Vec are on the one hand popular models for semantic as well as analogy tasks but on the other hand their properties are not fully investigated. Questions like the following remain: What has a model actually learned? How can we assess whether a result is meaningful? Answering these questions is essential, before we can use context-predicting models for scientific-entity relations like DDAs in innovative digital library services.

In this context we first proved that with an increasing distance the probability for a DDA decreases. We have shown that a sufficient AVG-precision can be achieved with 20-nearest-disease neighbors (NDNs) of an active substance. For example, the AVG-precision ranges between 60% for the 20-NDNs and 80% for the first one. Therefore, the threshold of 20-NDNs might be a good choice for a selection of DDAs because it is a trade-off between sufficiently good precision values and the number of future DDAs included in this set. Surprisingly most DDAs can't be distinguished with a distance-threshold because most false and true DDAs have a similar distance and the two sets overlap. We concentrated our investigation on the 20-NDNs and demonstrated that sets of false and true DDAs can be separated better. That, since many false DDAs have similar distances as true DDAs, led us to the question: Is it probable that a hidden and meaningful DDA relation has been learned? We investigated this question with a retrospective analysis. We have shown that a significant proportion of the false DDAs will actually become true in the future (increase of up to ∼17%). Additionally we have shown that with decreasing distance the probability for a DDA prediction increases. These results open up the possibility of predicting DDAs on the basis of co-contexts found in literature, which in turn can be of important benefit in the field of drug repurposing. Afterwards, we examined the distance range of this specific entities which we call *future* DDAs. We have shown that restricted to the 20-NDNs mean and median of future DDAs lies always in between the mean and median of false and true DDAs. The positions of the various values determined (median, mean) remain relatively stable over the periods and for different corpus sizes. In our future work we will examine if embedded diseases can reveal the intrinsic relationship between groups of embedded drugs investigated in our previous work [7]. And secondly, we want to explore the possibilities of DDA predictions and compare this method with state-of-the-art text mining approaches for DDA predictions.

References

1. Baroni, M., Dinu, G., Kruszewski, G.: Don't count, predict! A systematic comparison of context-counting vs. context-predicting semantic vectors. In: Proceedings of the 52nd Annual Meeting of the Association for Computational Linguistics: Long Papers, vol. 1, pp. 238–247 (2014)
2. Leaman, R., Islamaj Doğan, R., Lu, Z.: DNorm: disease name normalization with pairwise learning to rank. Bioinformatics 29(22), 2909–2917 (2013)
3. Zhang, W., et al.: Predicting drug-disease associations based on the known association bipartite network. In: 2017 IEEE International Conference on Bioinformatics and Biomedicine (BIBM), pp. 503–509. IEEE, November 2017
4. Lotfi Shahreza, M., Ghadiri, N., Mousavi, S.R., Varshosaz, J., Green, J.R.: A review of network-based approaches to drug repositioning. Brief. Bioinform. (2017). https://doi.org/10.1093/bib/bbx017
5. Jensen, L.J., Saric, J., Bork, P.: Literature mining for the biologist: from information retrieval to biological discovery. Nat. Rev. Genet. 7(2), 119 (2006)
6. Dudley, J.T., Deshpande, T., Butte, A.J.: Exploiting drug–disease relationships for computational drug repositioning. Brief. Bioinform. 12(4), 303–311 (2011)
7. Wawrzinek, J., Balke, W.-T.: Semantic facettation in pharmaceutical collections using deep learning for active substance contextualization. In: Choemprayong, S., Crestani, F., Cunningham, S.J. (eds.) ICADL 2017. LNCS, vol. 10647, pp. 41–53. Springer, Cham (2017). https://doi.org/10.1007/978-3-319-70232-2_4
8. Keiser, M.J., et al.: Predicting new molecular targets for known drugs. Nature 462(7270), 175 (2009)
9. Agarwal, P., Searls, D.B.: Can literature analysis identify innovation drivers in drug discovery? Nat. Rev. Drug Discov. 8(11), 865 (2009)
10. Ngo, D.L., et al.: Application of word embedding to drug repositioning. J. Biomed. Sci. Eng. 9(01), 7 (2016)
11. Lengerich, B.J., Maas, A.L., Potts, C.: Retrofitting distributional embeddings to knowledge graphs with functional relations. arXiv preprint arXiv:1708.00112 (2017)
12. Mikolov, T., Yih, W.T., Zweig, G.: Linguistic regularities in continuous space word representations. In: Proceedings of the 2013 Conference of the North American Chapter of the Association for Computational Linguistics: Human Language Technologies, pp. 746–751 (2013)
13. Mikolov, T., Chen, K., Corrado, G., Dean, J.: Efficient estimation of word representations in vector space. arXiv preprint arXiv:1301.3781 (2013)
14. Chiang, A.P., Butte, A.J.: Systematic evaluation of drug–disease relationships to identify leads for novel drug uses. Clin. Pharmacol. Ther. 86(5), 507–510 (2009)
15. Elekes, Á., Schäler, M., Böhm, K.: On the various semantics of similarity in word embedding models. In: 2017 ACM/IEEE Joint Conference on Digital Libraries (JCDL), pp. 1–10. IEEE, June 2017

16. Dumais, S.T.: Latent semantic analysis. Annu. Rev. Inf. Sci. Technol. (ARIST) **38**(1), 188–230 (2004). Association for Information Science & Technology
17. Larsen, P.O., Von Ins, M.: The rate of growth in scientific publication and the decline in coverage provided by Science Citation Index. Scientometrics **84**(3), 575–603 (2010)
18. Miller, G.A., Charles, W.G.: Contextual correlates of semantic similarity. Lang. Cogn. Process. **6**(1), 1–28 (1991)
19. Miller, G.A.: WordNet: a lexical database for English. Commun. ACM **38**(11), 39–41 (1995)
20. Rinaldi, F., Clematide, S., Hafner, S.: Ranking of CTD articles and interactions using the OntoGene pipeline. In: Proceedings of the 2012 BioCreative Workshop, April 2012

Towards Semantic Quality Enhancement of User Generated Content

José María González Pinto[✉], Niklas Kiehne, and Wolf-Tilo Balke

Institut für Informationssysteme, TU Braunschweig, Mühlenpfordstrasse 23,
28106 Brunswick, Germany
{pinto,balke}@ifis.cs.tu-bs.de, n.kiehne@tu-bs.de

Abstract. With the increasing amount of user-generated content such as scientific blogs, questioning-answering archives (Quora or Stack Overflow), and Wikipedia, the challenge to evaluate *quality* naturally arises. Previous work has shown the potential to evaluate automatically such content focusing on syntactic and pragmatic levels such as conciseness, organization, and readability. We push forward these efforts and focus on how to develop an intelligent service to ease the engagement of users in two *semantic attributes*: factual accuracy, e.g., whether facts are correct and validity, e.g., whether reliable sources support the content. To do so, we deploy a Deep Learning approach to learn citation categories from Wikipedia. Thus, we introduce an automatic mechanism that can accurately determine what *specific citation category* is needed to help users increase the value of their contribution at a semantic level. To that end, we automatically learn *linguistic patterns* from Wikipedia to support a broad range of fields. We extensively evaluated several machine learning models to learn from more than one million annotated sentences from the massive effort of Wikipedia contributors. We evaluate the performance of the different methods and present a profound analysis focusing on the balance accuracy achieved.

Keywords: Automatic quality enhancement · User-generated content · Data curation

1 Introduction

With the continuously growing of user-generated content on the Web, the challenge to verify quality content naturally arises. Previous work has shown that the quality of user-generated content is a combination of independent assessments from different indicators [13]. For instance, consider an article and the following indicators 'readability', 'factual accuracy' and 'validity.' Readability corresponds to a dimension called *syntactic* and is rather easy to assess because it is concerned with the structure of the content. In contrast, factual accuracy corresponds to the dimension *semantic* and is more difficult to assess, e.g., how do we know if the statements in the content in the article are correct? What about validity, e.g., whether reliable sources support the content? We argue that both of these issues could be tackled with proper citations, but how can a user decide if a statement - a claim - requires a citation and of which type: a book, a scientific paper, a journal paper? To answer these questions, we should look at

M. Dobreva et al. (Eds.): ICADL 2018, LNCS 11279, pp. 28–40, 2018.
https://doi.org/10.1007/978-3-030-04257-8_3

Wikipedia's remarkable example. Wikipedia is the most successful collaborative effort to create encyclopedic content freely available on the Web. Its popularity as a source of information as measured by Alexa[1] makes Wikipedia the top 5 ranked website in the world as stated in November 2017. Researchers assessed Wikipedia's quality for specific domains, and surprisingly it has been found to achieve comparable scores as expert-curated encyclopedias like, e.g., Encyclopedia Britannica [21]. On the other hand, in some cases, the completeness of the content of Wikipedia has been shown to be one of its drawbacks for more specific domains [5, 6, 16, 24]. In any case, as stated by Stvilia et al. [25] *"What makes special Wikipedia as a resource is that the quality discussions and processes are strongly connected to the data itself [...]"*.

Thus, even though no final agreement exists on what definitely can be 'the metric' that can measure the quality of Wikipedia, citations play a key role, i.e., valid citations provide *credibility* to the Wikipedia's content. As the Wikipedia 'citing sources' page[2] states: *"Wikipedia's verifiability policy requires inline citations for any material challenged or likely to be challenged and for all quotations, anywhere in article space"*. Moreover, in the Wikipedia's verifiability page[3] we find that *"[...] verifiability means that other people using the encyclopedia can check that the information comes from a reliable source. Verifiability, no original research and neutral point of view are Wikipedia's core content policies"*.

To motivate collaboration - and quality - on the content, Wikipedia uses the tag 'citation needed.' This tag is a request for other editors to verify a statement by a proper citation. Consider the following example[4]: *"Deep learning architectures are often constructed with a greedy layer-by-layer method [citation needed]."* Among the citations categories that exist on Wikipedia, what category would be needed here? A book, a journal, a conference paper? Is it possible to learn *citation categories accurately* from the linguistic patterns that exist on Wikipedia? If we could do it, then we could help users to enhance their content at the *semantic* level by tagging statements in need of a specific citation category! We argue that two of the semantic features defined in Dalip et al. [13] could be tackled: *factual accuracy*, e.g., whether facts are correct and *validity*, e.g., whether reliable sources support the content.

To this end, we focus on this paper in assessing the current state of the art machine learning approaches including classical techniques and deep leaning techniques exploiting different embedding word representations to learn citation categories automatically from Wikipedia. Our contributions are as follows:

- We introduce a novel automatic method with the potential to enhance user-generated content quality inspired by Wikipedia's successful qualitative practices.
- A comparative study of competitive methods to answer a simple but powerful question: what category of citation is needed?

---

[1] https://www.alexa.com/siteinfo/wikipedia.org.

[2] https://en.wikipedia.org/wiki/Wikipedia:Citing_sources.

[3] https://en.wikipedia.org/wiki/Wikipedia:Verifiability.

[4] https://en.wikipedia.org/wiki/Deep_learning.

- A detailed analysis and discussion that provide insights of what the best model can achieve and what this can tell us about the feasibility of an Intelligent Open Service available for the community to use.

2 Related Work

Our work draws motivation from recent qualitative studies on Wikipedia. Specifically, research efforts that use machine-based approaches to assess the quality of the massive effort behind Wikipedia. We will first start with a general discussion on information quality and then on the specific efforts related to our work: machine-based approaches to quantify the quality of Wikipedia.

There is a body of research on various aspects of information quality in information management sciences [10, 18, 19]. Quality is considered a multi-dimensional concept that involves different criteria such as accessibility, accuracy, authority, see [25] for a comprehensive discussion on the topic related to Wikipedia.

Dalip et al. [13] provided a Multiview framework for assessing the quality of collaboratively created content. As the authors stated in their extensive analysis of indicators "...it is clear that most of the effort to assess quality in collaborative repositories has focused on the syntactic and pragmatic levels. Indicators for these levels are normally easy to calculate, in contrast to semantic indicators that often require the use of expensive natural language processing techniques". Indeed, this is confirmed in several previous works to assess the content quality of Wikipedia automatically. Most of them use simple metrics such as article length, word count, sentence count, interlink count, and edition history. Herein we present some representative efforts that account for some of these features. For instance, the work of Adler and Alfaro [1] introduces a system to measure authors reputation of Wikipedia based on content. To measure an author's reputation, the researchers rely on the idea of "content evolution"; the assumption behind this approach is that content preserved should have more credibility. Concretely, authors lose reputation when their edits are rolled back or undone. This reputation mechanism aimed at introducing the idea of "flagging" new content as coming from an author with high-reputation or low-reputation. Such mechanism could in theory benefit jointly efforts of improving Wikipedia content by other volunteers to focus on content that comes from authors with low-reputation. Dang et al. [7] explored deep learning techniques for content-based analysis for classifying articles using the content assessment currently performed by Wikipedia's editors. The models they used did not consider citations or any other metadata for the task.

3 Approach and Problem Formulation

3.1 Problem Formulation

In this section, we define the problem and provide definitions to accomplish our goal: a machine-based approach to learn from linguistic patterns, Wikipedia citation categories.

Definition 1. Citation is a reference to an external source used to support what is mentioned in the text -usually a sentence- in a Wikipedia article. In Wikipedia there exist the following 16 categories of citations: web, news, book, journal, encyclopedia, episode, map, press release, video game, comic, conference, av. Media, court, thesis, mailing list, and newsgroup.

Definition 2. Claim: a claim in this work is a sentence in Wikipedia that needs or has a specific citation category.

Let k be the number of citation categories in Wikipedia. Our task is to find for a given claim c its corresponding citation category.

Claim Citation Categorization Problem. Formally, we want to learn a function: $f : \mathbb{R}^n \rightarrow \{1, \ldots, k\}$. When $y = f(x)$, the model assigns an input described by vector x to a category identified by numeric code y. The vector x in our case is a vector representation of a claim c. Different alternatives exist to learn from data such a function and we will explore some of them in this work.

3.2 Models

In this section, we describe the models we evaluated solve our problem. Firstly, we will start with the sequence-based models (LSTM and BiLSTM); secondly, we present non-recursive methods: Convolutional Neural Networks and Fully Connected Networks; and thirdly, we present other more "classical" machine learning approaches used as baselines. The model's architecture and source code used in the paper are available on request.

LSTM. One of the most widely successfully used recurrent neural networks is the Long-Short-Term-Memory (LSTM) by Hochreiter and Schmidhuber [14]. Researchers have applied LSTM to several sequence data problems, such as sentence embeddings for information retrieval [23], speech recognition from audio data [11] or the translation of sentences into different languages [2]. See the work of [12] for a recent extensive empirical study of different variations of LSTM's performance and tuning of its parameters.

Bidirectional LSTM. The bidirectional LSTM architecture is very similar to the unidirectional architecture. The only notable difference is how the input data is presented. In a common recurrent network, the data is processed from the beginning of the sequence to the end of it. Therefore, it is impossible for the model to know anything about the following sequence element before reaching it. In the case of natural language sentences, this restriction of context poses a problem since the semantics of a word usually depend on past and future context as well. To overcome this limitation of unidirectional recurrent networks a bidirectional layer is used. The idea is to add another LSTM parallel to an existing one, but with a reversed input. Both LSTMs work on their version of the input data, but their output is concatenated, such that any following layer will have access to both past and future context. Naturally, this doubles the number of weights and also the computation time needed, making this architecture even slower than a usual LSTM. The architecture used here consists of two bidirectional LSTM layers followed by three dense layers with a dropout of 25%. This model is by far the biggest architecture regarding weights.

Convolutional Neural Network. Convolutional neural networks (CNN) are known best for their use on image data, such as object detection [17] or even face recognition [26]. Recently, they have also shown to achieve state of the art results in sentence categorization. For instance, Kim [15] proposed not only to look at one specific amount of word vectors but also to use multiple context sizes in parallel. The idea here is as Zhang, and Wallace [27] demonstrated: to capitalize on the distributed representation of words embeddings. Zhang and Wallace provided practical guidelines of what can be achieved using CNN for text classification tasks. The implementation used here consists of four different context windows of two, three, four and five nearby words. Goodfellow et al. [9] have emphasized that three essential ideas motivate the use of CNN's in different machine learning tasks, including text classification: sparse interactions, parameter sharing, and equivariant representations. For text classifications task, sparse interactions allow for learning linguistic n-grams patterns; parameter sharing influences computation storage requirements, and equivariant representation allow for robustness in the patterns learned regarding of the position in the sentence.

Feed Forward Nets. These fully connected neural networks represent one of the most straightforward architectures available. The model uses fixed length input vectors from layer to layer sequentially, and with no recursion. These models are usually not able to compete with the more complex approaches for the sequence data, such as LSTMs. On the other hand, the simpler the model, the shorter is the training and inference time.

Other Classical Machine Learning Approaches. For the sake of completeness, we applied other well-known "classical" Machine Learning algorithms to the fixed size data set. AdaBoost, Random Forests, and Decision Trees were chosen from the Scikit-learn[5] Python library to provide alternatives for performance comparison.

4   Experimental Setup

We work on the Wikipedia dump introduced by Fetahu et al. in [8]. The data format consists of a big CSV file with six columns and a total of 8,797,947 rows of samples. In Table 1 we show the structure of this big table in CSV form.

4.1   Data Preprocessing

Sentence Representation. To use the models described in the previous section, we transformed the data into vectors or sequences of vectors. Since the original base data comprises an extensive vocabulary of over 700 k unique words (with capitalization) typical approaches like Bag of Words would result in massive vectors.

---

[5] http://scikit-learn.org/stable/.

Table 1. Raw data format

Column	Explanation
Entity	The Wikipedia article the current sample was taken from
Section	The name of the section the sentence was taken from
Sentence	The actual sentence encoded in Wikipedia markup language
Citation	Wikipedia markup describing the type of citation
URL	A hyperlink to the source that was referenced
Cite type	The category of citation that was used

Because a sentence usually consists of less than 100 unique words which cause the Bag of Words matrix to be extremely sparse. Instead of extremely sparse representation, we opted for the use of dense word vectors, also called word embeddings. In particular, for the word2vec algorithm by Mikolov et al. [22]. In a nutshell, word embeddings pack more information into far fewer dimensions. Researchers have shown [27] two approaches to take advantage of word embeddings for classification tasks: (1) learn word embeddings jointly with the problem at hand and (2) use embedding vectors from a precomputed embedding space that might exhibit useful properties (captures general aspects of language structure). In this work, we push this idea further by comparing precomputed vectors of word2vec (trained on Google News dataset) and FastText [4] (trained on Wikipedia) with our learned word2vec vectors. FastText is another neural language model that accounts for more syntactic properties in the language and deals with out of vocabulary words by learning representations of words as the sum of character n-grams vectors [4].

In the following, we describe all the necessary preprocessing steps to obtain sequences of word vectors. The steps are given in the order of their execution unless stated otherwise.

Duplicates Removal. We observed that there are sentences in the data that have more than one citation, even more than one citation category. Because in this work we restrict the problem to assign one category to each sentence, we used only sentences that have precisely one citation and are therefore suitable representatives of their respective classes. We leave the problem of assigning more than one category for future work. Thus, with this preprocessing, the corpus shrinks to 5,695,580 samples and 17 distinct citation categories as shown in Fig. 1.

Parsing and Tokenization. At this point, the sentences are still encoded in Wikipedia markup and therefore not immediately usable. To extract the natural language parts, we used the MediaWiki Parser[6]. After the extraction of the sentences, we tokenize them using the NLTK library. More specifically, the NLTK TreeBankWordTokenizer implementation and a PunktSentenceTokenizer [3]. The latter is needed to split paragraphs into multiple sentences which the word tokenizer then further splits down into

---

[6] https://github.com/earwig/mwparserfromhell.

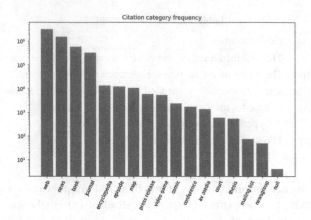

Fig. 1. Wikipedia citation category frequencies.

tokens. Our data now consists of 5,695,580 samples, with a total of 11,121,707 sentences and 264,943,821 tokens.

Punctuation Removal. After tokenization, we filter the punctuation out. Thus, the number of tokens reduces to 231,857,810.

Word2Vec Representation. A crucial part of the data preparation is the computation of word vector representations. The training is carried out by the Gensim Python[7] library which includes a fast and efficient implementation of the Word2Vec algorithm optimized for multiple CPUs. There is a multitude of parameters that strongly impact the quality of the vector representations, e.g., the dimensionality of the word vectors, the size of the context window, the learning rate, the numbers of training epochs or the number of negative samples. However, how can the quality of word vector representations be measured? Mikolov proposed a test based on analogical reasoning with which it is possible to test for semantic and syntactic analogies within the model. Such a test set contains multiple predefined relationships such as "Berlin is to Germany as Madrid is to Spain". If the model successfully learned the syntactic relationship between countries and their capitals, then the difference vector of Germany and Berlin should be very similar to the difference vector of Madrid and Spain.

Google released a collection of such analogies and are available on the author's website[8]. It contains 20k different examples that help to discover the strengths and weaknesses of any Word2Vec model. Google also supplied a model trained on approximately 100 billion words to use as a baseline. In Table 2, we show a comparison of the model trained on the Wikipedia sentences to Google's pre-trained model and a FastText' pre-trained model on Wikipedia. The result indicates that the model on Wikipedia has learned analogies and thus, is ready to use for word vector representation.

---

[7] https://radimrehurek.com/gensim/.

[8] https://github.com/nicholas-leonard/word2vec/blob/master/questions-words.txt.

Table 2. Comparison of word vector model performances

Category	Word2Vec Google	Word2Vec Wikipedia	FastText Wikipedia
capital-common-countries	0.8357	0.9571	0.9625
capital-world	0.8490	0.9431	0.9458
currency	0.3889	0.0000	0.0143
city-in-state	0.7558	0.6096	0.7364
family	0.9477	0.8708	0.8889
gram1-adjective-to-adverb	0.3730	0.2900	0.5517
gram2-opposite	0.4917	0.3889	0.6128
gram3-comparative	0.9143	0.8350	0.8534
gram4-superlative	0.8553	0.8476	0.8203
gram5-present-participle	0.8241	0.8034	0.7137
gram6-nationality-adjective	0.9679	0.9707	0.9869
gram7-past-tense	0.6776	0.7396	0.6684
gram8-plural	0.8067	0.7685	0.8908
gram9-plural-verbs	0.7138	0.6571	0.6779
Total	0.7728	0.7766	0.8104

Word2Vec Parameters. The parameters that performed best are a vector dimensionality of 300, a context window of 10 words and 15 negative samples. The learning rate started at 0.05 and was reduced by ten percent after each of the 20 epochs. Additionally, we discarded words that occurred less than five times in the corpus because there is not enough data to learn good vector representations for them.

Data Cleansing. Once the Word2Vec model is available for translating sequences of words into sequences of vectors, further cleaning of the data is required. To further improve the quality of the data, we discarded all samples that consist of more than one sentence (after tokenization). Focusing on single sentence samples lowers the number of total samples to 3,098,423.

Excluding Infrequent Categories. We also observed that some citation categories have a small number of samples. Consider for instance the categories mailing list, newsgroup with 33 and 17 samples respectively. In contrast, the category "journal" appears more than 400 K times. Following the suggested best practices of [9], we exclude categories with less than 5000 samples. Therefore, we reduce the total corpus size to 2,470,703 samples.

Citation Category Inconsistency. There is another quality aspect hidden inside the data. As shown in Fig. 1, the citation category "web" is the most frequent label, followed by "news", "book" and "journal". However, users wrongly used category "web" in some of the citations that originate from a newspaper, a book or a journal. One reason why this phenomenon happens is that all of these sources might also be available online. However, how to decide whether a citation belongs to the web category or not? Instead of solving this question the problem is dodged by splitting the corpus into two datasets. The first dataset is the corpus so far, but the second set excludes every sample labeled as web-content. The idea is simple: if the models perform significantly better on the second dataset, then it will confirm that the web category needs much cleaning to be of any use.

Sequence Representation. Many Machine Learning algorithms cannot operate on sequence data, whether the sequences have the same length or not. One solution is to summarize the sequences to map them to a fixed length vector. After preliminary experiments, we chose 30 as the fixed length. The mappings investigated here are the sum, mean or weighted sum of all the word vectors in a sentence. The latter operation multiplies each word vector by its corresponding TF-IDF [20] score before taking the sum which, in theory, should help to better represent a sentence as a sum of its words. The idea is to give more importance to those words that determine the content. Another important aspect is that these methods drastically reduce the memory consumption since every sequence of 30-word vectors is represented as a single vector. Finally, in Table 3 we show an overview of the main characteristics of the two datasets used for our experiments.

Table 3. Corpus statistics

	Web dataset	Non-web dataset
Number of samples	2,470,703	1,076,097
Number of classes	4	3

4.2   Results

We used different implementations of the algorithms to support a more diverse set of performance comparison using the two datasets. Each dataset comes in four variants: sequences, summed, averaged or weighted summed sequences. The shape of the raw sequence data is thirty-word vectors per sample whereas the shape of the summarized view is just one-word vector per sample.

Metrics. We applied two different metrics to measure the effectivity of the proposed architectures. The accuracy metric measures the percentage of right decisions a classifier made. However, the accuracy does not include the class frequencies. For example, in a two-class problem, if one of the classes occurs in 99% of the cases, the easiest way to achieve an accuracy of 0.99 would be to classify everything as the most frequent class. Naturally, such a classifier would not have learned any useful rules to distinguish the classes.

To measure whether a model has learned to differentiate the classes or not, we used balance-accuracy. The idea is to compute the mean per-class accuracy. So, the classifier in the example above would score the per class accuracies of 0.99 and zero, resulting in a balanced accuracy of 0.495. A classifier is considered right as soon as both metrics are comparatively high and do not differ by a high margin.

We show in Tables 4 and 5, the performances of the architectures outlined in previous sections. The Feed Forward models are abbreviated, so that "FF_sum_weighted"

Table 4. Overall results on the web dataset using dynamic Word2Vec

Model	Web	
	Accuracy	Bal. accuracy
LSTM	0.6501	0.5582
BILSTM	0.6522	0.5705
CNN	0.6239	0.4094
FF_sum	0.6657	0.5481
FF_mean	0.6687	0.5653
FF_sum_weighted	0.5768	0.3075
FF_mean_weighted	0.5816	0.3096

Table 5. Overall results without the "web" category using different word vector algorithms sorted by balanced accuracy. The dynamic Word2Vec model is abbreviated W2V, the static Google News GN and the static FastText on Wikipedia FT.

Model	Word vector model	No web	
		Accuracy	Bal. accuracy
BILSTM	W2V	0.7898	0.7664
LSTM	W2V	0.7872	0.7636
FF_MEAN	W2V	0.7806	0.7558
CNN	W2V	0.7606	0.7493
FF_SUM	W2V	0.7712	0.7450
BILSTM	FT	0.7777	0.7329
LSTM	GN	0.7697	0.7289
LSTM	FT	0.7676	0.7270
BILSTM	GN	0.7786	0.7269
FF_SUM	GN	0.7651	0.7174
CNN	GN	0.7411	0.7166
FF_SUM	FT	0.7541	0.7028
FF_MEAN	FT	0.7459	0.6955
FF_MEAN	GN	0.7634	0.6937
CNN	FT	0.7547	0.6913
AdaBoost	W2V	0.7616	0.6578
RandomForest	W2V	0.7651	0.6326
AdaBoost	GN	0.7353	0.6146
AdaBoost	FT	0.7314	0.6071
RandomForest	GN	0.7338	0.5813
RandomForest	FT	0.7300	0.5794
DecisionTree	W2V	0.7055	0.5781
DecisionTree	FT	0.6553	0.5295
DecisionTree	GN	0.6596	0.5293

stands for the Feed Forward architecture, using the weighted sum of word vectors dataset. We applied the algorithms Adaboost, Random Forest, and Decision Tree to the mean word vectors dataset without the web category. We used OneVsRest meta-algorithm because all of these algorithms are for binary classification tasks. OneVsRest trains one classifier for every class and chooses the class label with the highest confidence.

Discussion of the Results. First of all, there is a significant difference between the "web" and the "no-web" dataset. Any algorithm performs better when there is no web category. This observation leads to the conclusion that the web category is too noisy to use. The work of Fetahu et al. [8] confirms our findings: users have misinterpreted the web category; some articles that clearly should be in the "news" category are in the "web" category because the resources are online.

Secondly, on the web dataset, the best performing models are the Feed Forward architectures using the averaged or summed word vectors of the dynamic Word2Vec model. To our surprise, the most straightforward architectures available outperformed the more sophisticated recurrent or convolutional approaches. The averaged or summed word vectors worked better, even though they cover less information than the raw sequence data that the other architectures use. A simple Feed Forward net might not be that sensitive to such noise since it has fewer weights to adapt.

The BILSTM and its unidirectional version perform best on the "no-web" dataset. They both surpass the FF models. Still, the mean word vectors models give fierce competition to the LSTM and BILSTM nets. Considering the complexities of recurrent nets as compared to FF architectures, the difference in accuracy of 0.92% between FF_mean and BILSTM (Table 5) is remarkable. With fewer resources needed regarding disk space, GPU and GPU memory load, the Feed Forward architecture with averaged word vectors is very near to the recurrent nets. If resource consumption is not a concern, then the BILSTM would be the solution. Thirdly, the dynamic Word2Vec model outperforms the static GoogleNews and FastText models in most of the cases. The top 5 approaches all used W2V and outperformed the best static approach by more than 3%.

Lastly, the idea of using TF-IDF weighted sums or averages of word vectors failed. Two reasons might explain this phenomenon. Firstly, the semantics of word embeddings are so strong that incorporating TF-IDF adds no advantage to the classification task. Secondly, maybe because we are dealing with small documents (sentences) TF-IDF hurts the final representation of the document. However, to support our reasoning, we will need further experiments with other collections.

5   Conclusions and Future Work

In this work, we have introduced the idea of developing an intelligent service to spot citation categories automatically to enhance the quality of user-generated content at the *semantic* level. We hypothesized that the Wikipedia archive could provide a representative data source of several disciplines. Our experimental results revealed that three of Wikipedia representative citation categories do exhibit consistent patterns. We performed experiments with several algorithms to show that to a certain degree of success an intelligent service is feasible. We also confirmed that one of the current citation categories in Wikipedia requires a redefinition due to its misuse. Nevertheless, our current effort could ease the editing process in Wikipedia and any user-generated content.

References

1. Adler, B.T., de Alfaro, L.: A content-driven reputation system for the Wikipedia. In: Proceedings of the 16th International Conference on World Wide Web - WWW 2007, pp. 261–270 (2007)
2. Bahdanau, D., et al.: Neural Machine Translation by Jointly Learning to Align and Translate, pp. 1–15 (2014)
3. Bird, S., Loper, E.: NLTK: the natural language toolkit. In: Proceedings of the 42nd Annual Meeting of the Association for Computational Linguistics, pp. 1–4 (2004)
4. Bojanowski, P., et al.: Enriching word vectors with subword information. Trans. Assoc. Comput. Linguist. **5**, 135–146 (2017)
5. Brown, A.R.: Wikipedia as a data source for political scientists: accuracy and completeness of coverage. PS Polit. Sci. Polit. **44**(02), 339–343 (2011)
6. Clauson, K.A., et al.: Scope, completeness, and accuracy of drug information in Wikipedia. Ann. Pharmacother. **42**(12), 1814–1821 (2008)
7. Dang, Q.V., Ignat, C.-L.: Quality assessment of Wikipedia articles without feature engineering. In: Proceedings of 16th ACM/IEEE-CS on Joint Conference on Digital Libraries - JCDL 2016, pp. 27–30 (2016)
8. Fetahu, B., et al.: Finding News Citations for Wikipedia (2017)
9. Goodfellow, I., et al.: Deep learning. Nature **521**(7553), 800 (2016)
10. Gorla, N., et al.: Organizational impact of system quality, information quality, and service quality. J. Strateg. Inf. Syst. **19**(3), 207–228 (2010)
11. Graves, A., et al.: Speech recognition with deep recurrent neural networks. In: ICASSP, vol. 3, pp. 6645–6649 (2013)
12. Greff, K., et al.: LSTM: a search space odyssey (2016)
13. Dalip, D.H., et al.: A general multiview framework for assessing the quality of collaboratively created content on web 2.0. J. Assoc. Inf. Sci. Technol. **68**(2), 286–308 (2017)
14. Hochreiter, S., Urgen Schmidhuber, J.: Long short-term memory. Neural Comput. **9**(8), 1735–1780 (1997)
15. Kim, Y.: Convolutional Neural Networks for Sentence Classification, pp. 1746–1751 (2014)
16. Kräenbring, J., et al.: Accuracy and completeness of drug information in Wikipedia: a comparison with standard textbooks of pharmacology. PLoS One **9**(9), e106930 (2014)
17. Krizhevsky, A., et al.: ImageNet classification with deep convolutional neural networks. Adv. Neural. Inf. Process. Syst. **25**, 1–9 (2012)
18. Lee, Y.W., et al.: AIMQ: a methodology for information quality assessment. Inf. Manag. **40**(2), 133–146 (2002)
19. Madnick, S.E., et al.: Overview and framework for data and information quality research. ACM J. Data Inf. Q. **1**(1), 1–22 (2009)
20. Manning, C.D., Raghavan, P.: An Introduction to Information Retrieval (2009)
21. Mesgari, M., et al.: "The Sum of All Human Knowledge": A Systematic Review of Scholarly Research on the Content of Wikipedia (2015)

22. Mikolov, T., et al.: Efficient estimation of word representations in vector space. In: Proceedings of International Conference on Learning Representations (ICLR 2013), pp. 1–12 (2013)
23. Palangi, H., et al.: Deep sentence embedding using long short-term memory networks: analysis and application to information retrieval. IEEE/ACM Trans. Audio Speech Lang. Process. **24**(4), 694–707 (2016)
24. Royal, C., Kapila, D.: What's on Wikipedia, and what's not... ? Assessing completeness of information. Soc. Sci. Comput. Rev. **27**(1), 138–148 (2009)
25. Stvilia, B., et al.: Information quality work organization in Wikipedia. J. Am. Soc. Inf. Sci. Technol. **59**(6), 983–1001 (2008)
26. Sun, Y. et al.: Deep convolutional network cascade for facial point detection. In: Proceedings of the IEEE Computer Society Conference on Computer Vision and Pattern Recognition, pp. 3476–3483 (2013)
27. Zhang, Y., Wallace, B.: A Sensitivity Analysis of (and Practitioners' Guide to) Convolutional Neural Networks for Sentence Classification, pp. 253–263 (2015)

Query-Based Versus Resource-Based Cache Strategies in Tag-Based Browsing Systems

Joaquín Gayoso-Cabada, Mercedes Gómez-Albarrán,
and José-Luis Sierra$^{(\boxtimes)}$

Universidad Complutense de Madrid, 28040 Madrid, Spain
{jgayoso,mgomeza,jlsierra}@ucm.es

Abstract. Tag-based browsing is a popular interaction model for navigating digital libraries. According to this model, users select descriptive tags to filter resources in the collections. Typical implementations of the model are based on inverted indexes. However, these implementations can require a considerable amount of set operations to update the browsing state. To palliate this inconvenience, it is possible to adopt suitable cache strategies. In this paper we describe and compare two of these strategies: (i) a *query-based* strategy, according to which previously computed browsing states are indexed by sets of selected tags; and (ii) a *resource-based* strategy, according to which browsing states are indexed by sets of filtered resources. Our comparison focused on runtime performance, and was carried out empirically, using a real-world web-based collection in the field of digital humanities. The results obtained show that the resource-based strategy clearly outperforms the query-based one.

Keywords: Tag-based browsing · Cache strategy · Inverted indexes
Digital humanities

1 Introduction

Tag-based browsing [7, 27] is a popular interaction model adopted in many digital libraries [21]. According to this model, users can filter resources by employing descriptive *tags*. For this purpose, they can add new tags to shrink the current set of resources selected or to exclude tags in order to widen it. In consequence, the system updates the browsing state to provide: (i) the new set of filtered resources; and (ii) the new set of selectable tags.

A typical way to implement tag-based browsing is by using an *inverted index* [30]. An inverted index provides, for each tag, all the resources tagged with such a tag. In this way, after each user action the system can compute the new browsing state by performing several set operations involving the inverted index, the current browsing state, and, eventually, the overall underlying collection. Although there has been extensive research in performing these operations efficiently [5], the number of operations required can be appreciable, which can negatively impact user experience.

In order to decrease the cost of updating the browsing states, it is possible to use different cache strategies [8]. In particular, in this paper we will consider two of these strategies:

© Springer Nature Switzerland AG 2018
M. Dobreva et al. (Eds.): ICADL 2018, LNCS 11279, pp. 41–54, 2018.
https://doi.org/10.1007/978-3-030-04257-8_4

- *Query-based* strategy. This strategy uses the set of tags selected by the user (the *active tags*) as a cache index. Thus, it resembles the query-based caching mechanisms usually implemented in database systems [23]. The strategy is useful to identify *equivalent* browsing paths: two browsing paths are equivalent if they comprise the same set of active tags (although these tags may have been selected in a different order in each path). Since equivalent browsing paths lead to the same browsing state, by identifying a path to be equivalent to a previously explored one it is possible to reuse the cached information instead of re-computing it.
- *Resource-based* strategy. This strategy uses the set of filtered resources as the cache index. Thus, this strategy is able to detect paths leading to the same browsing state, even when they differ in their active tags. Therefore, the equivalency detection capability of this strategy outperforms that of the *query-based* one, since it is possible to have many distinct sets of active tags filtering the same set of resources. The disadvantage is the need to compute the set of filtered resources even for equivalent browsing paths.

In addition to describing these strategies, in this paper we will compare them using a real-world digital collection in the field of digital humanities (in particular, in the archeological domain). As it was mentioned above, and as we realized during our experience with several real-world collections in the field of digital humanities (see, for instance, [11]), response times during the updating of browsing states is a critical aspect that can directly impact user experience and satisfaction. Therefore, comparison will be focused on runtime performance, and, in particular, on the impact of each cache strategy on the time spent updating the information of the browsing states after each browsing action.

The rest of the paper is organized as follows: Sect. 2 surveys some works related to ours. Section 3 describes tag-based browsing in more detail. Section 4 describes the two cache strategies. Section 5 describes the empirical evaluation results. Finally, Sect. 6 provides some conclusions and lines of future work.

2   Related Work

Tag-based browsing naturally arises in digital collections organized as *semantic file systems* [28], in which resources are described using tags instead of being placed in particular folders or directories. In consequence, tag-based browsing resembles conventional directory-based navigation. Some works adopting this organization are [1, 7, 12, 24, 26]. These works typically use inverted indexes to organize the information and to speed up navigation. However, none of them discuss specific techniques concerning cache management in order to further enhance the browsing process.

Another field where tag-based browsing is extensively used is in digital collections supporting social tagging, in the style of Web 2.0 systems [6]. Some examples of works following this navigation model are [14–20]. Again, most of the systems described in this work use inverted indexes, but none of them focus on concrete techniques for dealing with the navigation cache.

In [8] we described an approach to enhancing tag-based browsing systems with inverted indexes and a cache strategy. By combining the cache-based and the resource-based strategy it is possible to obtain an improved version of the strategy proposed in that work. Finally, the work described in this paper is closely related to our previous work on *navigation automata* [9–11] for speeding up tag-based browsing. States in these automata correspond to sets of resources selected, while transitions correspond to the tags added by the users to shrink these sets. Navigation automata themselves are also closely related to *concept lattices* (as they are understood in *formal concept analysis* [3]), artifacts that have also been used to organize digital collections (e.g., [13, 29]). The approaches described in this paper can be understood as a dynamic expansion of these automata and lattices, which amortizes the overhead of their explicit construction during browsing, while also avoiding the construction of parts that will never be explored by the user.

3 Tag-Based Browsing

In this section we develop the aspects concerning tag-based browsing in more detail. Subsection 3.1 details the tag-based digital collection model proposed. Subsection 3.2 details the interaction technique itself.

3.1 Tag-Based Digital Collections

In this paper we will adopt a simple model of digital collection according to which a collection consists of:

– A set of *digital resources*. Resources are digital objects whose nature is no longer constrained by the model (e.g., media files like images, sound, video, etc., external resources identified by their URIs, or entities of a more abstract nature, such as tuples of a table in a relational database, records in a bibliographical catalog, elements in an XML document, rows from a spreadsheet, etc.).
– A set of *descriptive tags*. These tags are used to describe the resources. Notice that this cataloguing model, although simple, is not excessively limiting, since it is always possible to think of tags as terms or concepts taken from more sophisticated cataloguing schemata. For instance, we have followed this approach in *Clavy*, an experimental platform for managing digital collections with *reconfigurable* cataloguing schemata [9–11] presented as reconfigurable hierarchies of *element* types. Since the hierarchical structure of *Clavy* schemata can change unexpectedly, the internal implementation of the *Clavy* browsing system was assimilated into a tag-based one (in *Clavy*, *tags* corresponded with *element-value* pairs).
– The *annotation* of the resources. This annotation consists of associating tags with resources, which effectively catalogues these resources and, therefore, enables future uses of the collection (navigation, search, etc.).

Figure 1 outlines a small collection that follows this model. In this collection, resources are six image archives corresponding to artistic objects from the Prehistoric and Protohistoric artistic periods in Spain. Annotations are shown next to each resource. Tags describe the historic period (Prehistoric or Protohistoric), the artistic style (Cave-Painting, Megalithic, Tartesian, Punic, Phoenician), and the geographical area in which the object was discovered (Cantabrian, Levant, Plateau or Penibaetic).

Resources	Annotation	Resources	Annotation
r1 	Cave-Painting Cantabrian Prehistoric	r4 	Tartesian Plateau Protohistoric
r2 	Cave-Painting Levant Prehistoric	r5 	Phoenician Penibaetic Protohistoric
r3 	Megalithic Cantabrian Prehistoric	r6 	Punic Levant Protohistoric

Fig. 1. A small digital collection concerning prehistoric and protohistoric art in Spain

3.2 The Browsing Model

As indicated earlier, the tag-based browsing model adopted in this paper will allow the user to focus on a set of resources by adding and excluding descriptive tags. For this purpose, the user can carry out two different kind of actions:

Operation	Intended meaning
resources()	It provides all the resources in the collection.
tags()	It provides all the tags in the collection.
selectable_tags(R,T)	It determines which tags in T are selectable tags for the set of resources R (i.e., tags annotating *some*, but *not all*, of the resources in R).
next_user_action()	It returns the next interaction action carried out by the user (it will return $\perp$ when the user finishes interaction).
filter(R, t)	It returns all those resources in R annotated with t
query(F)	It returns the resources in the collection annotated with all the tags in F

Fig. 2. Basic operations supporting tag-based browsing

  – Adding a tag *t* to the set of *active tags*. This *add* action will be denoted by +*t*.
  – Removing the tag *t* from the set of active tags. This *remove* action will be denoted by ×*t*.

The browsing system will maintain a *browsing state* uniquely determined by the set of active tags $\mathbf{F}$. This state will have the following information items associated:

- The set of resources $\mathbf{R}^{\mathbf{F}}$ filtered by $\mathbf{F}$ (i.e., those resources in the collection annotated with all the tags in $\mathbf{F}$).
- The set of selectable tags $\mathbf{S}^{\mathbf{F}}$ that can intervene in an *add* action (i.e., those tags the user can use to further winnow down the current set of filtered resources). Each tag in $\mathbf{S}^{\mathbf{F}}$ will annotate some (but not all) the resources in $\mathbf{R}^{\mathbf{F}}$.

```
F ← ∅
Rᶠ ← resources ()
Sᶠ ← selectable_tags (Rᶠ, tags ())
do
    user_action ← next_user_action ()
    if user_action = +t
        F ← F ∪ {t}
        Rᶠ ← filter (Rᶠ,t)
        Sᶠ ← selectable_tags (Rᶠ,Sᶠ-{t})
    else if user_action = ×t
        F ← F - {t}
        Rᶠ ← query (F)
        Sᶠ ← selectable_tags (Rᶠ, tags ()-F)
    end if
until user_action = ⊥
```

Fig. 3. Algorithmic description of the tag-based browsing behavior

Figure 2 introduces a set of primitive operations in terms of which the browsing behavior can be described, and outlines its intended meaning. Figure 3 describes the browsing behavior itself. In this way:

- The browsing process begins by setting $\mathbf{R}^{\mathbf{F}}$ to all the resources in the collection, and $\mathbf{S}^{\mathbf{F}}$ to all the tags able to shrink these resources. Subsequently, the process proceeds until there are no more user actions available.
- To execute a $+t$ action, it is enough to: (i) add t to the set $\mathbf{F}$ of active tags; (ii) filter the resources in $\mathbf{R}^{\mathbf{F}}$ to those tagged with t; and (iii) update $\mathbf{S}^{\mathbf{F}}$ to the corresponding selectable tags (notice that t can be excluded as a selectable tag, since it will be shared by all the resources in the updated $\mathbf{R}^{\mathbf{F}}$; in addition, notice that all the resulting selectable tags must already be selectable *before* updating $\mathbf{S}^{\mathbf{F}}$).
- To execute a $\times t$ action, the steps to be carried out are: (i) remove t from $\mathbf{F}$; (ii) set $\mathbf{R}^{\mathbf{F}}$ to all those resources tagged by all the tags in the updated $\mathbf{F}$; and (iii) update $\mathbf{S}^{\mathbf{F}}$ (in this case, the potentially selectable tags are all the tags in the collection, with the exception of those in the updated $\mathbf{F}$).

Figure 4 outlines a tag-based browsing session for the collection in Fig. 1.

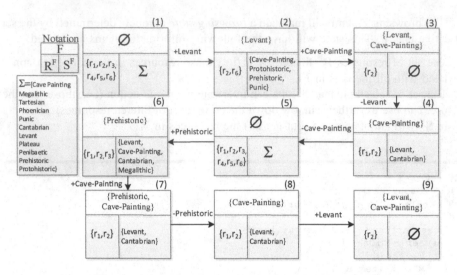

Fig. 4. A browsing session for the collection in Fig. 1

4 Cache Strategies

Updating the $\mathbf{R}^F$ and, especially, the $\mathbf{S}^F$ sets can be a costly process, since it can require several set operations (this fact is made apparent, for instance, in [8], where this process is implemented using inverted indexes). Therefore, the adoption of cache strategies like those aforementioned can substantially speed up this process. In this section we detail the abovementioned *query-based* strategy (Subsect. 4.1) and the *resource-based* one (Subsect. 4.2).

4.1 Query-Based Strategy

As suggested in Sect. 1, the query-based strategy binds sets of active tags $\mathbf{F}$ to the information for the resulting browsing state (i.e., the $\mathbf{R}^F$ and the $\mathbf{S}^F$ sets). Figure 5 describes the basic operations for managing the query-indexed cache, i.e., to store and retrieve the information. Using these operations, Fig. 6 describes the browsing strategy by extending the basic tag-based browsing process in Fig. 2 with cache capabilities. For this purpose, when the browsing system executes a browsing action:

- Firstly, it updates $\mathbf{F}$ accordingly (adding t for $+t$ actions, and removing t for $\times t$ actions).
- Afterwards, it uses the updated $\mathbf{F}$ to query the cache in the hope of retrieving the $\mathbf{R}^F$ and $\mathbf{S}^F$ values. If it fails to retrieve these values, (i) it updates them like the basic, un-cached, process described in Fig. 3; and (ii) it caches the updated values. Otherwise, it uses the retrieved values to update $\mathbf{R}^F$ and $\mathbf{S}^F$.

Therefore, each time the $\mathbf{F}$ set is updated, previously to computing the $\mathbf{R}^F$ and $\mathbf{S}^F$ sets, the cache is consulted. If this computation is finally carried out, this information is

Operation	Intended meaning
`cache_by_query(F,R`^{F}`,S`^{F}`)`	It stores $\mathbf{R}^F$ and $\mathbf{S}^F$ in the cache.
`retrieve_by_query(F)`	It retrieves the $(\mathbf{R}^F, \mathbf{S}^F)$ pair from the cache. If $\mathbf{F}$ is not cached, it returns $\bot$

Fig. 5. Operations for managing the query-indexed cache

```
F ← ∅
R^F ← resources()
S^F ← selectable_tags(R^F,tags())
cache_by_query(F,R^F,S^F)
do
    user_action ← next_user_action()
    if user_action ≠ ⊥
      if user_action = +t
         F ← F ∪ {t}
      else, let user_action = ×t in
         F ← F - {t}
      end if
      cached_info ← retrieve_by_query(F)
      if cached_info = ⊥
        if user_action = +t
           R^F ← filter(R^F,t)
           S^F ← selectable_tags(R^F,S^F-{t})
        else, let user_action = ×t in
           R^F ← query(F)
           S^F ← selectable_tags(R^F, tags()-F)
        end if
        cache_by_query(F,R^F,S^F)
      else
         (R^F,S^F) ← cached_info
      end if
    end if
until user_action = ⊥
```

Fig. 6. Tag-based browsing with a query-indexed cache

cached for subsequent use. In addition, since the cache indexes are the $\mathbf{F}$ sets of active tags, the order in which the tags are selected does not matter.

The strategy makes it possible, for instance, to avoid the computation of $\mathbf{R}^F$ and $\mathbf{S}^F$ in state (9) of Fig. 4, regardless of the fact that, when this information was cached -state (3)-, the sequence of tags selected was Levant followed by Cave-Painting, while in state (9) the selection order was inverted: first Cave-Painting, then Levant. It illustrates how this strategy is able to successfully deal with equivalent browsing paths, in the sense of leading to identical $\mathbf{F}$ sets. Concerning the other browsing states in Fig. 4, the strategy also avoids re-computing the $\mathbf{R}^F$ and $\mathbf{S}^F$ sets in states (5) and (8).

4.2 Resource-Based Strategy

While the query-based strategy successfully deals with browsing paths leading to identical sets of active tags, it fails to detect where two distinct sets of active tags filter the same set of resources. For instance, in the collection of Fig. 1 {Cave-Painting} and {Prehistoric, Cave-Painting} filter the same set of resources ({**r1, r2**}). However, the query-based strategy will be unaware of this fact. For instance, in state (7) of Fig. 4 it will re-compute $\mathbf{R}^F$ and $\mathbf{S}^F$, although these sets were already computed for state (4). The resource-based strategy alleviates this shortcoming. Figure 7 describes the resource-indexed cache managing operations required to implement the strategy. Figure 8 describes the resulting algorithmic behavior. In this case, the execution of a browsing action involves:

Operation	Intended meaning
cache_by_resources (**R, S**)	It binds the set of selectable tags **S** to the set of filtered resources **R** in the cache.
retrieve_by_resources (**R**)	It retrieves the set of selectable tags **S** for the resources **R** from the cache. If **R** is not cached, it returns ⊥

Fig. 7. Operations for managing the resources-indexed cache

```
F ← ∅
Rᶠ ← resources()
Sᶠ ← selectable_tags(Rᶠ,tags())
cache_by_resources(Rᶠ,Sᶠ)
do
   user_action ← next_user_action()
   if user_action ≠ ⊥
      if user_action = +t
         F ← F ∪ {t}
         Rᶠ ← filter(Rᶠ,t)
      else, let user_action = ×t in
         F ← F - {t}
         Rᶠ ← query(F)
      end if
      cached_sel_tags ← retrieve_by_resources(Rᶠ)
      if cached_sel_tags = ⊥
         if user_action = +t
            Sᶠ ← selectable_tags(Rᶠ, Sᶠ-{t})
         else, let user_action = ×t in
            Sᶠ ← selectable_tags(Rᶠ, tags()-F)
         end if
         cache_by_resources(Rᶠ,Sᶠ)
      else
         Sᶠ ← cached_sel_tags
      endif
   end if
until user_action = ⊥
```

Fig. 8. Tag-based browsing with a resource-indexed cache

- Firstly, updating $\mathbf{F}$ as in the query-based strategy in Fig. 6.
- Secondly, computing $\mathbf{R}^F$ as in the basic, un-cached, strategy in Fig. 3.
- Finally, querying the cache with $\mathbf{R}^F$ in the hope of getting a value for $\mathbf{S}^F$. If the query fails, $\mathbf{S}^F$ is computed as in Fig. 3, and then cached. Otherwise, $\mathbf{S}^F$ is updated to the value retrieved.

Therefore, notice that the resource-based strategy only avoids re-computing the $\mathbf{S}^F$ set, since it uses the set of filtered resources $\mathbf{R}^F$ as the cache index. However, as described in [8], the computation of $\mathbf{R}^F$ is usually much more agile than that of $\mathbf{S}^F$. Indeed:

- Once $\mathbf{R}^F$ is updated, the computation of $\mathbf{S}^F$ requires simulating the effect of an *add* action for *each* potentially selectable tag, i.e. (i) for each tag in the previous value for $\mathbf{S}^F$ (t excluded) if the user action was $+t$; or (ii) for each *non-active* tag (i.e., for each tag in the collection not present in $\mathbf{F}$) if the user action was a *remove* action.
- In consequence, the complexity of updating $\mathbf{S}^F$ is typically an order of magnitude greater than updating $\mathbf{R}^F$ (by using an inverted index, $\mathbf{R}^F$ can be updated by: (i) intersecting it with the entry in the inverted index for t if the user action was $+t$; or (ii) intersecting the entries for each surviving active tag if the action was $\times t$).

Concerning the browsing session in Fig. 4, the resource-based strategy will avoid re-computing $\mathbf{S}^F$ in (7), as well as in (5), (8) and (9).

5 Evaluation Results

This section describes an empirical comparison between the query based and the resource-based cache strategies oriented to assessing the differences in runtime performance between the two strategies. Subsection 5.1 describes the experimental setting. Subsection 5.2 presents the comparison results.

5.1 Experimental Setting

In order to carry out the comparison we implemented the two cache strategies in the aforementioned *Clavy* platform. In this context, we set an experiment concerning *Chasqui* [25],[1] a digital collection on Pre-Columbian American archeology. The current *Chasqui* version in *Clavy* consists of 2060 resources. The experimental setting allowed us to randomly generate browsing sessions. The generation process was based on the following random browsing process:

- In each browsing state in which both *add* and *remove* actions were allowed, a first, random decision on whether to choose one or another type of action was made (equal probability of 0.5 for each choice).

---

[1] http://oda-fec.org/ucm-chasqui.

- The generation of *add* actions was carried out by performing a second random decision, oriented to deciding whether to pick a tag between the 20 first selectable ones (probability of 0.8), or whether to pick a less significant tag (those placed from position 21 onwards). Finally, once the segment was determined, a tag in this segment was picked with equal probability.
- Concerning *remove* actions, random selection prioritized the most recently added tags: the last k-th added tag was picked with probability $0.8^{k-1} \times 0.2$ (i.e., following a geometric distribution with success probability p = 0.2).

These randomly generated browsing sessions allowed us to empirically check whether there were differences in the performances of the two strategies. Since our study was focused on runtime performance, we choose the total time spent for updating the browsing states during each browsing session (*cumulative browsing time*) as the primary comparison metric, since it provides all the time spent updating the browsing snapshot during each browsing session in a single measure. On the other hand, it is important to highlight that we were trying to assess which strategy provides responses faster than which others, not whether a particular tag-based collection (*Chasqui*, in this case) was correctly catalogued. This focus on time efficiency left out other resource and quality-based metrics which, like *precision* and *recall*, are typically used to evaluate information retrieval systems [22]. Indeed, both approaches (query-based and resource-based) are observationally equivalent from the point of view of the tag-based browsing model (i.e., when applied on the same sequence of browsing actions, both approaches will produce exactly the same sequence of browsing states, with the same R^F and S^F sets), which made it pointless to apply IR metrics like *recall* and *precision* in this study.

Next subsection summarizes the comparison results[2].

5.2   Comparison Results

The execution traces of the two strategies clearly suggested that the resource-based strategy outperformed the query-based one. For instance, Fig. 9 shows a representative example of these traces, displaying the cumulative browsing times for both strategies and for a browsing session consisting of 10000 user actions. In this particular execution the total computation time spent by the resource-based strategy (about 0.68 s) decreased the total time of the query-based approach (about 1.53 s) by about 55%.

After successive repetitions of the experiment, we observed similar behaviors, with improvements in favor of the resource-based strategy. More concretely, we measured the total execution times of both strategies for 500 browsing sessions, each one also containing 10000 user actions. The resource-based approach lowered the execution time in a range between 42% and 69% (Fig. 10). The average enhancement was of 54.8% (95% CI [54.8, 55.02]%). After running a Wilcoxon signed-rank test to compare the cumulative browsing times for the two strategies (query-based, mean rank = .00,

---

[2] All the measures reported were taken on a machine with an Intel® Core™ i5-4660S 2.9 GHz processor, RAM 16 GB and Windows 10 OS. Browsing software was programmed in Java. The browsing cache was maintained in memory using Java's HashMaps. Sets were managed using *roaring bitmaps* [4].

and resource-based, mean rank = 250.5), we realized that this perceived difference was clearly statistically significant (Z = −19.375, p = .000).

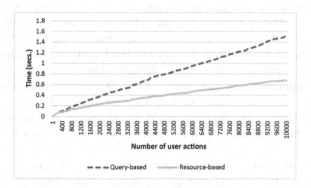

Fig. 9. Cumulative times for the query-based and the resource-based strategies for a randomly-generated browsing session

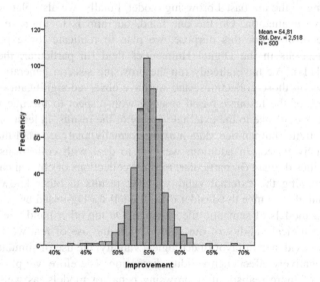

Fig. 10. Histogram of the improvement in time of the resource-based strategy

6   Conclusions and Future Work

In this paper we have described and compared two basic techniques to organize the browsing cache in tag-based digital collections. The first one, query-based strategy, is focused on caching browsing paths as set of active tags. In consequence, it is suitable for detecting equivalent browsing paths that involve exactly the same tags. However, it fails to detect paths that differ in some tag but that lead to the same set of resources.

This shortcoming is overcome by the resource-based strategy, by using sets of filtered resources, instead of sets of active tags, as indexing items. As side effects, it always recomputes the set of filtered resources. The experimental results obtained in this paper make it apparent that the resource-based approach can actually outperform the query-based one. Nevertheless, it does not exempt us from accepting this result with caution. In particular, the result is heavily dependent on the particular tag-based browsing model adopted. For instance, we can think of more restricted tag-based browsing models, like those followed in semantic file systems. Indeed, since in a semantic file system, browsing resembles the typical operations in a conventional file system, active tags can only be removed in reverse order to how they are added. Notice that, under this assumption, the query-based approach could provide better performance, since after *remove* actions, the information for the resulting state will always be in the query-indexed cache.

Currently we are working on improving the treatment of *remove* actions in order to reduce the number of set operations required. We are also working on combining the caching strategies with our previous work in navigation automata, as well as generalizing the approach to enable the navigation through links among resources. Also, we plan to combine browsing and Boolean searches, allowing users to browse search results according to the tag-based browsing model. Finally, we also plan to carry out a more exhaustive evaluation. On the one hand, our aim is to improve the external validity of the results. For this purpose, we plan to replicate the experiment with additional collections in the Digital Humanities field (in particular, the collections referred to in [11]). We have already run the browsing session generation and simulation processes on those collections, and we have observed significant differences in the performance of the resource-based strategy with respect to the query-based one. While it provides evidence to the external validity of the results, at least in reference to the domain of digital humanities, data must be formally analyzed, and the differences observed formally tested. In addition, we plan to deal with collections outside the Digital Humanities domain (in particular, medical collections of clinical cases [2]) with the aim of widening the external validity of the results to other knowledge fields. Finally, it would also be nice to consider other models for tag-based browsing (e.g., the aforementioned models of semantic file systems). On the other hand, we also want to improve the ecological validity of our study. While the use of real-world collections gave us positive evidence in favor of ecological validity, the use of simulated browsing traces could negatively affect such validity dimension. Therefore, we plan to carry out the simulation of more realistic user browsing behavior models, as well as real-user browsing traces. In addition, it would also be interesting to use additional metrics (e.g., the maximum response time for all that registered in a browsing trace), as well as experiments focusing on measuring user satisfaction.

Acknowledgements. This research is supported by the research projects TIN2014-52010-R and TIN2017-88092-R. Also, we would like to thank Mercedes Guinea and Alfredo Fernández-Valmayor (El Caño Foundation, Panamá), for their work on *Chasqui*.

References

1. Bloehdorn, S., Görlitz, O., Schenk, S., Völkel, M.: TagFS - tag semantics for hierarchical file systems. In: Proceedings of the 6th International Conference on Knowledge Management (I-KNOW 2006) (2006)
2. Buendía, F., Gayoso-Cabada, J., Sierra, J.-L.: Using digital medical collections to support radiology training in e-learning platforms. In: Pammer-Schindler, V., Pérez-Sanagustín, M., Drachsler, H., Elferink, R., Scheffel, M. (eds.) EC-TEL 2018. LNCS, vol. 11082, pp. 566–569. Springer, Cham (2018). https://doi.org/10.1007/978-3-319-98572-5_46
3. Carpineto, C., Romano, G.: Concept Data Analysis: Theory and Applications. Wiley, Hoboken (2004)
4. Chambi, S., Lemire, D., Kaser, O., Godin, R.: Better bitmap performance with Roaring bitmaps. Softw.-Pract. Exp. **46**(5), 709–719 (2016)
5. Culpepper, J.-S.; Moffat, A.: Efficient set intersection for inverted indexing. ACM Trans. Inf. Syst. **29**(1), Article no. 1 (2010)
6. Dimitrov, D., Helic, D., Strohmaier, M.: Tag-based navigation and visualization. In: Brusilovsky, P., He, D. (eds.) Social Information Access. LNCS, vol. 10100, pp. 181–212. Springer, Cham (2018). https://doi.org/10.1007/978-3-319-90092-6_6
7. Eck, O., Schaefer, D.: A semantic file system for integrated product data management. Adv. Eng. Inform. **25**(2), 177–184 (2011)
8. Gayoso-Cabada, J., Gómez-Albarrán, M., Sierra, J.-L.: Tag-based browsing of digital collections with inverted indexes and browsing cache. In: Proceedings of the 6th Edition of the Technological Ecosystems for Enhancing Multiculturality Conference (TEEM 2018) (2018)
9. Gayoso-Cabada, J., Rodríguez-Cerezo, D., Sierra, J.-L.: Multilevel browsing of folksonomy-based digital collections. In: Cellary, W., Mokbel, Mohamed F., Wang, J., Wang, H., Zhou, R., Zhang, Y. (eds.) WISE 2016. LNCS, vol. 10042, pp. 43–51. Springer, Cham (2016). https://doi.org/10.1007/978-3-319-48743-4_4
10. Gayoso Cabada, J., Rodríguez-Cerezo, D., Sierra, J.-L.: Browsing digital collections with reconfigurable faceted thesauri. In: 25th International Conference on Information Systems Development (ISD), Katowize, Poland (2016)
11. Gayoso-Cabada, J., Rodríguez-Cerezo, D., Sierra, J.-L.: Browsing digital collections with reconfigurable faceted thesauri. In: Gołuchowski, J., Pańkowska, M., Linger, H., Barry, C., Lang, M., Schneider, C. (eds.) Complexity in Information Systems Development. LNISO, vol. 22, pp. 69–86. Springer, Cham (2017). https://doi.org/10.1007/978-3-319-52593-8_5
12. Gifford, D.K., Jouvelot, P., Sheldon, M.A., O'Toole, J.W.: Semantic file systems. SIGOPS Oper. Syst. Rev. **25**(5), 16–25 (1991)
13. Greene, G.-J., Dunaiski, M., Fischer, B.: Browsing publication data using tag clouds over concept lattices constructed by key-phrase extraction. In: Proceedings of Russian and South African Workshop on Knowledge Discovery Techniques Based on Formal Concept Analysis (RuZA 2015) (2015)
14. Helic, D., Trattner, C., Strohmaier, M., Andrews, K.: On the navigability of social tagging systems. In: 2010 IEEE Second International Conference on Social Computing (SocialCom 2010), pp. 161–168 (2010)
15. Hernandez, M.-E., Falconer, S.-M., Storey, M.-A., Carini, S., Sim, I.: Synchronized tag clouds for exploring semi-structured clinical trial data. In: Proceedings of the 2008 Conference of the Center for Advanced Studies on Collaborative Research: Meeting of Minds (CASCON 2008) (2008)

16. Kammerer, Y., Nairn, R., Pirolli, P., Chi, E.H.: Signpost from the masses: learning effects in an exploratory social tag search browser. In: Proceedings of the SIGCHI Conference on Human Factors in Computing Systems (CHI 2009) (2009)
17. Kleinberg, J.: Navigation in a small world. Nature 406(6798), 845 (2000)
18. Koutrika, G., Zadeh, Z.-M., Garcia-Molina, H.: CourseCloud: summarizing and refining keyword searches over structured data. In: Proceedings of the 12th International Conference on Extending Database Technology (EDBT), pp. 1132–1135 (2009)
19. Leone, S., Geel, M., Müller, C., Norrie, M.C.: Exploiting tag clouds for database browsing and querying. In: Soffer, P., Proper, E. (eds.) CAiSE Forum 2010. LNBIP, vol. 72, pp. 15–28. Springer, Heidelberg (2011). https://doi.org/10.1007/978-3-642-17722-4_2
20. Lin, Y.-L., Brusilovsky, P., He, D.: Finding cultural heritage images through a Dual-Perspective Navigation Framework. Inf. Proc. Manag. 52(5), 820–839 (2016)
21. Redden, C.S.: Social bookmarking in academic libraries: trends and applications. J. Acad. Librariansh. 36(3), 219–227 (2010)
22. Salton, G., McGill, M.J.: Introduction to Modern Information Retrieval. McGraw-Hill, New York (1986)
23. Schwartz, B., Tkachenko, V., Zaitsev, P.: High Performance MySQL, 3rd edn. O'Reilly Media, Sebastopol (2012)
24. Seltzer, M., Murphy, N.: Hierarchical file systems are dead. In: Proceedings of the 12th Conference on Hot Topics in Operating Systems (HotOS 2009) (2009)
25. Sierra, J.-L., Fernández-Valmayor, A., Guinea, M., Hernanz, H.: From research resources to learning objects: process model and virtualization experiences. Educ. Technol. Soc. 9(3), 56–68 (2006)
26. Sim, H., Kim, Y., Vazhkudai, S.S., Vallée, G.R., Lim, S.-H., Butt, A.R.: Tagit: an integrated indexing and search service for file systems. In: Proceedings of the International Conference for High Performance Computing, Networking, Storage and Analysis (SC 2017) (2017)
27. Trattner, C., Lin, Y., Parra, D., Yue, Z., Real, W., Brusilovsky, P.: Evaluating tag-based information access in image collections. In: Proceedings of the 23rd ACM Conference on Hypertext and Social Media (HT 2012), pp. 113–122 (2012)
28. Watson, R., Dekeyser, S., Albadri, N.: Exploring the design space of metadata-focused file management systems. In: Proceedings of the Australasian Computer Science Week Multiconference (ACSW 2017) (2017)
29. Way, T., Eklund, P.: Social tagging for digital libraries using formal concept analysis. In: Proceedings of the 17th International Conference on Concept Lattices and Their Applications (CLA 2010) (2010)
30. Zobel, J., Moffat, A.: Inverted files for text search engines. ACM Comput. Surv. 33(2), Article 6 (2006)

Automatic Labanotation Generation, Semi-automatic Semantic Annotation and Retrieval of Recorded Videos

Swati Dewan[(✉)], Shubham Agarwal, and Navjyoti Singh

International Institute of Information Technology, Hyderabad, Hyderabad, India
{swati.dewan, shubham.agarwal}@research.iiit.ac.in,
navjyoti@iiit.ac.in

Abstract. Over the last decade, the volume of unannotated user-generated web content has skyrocketed but manually annotating data is costly in terms of time and resources. We leverage the advancements in Machine Learning to reduce these costs. We create a semantically searchable dance database with automatic annotation and retrieval. We use a pose estimation module to retrieve body pose and generate Labanotation over recorded videos. Though generic, it provides an essential application due to large amount of videos available online. Labanotation can be further exploited to generate ontology and is also very relevant for preservation and digitization of such resources. We also propose a semi-automatic annotation model which generates semantic annotations over any video archive using only 2–4 manually annotated clips. We experiment on two publicly available ballet datasets. High-level concepts such as ballet pose and steps are used to make the semantic library. These also act as descriptive meta-tags making the videos retrievable using a semantic text or video query.

Keywords: Searchable dance video library · Labanotation
Automatic annotation · Semantic query retrieval

1 Introduction

Representation and annotation of multimedia content are important steps towards visual media analysis. However, annotation incurs heavy cost in terms of time and other resources (motion capture sensors, annotators, etc.). This motivates heavy research efforts towards automatic multimedia content annotation. While there are frameworks that bridge the gap between natural human language annotations and ontology development, there is a need for multimedia semantic annotations especially videos that require frame level supervision. With the progress in machine learning and its applications, we leverage its automation and computation power towards faster content annotation. Here, we work on a relatively unexplored and novel domain to generate semantically informative annotations over a dance dataset. We work on ballet but the framework can be easily extended to any other dance format. We propose 2 tasks, (1) Automatic Labanotation generation, (2) Semi-automatic semantic annotations for a dance format given a semantic vocabulary.

© Springer Nature Switzerland AG 2018
M. Dobreva et al. (Eds.): ICADL 2018, LNCS 11279, pp. 55–60, 2018.
https://doi.org/10.1007/978-3-030-04257-8_5

1.1 Related Work

Different handcrafted feature based methods have been proposed [1–4] for human activity analysis, where a generic classifier like SVM [5] is used for classification. In [6], the idea of two-stream CNN was introduced and many state-of-the-art algorithms [7–9] extended over it. Here, we focus on LMA formalization. The most relevant analytical work in formalizing LMA [10] has been [11–13]. Also, there are frameworks that make manual annotation fast, e.g. [13] which is similar to ours but we require minimal manual annotations at the cost of a simpler semantic vocabulary. However, all these works require a lot of manual annotation. We haven't seen much work done on automatic semantic annotation in the area of video analysis. Also, we do not directly build ontologies over our framework because works like [15, 16] have already built very detailed dance ontologies. Most works that target automation of ontological or semantic discovery have been in the domain of text and document analysis or linguistics [17, 18]. However, the most impactful and relevant works in the domain of automatic video semantic analysis have been [13, 19, 20]. We draw inspirations for these works to use them in a video context.

2 Methodology

2.1 3D Skeleton from Recorded Ballet Videos

We follow the approach from [11] where they used a 2D human pose estimation approach further extended into a 3D human pose estimation model. We use a state-of-the-art depth regression model [21] to convert the 2D pose into 3D. Stochastic gradient descent optimization is used for training. We use a pre-trained model trained on Human3.6M dataset [22, 23], and fine-tune it with manually annotated data.

2.2 LMA Based Feature Extraction and Labanotation

Adapting LMA Theory into Laban Features: LMA is a multidisciplinary system that draws on Rudolph Laban's theories to describe, interpret and document human movements. It is divided into 4 categories: Body, Effort, Shape, Space. It provides a language to observe, describe, index and record human motion with applications in understanding interpersonal human behavior, animating virtual characters, digitizing and preserving traditional dance, etc. We use our approach in [11] to formalize LMA theory and generate meaningful spatio-temporal Laban features.

Labanotation: To generate Labanotation we use feature matching between features of consecutive frames and detect key frames by measuring the dissimilarity level. The video is divided into windows (0.2 s) and the key frames detected in each are used to write motion change over the Laban staff. As we work on skeletal data, one may use tools like GenLaban [24] to generate Labanotation from motion capture data. In this paper, we don't build our own ontological system towards Labanotation as works [15, 16] have already built great and extensive ontologies over it.

2.3 Semantic Annotations, Semi-automatic Tagging, Approach for Retrieval

Dataset and Semantic Vocabulary: We create a ballet dataset by taking videos from 2 sources [25–27] and manually labeling them with semantic annotations. One limitation in our work is the focus on a single performer per frame. The combined dataset contains a total of 83 videos at present. We use a total of 22 semantic annotations to divide the dataset, however, more will be added as the dataset and the vocabulary will grow with more manual annotations. Of these, 14 are dynamic (dance sequences) while 8 are static (dance pose). We find the semantic events such that they can be identified using visual cues and find strong relevance in semantics for retrieval.

Semi-automatic Annotation Model: We manually annotate a very small number of examples (2–4) per semantic event. This forms our training data. We use *LSTM* as a sequence learning model to learn the classification problem. We stack the Laban features for every frame to form a video descriptor. We train the LSTM with these descriptors. To generate fine-grained annotations, we use a sliding window architecture. To generate annotations for static ballet pose, we use the normalized pose as a feature vector and use correlation to match it to a pose from the vocabulary.

Retrieval and a Searchable Dance Library: The semantic annotations can act as *descriptive meta-tags* for a dance format which is relevant in retrieval. Towards this application, we built a *semantically searchable database*[1] over the ballet dataset. The search can be: *(i)* semantic text: word from the semantic vocabulary; *(ii)* video: a video of some ballet action sequence. This database also acts as an educational source to learn dance as it provides videos corresponding to a query to study. We plan to extend this database to hold more dance formats and grow it into a big Digital Library.

2.4 Evaluation and Performance

Table 1 compares the performance of our STLF-LSTM [11] model with the state-of-the-art on three datasets: KTH [9], ballet, ICD [28]. The model performs comparable to state-of-the-art for coarse-action recognition tasks. We obtain a *mAP of 94.56%* on the ballet dataset which is the only dataset with a semantically meaningful vocabulary. We infer that the model performs with great precision on ballet videos and can be used to generate the proposed semantic annotations accurately and in a fine-grained manner. The code to reproduce our work can be found here[2]. The approach is *semi-automatic* because we need to predefine the semantic events (samples from any annotated archive) and *manually annotate* few videos (2–4 per event) in their entirety and train the model. Then we can automatically detect and label the predefined semantic events in unseen videos using the then trained model.

---

[1] [https://shubhamagarwalwork.wixsite.com/dancelib] At present, this web-page is a prototype and does not support video queries but that will be extended soon with more data.

[2] https://drive.google.com/open?id=1lG0j0td7pD6QBAcUxd9CKPIAllFbw0Rp.

Table 1. Performance of STLF and state-of-the-art over different datasets

Method	KTH	ICD	Ballet
CNN+LSTM	89.60	83.48	–
TS-LSTM [6]	95.20	**88.99**	90.01
Ours (STLF [11])	**97.60**	86.41	**94.56**

3 Conclusions and Future Work

This work is a great example of the potential of applications that can be built at the crossroads of Digital Humanities and Machine Learning. The model performs well to generate fine-grained semantic annotations from a pre-defined semantic vocabulary for ballet and can be extended to more dance formats given more annotated content. Each step in the pipeline can be expanded into an application in the future. The pose estimation module provides applications such as automatic annotation of ontologies based directly on motion information. The Laban feature extraction module has already been implemented and used in its variations [16, 29] and can be expanded into a fully automatic process to generate Labanotation for videos. Finally, the semi-automatic fine-grained semantic event annotation model can be expanded to cover different forms of cultural heritage with support for more semantic events. However, The main limitations of this work is the limited annotated content, the dependence on a good pose estimation module and the restriction to a single performer in a frame. The ambitious goal for this project is a big semantically searchable Knowledge Library which will hold many different dance formats across the world.

References

1. Dewan, S., Agarwal, S., Singh, N.: Spatio-temporal Laban features for dance style recognition. In: ICPR, Beijing, China (2018)
2. Laban, R., Ullmann, L.: The Mastery of Movement. ERIC, Plays, Inc., Boston (1971)
3. Wang, Y., Mori, G.: Human action recognition by semi-latent topic models. IEEE Trans. Pattern Anal. Mach. Intell. **31**, 1762–1774 (2009)
4. Sgouramani, E., Vatakis, A.: "Flash" dance: how speed modulates perceived duration in dancers and non-dancers. Acta Psychol. **147**, 17–24 (2014)
5. Vatakis, A., Sgouramani, E., Gorea, A., Hatzitaki, V., Pollick, F.E.: Time to act: new perspectives on embodiment and timing. Procedia - Soc. Behav. Sci. **126**, 16–20 (2014)
6. Ionescu, C., Papava, D., Olaru, V., Sminchisescu, C.: Human3.6M: large scale datasets and predictive methods for 3D human sensing in natural environments. IEEE Trans. Pattern Anal. Mach. Intell. **36**(7), 1325–1339 (2014)
7. Ionescu, C., Li, F., Sminchisescu, C.: Latent structured models for human pose estimation. In: International Conference on Computer Vision (2011)
8. Zhou, X., Huang, Q., Sun, X., Xue, X., Wei, Y.: Towards 3D human pose estimation in the wild: a weakly-supervised approach. In: The IEEE International Conference on Computer Vision (ICCV), October 2017

9. Schuldt, C., Laptev, I., Caputo, B.: Recognizing human actions: a local SVM approach. In: ICPR (2004)
10. Samanta, S., Purkait, P., Chanda, B.: Indian classical dance classification by learning dance pose bases. In: 2012 IEEE Workshop on the Applications of Computer Vision (WACV), Breckenridge, CO, pp. 265–270 (2012)
11. Ma, C.-Y., Chen, M.-H., Kira, Z., AlRegib, G.: TS-LSTM and temporal-inception: exploiting spatio-temporal dynamics for activity recognition. CoRR, abs/1703.10667 (2017)
12. Aristidou, A., Stavrakis, E., Charalambous, P., Chrysanthou, Y., Himona, S.L.: Folk dance evaluation using Laban movement analysis. J. Comput. Cult. Herit. (JOCCH) **8**(4), 20:1–20:19 (2015)
13. Aristidou, A., Chrysanthou, Y.: Motion indexing of different emotional states using LMA components. In: SIGGRAPH Asia 2013 Technical Briefs (SA 2013), pp. 21:1–21:4. ACM, New York (2013)
14. Handschuh, S., Staab, S., Ciravegna, F.: S-CREAM—Semi-automatic CREAtion of metadata. In: Gómez-Pérez, A., Benjamins, V.R. (eds.) EKAW 2002. LNCS (LNAI), vol. 2473, pp. 358–372. Springer, Heidelberg (2002). https://doi.org/10.1007/3-540-45810-7_32
15. Navigli, R., Ponzetto, S.P.: BabelNet: the automatic construction, evaluation and application of a wide-coverage multilingual semantic network. Artif. Intell. **193**, 217–250 (2012). https://doi.org/10.1016/j.artint.2012.07.001
16. Ballan, L., Bertini, M., Bimbo, A., Seidenari, L., Serra, G.: Event detection and recognition for semantic annotation of video. Multimed. Tools Appl. **51**(1), 279–302 (2011). https://doi.org/10.1007/s11042-010-0643-7
17. Yildirim, Y., Yazici, A., Yilmaz, T.: Automatic semantic content extraction in videos using a fuzzy ontology and rule-based model. IEEE Trans. Knowl. Data Eng. **25**(1), 47–61 (2013)
18. Raheb, K.E.: Dance ontology: towards a searchable knowledge base. In: Workshop on Movement Qualities and Physical Models Visualization, IRCAM Centre Pompidou, Paris (2012)
19. El Raheb, K., Mailis, T., Ryzhikov, V., Papapetrou, N., Ioannidis, Y.: BalOnSe: temporal aspects of dance movement and its ontological representation. In: Blomqvist, E., Maynard, D., Gangemi, A., Hoekstra, R., Hitzler, P., Hartig, O. (eds.) ESWC 2017. LNCS, vol. 10250, pp. 49–64. Springer, Cham (2017). https://doi.org/10.1007/978-3-319-58451-5_4
20. Dewan, S., Agarwal, S., Singh, N.: Laban movement analysis to classify emotions from motion. In: ICMV, Vienna, Austria (2017)
21. Lea, C., Vidal, R., Reiter, A., Hager, G.D.: Temporal convolutional networks: a unified approach to action segmentation. In: Hua, G., Jégou, H. (eds.) ECCV 2016. LNCS, vol. 9915, pp. 47–54. Springer, Cham (2016). https://doi.org/10.1007/978-3-319-49409-8_7
22. Balakrishnan, R., Rajkumar, K.: Semi-automated annotation and retrieval of dance media objects. Cybern. Syst. **38**(4), 349–379 (2007). https://doi.org/10.1080/01969720701291189
23. Choensawat, W., Nakamura, M., Hachimura, K.: GenLaban: a tool for generating Labanotation from motion capture data. Multimed. Tools Appl. **74**, 10823 (2015). https://doi.org/10.1007/s11042-014-2209-6
24. Jalal, A., Kamal, S., Kim, D.: A depth video sensor-based life-logging human activity recognition system for elderly care in smart indoor environments. Sensors **14**, 11735–11759 (2014)
25. Jalal, A., Sarif, N., Kim, J.T., Kim, T.S.: Human activity recognition via recognized body parts of human depth silhouettes for residents monitoring services at smart home. Indoor Built Environ. **22**, 271–279 (2013)
26. Li, J., Allinson, N.: Building recognition using local oriented features. IEEE Trans. Industr. Inform. **9**(3), 1697–1704 (2013)

27. Jalal, A., Kamal, S., Kim, D.: Shape motion features approach for activity tracking and recognition from kinect video camera. In: IEEE 29th International Conference on Advanced Information Networking and Applications Workshops, Gwangju, pp. 445–450 (2015)
28. Wang, L., et al.: Temporal segment networks: towards good practices for deep action recognition. In: ECCV (2016)
29. Fleichtenhofer, C., Pinz, A., Zisserman, A.: Convolutional two-stream network fusion for video action recognition. In: CVPR (2016)

Quality Classification of Scientific Publications Using Hybrid Summarization Model

Hafiz Ahmad Awais Chaudhary[1] , Saeed-Ul Hassan[1(✉)] ,
Naif Radi Aljohani[2] , and Ali Daud[2]

[1] Information Technology University, Lahore, Pakistan
saeed-ul-hassan@itu.edu.pk
[2] King Abdulaziz University, Jeddah, Saudi Arabia

Abstract. In this paper (Note that the dataset and code to reproduce the results can be accessed at the following URL: https://github.com/slab-itu/hsm), we intend to assess the quality of scientific publications by measuring the relationship between full text papers with that of their abstracts. A hybrid summarization model is proposed that combines text summarization and information retrieval (IR) techniques to classify scientific papers into different ranks based on their abstract correctness. Using the proposed model, we study the relationship between a correctly written abstract (in accordance with full-text) and the scholarly influence of scientific publications. The proposed supervised machine learning model is deployed on 460 full-text publications - randomly downloaded from Social Science Research Network (SSRN). In order to quantify the scholarly influence of publications, a composite score provided by SSRN is used that combines usage indicators along with citation counts. This score is then used to label the publications into high and low ranks. The results determine that the papers having abstracts in accordance with full text also show high scholarly rank with an encouraging accuracy of 73.91%. Finally, 0.701 Area Under the Curve (AUC) for receiver-operating characteristic is achieved that outperforms the traditional IR and summarization models with AUC of 0.536 and 0.58 respectively. Overall our findings suggest that a correctly written abstract in accordance to its full text have a high probability to attract more social usage and citations and vice versa.

Keywords: Hybrid summarization model
Classification of scientific publications · Information retrieval · Summarization
Social Science Research Network

1 Introduction

Document summarization has become an important and timely tool for assisting and interpreting text information in today's fast growing information age [1]. Recent works on summarization are on technical documents that provide early insight on various features that are helpful in finding salient parts of documents [2]. Initially, most of the systems assumed feature independence but with the emergence of data mining and machine learning techniques in natural language processing, a series of influential papers has been published that engaged statistical techniques to summarize documents [3].

© Springer Nature Switzerland AG 2018
M. Dobreva et al. (Eds.): ICADL 2018, LNCS 11279, pp. 61–67, 2018.
https://doi.org/10.1007/978-3-030-04257-8_6

In the modern age, with the revolution of device-to-device communication and the invention of economical storages, the amount of information has grown largely and manual handling of such an enormous data is nearly impossible. Hence, the data lakes will sooner be converted into data swamps if not handled properly. Hence, summarization has become demanding and popular in web searches and an automated human like summary generation is still a promising research area for new researchers.

The World Wide Web and social media has become the most frequent and substantial source of information in modern age, where millions of users from all over the world interact with different varieties of information and search engines provide them relevant information. The search engines do not process every single bit of information [4], instead they use IR techniques to query the already generated summaries against documents [5]. Now the question is how accurate are these summaries written? If the summary or abstract is not written correctly, then the search engines might not provide relevant results.

Given the crucial need for improved summarization techniques, this article presents a novel hybrid model that combines traditional feature-oriented summarization with the recent IR techniques. Following is the contribution of this work: (a) Application of summarization and IR for quality classification of scientific papers by exploiting abstract correctness instead of traditional citation counts or link weight based methods, (b) Investigation of the relationship between correctly written abstract (in accordance with full text) and scholarly influence of scientific paper.

2 Literature Review

In spite of, text summarization being an active area of research for more than 50 years, researchers are still investigating and introducing new techniques to improve the domain [6]. A survey on automatic text summarization suggests that its foundation laid on IR techniques [3]. Therefore, IR is not entirely an exclusive domain compared with summarization [1].

Although the techniques for summarization are constantly evolving and based upon types, these can be categorized into; Extractive methods [7], abstractive methods, general short summaries [8], centroid-based summaries [1], single document and multi-document summarization [3], rich features and decision trees [3], Naïve-Bayes methods, hidden Markov models [9] and deep natural language analysis methods [3]. Information overload has created an acute need for summarization. Typically, either the same information is present across multiple documents or various aspects of the same information is discussed in multiple documents. So the need for single vs. multiple document summarizations varies from domain to domain. Extending summarization to multi-document presents some additional challenges such as removing redundancies, sentence ranking and name filters for duplication removal [10]. During the training of system, the researchers used a combination of features [6] like term frequency [1], inverse document frequency [11], term position [7] and sentence length [7] for the calculation and assignment of scores to sentences.

The IR models can be categorized into set-theoretic, algebraic and probabilistic [12] and known models among them are standard boolean, extended boolean, fuzzy retrieval and vector space model (VSM) [13]. The majority of IR systems are built by standard or extended Boolean models because of its simplicity and intuitively [14]. We have discussed important summarization and IR techniques. Although they are used in different areas of research but are hardly explored for quality classification of scientific papers.

3 Methodology

Our proposed model HSM is a hybrid model, consisting of feature-oriented summarization and IR methods for quality classification of papers using supervised machine learning approach. For ranking mechanism, the model assigns the score to every sentence based upon the features obtained from summarization and IR methods. Finally, HSM generates a brief extractive summary for calculation of similarity coefficients and apply decision tree for classification of papers.

3.1 Data Set

We downloaded[1] full-text research papers from Social Science Research Network (SSRN). SSRN is an open source repository devoted to scholarly research in humanities and social sciences and was ranked as the world's top open access repository in 2013. SSRN also provides a composite score that combines altmetrics related indicators along with citation counts. This composite score was used to rank the publications. Additionally, we downloaded 460 papers of social science domain that contain abstracts in their full-text. Note the tool used for data cleaning and training of model is Visual Studio 2013 using C#. For experimentation and evaluation, we used R-studio and R-Language. The experimentation, representation and graph plotting was also carried out through IBM SPSS version 21 and Tableau.

3.2 Proposed Hybrid Model

This section contains the detail of our proposed HSM. Firstly, we trained our model on training data, which is later, used for making the predictions on testing data. The dataset is divided into two sections for training and testing purpose. The proposed model has two sub-modules, summarization and IR modeling. While modeling summarization, we calculated the key summarization parameters; term frequency, sentence position, and sentence length.

Term frequency is one of the most important summarization parameters, which is a part of almost every summarization system. It is frequency or count of keywords in a document to highlight the concept of the document. *Sentence length* plays an important role in the selection of sentences for final summary. Sentences with average length are best fit for final summary. The reason behind ignorance of very short sentences is that the isolated sentences with two or three words will not convey any meaning, similarly

---

[1] The data was downloaded from http://www.ssrn.com/ on Feb 16, 2015.

very long sentences do not qualify for the criteria of summary, as summary should be precise. *Sentence positions* also represent the importance of sentences. Majorly, the sentences from the top most section of the text and lowest portion are considered important as they contain the opening remarks and conclusion of the document. Therefore, we assigned score 100 and 75 to the initial and the final sentence of document respectively. The remaining sentences get the score in-between with the minimum score of 40 for the middle section as they usually contain details and explanations. After calculating the parameters, normalization is applied to get values in between 0 to 100. A brute force approach is used to get the optimal weights. This is done by assessing all combination of weights in accordance with the given abstract with the granularity of 10 so that the importance of every single parameter can be examined. The first summary (FS) is then generated against each paper by selecting N sentences with top scores, where N was empirically selected as 1.5 times of abstract's length.

Our IR model utilizes ensemble methods to achieve the maximum accuracy. In the ensemble method, we implemented Boolean Model, Extended Boolean Model and, VSM in a way that each sentence of abstract is treated as a query to extract most relevant sentences from the full text. This made each sentence to have an accumulative score given by abstract queries from different IR models on basics of similarity. Then the second summary (SS) is generated against each paper by selecting again N sentences with the maximum accumulative score. Lastly, a brief extractive final summary (FF) was generated by the union of summaries FS and SS generated by the summarization and IR model, respectively. For quality ranking, we calculated similarity coefficients, Levenshtein Distance, Jaccard Distance (JD), Ratcliff Obershelp (RO) Similarity and Sorensen Dice Distance between abstract and generated Final Summary (FF) for each paper and feed these coefficients along with SSRN altmetrics to decision tree algorithm. We used the SSRN score to label training documents rank as high or low. The algorithm tuned these coefficients on training data and calculated threshold values of coefficients for class variable i.e. rank.

4 Results and Discussion

We used a composite score provided by SSRN to label training documents into class variables as high and low ranks. Further, these ranks are used to evaluate the effectiveness of our model in identifying the relation between a correctly written abstract and the influence of scientific paper. The dataset was divided into two parts: 368 files (80%) for the training and 92 files (20%) for testing. In the training phase, our goal was to calculate optimal weights/threshold values for the similarity coefficients and then further use them in testing. Initially, multiple similarity coefficients were considered for labeling, but we observed that the impact of these coefficients is not identical and hence, a mechanism is required to finalize the coefficients and threshold values.

Therefore, the decision tree with k-fold cross-validation was applied to choose the best coefficients in order to achieve the optimal results. Hence, JD and RO were finalized as similarity coefficients for labeling of test data. Moreover, for the evaluation of model, we applied proposed HSM on testing dataset, predict their rank using trained decision tree parameters, and calculated the accuracy.

Table 1 shows the results of testing data with different k-fold iterations and the overall accuracy of the system remains the same, across all k-fold i.e. $\sim 67\%$. Finally, Receiver operating characteristic (ROC) curve was generated to examine the accuracy and ability of the model to discriminate among the various classes. Figure 1 shows the AUC comparison and the maximum independent coverage of models i.e. 53.6% for SM and 58% for IR. However, the HSM is covering the maximum area under the curve that is maximum 70.1% for some points. So, it can be deduced that the performance of HSM is maximum as compared to other models.

Table 1. Test results of hybrid summarization model

K-fold	Testing examples	Correct prediction	Wrong prediction	Mean absolute error	Accuracy
3	460	312	148	0.425	67.82%
10	460	309	151	0.432	67.17%
25	460	310	150	0.430	67.39%

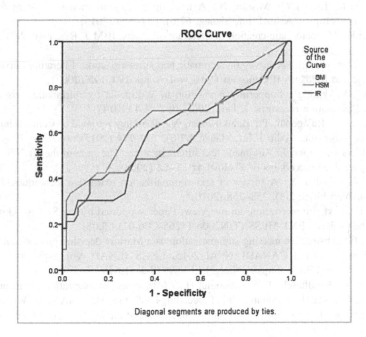

Fig. 1. ROC curve of SM, IR and HSM.

5 Concluding Remarks

We have proposed an HSM that combines summarization and IR techniques to classify scientific papers into different ranks based on their abstract correctness. The model examines the relationship between the scholarly influence of scientific paper and a correctly written abstract in accordance with full text. To quantify the scholarly influence of papers, we used a composite score provided by SSRN. This score was then used to label the publications into high and low ranks. Our proposed machine-learning model classifies the scientific papers into ranks based on the relevancy of their abstract with full text. Furthermore, HSM shows relatively high 0.701 area under the curve compared with the traditional ones i.e. 0.58 area under the curve for the summarization method and 0.536 area under the curve for IR method.

In future, we plan to increase the training and testing data of the system. This will not only improve the accuracy of the system but will also reach a level of expert tool. Similarly, tweaking the selection of parameters and algorithms may provide us with better results.

References

1. Chang, H.T., Liu, S.W., Mishra, N.: A tracking and summarization system for online Chinese news topics. Aslib J. Inf. Manag. **67**(6), 687–699 (2015)
2. Luhn, H.P.: The automatic creation of literature abstracts. IBM J. Res. Dev. **2**(2), 159–165 (1958)
3. Das, D., Martins, A.F.: A survey on automatic text summarization. Literature Survey for the Language and Statistics II Course at CMU, vol. 4, pp. 192–195 (2007)
4. Wu, I.C., Vakkari, P.: Supporting navigation in Wikipedia by information visualization: extended evaluation measures. J. Doc. **70**(3), 392–424 (2014)
5. Ravana, S.D., Rajagopal, P., Balakrishnan, V.: Ranking retrieval systems using pseudo relevance judgments. Aslib J. Inf. Manag. **67**(6), 700–714 (2015)
6. Ježek, K., Steinberger, J.: Automatic text summarization (The state of the art 2007 and new challenges). In: Proceedings of Znalosti, pp. 1–12 (2008)
7. Gupta, V., Lehal, G.S.: A survey of text summarization extractive techniques. J. Emerg. Technol. Web Intell. **2**(3), 258–268 (2010)
8. Lloret, E.: Text summarization: an overview. Paper supported by the Spanish Government under the project TEXT-MESS (TIN2006-15265-C06-01) (2008)
9. Murray, G.: Abstractive meeting summarization as a Markov decision process. In: Barbosa, D., Milios, E. (eds.) CANADIAN AI 2015. LNCS (LNAI), vol. 9091, pp. 212–219. Springer, Cham (2015). https://doi.org/10.1007/978-3-319-18356-5_19
10. Fiszman, M., Rindflesch, T.C., Kilicoglu, H.: Abstraction summarization for managing the biomedical research literature. In: Proceedings of the HLT-NAACL Workshop on Computational Lexical Semantics, pp. 76–83. Association for Computational Linguistics (2004)
11. Hjørland, B., Nissen Pedersen, K.: A substantive theory of classification for information retrieval. J. Doc. **61**(5), 582–597 (2005)
12. Galvez, C., de Moya-Anegón, F., Solana, V.H.: Term conflation methods in information retrieval: non-linguistic and linguistic approaches. J. Doc. **61**(4), 520–547 (2005)

13. Pontes, E.L., Huet, S., Torres-Moreno, J.-M., Linhares, A.C.: Automatic text summarization with a reduced vocabulary using continuous space vectors. In: Métais, E., Meziane, F., Saraee, M., Sugumaran, V., Vadera, S. (eds.) NLDB 2016. LNCS, vol. 9612, pp. 440–446. Springer, Cham (2016). https://doi.org/10.1007/978-3-319-41754-7_46
14. Bordogna, G., Pasi, G.: Application of fuzzy set theory to extend boolean information retrieval. In: Crestani, F., Pasi, G. (eds.) Soft Computing in Information Retrieval. Studies in Fuzziness and Soft Computing, vol. 50, pp. 21–47. Physica, Heidelberg (2000). https://doi.org/10.1007/978-3-7908-1849-9_2

Social Media, Web, and News

Investigating the Characteristics and Research Impact of Sentiments in Tweets with Links to Computer Science Research Papers

Aravind Sesagiri Raamkumar$^{(\boxtimes)}$ (iD), Savitha Ganesan,
Keerthana Jothiramalingam, Muthu Kumaran Selva, Mojisola Erdt (iD),
and Yin-Leng Theng (iD)

Wee Kim Wee School of Communication and Information,
Nanyang Technological University, Singapore 637718, Singapore
{aravind0002, savitha002, keerthan004, sath0018,
mojisola.erdt, tyltheng}@ntu.edu.sg

Abstract. Research papers are often shared in Twitter to facilitate better readership. Tweet counts are embedded in journal websites and academic databases, to emphasize the impact of papers in social media. However, more number of tweets per paper is doubted as an indicator of research quality. Hence, there is a need to look at the intrinsic factors in tweets. Sentiment is one of such factors. Earlier studies have shown that neutral sentiment is predominantly found in tweets with links to research papers. In this study, the main intention was to have a closer look at the non-neutral sentiments in tweets to understand whether there is some scope for using such tweets in measuring the interim quality of the associated research papers. Tweets of 53,831 computer science papers from the Microsoft Academic Graph (MAG) dataset were extracted for sentiment classification. The non-neutral sentiment keywords and the attributed aspects of the papers were manually identified. Findings indicate that although neutral sentiments are majorly found in tweets, the research impact of papers which had all three sentiments was better than papers which had only neutral sentiment, in terms of both bibliometrics and altmetrics. Implications for future studies are also discussed.

Keywords: Twitter · Tweet sentiments · Research impact · Computer science
Research metrics

1 Background

Social media has become a widely accessible information source since it enables users to post their opinions and multimedia content without much external verification [1]. Social media has transformed the communication between scholars and the public by facilitating access to research articles at a comparatively lesser cost and faster pace [2]. Accordingly, readers tend to recommend research articles which are relevant and useful to other users in their social media networks [3]. As a popular example, the microblogging platform Twitter is used by researchers and academicians to network with people of similar interests and to share information with wider audience.

© Springer Nature Switzerland AG 2018
M. Dobreva et al. (Eds.): ICADL 2018, LNCS 11279, pp. 71–82, 2018.
https://doi.org/10.1007/978-3-030-04257-8_7

It is well know that the impact of research outputs is measured using traditional indicators known as Bibliometrics [4]. On the other hand, the rise of social media platforms and increasing online activity of users, have led to the development of a new set of indicators called Altmetrics, a term proposed in 2010 [5]. Popular examples of these social media metrics include tweets count, Mendeley readers count, bookmarks count for the corresponding research papers. Subsequently in recent years, research has been conducted on themes such as investigating researchers' intent behind social media sharing and outreach [6, 7]. Studies have shown that these metrics are weak indicators of research impact due to the lack of meaningful context while sharing research papers in social media platforms [8].

The Matthew effect in citations leads to highly cited papers to be cited even more [9]. This effect is facilitated by academic search engines and databases which rank papers based on higher number of citations. Unless the user changes the sort options to rank papers by recency, the highly cited papers keep attracting user's attention. Social media impact indicators can be perceived as an alternative to rank papers in academic systems. However, these sources are not used by everyone in the research community. For instance, Twitter is banned in some countries where they have their own microblogging platforms (e.g., Weibo). Mendeley is not widely used as Endnote. Most importantly, these metrics do not assure quality. A high altmetric score for a research paper indicates that the paper is popular in different social media platforms. Among the different altmetric indicators, only Mendeley readers count has been found to be correlated with citations count [10]. Other social media metrics mostly have weak positive correlations [11, 12]. Hence, the impetus is to mine deeper into the social media data to get better insights on the quality of the papers.

In this study, the focus is on Twitter since it is one of the popular social media platforms for researchers. It is often observed that a research paper with more number of tweets has a high aggregated altmetric score. Tweet count is the main Twitter metric. Some of the associated disadvantages of relying solely on tweet counts have already been underlined in earlier studies [8]. Apart from the tweet count, retweets count and favorites count are other Twitter metrics whose use is restricted due to high data sparsity. Apart from these metrics, the tweet content can be used for gleaning insights about the opinions of Twitter users about the research papers that are shared through the tweets. Twitter content analysis has been an area of research conducted to study different type of events such as pandemics [13] and politics [14], to name a few. One of the methods of content analysis, sentiment analysis is a way of determining the sentiment or opinion about a product or subject in a discussion or conversation [15]. An opinion is "simply a positive or negative sentiment, view, attitude, emotion, or appraisal about an entity or an aspect of the entity" [16]. This method has been used with the content from social media platforms as well [17, 18].

Although Twitter content analysis studies are frequently conducted, studies on sentiment analysis of tweets containing links to research papers are very few. Three studies have been conducted on this topic. In the earliest study [19], a manual content analysis was conducted on 270 tweets from papers published in 2012. 96% of the tweet had neutral sentiments while the remaining 4% tweets had positive sentiments. There were no negative sentiment tweets found. In this study, other facets such as main content of tweet, authorship attribution and expression of interest were also identified.

In the next study [20], sentiment analysis was done on an extract of 1,000 tweets using the SentiStrength[1] tool. In this study, 94.8% of the tweets had neutral sentiment while positive and negative sentiments were found in 4.3% and 0.9% of the tweets respectively. The authors conclude that sentiment analysis tools do not perform an adequate identification of negative tweets. In another study conducted by the same authors [21], a larger extract of 487, 610 tweets were classified. The percentage of positive tweets is the highest in this study with 11% and even negative tweets were identified for 7.3% of the tweets while neutral sentiment tweets were at 81.7%. Since this study was conducted on papers from different disciplines, authors identify that the highest percentage of negative tweets were found in social sciences and humanities disciplines. However, this study lacks in-depth analysis of the tweets containing non-neutral sentiments.

2 Research Objectives

In this study, we have attempted to understand the role and nature of sentiments in tweets by starting with a qualitative analysis of tweets with non-neutral sentiments. In addition, we have also compared the performance of papers with all sentiments against papers with just neutral sentiment in tweets. These two objectives were conceptualized due to the need for identifying new metrics or data items from Twitter, which could be used as proxy measures for ascertaining quality of research papers. For this study, we wanted to focus on Computer Science (CS) research papers since CS papers are popular in Twitter. The research reported in this paper addresses the following questions.

RQ1: How are the sentiments represented in the tweets, in terms of composition, keywords and attributed aspects?

RQ2: How do papers with all three sentiments compare against papers with only neutral sentiments in terms of impact indicators?

3 Methodology

3.1 Data Collection and Pre-processing

The Microsoft Academic Graph (MAG) dataset provided by Microsoft Research [22] was used for this study. The dataset version used in this paper was released on February 2016. Computer science (CS) related papers were extracted from the MAG dataset using the CS venue entries indexed in DBLP, a bibliographic database which covers publications from major CS journals and conference proceedings. The citation counts of the extracted papers were calculated with the MAG dataset internally. From this initial extract of CS papers, the papers published since 2012 were shortlisted ($n = 53,831$) as most papers published before that period, tend to have very minimal social media data. The altmetric impact indicators of these papers were extracted using

---

[1] SentiStrength http://sentistrength.wlv.ac.uk/.

the APIs provided by Altmetric.com and PlumX. From these 53,831 papers, it was found that only 13,809 papers (25.65%) had tweets. Bot and spam accounts are a well-known phenomenon in Twitter [23]. To remove such accounts, the twitter user's description field was used. Keywords such as bot and robot were employed for this filtering purpose. In the next stage, the paper titles were removed from the tweets. At this stage, there were 77, 914 tweets. In the next step, retweets were also removed and the final extract of tweets to be classified and analyzed stood at 49,849 tweets for 12, 967 associated papers.

3.2 Determining Sentiment Polarity and Score

The TextBlob[2] package in Python was used for determining the sentiment polarity of tweets. The TextBlob module has a scoring scale range from −1 to +1. This range was initially divided into five equal parts and classified as shown in Table 1. To verify the current classification scheme used, manual annotation process was carried out on entries which fell under the positive and negative sentiment category. When comparing the manually annotated sentiment category tweets, it was found that some of the neutral tweets were classified as either positive or negative. Through further analysis, it was found that actual neutral tweets had a sentiment score between −0.3 and 0.3. The score scheme was adjusted accordingly. The modified scoring scheme has been included in Table 1.

The existing sentiment classification tools and libraries used in general domains, are not directly applicable for classifying tweets that contains links to research papers. The main reason being the presence of paper titles in the tweets [19], which could be resolved to some extent by data cleaning. The secondary reason being the training model built with data from other domains. In the current study's classification phase, it was decided that the tweets which are initially classified as neutral could be left unchanged. The positive and negative tweets were manually checked to reclassify certain tweets to the neutral category. Thus, the modified sentiment score range could be adopted in future studies where the TextBlob library is used to classify sentiments.

3.3 Extraction of Sentiment Keywords and Identification of Aspects

After the sentiment classification exercise was completed, the next step was to extract the keywords representing positive and negative sentiments in the tweets. Along with these keywords, the aspect of the papers for which the sentiment was expressed, was also identified for each non-neutral tweet. The identification of aspects was first performed by a single coder and later validated and corrected by two other coders. For this coding exercise, coding book was not employed, instead the coders decided the aspect codes through a grounded theory approach [24].

---

[2] TextBlob: Simplified Text Processing https://textblob.readthedocs.io/en/dev/.

Table 1. Initial and modified sentiment score ranges

Initial sentiment score range	Modified sentiment score range	Sentiment category
> 0.5 and ≤ 1.0	>0.5 and ≤ 1.0	Extremely positive
> 0.0 and ≤ 0.5	>0.3 and ≤ 0.5	Positive
= =0.0	≥ −0.3 and ≤ 0.3	Neutral
<0.0 and ≥ −0.5	<−0.3 and ≥ −0.5	Negative
<−0.5 and ≥ −1.0	<−0.5 and ≥ −1.0	Extremely negative

4 Results

4.1 Representation of Sentiments in Tweets

In Table 2, the statistics related to the distribution of the sentiment categories in tweets are listed along with the associated papers count and averages of likes count and retweets count of the tweets. A vast majority of the tweets had neutral sentiment (97.16%) which is even more than the previous studies [19, 20]. Positive sentiments accounted for about 2.8% of the tweets while negative sentiments were found in a meagre 0.05% of the tweets. Among the tweets classified for the total 12,973 papers, non-neutral sentiments were found in 991 papers (7.8%). Interestingly, non-neutral tweets had more likes and retweets than neutral tweets at an average level. It is re-iterated that the retweets were removed from the extract before the data was analyzed.

The extracted keywords from the positive and negative sentiment tweets are illustrated as tag clouds in Figs. 1 and 2 respectively. 92 positive and 18 negative unique keywords were extracted from the 2,709 non-neutral tweets. The existence of common positive keywords such as *interesting, nice, good* and *great* was apparent since these keywords are used as a general form of appreciation in conversations. Comparatively, negative keywords such as *stupid, bad* and *terrible* were found to be used with more intent. In Tables 3 and 4, the top 5 aspects and corresponding key-words along with examples are listed for positive and negative tweets respectively.

In the case of positive sentiments, the most commonly attributed aspect was the *overall paper*. There are two main reasons for the prominence of this aspect. Due to the character limit imposed in Twitter, end-users tend to tweet in a terse manner. Secondly, the readers might be just indicating the initial impression of these papers [solid ending needed]. The other prominent aspects were *readership, review, work* and *study*. The *readership* aspect can be considered a derivative of the *overall paper* aspect, but it adds more credibility since the users indicate they have read the papers. The *review* aspect is applicable for literature review/survey papers which tend to quite popular among readers. The next two aspects are more intrinsic in nature. In the *work* aspect tweets, the workmanship was appreciated while the *study* aspect tweets indicate the superior quality of the research study described in the associated papers. Among these five aspects, *work, study* and *readership* are aspects that highlight the sound quality of research conducted in the tweeted research studies.

The number of aspects identified for negative sentiment tweets was low due to the overall lesser number of negative tweets. Similar to the positive sentiment tweets, the

Table 2. Sentiment classification stats

Sentiment	Tweet count	Associated paper count	Likes count (μ)	Retweets count (μ)
Positive	866 (1.74%)	579	1.15	1.03
E. Positive	527 (1.06%)	393	1.65	1.58
Negative	15 (0.03%)	12	1.73	0.93
E. Negative	9 (0.02%)	7	0.78	3.33
Neutral	48432 (97.16%)	12791	0.94	0.83

Fig. 1. Positive keywords in tweets

Fig. 2. Negative keywords in tweets

presence of aspects *overall papers* and *study* was apparent. The other three aspects were *opinion on authors, paper length* and *paper title*. Unlike positive sentiment aspects, the aspects *overall paper* and *study* could be considered as indicators of inferior research quality. The other three aspects appear to be lot more biased and

Table 3. Aspects and keywords in positive tweets

Aspect	Keywords used	Example tweets*
Overall paper	awesome, great, interesting, fascinating, nice, new	*A paper published on cloud biolinux. awesome. [URL]*
		This is really good. simple rules for better figures [URL] great tips with examples
Readership	good, great, interesting, nice, worth	*[TH] [TH] the value of draft picks. nerdy but a great read [URL]*
		Looks worth a read #ploscompbio: [Paper] [URL] #oxcompbio
Review	awesome, good, great, interesting, nice	*Adjusting confounders in ranking #biomarkers: a model-based roc approach - #awesome review [TH] [URL]*
		a nice review paper about image segmentation on gpus [TH] [TH] #gpgpu [URL]
Work	amazing, excellent, impressive, interesting, nice	*[TH] just read article on usability testing serious games [URL] excellent work. will be sharing with my students.*
		Brainbrowser: distributed, web-based neurological #dataviz. impressive work via [TH] w/[TH] and more. [URL]
Study	beautiful, best, cool, interesting, nice	*Beautiful study on how the canary sings! relevant to sequence organization in animal behavior in general. [URL]*
		Cool study by browning harmer suggesting anxiety disrupts the expectancy learning process (for threat info) - [URL]

Note. [TH] stands for Twitter handle, [Paper] refers to paper title

personal in nature. However, such comments could end up being a precursor to undermine the impact of the corresponding research papers in the future.

4.2   Comparison of Paper Groups with Impact Indicators

The papers were classified into two groups. The first group included the papers ($n = 901$) which had tweets with all three sentiments while the second group included papers ($n = 12066$) which had tweets with only neutral sentiment. The two groups' impact performance was compared with six indicators. Citations was the singular bibliometric indicator while the other five were social media metrics (altmetrics). They were usage total (paper views and downloads count), likes count and retweets count from Twitter, Mendeley readers count and the Altmetric score (an aggregated score calculated by Altmetric.com[3]). The usage total data was extracted using PlumX API,

---

[3] How is the Altmetric Attention Score calculated https://help.altmetric.com/support/solutions/articles/6000060969-how-is-the-altmetric-attention-score-calculated-.

Table 4. Aspects and keywords in negative tweets

Aspect	Keywords used	Example tweets*
Overall paper	fool, seriously, shit, terrible, fuck	*This is terrible science ignore it: [URL] the article ([URL] even cites wakefield (2002)*
		#roundup has gone and fucked up. - has anybody else seen this published 4/18/13, linking roundup weed killer to... [URL]
Study	bad, stupid	*Another bad study on narcissism social media [URL] 19 yr use twitter, 35 yr facebook. lots p surveys not comparable*
		This study should be called, facebook making us stupid [URL]
Opinion on authors	idiot	*[TH] here is one. so you are totally [URL] why am i arguing with an idiot who thinks he speaks for science*
Paper length	stupid	*Keep it long and complicated, stupid. [URL]*
Paper title	horrible	*[Paper]. [URL] pevzner group. cool. (but what a horribly overloaded name!)*

Note: [TH] stands for Twitter handle, [Paper] refers to paper title

likes and retweets count were extracted using web scraping with tweet URLs while all the other social media metrics data were extracted using Altmetric.com API.

The mean values and median values of the two groups are listed in Tables 5 and 6 respectively. The two groups were compared using arithmetic mean (average) and median values. The mean differences were found to be statistically significant using a t-test at $p < 0.05$ level. Results indicate that the citations count of group 1 ($\mu = 13.52$) was higher than group 2 ($\mu = 9.09$). For the five other social media indicators, the values for group 1 were considerably higher than group 2. Papers in group 1 were viewed (usage total [$\mu = 1765.78$]) and read (Mendeley [$\mu = 91.62$]) more than group 2 (usage total [$\mu = 557.51$]); Mendeley [$\mu = 48.77$]). Hence, the altmetric score was also considerably higher for group 1 ($\mu = 28.85$) in comparison to group 2 ($\mu = 3.97$). The median values comparison results were also similar. However, the citation count of group 1 ($\tilde{x} = 5$) was closer to group 2 ($\tilde{x} = 4$). All the other indicator median values of group 1 was considerably higher than group 2, except for likes count and retweets count since zero values seem to be prevalent for most papers in both the groups.

5   Discussion

The existing sentiment classification tools and libraries used in general domains, are not directly applicable for classifying tweets that contains links to research papers. The main reason being the presence of paper titles in the tweets [19], which could be resolved to some extent by data cleaning. The secondary reason being the training model built with data from other domains. In the current study's classification phase, it was decided that the tweets which are initially classified as neutral would be left

Table 5. Mean values of the two groups

Paper group	Citations	Usage total	Likes count	Retweets count	Mendeley readers	Altmetric score
All sentiments (group 1)	13.52	1765.78	1.83	1.73	91.62	28.85
Only neutral (group 2)	9.09	557.51	0.66	0.56	48.77	3.97

Table 6. Median values of the two groups

Paper group	Citations	Usage total	Likes count	Retweets count	Mendeley readers	Altmetric score
All sentiments (group 1)	5	92	0	0	53	6
Only neutral (group 2)	4	65.5	0	0	30	1.25

unchanged. The positive and negative tweets were manually checked to reclassify certain tweets to the neutral category. Thus, the modified sentiment score range could be adopted in future studies where the TextBlob library is used to classify sentiments in tweets.

It was a tad surprising to find more neutral tweets (97.16%) in the current study. In previous studies, neutral tweets accounted for 81.7% [21] and 96% [19] of the total tweets. The general practice for Twitter users is to share informative web links to their network with very little commentary [8]. Hence, neutral sentiment is expected to be prevalent. Positive sentiment tweets were more visible than the negative sentiments. Yet, the percentage in the study (2.8%) was lower than both the earlier studies. The presence of negative sentiments continues to be meagre. Public criticism of research in social media does not seem to be a customary practice. Therefore, the likelihood for witnessing negative opinions on research papers will be low.

Sentiments are attributed to certain aspects of research papers. These aspects were identified for the positive and negative tweets by the coders. The aspects *overall paper* and *study* were common for both non-neutral sentiments. Providing opinion on the research paper is probably the most convenient method for a Twitter user as he/she might can post the initial thoughts on the paper. In [19], it is reported that 82% of the tweets did not attribute authorship. The same observation was made in this study where tweets had very little author-related information. If the Twitter users were colleagues or friends of the authors, they would have tagged such users. Yet, this type of tagging was not witnessed. Hence, it could be assumed that such positive/negative tweets were posted by researchers from the public domain. The *review* aspect among positive tweets is very similar to the *overall paper* aspect and the main difference being that this aspect is specifically for literature review/survey papers. The *readership* aspect among positive tweets, indicates that the Twitter users have read the papers and accordingly, such tweets carry more weightage than the aforementioned two positive aspects.

Among the positive tweets, the remaining two aspects *work* and *study* are probably the most detailed aspects since such tweets contain specific opinion on the quality of the conducted research. The *study* aspect is also found among negative tweets.

For ascertaining the research impact performance, the papers were split into two groups – the first group with papers which had all three sentiment tweets and the second group which had only neutral sentiment tweets. The naïve hypothesis was that group 1 papers would have better values than group 2. Even though, the sample size of second group was comparably lesser than group 1, the difference in the means was statistically significant. For all the six indicators, group 1 had higher mean values than group 2. The difference was small only for the citation count while for the other social media metrics, the difference was substantial. The reason for this difference could be due to the higher number of tweets per paper for group 1 which had all three sentiments. More chatter in social media leads to more views and downloads, more readership in Mendeley and subsequently, higher aggregated altmetric score. However, the bibliometric indicator citations count also supports the better performance for group 1. Hence, for the papers in group 1, altmetric impact leads to a better bibliometric impact (i.e. more citations). This observation is new for research metric studies where earlier works haven't managed to show that higher altmetric scores correlate with higher citations count [11, 12]. From the analyses that were conducted, we posit that the non-neutral sentiment and aspect pair from tweets can be used to boost the weightage of papers when they are retrieved or recommended in academic search engines, databases and digital libraries.

There are a few limitations in this study. By the end of 2017, Twitter increased the character count in tweets to 280 from the earlier 140 characters. Hence, users can post more descriptive content and tag more users in their tweets. Therefore, this user-interface (UI) level change could possibly alter the usage dynamics of Twitter users. Secondly, the sentiment classification was performed only for computer science research papers in this study. This exercise needs to be extended to other disciplines for validating the findings.

6   Conclusion

Research performance has been traditionally measured using bibliometric indicators. These indicators take time to be measured as they are predominantly based on scientific citations. On the other hand, social media-based altmetric research indicators are often readily available but these indicators accurately represent mainly the popularity of the research papers and not necessarily the quality. Hence, there is a need to look at detailed level of social media data for ascertaining the quality of papers. In this study, tweet sentiments of 53,831 computer science papers from the Microsoft Academic Graph (MAG), were analyzed for this purpose. On expected lines, neutral sentiment accounted for about 97% of tweets. The keywords from the non-neutral tweets were extracted along with the attributed aspects of the papers. It was found that sentiments were mostly attributed to the overall paper followed by opinions on the study and research work. To test whether papers with all sentiments performed better than papers with only neutral tweets, six bibliometric and altmetric indicators were compared.

Results indicated that papers with all sentiments performed better both in terms of citations and altmetric footprint. Through this study, we make a case for using non-neutral sentiment-aspect pairs as a proxy measure of quality. This filtered information could be used to appropriately rank recent papers in academic search engines, digital libraries and databases. In our future studies, we will be working on methods and techniques for incorporating non-neutral sentiment-aspect pairs in scientific paper retrieval and recommender systems.

Acknowledgements. The research project "Altmetrics: Rethinking And Exploring New Ways Of Measuring Research" is supported by the National Research Foundation, Prime Minister's Office, Singapore under its Science of Research, Innovation and Enterprise programme (SRIE Award No. NRF2014-NRF-SRIE001-019).

References

1. Viviani, M., Pasi, G.: Credibility in social media: opinions, news, and health information - a survey. Wiley Interdiscip. Rev. Data Min. Knowl. Discov. **7**, e1209 (2017)
2. Laakso, M., Welling, P., Bukvova, H., Nyman, L., Björk, B.-C., Hedlund, T.: The development of open access journal publishing from 1993 to 2009. PLoS ONE **6**, e20961 (2011)
3. Liu, X.Z., Fang, H.: What we can learn from tweets linking to research papers. Scientometrics **111**, 349–369 (2017)
4. Haustein, S., Larivière, V.: The use of bibliometrics for assessing research: possibilities, limitations and adverse effects. In: Welpe, I.M., Wollersheim, J., Ringelhan, S., Osterloh, M. (eds.) Incentives and Performance, pp. 121–139. Springer, Cham (2015). https://doi.org/10. 1007/978-3-319 09785 5_8
5. Priem, J., Taraborelli, D., Groth, P., Neylon, C.: Altmetrics: a manifesto. http://altmetrics. org/manifesto/
6. Veletsianos, G., Kimmons, R.: Scholars in an increasingly open and digital world: how do education professors and students use Twitter? Internet High. Educ. **30**, 1–10 (2016)
7. Mohammadi, E., Thelwall, M., Kwasny, M., Holmes, K.L.: Academic information on Twitter: a user survey. PLoS ONE **13**, e0197265 (2018)
8. Robinson-Garcia, N., Costas, R., Isett, K., Melkers, J., Hicks, D.: The unbearable emptiness of tweeting—About journal articles. PLoS ONE **12**, e0183551 (2017)
9. Merton, R.K.: The Matthew effect in science. Science **159**, 59–63 (1968)
10. Thelwall, M.: Why do papers have many Mendeley readers but few scopus-indexed citations and vice versa? J. Librariansh. Inf. Sci. **49**, 144–151 (2017)
11. Costas, R., Zahedi, Z., Wouters, P.: Do "Altmetrics" correlate with citations? Extensive comparison of altmetric indicators with citations from a multidisciplinary perspective. J. Assoc. Inf. Sci. Technol. **66**, 2003–2019 (2015)
12. Ortega, J.L.: Relationship between altmetric and bibliometric indicators across academic social sites: the case of CSIC's members. J. Informetr. **9**, 39–49 (2015)
13. Chew, C., Eysenbach, G.: Pandemics in the age of Twitter: content analysis of tweets during the 2009 H1N1 outbreak. PLoS ONE **5**, e14118 (2010)
14. Small, T.A.: What the Hashtag? A content analysis of Canadian politics on Twitter. Inf. Commun. Soc. **14**, 872–895 (2011)
15. Pang, B., Lee, L.: Opinion mining and sentiment analysis. Found. Trends® Inf. Retr. **2**, 1–135 (2008)

16. Bing, L.: Web Data Mining: Exploring Hyperlinks, Contents, and Usage Data. Springer, Heidelberg (2007). https://doi.org/10.1007/978-3-540-37882-2
17. Kouloumpis, E., Wilson, T., Moore, J.: Twitter sentiment analysis: the good the dad and the OMG! In: Proceedings of the Fifth International AAAI Conference on Weblogs and Social Media (2011)
18. Thakkar, H., Patel, D.: Approaches for sentiment analysis on Twitter: a state-of-art study (2015)
19. Thelwall, M., Tsou, A., Weingart, S., Holmberg, K., Haustein, S.: Tweeting links to academic articles. Cybermetrics Int. J. Sci. Inf. Bibliometr. **17**, 1–8 (2013)
20. Friedrich, N., Bowman, T.D., Stock, W.G., Haustein, S.: Adapting sentiment analysis for tweets linking to scientific papers (2015)
21. Friedrich, N., Bowman, T.D., Haustein, S.: Do tweets to scientific articles contain positive or negative sentiments? In: The 2015 Altmetrics Workshop, Amsterdam (2015)
22. Sinha, A., et al.: An overview of microsoft academic service (MAS) and applications. In: Proceedings of the 24th International Conference on World Wide Web - WWW 2015 Companion, pp. 243–246. ACM Press, New York (2015)
23. Chu, Z., Gianvecchio, S., Wang, H., Jajodia, S.: Who is tweeting on Twitter: human, bot, or cyborg? In: Proceedings of the 26th Annual Computer Security Applications Conference on - ACSAC 2010, p. 21. ACM Press, New York (2010)
24. Charmaz, K., Belgrave, L.L.: Grounded theory. In: The Blackwell Encyclopedia of Sociology. Wiley, Oxford (2015)

Predicting Social News Use: The Effect of Gratifications, Social Presence, and Information Control Affordances

Winston Jin Song Teo[(⊠)] ID

Department of Media and Communication, University of Auckland,
Auckland, New Zealand
w.teo@auckland.ac.nz

Abstract. Social media applications such as Facebook allow its users to engage in news content from three dimensions: news consumption, news participation, and news production. Borrowing from literature on uses and gratifications theory, social presence theory, as well as the concept of self-presentation and information control, the study investigates how individual and media factors influence news-related activities on social media. A national survey was designed and administered to young Singaporean adults through means of stratified cluster sampling. Results from multiple regression analyses revealed that respondents who were driven by gratifications of information-seeking were more likely to engage in news consumption whereas respondents who were driven by gratifications of status-seeking and socialising were more like to engage in news participation and production. In addition, participants who experienced a greater sense of social presence were more likely to engage in all forms of news activities on social media and those who perceive a greater sense of information control were found to participate in news consumption and production. Implications and directions for future work are discussed.

Keywords: Social media · News · Motivations · Social presence
Information control · Gratifications

1 Introduction

The pervasiveness of social media as a popular communication medium is having a significant impact on online news distribution and consumption. The results of Reuters' most recent digital news report revealed that the use of social media as a news source has risen globally from 27% in 2013 to 51% in 2016 [1]. Conversely, news consumption via printed newspapers, television and other online platforms have either plateaued or declined. However, despite the use of social media for news-related activities – or social news use – becoming increasingly prevalent in recent years, existing scholarly research have primarily focused on one aspect of news participation (such as 'sharing'), and do not venture far from investigating the effects of human factors such as age, gender, and social or psychological needs [2–5]. Further understanding and determining how the affordances of the medium can facilitate social new use would lead to a better explanation of the implications of this rising trend.

© Springer Nature Switzerland AG 2018
M. Dobreva et al. (Eds.): ICADL 2018, LNCS 11279, pp. 83–98, 2018.
https://doi.org/10.1007/978-3-030-04257-8_8

The present research contributes to the existing body of research on social media and citizen participation by examining how both media (social presence and information control) and social-psychological (motivations) factors predict social news use. Social presence, defined as the extent to which a medium facilitates the experience of direct or indirect human contact [6], has often been identified as a key predictor in a range of virtual environments and is therefore a likely factor affecting social news use [7, 8]. Similarly, empirical studies in computer-mediated communication (CMC) have demonstrated how the affordances offered by social media – particularly controls which enable users to limit or regulate information about oneself – can have a positive impact on its usage [9]. Given the commonly accepted understanding that individuals undertake a daily "information game" whereby their expertise in communicating facets of their real core selves influence the impressions others form of them [10], the affordance of information control would be more relevant to those who engage regularly with materials that are potentially contentious [11, 12].

Additionally, while preceding studies on social news use have frequently invoked the uses and gratifications (U&G) perspective of mass communication, none to the best of the author's knowledge has simultaneously considered the influence of individuals' motivations (i.e., information-seeking, socialising, status-seeking and entertainment), and the nature of the social interactions offered by these technologies. By modelling the implications of social news use through both social-psychological and technical dimensions this study hopes to develop a more coherent theoretical model and help the field gain interpretive strength.

2   Literature Review

2.1   Social News Use

While the use of social media has become a widespread phenomenon, there remains no unanimous interpretation of the medium. For this study, I adopt the popular definition advanced by [13]: A group of internet-based applications that facilitates the creation and exchange of User-Generated Content (UGC), and that allows its users to communicate, collaborate and interact with each other. These applications include blogs or microblogs, social networking sites, online collaborate projects, content communities, virtual social worlds, and virtual game worlds. The applications of particular interest in this study are social networking sites (SNSs) as they are by far the most popular social media platforms for news use [1] and have received considerable attention in scholarly literature [14, 15].

Scholarship suggests a growing trend in not only understanding individuals' motives for engaging in social media [e.g. 12, 16], but also its role in online news consumption and distribution [e.g. 17, 18]. However, despite the popularity of social media and the developing interest in explaining the use of social media for political or news-related activities, only a handful of research has begun to recognise the varied ways in which an individual may participate in this platform [2, 19, 20]. Given that social media is used to share the gamut of human experiences – not just news – generally discussing the medium as it is one singular element is neither helpful nor realistic. A more detailed distinction and operationalisation of social media use is required to address and expand upon previous limited research on young adults.

To study the different antecedents and effects of news-related activities on social media – or social news use – this research first identifies news as information relating to local politics or public affairs. I focus on this particular type of content as earlier studies have consistently found a connection between consumption of such materials and civic involvement [21–23]. Secondly, I readapt the classification of social media use as proposed by [2] and [24]. The three primary types of news engagement typically performed on social media are: news consumption, news participation and news production. Consumption refers to isolated activities such as reading, watching or viewing news content with no apparent contribution. News participation consists of user-to-user interaction and/or user-to-content interaction (such as sharing links of news stories from other online sources or responding with a 'like' to related stories). News production activities refer to any form of UGC initiated by the user and disseminated to a mass audience (such as publishing original news-related articles or videos). [24] posits that while these classes of activities are progressively more demanding – with consuming and producing being the lowest and highest tier respectively – not all users who consume will eventually become producers. This can be attributed to both individuals' purpose for social news use, as well as the technical structure and affordances of the platform.

2.2   Social Presence

Many scholars agree that virtual co-presence is an essential concept in understanding active engagement in online media use [25, 26]. In CMC studies, perceived social presence is a psychological variable that goes beyond the virtual presence of other social actors and generates subjective experiences of closeness and connectedness [27, 28]. This study adapts the definition from preceding research and regards perceived social presence as the extent to which a medium facilitates the experience of being psychologically present with others and the perceptual illusion of non-mediation [29, 30].

The influence of perceived social presence on user behaviours or intentions has been widely examined in the context of social media. For instance, [31] demonstrated that social presence was a strong predictor of We-intention, or the intention to participate or interact with other users in a specific Facebook group. Similarly, [32] identified co-presence, intimacy, and immediacy as a function of social presence and found that these three factors had a positive impact on user attitude and usage behaviour on SNSs. In a series of experiments conducted within a Facebook game application, [33] showed that designs or features which facilitate the presence of other players - such as photos, names or opportunities for communication – increased commitment to the site and encouraged longer participation.

These findings not only identify social presence as a crucial construct to be examined in relation to social news use but also draw attention to the multiple inter-activity features within social media [5, 34]. Communicative functions - such as 'likes' or a comment (on a post) – facilitate affective exchanges between users, thereby emphasizing the presence of other users' involvement or feelings of human contact

[35]. Some scholars have argued that this awareness often contributes to a much more pleasurable or fulfilling experience, thereby influencing users' behavioural intentions or actual usage [26, 36].

2.3   Self-presentation and Information Control

Self-presentation refers to the process by which individuals engage in controlling for their face, or information about themselves which influences impressions others form of them [37]. Self-presentation thus, is a goal-driven behaviour [38], a strategic effort to convince others to view them, or to continue to view them positively and/or to present themselves in a way that is socially acceptable. This impression-management behaviour can be categorised into two primary actions of information control: (1) expressive, which refers to controlling the flow of revealed information as required and (2) privacy, which means to withhold or prevent information from being shared as required [39, 40]. An unregulated face will likely result in unfavourable social encounters, such as offense or embarrassment, regardless of whether it occurs in a Face-to-Face (FtF) or mediated context. As [41] argues, an awkward encounter arises when "there is too much variance between the role the actor (an individual) assumes and what is already known about the actor or what he comes unwittingly to reveal about himself". Thus, it is contended that under normal circumstances, individuals have a tendency to want to be well-received and will act accordingly to present favourable or appropriate images to others.

Several scholars have posited that the affordances featured on social media present novel opportunities for self-presentation [42, 43]. Unlike FtF interactions, social media users have greater capacity to reveal, omit, or regulate information about themselves in an ideal and intended manner [44]. Indeed, while individuals can attempt to make salient certain aspects of themselves in FtF interactions, they are disadvantaged as they have to dedicate additional cognitive resources to monitor non-verbal expressions or effects of response latencies. Accordingly, prior research has found that individuals do emphasize aspects of their lives online that are difficult to replicate or maintain consistently in FtF contexts, including intentionally selecting appealing or edited photos of themselves for their social media profiles [45], and limiting the audience to whom messages are transmitted [46].

These studies illustrate that individuals are concerned with impression management online and will leverage on the affordances of the medium to express or withhold information about themselves. More importantly, the literature suggests that if users believe they are unable to control the reach of their disclosure, it is likely they will withdraw from use or reduce the amount of information revealed. This expectation is in tandem with previous research that found that users' presentation behaviours were predicted by their perceived ability to use Facebook affordances to control information [9]. Conversely, [47] have shown that individuals' concerns over privacy and sharing controls on SNSs have a strong, negative effect on its use. Similar findings were reported in a qualitative study by [12], observing that youths' awareness of social contexts collapse on Facebook led them to limit sharing of political content to private groups or lists. Hence this study expects both expressive and privacy information control to be crucial concepts to be examined in the context of social news use.

2.4 Gratifications

One of the most seminal theories addressing the relationship between human factors and media usage behaviours is the uses & gratifications theory (UGT) [48]. A key assumption of UGT is that all media consumers are goal-directed [49], deliberately interacting with media and interpreting the messages they receive for their own benefit [50]. While UGT was originally developed to identify the underlying motivations behind traditional media use [48, 51], its theoretical relevance is particularly poignant in the age of the internet. In contrast to traditional media, web-based applications such as social media are more likely to be intentionally consumed, as users must make conscious decisions about not only which platform to visit but also how they will process the news media content.

Prior research on online news browsing have identified overlapping motivations: entertainment, interpersonal communication, information seeking, information learning [52], and information seeking/surveillance, socialization and entertainment [53]. Extending upon these findings, a recent study by [2] distinguishes motivations for news-related activities on SNSs. According to this strand of literature, the motivation of "surveillance" and "socialising" were found to be significant determinants of news reading, posting and endorsing activities, whereas the motivation of "getting recognition" was reported to be positively associated with news posting activities only. His work corresponds largely to the motivations of social media use [5] identified among Singaporean college students: information-seeking, socializing, entertainment and status-seeking. In the latter, the researchers found out that only respondents who were seeking entertainment gratifications were unlikely to share news on social media.

The studies reviewed suggests four common motivations for participating in social news use: information-seeking/surveillance, socialising, status-seeking, entertainment. Information-seeking refers to the extent in which participating in social news use is able to provide desirable information and fulfil the desire to learn [54]. Socialising is related to how social news use is able to gratify people's intrinsic need to form and maintain relationships with others [55]. Status-seeking describes how social news use can help one to gain acceptance and approval from other users, or improve his/her social status within the community by contributing to it [56]. Entertainment refers to hedonistic gratifications such as escape and diversion from reality [24].

Based on the aforementioned literature, I espouse the commonly used motivations as well as the affordance of social presence and information control in this study. Therefore, I put forward the following research questions:

RQ 1: How are media (perceived social presence and information control) and social-psychological (motivations) factors associated with social news consumption?

RQ 2: How are media (perceived social presence and information control) and social-psychological (motivations) factors associated with social news participation?

RQ 3: How are media (perceived social presence and information control) and social-psychological (motivations) factors associated with social news production?

2.5 The Singapore Context

As an economically and technologically advanced city-state, Singapore enjoys almost universal internet access, with more than 87% of resident households having access to at least one computer at home and an internet connection [57]. Unsurprisingly, the use of social media is vastly popular, with seven in 10 internet users assessing Facebook regularly in 2018, up 27% from two years ago [58, 59]. For other social media platforms such as WhatsApp, Youtube, and Instagram, the corresponding figures were 73%, 71%, and 44%. Local industry research has revealed that youths in particular (defined as residents aged between 15–34 years of age) form the biggest proportion of users on social networking sites and instant-messaging applications [57]. The consumption of online news has also risen recently among this cohort, with 36% for those aged 15–24 and 48% in the 25–34 age range now engaging in this activity. The statistics show that new media, especially social media, is frequently used by a large percentage of this demographic.

While preceding studies have suggested that certain individual traits and motivations can be an impetus for news-related activities on social media, a comprehensive overview of literature by [60] revealed a strong focus on US-Americans in this domain (>50%). This study thus attempts to fill in this knowledge gap and add an Asian perspective from a predominantly Western demographic in this area of research. Singapore, with its highly developed communication infrastructure and high social media penetration, represents an appropriate research site to investigate the antecedents of social news use among young adults.

3 Methodology

3.1 Procedure and Sample

A one-on-one survey was collected in Singapore from eligible voters under the age of 36 years old and have had some prior experience with social news use. Participants in this study were recruited through means of stratified cluster sampling [61]. In the first stage, only residential districts containing Housing Development Board (HDB) blocks - public housing apartment blocks - were included in the study. Thus, only 24 out of 28 districts were included in the sampling in this research.

Subsequently, a specific number of HDB blocks were randomly selected from each district based on the proportion of the number of HDB blocks in each district to the number of HDB blocks nation-wide. Next, the selection was narrowed down to every second household of the apartment block; finally, in each household, the youngest millennial of voting age was requested to participate in the study. As an incentive to participate, respondents were offered a shopper voucher of SGD $5 upon completion. In the event that the selected unit was unoccupied or none of the residents were able to participate in the survey, the immediate next unit was selected and so forth.

All prospective respondents were briefed about the purpose of the research and provided with information regarding the confidentiality of their participation. Following their consent, the first part of the survey included questions on demographic as well as general social news use activities to determine their eligibility for the study. The survey was terminated if participants were found to be ineligible (i.e. below 21 years old, are not Singaporeans, and/or did not use social media).

The final sample consisted of 199 males (49.8%) and 201 females (50.2%). Respondents ranged in age from 21 to 35 years old (M = 27.7, SD = 4.36). The sample was found to reasonably approximate the general population in terms of gender and race, and it also reasonably approximated the youth population in terms of education level [62]. On average, participants spent once a day on social news use and the primary social media platform used by most participants for social news use was Facebook (71.5%). The demographic profiles of the participants are summarised in Table 1.

Table 1. Sample demographics (N = 400).

Demographic variables	N	(%)
Gender		
Male	199	49.8
Female	201	50.2
Age		
21–25	148	37
26–30	136	34
31–35	116	29
Race		
Chinese	294	73.5
Malay	58	14.5
Indian	35	8.8
Others	13	3.3
Primary social news platform		
Facebook	286	71.5
Twitter	28	7.0
WhatsApp	25	6.3
Youtube	24	6.0
Instagram	16	4.0
Others	21	5.2

3.2   Measures

All major constructs have been developed or adapted based on previous studies in various areas of social sciences. The instrument assessing social news use was drawn from various work in UGC and social news use literature [2, 5, 24]. The 10-item self-report consisted of three subscales: news consumption, participation and production. Respondents were asked to indicate their responses on a 7-point response scale (1 = Never, 7 = Always) to questions such as, "How often do you click on links to news stories that you receive on social media," "How often do you share news links from other online news sources," and "How often do you post or repost news links together with your own thoughts or comments about the story's content." Scores for each item were summed up to create an index of the three types of news-related activities respectively. Reliability analysis revealed acceptable to excellent reliability ($\alpha = .75$ to $.91$) in the current study. Additionally, a principal component factor analysis with varimax rotation was conducted on all 10 social news use activity items. Three factors emerged with eigenvalues greater than 1.00, explaining a total of 73.1% of the variance. Two items however were dropped due to issues of cross-loading.

Social presence was measured using a 4-item additive scale adapted from [63]. They include: "I feel like many people are also reading or watching the same news content with me when I engage in social news use", "I feel like I'm communicating with friends when I engage in social news use", and "I feel like I'm a participant in a national dialogue when I engage in social news use". All statements were asked on a Likert-type scale anchored by "strongly disagree" (1) to "strongly agree" (7). The study showed good reliability for values ($\alpha = .84$).

Respondents' perceived information control was measured by two separate but complementary impression-management affordance scales: expressive and privacy information control [9]. Both variables consisted of 4 items each on a 7-point scale (1 = strongly disagree, 7 = strongly agree). Respondents indicated their agreement to statements such as: "I am able to communicate in ways that I feel are most suitable to the situation with the features available" and "I can generally hide any information that I do not wish to be disclosed with the features available". Cronbach α for expressive and privacy information control were .93 and .89 respectively.

Based on pre-validated measurement items from previous studies in news consumption and sharing on social media [2, 5], social news use motivations was measured with four scales representing the sub-dimensions of information-seeking, socialising, entertainment and status-seeking. All motivations were measured with four items respectively with items such as, "I partake in social news use to keep up with the latest issues and events", "I partake in social news use to exchange ideas with other people", "I partake in social news use to entertain myself", and "I partake in social news use to gain support and respect". A 7-point Likert scale was used to indicate responses (1 = strongly disagree, 7 = strongly agree) and all items were added to create an index of information-seeking, socialising, entertainment, and status-seeking motivation respectively. The scales showed excellent reliability ($\alpha = .90$ to $.91$) in the current study.

4   Results

Three hierarchical multiple regression analyses were conducted to examine the influence of various factors on social news consumption, participation, and production (see Table 2). Respondents' age, ethnicity, education background, and monthly household income were controlled in the first block. Next media technical factors – social presence, privacy and expressive information control – were in the second block. Finally, the motivations of information-seeking, socialising, status-seeking, and entertainment were entered in the third block.

Table 2. Results of regression analysis

Independent variables	News consumption	News participation	News production
	β	β	β
Block 1: demographics			
Gender (1 = Male; 0 = Female)	.08	.14**	.16**
Ethnicity (1 = Chinese; 0 = Non-Chinese)	.01	−.01	.01
Educational attainment	.13*	.05	.06
Monthly income	.12*	−.04	.02
ΔR^2	.05***	.02	.03*
Block 2: with technical factors			
Gender	.01	.06	.09*
Ethnicity	.04	.01	−.00
Educational attainment	.08	−.01	−.00
Monthly income	.07	−.09*	−.02
Social presence	.34***	.46***	.41***
Information control			
• Privacy information control	.25***	.14**	−.06
• Expressive information control	.13**	.11*	.27***
ΔR^2	.35***	.36***	.30***
Block 3: with motivations			
Gender	.03	.05	.06
Ethnicity	.05	.03	.03
Educational attainment	.08	−.01	−.01
Monthly income	.09*	.08	−.02
Social presence	.18**	.36***	.39***
Information control			
• Privacy information control	.12*	.10	−.02
• Expressive information control	.10*	.08	.23***
Motivations			
• Information-seeking	.21**	−.11	−.27***
• Socialising	.12	.11	.17*
• Status-seeking	.10	.14*	.16**
• Entertainment	−.00	.08	−.07
ΔR^2	.06***	.03**	.06***
Total R^2	.45	.41	.39
Total adjusted R^2	.44	.39	.37

*p < .05, **p < .01, *** p < .001

None of the motivations except information-seeking positively and significantly predicted news consumption (β = .21, p < .01). News consumption was also positively associated with perceived social presence (β = .18, p < .01), privacy information control (β = .12, p < .05), expressive information control (β = .10, p < .05). The overall regression model (adjusted) predicting news consumption accounted for 44% of the variance, with the motivations block explaining only 6%, and the media factors block explaining 35%.

For news participation, the motivation of status-seeking (β = .14, p < .05) and perceived social presence (β = .36, p < .001) were significant and positive predictors of the activity. The overall regression model (adjusted) predicting news consumption accounted for 39% of the variance, with the motivations block explaining only 3%, and the media factors block explaining 36%.

The findings also showed that news production was positively associated with perceived social presence (β = .39, p < .001), expressive information control (β = .23, p < .001), socialising (β = .17, p < .05), and status seeking (β = .16, p < .01). Interestingly, news production was also negatively associated with information-seeking (β = $-$ .27, p < .001). The overall regression model (adjusted) predicting news production accounted for 37% of the variance, with the motivations block explaining only 6%, and the media factors block explaining 30%.

5   Discussion

The present study explored why social media users engage with news content on the platform differently. To answer this question, it distinguished between three main types of social news use and investigated the influences of information-seeking, socialising, entertainment, status-seeking, information control, and social presence on the former. In general, the results suggest that different user motivations and technological affordances can encourage different social news practices.

In interpreting the findings, first, it is notable that user involvement in news content depends on the social affordances of the site, particularly those that facilitate the presence of other users and those that enable users to take an active role in reproducing news content with their networks. Social presence was found, with statistical significance, to be the sole consistent antecedent driving all social news use activities. Indeed, aside from news consumption, the beta coefficient for this variable is the largest in the final model, suggesting that it is the most salient factor predicting social news use. These findings are aligned with earlier research that a sense of others is an important concept to understand the social motives of media use [31, 64]. While social media has primarily been seen as a tool for maintain personal relationships [4], the results of this study show that the sense of awareness that others are also present and are able to respond is an equally important impetus of news-related activities too.

Moreover, the findings also show that expressive information control was positively associated with news consumption and production while privacy information control was a significant predictor for news consumption only. The significant influence of expressive information control indicates that users who proactively engage with news content are more likely to perceive greater control over how they communicate. This is consistent with [41]'s theory of self-presentation and suggests that people may be engaging in social news use as a form of impression management behaviour. The lack of a significant relationship between privacy controls and a more active social news use appear to be inconsistent with preceding research that demonstrates a negative relationship between privacy concerns and information disclosure online [47, 65, 66]. However, rather than interpreting from these results that young adults are not cognisant or concerned about who is in their potential audience, I reason that young adults do not simply rely on privacy settings to circumvent unwanted interaction. Indeed, research has shown that instead of cutting down on the amount of information revealed, young adults also engage in other privacy-protecting tactics such as "content encoding" or "the lowest common denominator" [67, 68]. In the former, users reduce the information to be interpretable to a selected audience whereas in the latter, users only disclose information that is appropriate to all members of the network. Future research would benefit from a content analysis to explore how these strategies apply in a social news context.

Another notable finding concerns the influence status-seeking on news participation and production. This finding is consistent with earlier studies on the gratifications attained from news consumption/sharing on social media [2, 5]. As discussed earlier, media users are inclined to exploit the features of a medium to manage the impressions of others. In the context of social news use, those who make news more personally relevant to their networks by reproducing it may be motivated by the desire to obtain a reputation as a gatekeeper or opinion leader [69]. While they might not necessarily be the original sources of information, by posting news stories and sharing it to their contacts, these individuals may be viewed as sources by their networks and receive important psychological benefits. The motivation of socialising was the other significant predictor of news production. The concept of socialising around news content is not a recent phenomenon. Early media research has posited that receiving news information offers resourceful topics for offline discussion and that these two activities reinforce each other [70]. Our findings suggest that news engagement remains "socially driven" [71]. However, in contrast to traditional media where news engagement was primarily sequential, social media supports interpersonal interaction with features that allow users to proactively engage with news content.

Somewhat surprisingly, the study found that information-seeking was positively associated with news consumption but negatively associated with news production. This reinforces the observation that social media use – or social news use – consists of heterogenous practices derived from varying motivations [72]. While receiving news on social media may satisfy users' needs to stay informed of the political environment or verify existing decisions, it is not necessarily a source for news production activities. Given that those who are involved in the latter activity are motivated by status-seeking gratifications, it is likely they will gain that sense of agency simply by consuming and passing along information that is already circulating widely in their network. Instead, they may be adapting news consumed elsewhere. This is plausible as recent research has also shown that those who contribute their own news content on SNSs are likely to have a larger media repertoire – including traditional news media such as network and cable television, as well as other digital platforms [2, 73].

The results presented in this study have both academic and practical implications. From an academic perspective, this is one of the few studies that adapts an interdisciplinary approach (i.e. information science and communication) in investigating the antecedents of social news use. This study builds off from an earlier study by [5] in

Singapore, of which the authors primarily focused on a user-oriented approach. As noted by [60] in their literature review of news sharing on social media, the effects of individuals' personal traits need to be understood in conjunction with the social structures and characteristics of social media platforms. This study thus responds to that recommendation by showing that UGT, social presence theory and processes in information control work concurrently in explaining social news use. The research model in this study provides a preliminary step from which to further explore how the different media and individual social-psychological factors interact to influence social news use behaviour. Further, the current study contributes to literature by also being one of the few studies to adopt a multi-dimension perspective of news-related activities on social media.

From a practical standpoint, the positive influence of social presence and information control not only lends support to propositions and research findings that Singaporean youth are more inclined towards social media to keep abreast of news events [57, 74], but also imply that creating awareness of other social news users can support the continuance of such activities. This could serve as a reference to social media service providers when developing or enhancing their current platforms. For SNSs such as Facebook, this could include an automated mechanism to allow users to know who are reading the same news material that they are also consuming, instead of relying on manual response functions such as "likes" or "share". Similarly, because the success of any social media platform is dependent on the amount of activity and content that its users (co)produce, including news materials, it is imperative to empower users to have more control to interact on these platforms as desired.

6 Limitations and Future Directions

This study does have some limitations that should be considered. The first limitation lies in the sampling method. This study focused only on residents in public housing where at least 80% of the population live. However, to compensate for this limitation and to provide a more accurate representation of the young adult population, the current study based the sample on three census demographic variables: gender, race and education. Additionally, while this study has provided an Asian perspective in regards to the current social news use phenomenon, future studies would benefit from exploring how cultural identity might contribute to these activities. Indeed, cross-cultural studies have demonstrated that individuals from both collectivist and individualistic cultures differ in self-presentation strategies on social media [75]. It is likely that this difference may extend towards news-related activities on the same platform. Moreover, the distinction between the different types of social media platforms were not considered. Indeed, while each social media platform facilitates online, social interaction, they offer different communicative affordances. A specific or comparative social news platform study is warranted. Finally, self-reported data may not accurately reflect users' actual social news behaviour. In future, more objective measurements of sharing in social media, like the collection of activity logs from these sites could be used in conjunction with the existing scales to provide more detailed information on the relationship between social news use and individual and media factors.

References

1. Newman, N., Fletcher, R., Levy, D.A.L., Nielsen, R.K.: Reuters institute digital news report 2016 (2016)
2. Choi, J.: Why do people use news differently on SNSs? An investigation of the role of motivations, media repertoires, and technology cluster on citizens' news-related activities. Comput. Hum. Behav. **54**, 249–256 (2016)
3. Choi, J., Lee, J.K., Metzgar, E.: Networks versus news media, or networks and news media? The interactive effects of network heterogeneity and news sharing on social networking services (SNSs) on citizens' participatory activities. Presented at the 2013 Association for Education in Journalism and Mass Communication (AEJMC), Washington, D.C., August 2013
4. Glynn, C.J., Huge, M.E., Hoffman, L.H.: All the news that's fit to post: a profile of news use on social networking sites. Comput. Hum. Behav. **28**, 113–119 (2012)
5. Lee, C.S., Ma, L.: News sharing in social media: the effect of gratifications and prior experience. Comput. Hum. Behav. **28**, 331–339 (2011)
6. Gefen, D., Straub, D.: Managing user trust in B2C e-Services. e-Serv. J. **2**, 7–24 (2003)
7. Kear, K., Chetwynd, F., Jefferis, H.: Social presence in online learning communities: the role of personal profiles. Res. Learn. Technol. **22** (2014)
8. Chung, N., Han, H., Koo, C.: Adoption of travel information in user-generated content on social media: the moderating effect of social presence. Behav. Inf. Technol. **34**, 902–919 (2015)
9. Kuo, F.-Y., Tseng, C.-Y., Tseng, F.-C., Lin, C.S.: A study of social information control affordances and gender difference in Facebook self-presentation. Cyberpsychol. Behav. Soc. Netw. **16**, 635–644 (2013)
10. Goffman, E.: The Presentation of Self in Everyday Life. Overlook Press, Woodstock (1973)
11. Hayes, R.A., Smock, A., Carr, C.T.: Face[book] management: self-presentation of political views on social media. Commun. Stud. **66**, 549–568 (2015)
12. Storsul, T.: Deliberation or self-presentation? Young people, politics and social media. Nord. Rev. **35**, 17–28 (2014)
13. Kaplan, A.M., Haenlein, M.: Users of the world, unite! The challenges and opportunities of social media. Bus. Horiz. **53**, 59–68 (2010)
14. Theocharis, Y., Lowe, W.: Does Facebook increase political participation? Evidence from a field experiment. Inf. Commun. Soc. **19**, 1–22 (2015)
15. Yang, H., Dehart, J.L.: Social media use and online political participation among college students during the US election 2012. Soc. Media Soc. **2**, 1–18 (2016)
16. de Oliveira, M.J., Huertas, M.K.Z., Lin, Z.: Factors driving young users' engagement with Facebook: evidence from Brazil. Comput. Hum. Behav. **54**, 54–61 (2016)
17. Mitchell, A., Page, D.: The role of news on Facebook (2013)
18. Pentina, I., Tarafdar, M.: From "information" to "knowing": exploring the role of social media in contemporary news consumption. Comput. Hum. Behav. **35**, 211–223 (2014)
19. Beheshti-Kashi, S., Makki, B.: Social media news: motivation, purpose and usage. Int. J. Comput. Sci. Inf. Technol. **5**, 97–105 (2013)
20. Skoric, M.M., Zhu, Q.: Social media and offline political participation: uncovering the paths from digital to physical. Int. J. Public Opin. Res. **28**, 415–427 (2016)
21. Kenski, K., Stroud, N.J.: Connections between internet use and political efficacy, knowledge, and participation. J. Broadcast. Electron. Media. **50**, 173–192 (2006)
22. Shah, D.V., Mcleod, J.M., Yoon, S.-H.: Communication, context, and community: an exploration of print, broadcast, and internet influences. Commun. Res. **28**, 464–506 (2001)

23. Skoric, M.M., Pan, J., Poor, N.D.: Social media and citizen engagement in a city-state: a study of Singapore. Presented at the Sixth International AAAI Conference on Weblogs and Social Media, Dublin, Ireland, May 2012
24. Shao, G.: Understanding the appeal of user-generated media: a uses and gratification perspective. Internet Res. **19**, 7–25 (2009)
25. Kim, T., Biocca, F.: Telepresence via television: two dimensions of telepresence may have different connections to memory and persuasion. J. Comput. Commun. **3** (1997)
26. Song, J.H., Hollenbeck, C.R.: The value of social presence in mobile communications. Serv. Ind. J. **35**, 611–632 (2015)
27. Heeter, C.: Being there: the subjective experience of presence. Presence: Teleoperators Virtual Environ. Abbr. **1**, 262–271 (1992)
28. Lombard, M., Ditton, T.: At the heart of it all: the concept of presence. J. Comput. Commun. **3** (1997)
29. Rogers, P., Lea, M.: Social presence in distributed group environments: the role of social identity. Behav. Inf. Technol. **24**, 151–158 (2005)
30. Hassanein, K., Head, M.: The impact of infusing social presence in the web interface: an investigation across product types. Int. J. Electron. Commer. **10**, 31–55 (2006)
31. Cheung, C.M.K., Chiu, P.-Y., Lee, M.K.O.: Online social networks: why do students use Facebook? Comput. Hum. Behav. **27**, 1337–1343 (2011)
32. Al-Ghaith, W.: Understanding social network usage: impact of co-presence, intimacy, and immediacy. Int. J. Adv. Comput. Sci. Appl. **6**, 99–111 (2015)
33. Farzan, R., Dabbish, L., Kruat, L., Postmes, T.: Increasing commitment to online communities by designing for social presence. In: Proceedings of ACM 2011 Conference on Computer Supported Cooperative Work, pp. 321–330 (2011)
34. Leonardi, P.M.: Activating the informational capabilities of information technology for organizational change. Organ. Sci. **18**, 813–831 (2007)
35. Yoo, Y., Alavi, M.: Media and group cohesion: relative influences on social presence, task participation, and group consensus. MIS Q. **25**, 371–390 (2001)
36. Bulu, S.T.: Place presence, social presence, co-presence, and satisfaction in virtual worlds. Comput. Educ. **58**, 154–161 (2012)
37. Goffman, E.: The Presentation of Self in Everyday Life. Doubleday Anchor Books, Garden City (1959)
38. Leary, M.R., Kowalski, R.M.: Impression management: a literature review and two-component model. Psychol. Bull. **107**, 34–47 (1990)
39. Petronio, S.: Boundaries of Privacy: Dialectics of Disclosure. State University of New York Press, Albany (2002)
40. Rui, J., Stefanone, M.A.: Strategic image management online: self-presentation, self-esteem and social network perspectives. Inf. Commun. Soc. **16**, 1286–1305 (2013)
41. Goffman, E.: Communication conduct in an island community (1953). http://search.proquest.com.ezproxy.auckland.ac.nz/pqdtglobal/docview/302075487/citation/692F2994E1F04BF0PQ/1
42. Bartsch, M., Subrahmanyam, K.: Technology and self-presentation. In: Rosen, L.D., Cheever, A., Carrier, L.M. (eds.) The Wiley Handbook of Psychology, Technology, and Society, pp. 339–357. Wiley, Chichester (2015)
43. Fox, J., Vendemia, M.A.: Selective self-presentation and social comparison through photographs on social networking sites. Cyberpsychol. Behav. Soc. Netw. **19**, 593–600 (2016)

44. Walther, J.B., Van Der Heide, B., Ramirez, A., Burgoon, J.K., Peña, J.: Interpersonal and hyperpersonal dimensions of computer-mediated communication. In: Sundar, S.S. (ed.) The Handbook of the Psychology of Communication Technology, pp. 1–22. Wiley, Chichester (2015)

45. Young, K.: Online social networking: an Australian perspective. Int. J. Emerg. Technol. Soc. **7**, 39–57 (2009)

46. Stutzman, F., Kramer-Duffield, J.: Friends only: examining a privacy-enhancing behavior in Facebook. Presented at the 2010 SIGCHI Conference on Human Factors in Computing Systems, Atlanta, GA, April 2010

47. Staddon, J., Huffaker, D., Brown, L., Sedley, A.: Are privacy concerns a turn-off? Engagement and privacy in social networks. In: Proceedings of the Eighth Symposium on Usable Privacy and Security, 1–13 July 2012, p. 10 (2012)

48. Katz, E., Blumer, J.G., Gurevitch, M.: Uses and gratifications research. Public Opin. Q. **37**, 509–523 (1973)

49. Stanley, J.B., Davis, D.K.: Mass Communication Theory: Foundations, Ferment, and Future. Wadsworth Publishing Company, Belmont (2006)

50. Abercrombie, N., Longhurst, B.: The Penguin Dictionary of Media Studies. Penguin Books, London (2007)

51. Katz, E., Blumer, J.G., Gurevitch, M.: Utilization of mass communication by the individual. In: Blumer, J.G., Katz, E. (eds.) The Uses of Mass Communications: Current Perspectives on Gratifications Research, pp. 19–34. Sage, London (1974)

52. Lin, C., Michael, S., Rasha, A.: Uses and gratifications of online and offline news: new wine in an old bottle? In: Michael, S., Garrison, B., Mahwah, D. (eds.) Online News and the Public, pp. 221–236. Lawrence Erlbaum Associates, Mahwah (2005)

53. Diddi, A., LaRose, R.: Getting hooked on news: uses and gratifications and the formation of news habits among college students in an internet environment. J. Broadcast. Electron. Media. **50**, 193–210 (2006)

54. Nambisan, S., Baron, R.A.: Virtual customer environments: testing a model of voluntary participation in value co-creation activities. J. Prod. Innov. Manag. **26**, 388–406 (2009)

55. Han, S., Min, J., Lee, H.: Antecedents of social presence and gratification of social connection needs in SNS: a study of Twitter users and their mobile and non-mobile usage. Int. J. Inf. Manag. **35**, 459–471 (2015)

56. Dholakia, U.M., Bagozzi, R.P., Pearo, L.K.: A social influence model of consumer participation in network- and small-group-based virtual communities. Int. J. Res. Mark. **21**, 241–263 (2004)

57. Infocomm Media Development Authority: Annual survey on infocomm usage in households and by individuals for 2015 (2017)

58. Kemp, S.: Digital in 2016 (2016)

59. Kemp, S.: Digital in 2018 (2018)

60. Kümpel, A.S., Karnowski, V., Keyling, T.: News sharing in social media: a review of current research on news sharing users, content, and networks. Soc. Media Soc. **1**, 1–14 (2015)

61. Babbie, E.: The practice of social research. Wadsworth Cengage Learning, Canada (2013)

62. Ministry of Manpower: Manpower Research and Statistics Department: Labour Force in Singapore 2017 (2018)

63. Hwang, Y., Lim, J.S.: The impact of engagement motives for social TV on social presence and sports channel commitment. Telemat. Inform. **32**, 755–765 (2015)

64. Xu, C., Ryan, S., Prybutok, V., Wen, C.: It is not for fun: an examination of social network site usage. Inf. Manag. **49**, 210–217 (2012)

65. Krasnova, H., Spiekermann, S., Koroleva, K., Hildebrand, T.: Online social networks: why we disclose. J. Inf. Technol. **25**, 109–125 (2010)
66. Nemec Zlatolas, L., Welzer, T., Heričko, M., Hölbl, M.: Privacy antecedents for SNS self-disclosure: the case of Facebook. Comput. Hum. Behav. **45**, 158–167 (2015)
67. Marwick, A.E., Boyd, D.: Networked privacy: how teenagers negotiate context in social media. New Media Soc. **16**, 1051–1067 (2014)
68. Hogan, B.: The presentation of self in the age of social media: distinguishing performances and exhibitions online. Bull. Sci. Technol. Soc. **30**, 377–386 (2010)
69. Burke, M., Marlow, C., Lento, T.: Feed me: motivating newcomer contribution in social network sites. In: Proceedings of the 27th International Conference on Human Factors in Computing Systems, Boston, USA, pp. 945–954. ACM (2009)
70. McLeod, J.M., Scheufele, D.A., Moy, P.: Community, communication, and participation: the role of mass media and interpersonal discussion in local political participation. Polit. Commun. **16**, 315–336 (1999)
71. Purcell, K., Rainie, L., Mitchell, A., Rosenstiel, T., Olmstead, K.: Understanding the participatory news consumer. http://www.gabinetecomunicacionyeducacion.com/sites/default/files/field/adjuntos/understanding_the_participatory_news_consumer.pdf
72. Dhavan, V.S., Kwak, N., Holbert, R.L.: "Connecting" and "disconnecting" with civic life: patterns of internet use and the production of social capital. Polit. Commun. **18**, 141–162 (2001)
73. Mitchell, A., Kiley, J., Gottfried, J., Guskin, E.: The role of news on Facebook: common yet incidental. http://www.journalism.org/2013/10/24/the-roleof-news-on-facebook/
74. Soon, C., Samsudin, S.N.: General election 2015 in Singapore: what social media did and did not do. Round Table **105**, 171–184 (2016)
75. Rui, J., Stefanone, M.A.: Strategic self-presentation online: a cross-cultural study. Comput. Hum. Behav. **29**, 110–118 (2013)

Aspect-Based Sentiment Analysis of Nuclear Energy Tweets with Attentive Deep Neural Network

Zhengyuan Liu and Jin-Cheon Na[⊠]

Wee Kim Wee School of Communication and Information,
Nanyang Technological University, 31 Nanyang Link,
Singapore 637718, Singapore
zhengyua001@e.ntu.edu.sg, tjcna@ntu.edu.sg

Abstract. Opinion mining of social networking sites like Facebook and Twitter plays an important role in exploring valuable online user-generated contents. In contrast to sentence-level sentiment classification, the aspect-based analysis which can infer polarities towards various aspects in one sentence could obtain more in-depth insight. However, in traditional machine learning approaches, training such a fine-grained model often needs certain manual feature engineering. In this article, we proposed a deep learning model for aspect-level sentiment analysis and applied it to nuclear energy related tweets for understanding public opinions towards nuclear energy. We also built a new dataset for this task and the evaluation results showed that our attentive neural network could obtain insightful inference in rather complex expression forms and achieve state-of-the-art performance.

Keywords: Deep learning · Sentiment analysis · Social network
Natural language processing

1 Introduction

Online social media has become one of the leading channels where people share their ideas, thoughts and attitudes. These web platforms like Twitter provide an opportunity, a friendly environment, and encourage everyone to make contributions. Thus, the user-generated contents tend to contain the latest information, and reflect holistic social trends rapidly. As a result, sentiment analysis or opinion mining of social networks becomes increasingly important for organizations to make fast and effective decisions.

Nuclear energy has been a hot and controversial topic for a long term. On the one hand, the number of nuclear power plants is estimated to reach thousands worldwide. On the other hand, people are paying more attention to nuclear reliability and waste. They often worry about the hidden peril of nuclear energy like leaking disasters. As it is a double-edged sword, the development of this kind of technology needs careful consideration. Public attitudes and perceptions should be taken into account, and the government could adjust their policies based on the opinion analysis.

© Springer Nature Switzerland AG 2018
M. Dobreva et al. (Eds.): ICADL 2018, LNCS 11279, pp. 99–111, 2018.
https://doi.org/10.1007/978-3-030-04257-8_9

Many studies on automatic sentiment analysis of the textual content are primarily using traditional supervised machine learning approaches like Naïve Bayesian classifier and Support Vector Machine (SVM) that have shown good performance on document-level and sentence-level. However, these coarse-grained methods may introduce errors when people comment on more than one aspect, especially when their attitudes towards these aspects are different. This becomes more prominent in public opinion mining because tweets often contain clauses with different sentiments toward different aspects (e.g., positive towards cost, and negative towards safety). Enhancing those traditional models with manually-refined rules and features could be useful, but it becomes time-consuming and needs expertise in the target domain.

Recently, deep neural networks have brought breakthroughs to multiple fields. With their robust learning capability, we can obtain high-availability and high-performance models in the end-to-end way. In the text classification, methods like recurrent neural networks (RNNs) are introduced to make predictions with latent representation of sequential information and contextual fusion. Moreover, models with attention mechanism can handle more complex tasks, such as aspect-based sentiment classification.

In this article, our objective is to develop an accurate aspect-level sentiment classifier with a deep learning approach and apply it to explore online public opinion towards nuclear energy on a social media platform, i.e. Twitter. For this domain-specific task, we collected tweets from scratch, developed a deep neural network model with attention mechanism, evaluated its performance, and took some quantitative content analysis with additional recent tweets.

2   Related Work

We have witnessed the power of opinionated postings in social networking websites, which can affect business, sway public perception and even impact the political systems. Therefore, researchers have showed strong interests in opinion mining on these user-generated contents and developed a wide range of applications such as predicting elections [1] and tracking diseases and disasters [2].

The essential task of opinion mining is sentimental polarity classification. Even though postings with "thumbs up" or retweets to support others' opinions are easily observable, intricate opinions are "hidden" in free text [3]. Thus, in the natural language processing (NLP), researchers try to model and analyze these contents at different levels of granularity. Among the various levels, aspect-based sentiment classification becomes a hot area [4]. The shortcoming of detecting polarity from the entire sentence is that it pays little attention to particular entities or aspects, thus leading to low accuracy when it is necessary to predict the sentiment of a specific aspect of a sentence. One approach to solve this fine-grained problem is building various features manually, like using optimized SVM with well-defined features [5] and combing linguistic modelling with SentiWordNet [6]. However, these methods require substantial manual work and complex syntactic information of sentences, and may not be suitable for the tweets with a lot of lax expressions.

The trendy alternative is to apply neural networks such as the RNN [7] which works well in many NLP tasks. Generally, in deep learning, textual contents are represented in semantic vector spaces like word embedding [8]. Long short term memory (LSTM) was introduced to enhance RNN's capability of handling longer contextual dependency [9]. In order to concentrate on proper context with conditional targets, attention mechanisms [10] were proven effective in the machine translation [11] and question answering systems [12]. For aspect-level classification, several models were proposed like the ATAE-LSTM [13] which combines attention calculation with LSTM.

The tweets of nuclear energy were studied in [14], however, their method was at sentence level and based on the descriptive statistics of sentimental words with a limited dataset and an insufficient generalization capability. In our work, we collected a larger dataset, developed an attentive neural network model, and conducted aspect-level sentiment analysis to have deeper insights into nuclear energy related tweets.

3 Building Dataset

3.1 Aspect Definition

In aspect-based sentiment analysis tasks like Semeval-2014 task 4 [4], involving the reviews of restaurants and laptops, proposed aspect terms were noun words in a given sentence such as service and battery. However, in our pilot analysis of the nuclear energy related tweets (about 1,500 samples), their aspect terms were largely dissimilar with ones in the product reviews. One major difference was that in over 90% of the samples, only adjective words carried aspect information. For instance, when talking about nuclear safety, people preferred to use an adjective term as in the post "*It is not safe*" instead of using a noun term in the post "*Its safety is not good*". To adapt labeling task to this characteristic, we expanded the original aspect definition in [4]. Specifically, in addition to aspect-related nouns, we tagged adjective terms containing aspect information as aspect target terms.

Firstly, we used common keywords like "*nuclear energy*" for searching nuclear energy related tweets, and then investigated relevant and important aspect terms people mentioned frequently. While collecting the data, we refined a list of aspect terms, and merged similar terms into a relevant aspect category. Finally, we identified six main aspects of nuclear energy related tweets, as shown in Table 1.

Table 1. Definition of aspects of nuclear energy related tweets

Aspect	Definition
Cost	Development and maintenance price and its subsidy
Efficiency	Energy productive efficiency
Emission	CO_2, carbon emission and green energy
Radiation	Nuclear radiation and radio-active pollution
Safety	Nuclear safety, reliability, risk and disaster
Waste	Nuclear waste and its dump

3.2 Data Collecting

Twitter offered the advanced searching interface which supported Boolean queries, and we used the appropriate combinations of keywords to obtain available contents. As shown in Table 2, for each search query, we combined aspect specific keywords with a common word, like *"Nuclear energy AND expensive OR cheap OR subsidy"*. Time span of searching was from 2013 to 2017 and tweets in non-English languages were not considered. We obtained more than 13,500 tweets with this searching strategy.

Table 2. Keywords for searching nuclear energy related tweets

Common words	Nuclear energy; nuclear power; nuclear power plants; nukes
Aspect	Aspect keywords
Cost	Cost; expensive; cheap; price; subsidy
Efficiency	Efficiency; efficient; cost-efficients
Emission	Emission; zero carbon; carbon free; clean; green
Radiation	Radiation; radio-active; poisoning; harmful
Safety	Safety; safe; reliable; risky; dangerous; disastrous
Waste	Waste; waste dump

3.3 Text Preprocessing

Unstructured texts from the Internet are often not standardized and clean, therefore, text preprocessing is necessary. As our proposed model infers the meaning of a sentence from contextual dependency of words, operations which would introduce some loss of semantic information like lemmatization and stemming were avoided. In this stage, the following steps were conducted by using regular expressions, and after the process we obtained about 9,890 samples:

1. Filtering non-English characters, emojis, hashtags, hyperlinks, and @ tags.
2. Filtering replicated tweets having more than 95% similarity and tweets shorter than 8.
3. Adding blank space between words and punctuations.
4. Standardizing negative expression, like replacing "don't" with "do not", and normalizing some abbreviation patterns, like replacing "they're" with "they are".
5. Standardizing some Twitter abbreviations, like replacing "w/o" with "without".

Worth mentioning, from the sentence level, some hashtags were useful to extract sentiment like "#smile" and "#nonuclear". However, in the aspect level, as most hashtags were found at the end of tweets, they may be too spatially far apart from relevant context terms which could lead to misunderstanding. Moreover, many hashtags could not be indexed to corresponding vectors in the general embedding library. Thus, we directly removed them.

3.4 Aspect Extracting and Sentiment Labeling

The aspect keywords in Table 2 were used for automatic aspect extracting. When we traversed each sentence, a new corresponding sample would be generated once there was a certain aspect keyword. When there was more than one aspect in a sentence, several samples with different target aspects were created.

After aspect detection, all the tweets' sentiments toward target aspects were labeled individually by two coders. Non-subjective sentences, such as "*There is a new subsidy policy of nuclear power plants*", and the irrelevant ones talking about nuclear warship or weapons were filtered out. The intercoder agreement of Cohen's kappa coefficient is 0.92 and conflicting samples were reviewed and re-classified by the two coders.

As shown in Fig. 1, in the labeled data, nuclear efficiency and waste aspects drew the most attention while emission and radiation drew the least. Moreover, in nuclear efficiency, positive tweets were nearly triple of negative ones, and people mostly held negative opinions when mentioning nuclear waste.

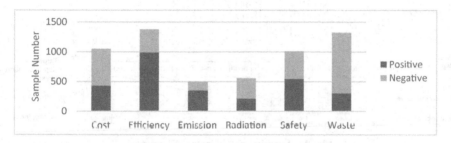

Fig. 1. Polarity distribution of labeled dataset

Sample imbalance might bring negative influence on the model training, so we removed some tweets with high similarity scores (>0.9) in efficiency and waste aspects to mitigate the polarity disproportion of the samples. This allowed the whole dataset (5,208 samples) to have balanced positive and negative tweets as shown in Table 3.

Table 3. Statistic of labeled balanced dataset

	Cost	Efficiency	Emission	Radiation	Safety	Waste	Summary
Positive	431	689	350	211	546	304	2531
Negative	620	391	151	345	464	706	2677
Summary	1051	1080	501	556	1010	1010	5208

4 Attentive Deep Neural Network

We adopted the idea from dynamic memory network (DMN) which usually works well in question answering (QA) [15] and redesigned it to fit into aspect-level sentiment classification task. As shown in Fig. 2, the proposed model contains six main components: Embedding Layer, Input Representation, Target Representation, Attention Layer, Episode Memory Layer, and Answer Layer. The input is a pair of sentence and aspect term, and the output is a classification label, i.e. positive or negative polarity.

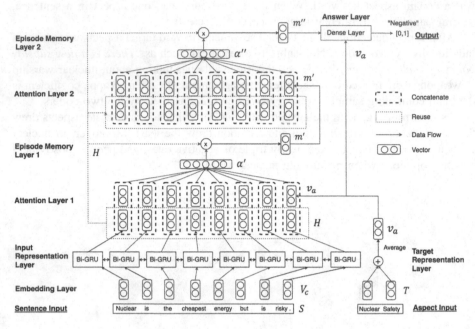

Fig. 2. Attentive neural network structure

- Embedding Layer

Word embedding is a semantic vector space where terms are mapped to real numbers. Unlike one-hot encoding which vectorizes words by simply distinguishing each term from others in a vocabulary, it can help semantic calculation and boost performance in NLP tasks [8]. The pre-trained embedding sets were widely applied in small scale training, and here we imported the GloVe [16].

Given an input $S = \{w_1, w_2, w_3 \ldots w_t\}$ where t is a variable sentence length, each token w_i was converted into a vector v_i by looking up in the embedding set $D \in R^{|V| \times d}$, where $|V|$ is the vocabulary size and $d = 300$ is the embedding dimension. Moreover, for the batch training, zeros were used for padding inputs to a fixed length $n = 65$ which is set to be larger than the longest sentence size in the whole dataset. After this layer, a sentence became into an embedding list $V_c = \{v_1^c, v_2^c, v_3^c \ldots v_n^c\}$ where $v_i^c \in R^d$.

- Input Representation Layer

Gated Recurrent Unit (GRU), a variance of LSTM, is to handle the loss of long term memory and vanishing gradient problem which occurred in traditional RNNs. It exposes the complete hidden output without any auxiliary control and has fewer

parameters than LSTM [17]. Thus, it exhibits faster convergence and better performance on smaller datasets and is more suitable for our dataset.

The input representation layer is a sequence encoder with bi-directional GRUs,
transforming the embedding list $V_c = \{v_1^c, v_2^c, v_3^c \ldots v_n^c\} \in R^{n \times d}$ into the contextual
sequence $H = \{h_1, h_2, h_3 \ldots h_n\} \in R^{n \times d}$. The bi-directional structure helps to obtain
both forward and backward information, and their outputs were merged.

$$h_i = Forward\_GRU\left(v_i^c\right) + Backward\_GRU\left(v_i^c\right). \tag{1}$$

- Target Representation Layer

In the QA system, questions like *"What is the weather today?"* could be encoded in
the same way as the context sentence H. However, in the aspect-level task, a target is a
phrase such as *"nuclear cost"*, containing little syntactic structure. In this case, the
aspect vector $v_a \in R^d$ was directly calculated as the mean of the phrase's embedding
list $T = \{v_1^a, v_2^a \ldots v_m^a\} \in R^{m \times d}$ where m is the phrase's length.

$$v_a = \frac{1}{m} \sum_m \{v_1^a, v_2^a \ldots v_m^a\}. \tag{2}$$

- Multi-hop Episode Memory Layer with Attention Mechanism

We stacked two hops of episode memory layer which integrates the attention layer
since this strategy proved to elevate performance, especially for long sentences

The first attention layer obtained the correlation scores between the target v_a and
each part of the contextual sequence H. Two dense layers with hyperbolic tangent
activation were stacked. The output called the attentive vector is
$\alpha' = \{a_1', a_2' \ldots a_n'\} \in R^{n \times 1}$, indicating the weights of term importance. The sum of
attention scores in one sentence should be 1.0, so a softmax operation was applied for
normalization.

$$\alpha_i' = softmax\left(W'^{(2)} \tanh\left(\left(W'^{(1)}[v_a; h_i] + b'^{(1)}\right)\right) + b'^{(2)}\right) \tag{3}$$

where $W'^{(1)} \in R^{d \times 2d}$, $W'^{(2)} \in R^{1 \times d}$ are the weights and $b'^{(1)} \in R^d$, $b'^{(2)} \in R$ are biases
of dense layers, and $[;]$ is the concatenate operation.

Then, the first episode memory $m' \in R^d$ could be generated by multiplying attentive
vector $\alpha' \in R^{n \times 1}$ with the context sentence $H \in R^{n \times d}$.

$$m' = \alpha'^T H. \tag{4}$$

The second attention layer used m' as target input instead of v_a, and reused the
contextual sequence H. Its output, the attentive vector α'', was multiplied with H to
generate the final memory m''.

- Answer Layer

For the classification task, the output is a one-hot vector indicating sentiment polarity. More specifically, positive and negative labels were encoded as $[1,0]$ and $[0,1]$ respectively. In this step, the final memory m'' was concatenated with the aspect vector v_a, squeezed via a dense layer, and then normalized by a softmax operation to probability values between 0 and 1.

$$p = \text{softmax}\left(W^{(\text{aw})}[m''; v_a] + b^{(\text{aw})} \right). \tag{5}$$

where $W^{(\text{aw})} \in R^{2 \times 2d}$ and $b^{(\text{aw})} \in R^{2 \times 1}$ are the weight and bias respectively.

5 Model Training

5.1 Loss Function

The model was trained via gradient backpropagation with the cross-entropy loss function which measures the distance of two distributions. Specifically, when y is the expected polarity distribution and $\hat{y}$ is the predicted distribution from the model, the goal of training was to minimize the loss between them for all sentences:

$$loss = -\sum_i \sum_j y_i^j \log \hat{y}_i^j + \lambda ||\theta||^2. \tag{6}$$

where i is the index of a sample sentence, j is the index of its category, λ is the L2-regularization term and θ is the trainable parameter set in the neural network.

5.2 Training Configuration

The loss function was optimized by Adam algorithm [18] with 0.001 learning rate. The whole dataset was split into a training set and test set with a ratio of 9:1. Batch size was 100 and we re-shuffled all samples in each epoch. The percentage of out-of-vocabulary words was below 0.2%, and they were replaced with zero vectors.

The L2-norm regularization (value = 0.002) and the dropout with 0.9 rate were applied to mitigate overfitting. Besides, we adopted early stop strategy when a slight overfitting occurred, and the average training epoch was around 20 times.

6 Model Evaluation

6.1 Evaluation on the Twitter Dataset

We evaluated our attentive model on the labeled Twitter dataset and compared it with two sentence-level methods: SVM and regular LSTM, which do not capture any aspect information. SVM is a traditional approach used bag-of-words matrix to represent sentences. We implemented it with the term frequency inverse document frequency (TF * IDF) and L2 normalization of sentence length. Worth mentioning, it was incapable to utilize word embedding, so we added some feature refinement like removing stop words and applying tokenization and lemmatization. Besides, a regular LSTM model without attention mechanism was tested. In it, word embedding layer with pretrained GloVe was used as well. The basic training configuration like learning rate and dropout rate were the same as in our attentive model.

Comparison on the Original Twitter Dataset. Firstly, we evaluated the three models with the labeled nuclear tweets. To reduce sample difference from random shuffling, training and test sets were kept the same during the comparison. We summarized the test accuracy and F1 scores of the six aspect categories in Tables 4 and 5. Surprisingly, these three models did not show significant differences. After reviewing the dataset with scrutiny, we found two possible reasons for the unexpected results:

1. Although different aspects were mentioned in a sentence, they usually shared the same sentiment polarity. For instance, the sentence "*Nuclear is the future! It's safe and efficient!*" contained two different aspects with the same positive polarity.
2. Due to the limited sample size of our collection, a large proportion of the samples contain only one aspect, namely, people usually commented one aspect at one time. In this case, our model could not take advantage of its attentive feature.

Table 4. Performance comparison on the original twitter dataset

Model	Type	Test accuracy	Macro-F1
Attentive model	Aspect-level	0.790	0.772
SVM	Sentence-level	0.778	0.768
LSTM	Sentence-level	0.773	0.764

Comparison on the Augmented Twitter Dataset. To verify the advantage of our attentive model in the aspect-level analysis, we augmented the dataset by combining two sentences which contained different aspects as well as different polarities. The augmented dataset contains 10,416 sentences, doubling the size of the original one and the shortcomings of data as mentioned above would be alleviated.

We conducted another round of training and test processes and summarized the results in Table 6. The test accuracy and F1 scores of the SVM and LSTM dropped dramatically from around 0.77 (shown in Table 5) to around 0.5. This significant difference could be explained by the fact that the SVM and LSTM models could only get one correct judgment on the overall sentiment of a sentence, whereas the proposed model could adapt to the given target aspect of the sentence. In this case, the attentive neural network largely outperformed.

Table 5. Aspect-level F1 scores

	Cost	Efficiency	Emission	Radiation	Safety	Waste
Attentive model	0.775	0.868	0.888	0.701	0.795	0.607
SVM	0.673	0.774	0.914	0.830	0.764	0.656
LSTM	0.774	0.829	0.869	0.681	0.729	0.705

Table 6. Performance comparison of augmented twitter dataset

Model	Type	Test accuracy	Macro-F1
Attentive model	Aspect-level	0.810	0.798
SVM	Sentence-level	0.500	0.500
LSTM	Sentence-level	0.499	0.499

6.2   Evaluation on a Public Dataset

Additionally, we trained the attentive model on the restaurant review dataset from Semeval-2014 task 4 [4] and compared the results with which of several state-of-the-art models in [13]. As shown in Table 7, our model performed competitively.

Table 7. Performance comparison on a public dataset (* denotes results from [13])

Model	Type	Test accuracy
Attentive model	Aspect-level	0.770
LSTM	Sentence-level	0.743*
AE-LSTM	Aspect-level	0.766*
ATAE-LSTM	Aspect-level	0.772*

6.3   Analysis with Attention Visualization

To evaluate the performance of attention mechanism in our model, we plotted the attention vector α'', which mainly affected the final prediction. As shown in Fig. 3, darker colors indicate higher attention scores, and influence more on the polarity judgment. With the aspect "*nuclear cost*", the attention layer concentrated on the subsections "*nuclear not cheap*" and "*cheaper than nuclear*" separately and judged the sentences as negative. It shows that the model could put more attention to the relevant terms of the target aspect and determine the aspect-based sentiment polarity.

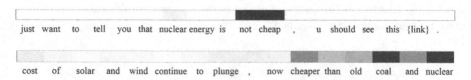

Fig. 3. Attention visualization examples (target: nuclear cost, polarity: negative)

7   Model Deployment

Finally, we deployed the aspect-based sentiment classification model. With the aforementioned search strategy and data preprocessing, we collected the latest tweets from January to March in 2018 that were conveying the public opinion on nuclear energy. The details of the collected tweets were summarized in Table 8. It showed that people discussed nuclear energy more in March. In each month, emission was the aspect people paid the most attention to, followed by cost and safety, while efficiency drew the least discussion. This was largely dissimilar with the previous data shown in Fig. 1. This interesting phenomenon to some extent represented the changes of topic trends as time goes by.

Table 8. Details of the collected tweets (from 2018.01 to 2018.03)

	Cost	Efficiency	Emission	Radiation	Safety	Waste	Summary
January	43	2	71	8	32	9	165
February	29	3	44	3	26	7	112
March	61	8	83	11	53	20	236

Then we conducted fine-grained sentiment analysis which could help gather more in-depth insight into public thoughts, and the results were summarized in Fig. 4. Across the first quarter of 2018, people held different attitudes towards the top three aspects of nuclear energy: safety, emission and cost. The polarity of nuclear safety was fifty-fifty, and much more postings held positive opinion towards emission. When it came to cost, people tended to have more concerns. Based on this analysis, relevant organizations could adjust their strategies to help the public obtain more comprehensive and correct information about nuclear energy.

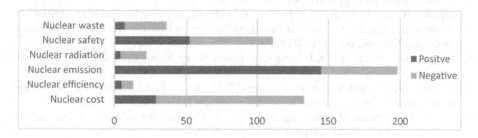

Fig. 4. Polarity analysis on nuclear energy (from 2018.01 to 2018.03)

8   Conclusion and Future Work

We have developed the attentive neural network for aspect-based sentiment classification and conducted a practical analysis task on nuclear energy related tweets. The main contribution of this paper is that we introduced a novel neural network approach for aspect-level sentiment classification. With sufficient training data, the proposed model could learn to concentrate on the proper parts of a sentence when different target aspects were given. Therefore, it was more competitive for an aspect-level classification task. Experimental results showed that it obtained superior performance over the sentence-level models.

However, the model that works well in one specific domain may need to re-train for another, especially there is a huge gap between datasets. It is still challenging for machine learning models to take the transfer learning. Thus, one direction of our future work can be combining current approach with other linguistic models to enhance its generalization capability. This will help the model to be applied in different domains with more flexibility and less supervision.

References

1. Tumasjan, A., Sprenger, T.O., Sandner, P.G., Welpe, I.M.: Predicting elections with Twitter: what 140 characters reveal about political sentiment. Icwsm 10(1), 178–185 (2010)
2. Sakaki, T., Okazaki, M., Matsuo, Y.: Earthquake shakes Twitter users: real-time event detection by social sensors. In: Proceedings of the 19th International Conference on World Wide Web, pp. 851–860. ACM (2010)
3. Liu, B.: Sentiment analysis and opinion mining. Synth. Lect. Hum. Lang. Technol. 5(1), 1–167 (2012)
4. Pontiki, M., Galanis, D., Pavlopoulos, J., Papageorgiou, H., Androutsopoulos, I., Manandhar, S.: SemEval-2014 task 4: aspect based sentiment analysis. In: Proceedings of the 8th International Workshop on Semantic Evaluation (SemEval 2014), pp. 27–35 (2014)
5. Mohammad, S.M., Kiritchenko, S., Zhu, X.: NRC-Canada: building the state-of-the-art in sentiment analysis of tweets. arXiv preprint arXiv:1308.6242 (2013)
6. Thet, T.T., Na, J.C., Khoo, C.S.: Aspect-based sentiment analysis of movie reviews on discussion boards. J. Inf. Sci. 36(6), 823–848 (2010)
7. Dzmitry, B., Cho, K., Bengio, Y.: Neural machine translation by jointly learning to align and translate. arXiv preprint arXiv:1409.0473 (2014)
8. Mikolov, T., Sutskever, I., Chen, K., Corrado, G.S., Dean, J.: Distributed representations of words and phrases and their compositionality. In: Advances in Neural Information Processing Systems, pp. 3111–3119 (2013)
9. Hochreiter, S., Schmidhuber, J.: Long short-term memory. Neural Comput. 9(8), 1735–1780 (1997)
10. Rocktäschel, T., Grefenstette, E., Hermann, K.M., Kočiský, T., Blunsom, P.: Reasoning about entailment with neural attention. arXiv preprint arXiv:1509.06664 (2015)
11. Luong, M.T., Pham, H., Manning, C.D.: Effective approaches to attention-based neural machine translation. arXiv preprint arXiv:1508.04025 (2015)
12. Sukhbaatar, S., Weston, J., Fergus, R.: End-to-end memory networks. In: Advances in Neural Information Processing Systems, pp. 2440–2448 (2015)
13. Wang, Y., Huang, M., Zhao, L.: Attention-based LSTM for aspect-level sentiment classification. In: Proceedings of the 2016 Conference on Empirical Methods in Natural Language Processing, pp. 606–615 (2016)
14. Kim, D.S., Kim, J.W.: Public opinion sensing and trend analysis on social media: a study on nuclear power on Twitter. Int. J. Multimed. Ubiquitous Eng. 9(11), 373–384 (2014)

15. Kumar, A., et al.: Ask me anything: dynamic memory networks for natural language processing. In: International Conference on Machine Learning, pp. 1378–1387 (2016)
16. Pennington, J., Socher, R., Manning, C.: Glove: global vectors for word representation. In: Proceedings of the 2014 Conference on Empirical Methods in Natural Language Processing (EMNLP), pp. 1532–1543 (2014)
17. Cho, K., et al.: Learning phrase representations using RNN encoder-decoder for statistical machine translation. arXiv preprint arXiv:1406.1078 (2014)
18. Kingma, D.P., Ba, J.: Adam: a method for stochastic optimization. arXiv preprint arXiv: 1412.6980 (2014)

Where the Dead Blogs Are
A Disaggregated Exploration of Web Archives to Reveal Extinct Online Collectives

Quentin Lobbé$^{(\boxtimes)}$ (iD)

LTCI, Télécom ParisTech, Université Paris Saclay & Inria, Paris, France
quentin.lobbe@telecom-paristech.fr

Abstract. The Web is an unsteady environment. As Web sites emerge and expand every days, whole communities may fade away over time by leaving too few or incomplete traces on the living Web. Worldwide volumes of Web archives preserve the history of the Web and reduce the loss of this digital heritage. Web archives remain essential to the comprehension of the lifecycles of extinct online collectives. In this paper, we propose a framework to follow the intern dynamics of vanished Web communities, based on the exploration of corpora of Web archives. To achieve this goal, we define a new unit of analysis called *Web fragment*: a semantic and syntactic subset of a given Web page, designed to increase historical accuracy. This contribution has practical value for those who conduct large-scale archive exploration (in terms of time range and volume) or are interested in computational approach to Web history and social science. By applying our framework to the Moroccan archives of the e-Diasporas Atlas, we first witness the collapsing of an established community of Moroccan migrant blogs. We show its progressive mutation towards rising social platforms, between 2008 and 2018. Then, we study the sudden creation of an ephemeral collective of forum members gathered by the wave of the Arab Spring in the early 2011. We finally yield new insights into historical Web studies by suggesting the concept of *pivot moment of the Web*.

Keywords: Web archives · Digital heritage
Online migrant collectives

1 Introduction

At the end of the 90's, the development of the Information and Communication Technologies (ICT) reshaped the notion of time, space, and border. The rises of Internet, electronic messaging, and mobile phones provided new remote tools of communication and organisation to worldwide migrant collectives. The Web then became an environment favourable to the establishment of online hubs for migrants to connect with each other or to preserve pieces of a scattered collective memory. In 2012, the e-Diasporas Atlas [7], directed by Diminescu, revealed diasporic collectives that organize first and foremost on the Web, as

© Springer Nature Switzerland AG 2018
M. Dobreva et al. (Eds.): ICADL 2018, LNCS 11279, pp. 112–123, 2018.
https://doi.org/10.1007/978-3-030-04257-8_10

networks of migrant websites, connected to each other through hypertext links. The atlas led to the observation of 10,000 migrant Web sites distributed along 30 diasporic networks (Moroccan, Tunisian, Egyptian, etc.) called *e-Diasporas*[1]. But facing, month after month, the partial or total disappearance of some of the observed migrant Web sites, it was decided to start archiving them to ensure the preservation of their digital history and to allow forthcoming researche.

Web Archiving. Since the creation of the Web in the early 90's [5], the loss of the digital content that constitutes the Web itself has been considered a major issue. Started as a volunteer initiative with the creation of Internet Archive [9], Web archiving was gradually assumed by various states. Shortly after the recognition of the *Charter on the Preservation of the Digital Heritage* by UNESCO [18], terabytes of Web pages were saved worldwide by archiving the genesis of the Web. But after 20 years of Web archiving, it must be said that there is an asymmetry between works focused on upstream archive acquisition [13] and analysis of existing Web archives corpora [17]. In practice, most national libraries allow limited consultation points with no remote access to their archived corpora. The online portal of the WayBack Machine[2] only provides a restrictive search-by-URL system without any full-text search facility. Existing tools are designed and effective for refining past versions of a known URL, not for proceeding to a large-scale exploration. Thus, related research based on Web archives chooses to manually track a set of URLs [16] or to focus on the visual aspects of an archived Web page [1]. As a new insight, Brügger introduces the notion of *analytical Web strata* [3]. He then suggests the possibility of building a dynamic system to resize historical studies from an archived Web page to its individual Web elements

Summary of Main Contributions In this paper, we propose a framework based on the exploration of corpora of Web archives, to follow the internal dynamics of extinct online migrant collectives: communities for which too few or incomplete traces remain on the living Web. We hypothesize that their structure is permeable to the impact of exogenous events or shocks. Our aim is to search for correlations between a given political and social context and the topographic evolutions of a vanished community. We will study two online migrant collectives extracted from the Moroccan section of the e-Diasporas Atlas archives[3]: an established blogosphere (Sect. 4) and an ephemeral group of forum members (Sect. 5). They both vanished from the Web at some point before 2018. The Moroccan *e-Diaspora* is a network of 254 Web sites, built on hypertext citations, created or managed by Moroccan migrants or that deal with them, and initially mapped in 2008 (Fig. 1). It can be divided in 3 clusters: (1) Institutional Web sites managed by the Moroccan government, (2) Associations and NGOs, (3) The blogosphere edited by citizens. The forum *yabiladi.com* can be seen as a hub between the 3 clusters, *larbi.org* is depicted as one of the leading blogs. The

---

[1] http://www.e-diasporas.fr/.

[2] https://archive.org/web/.

[3] Available at http://www.e-diasporas.fr/wp/moroccan.html.

whole network was then weekly archived from March 2010 to September 2014: we count 2,683,928 archived pages for *yabiladi.com* and 78,311 for *larbi.org*. We start by introducing, in Sect. 2, an entity called *Web fragment*: a new unit to explore archived corpora that results from the segmentation of a Web page. We then discuss the benefits of using it in comparison to existing approaches. We show, in Sect. 3, the way we can extract and shape Web fragments out of archived Web pages. We then depict the technical implementation of the whole framework. In Sect. 4, we witness the collapsing of the Moroccan blogosphere. We show its progressive mutation towards rising social platforms, between 2008 and 2018. In Sect. 5, we study the creation of an ephemeral collective of members of the forum *yabiladi.com* gathered by the wave of Arab Spring[4]. In particular, we show how some old users converged suddenly around the online organisation of the demonstration of February 20th 2011. Finally, we discuss in Sect. 6 the limitations of Web archives as a source of information and introduce the notion of *pivot moment of the Web*.

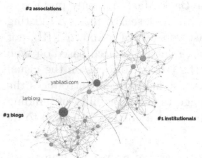

Fig. 1. The Moroccan e-Diasporas (mapped by D. Diminescu, M. Renault and M. Jacomy)

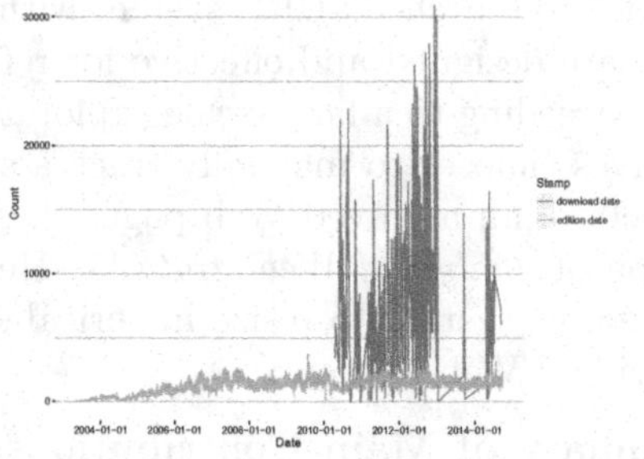

Fig. 2. Distribution of the archives of *yabiladi.com* using download dates vs edition dates (Color figure online)

2   The Web Fragment

In the following, we introduce the Web fragment and discuss the benefits of upscaling the historical analysis of Web archives by using the Web fragment instead of the Web page as new unit of exploration.

2.1   Definition

Considering the Web page as the basic unit of access to the World Wide Web, built using its own digital writing modalities, and noticing that from the point of

---

[4] The Arab Spring was a revolutionary wave of protests in North Africa and the Middle East between 2010 and 2012 (https://en.wikipedia.org/wiki/Arab_Spring).

view of human perception [14] a Web page is the result of the logical arrangement of distinct semantic components, we define a Web fragment as a semantic and syntactic subset of a given Web page. There is a scale relationship between a Web page and its Web fragments. A Web fragment is a coherent set of textual, visual, audio or animated contents extracted from a Web page. The Web fragment should be comprehensible on its own. Within the same Web page, two fragments cannot overlap, even partially. A Web fragment must go with an associated set of extracted meta contents (an author, a title, an edition date, etc.) and it must also encompass all the writing and sharing elements used for publishing this content on the Web (CMS widgets, integrated text editor, hypertext links, rss feed, etc.).

2.2   Upscaling the Exploration

Assumptions. Archive file formats[5] are basically a collection of crawled HTML pages associated with a download date. In existing Web archive explorer tools (such as the Wayback Machine), the results are stamped by download date. By contrast, a Web fragment is related to an edition date: the date when it was created or published on the living Web. The many difficulties to retrieve edition dates have already been addressed by [8], but the benefits in term of historical accuracy are impressive. From this point, we will anticipate the possibility of extracting Web fragments (see Sect. 3 for a technical implementation).

Reducing Crawl Blindness. We call here *crawl blindness* the action of mis-timestamping a change on a page after a crawl. A change can be the creation, the update, or the deletion of all or part of a Web page [6]. As a proposition, we first call the process of downloading the Web pages $\{p_1,...,p_n\}$ of an entire Web site a crawl c_i. We then assume that a corpus of Web archives is the result of one or several successive crawls $\{c_1,...,c_l\}$. An archived Web site consists of n Web pages numbered $\{p_1,...,p_n\}$. The time taken for downloading pages is neglected. We call $t_i(p_j)$ the download date of page p_j during crawl c_i. We assume to know the last modified stamp of page p_j denoted $\mu_i(p_j)$ during crawl c_i (having $\mu_i(p_j) \leq t_i(p_j)$). Here, we argue that a page p_j consists of m Web fragments numbered $\{f_{j1},...,f_{jm}\}$. We also assume to know the edition date of each Web fragment $\phi(f_{j1}),...,\phi(f_{jm})$, where c_i is a crawl in which f_{jk} exists, so that an edition date will always be more historically accurate than a download date:

$$\forall p_j, f_{jk} \exists \phi(f_{jk}) : \phi(f_{jk}) \leq \mu_i(p_j) \leq t_i(p_j)$$

Increasing the Historical Accuracy. We now assume that the first download date of page p_j is denoted as $\min_i t_i(p_j)$ and we approximate its creation date by its first edition date $\min_k \phi(f_{jk})$. As an experiment, we select the 109,534 archived Web pages of the forum section of *yabiladi.com* stamped by first download date.

---

[5] WARC (Web ARChive) or DAFF (Digital Archive File Format) file formats.

We split them into 422,906 deduplicated Web fragments stamped by edition dates. To be more specific, the remaining Web fragments can be seen as single archived forum messages associated with a publication date. In Fig. 2, we compare the temporal distribution of the archived pages stamped by first download dates (red line) versus their corresponding first edition dates (blue line). First of all, we witness a crawl blindness around 2013 (red line): the crawler stopped archiving during many months. This crawl legacy can be attenuated by switching to the edition dates (blue line). Then, as archived pages keep the traces of past messages, we can extend the comprehension of our corpus (archived since 2010) to consider contents written up to 2003 (blue line). If we calculate the difference $\min_i t_i(p_j) - \min_k \phi(f_{jk})$ in days, the corresponding quartiles are: (Q1) 256, (Q2) 777, (Q3) 1340. With our framework, doing an exploration on top of Web fragments stamped by edition dates will always be more historically accurate than looking at the original Web pages stamped by download dates.

3   Disaggregating Web Archives

In the following, we will move to the practical implementation of our framework and discuss our method for extracting and framing Web fragments.

Implementation. Our architecture is released under an open-source license[6] and follows a classical implementation model[7]: (1) archives files are grabed by a Java extractor and then uploaded into a Hadoop Distributed File System (HDFS). (2) A Spark pipeline ingests the HDFS and filters the archives. (3) A dedicated library extracts the Web fragments out of the archived pages. (4) Then the text content of each Web fragment is indexed into a Solr search engine.

Extraction of Web Fragments. Here, we consider an archived Web page as a finite set of m HTML nodes $\{n_1, ..., n_m\}$, organized as a DOM tree t and associated with some CSS style rules. First, we clean t using the boilerplate method of [11] to filter out ads and navigation nodes. We then follow user-centric scraping strategies[8]: Mozilla's Readability and Fathom projects. As Readability was designed to find the most important part of a Web page (like an article), we extend it using the Fathom agglomerative clustering algorithm to find all the coherent clusters of HTML nodes. In the Fathom algorithm, all the HTML nodes are initially stored in an $m \times m$ sparse adjacency matrix called A. An agglomerative clustering is then applied node by node, having the rows of A incrementally going from single nodes to clusters of nodes. A pseudo-code implementation of it is given in Algorithm 1. We call d the distance function resulting of the depth difference between two nodes in the DOM tree t. We assume the existence of a function named *closestRows* that returns the two closest rows of A based on the

[6] https://github.com/lobbeque/archive-miner   and   https://github.com/lobbeque/archive-search.
[7] Using Hadoop (http://hadoop.apache.org/), Spark (https://spark.apache.org/) and Solr (http://lucene.apache.org/solr/).
[8] https://github.com/mozilla/readability and https://github.com/mozilla/fathom.

distance between their respective nodes. The variable $minDist$ is the minimal distance to allow for agglomerate two nodes. As a contribution, we extend the distance function d of Readability with visual-based penalties introduced by [4] and tag-based penalties introduced by [8] to handle the *"human perception"* part of the Web fragment. In practice, we initialize the variable $minDist$ for each Web site after human validation. For each remaining cluster, we parse the HTML and CSS class-names of all the constitutive nodes using a set of dedicated regular expressions to identify and extract edition dates. Finally, we index the text contents as well as all the HTML id and class names[9]. To sum up, a Web fragment is a coherent cluster of HTML nodes.

> **while** $rows(A) > 1$ *and* $closestRows(A) < minDist$ **do**
> $\quad \{r_i, r_j\} = closestRows(A)$
> $\quad newRow = \{\}$
> $\quad$ **for** $r \in rows(A)$ **do**
> $\quad\quad$ **if** $r \neq r_i$ and $r \neq r_j$ **then**
> $\quad\quad\quad newRow[r] = \min(d(r_i, r), d(r_j, r))$
> $\quad\quad$ **end**
> $\quad$ **end**
> $\quad remove(A[r_i])$
> $\quad remove(A[r_j])$
> $\quad remove(A[*][r_i])$
> $\quad remove(A[*][r_j])$
> $\quad append(A, newRow)$
> **end**

Algorithm 1: Fathom agglomerative clustering

4   Archived Traces of Digital Mutation

We now transition to the question of extinct online migrant collectives. In particular, we focus on analysing the collapsing of an old-established community of migrant Moroccan blogs between 2008 and 2018.

An Old-Established Blogosphere. In 2008, a set of 47 blogs (linked together by hypertext citations and created or managed by Moroccan migrants) was discovered and mapped as illustrated by Figs. 1 (full network) and 3 (close up, left). The political blog *larbi.org* possessed the highest in-degree[10] and occupied a central position in the community. The 47 blogs used French as a main language and produced a bundle of political thoughts and daily moods. In 2015, a report [10] induced that many of the blogs were no longer active. By updating this survey in 2018, we show that 20 blogs are now dead, 22 have not been updated since at least 2 years and only 5 are still alive (see Fig. 3, right).

---

[9] See https://github.com/lobbeque/rivelaine for the whole implementation and https://frama.link/XYj1FNSY for the set of regular expressions.

[10] The number of edges incoming to a vertex.

Exploration Task. We emit two hypotheses: (1) the authors of the blogs deleted them and moved away from the Web, (2) the authors migrated from one Web territory to another (such as Twitter or Facebook). As we know that Facebook groups where contemporary of this set of blogs [12], we define our task of exploration as finding the past traces of a digital mutation. We choose to target the first traces of social media in the whole archives. In our framework, we request for fragments containing HTML nodes related to social networks like *<span class="Twitter"></span>*, *<button class="Fb-share"></button>*, or directly mentioning *facebook, youtube, pinterest, etc.* inside their textual contents.

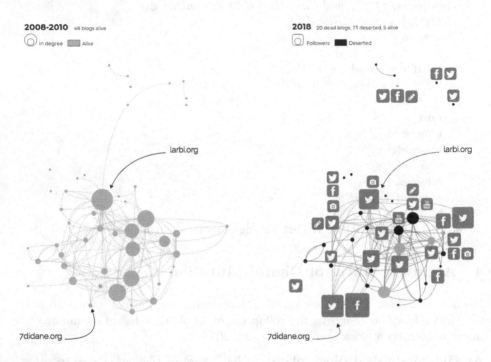

Fig. 3. Evolution of the Moroccan blogosphere between 2008 (left) and 2018 (right) with a kept position

The Recomposition of the Community. The results consist in a filtered set of Web fragments timestamped and grouped by blogs. Some of them contain the URL or the account name of a linked social media. We use the WayBack Machine to visually validate each URL and deliver a qualitative analysis[11]. After managing a blog of their own, 20 authors moved to a social platform: 8 have a Facebook standalone page, 16 are on Twitter (Fig. 3). Created between 2005 and 2007, the blogs slowly died around the early 2010's. Keeping alive its digital

---

[11] The results can be download here https://frama.link/FP-T6Z8_.

identity is a shared characteristic in this community, as all the authors reused their pseudonyms (or a close variation of them) on the social media. The online expression is now fragmented and specialized by type of medium. Some choose to have both a Facebook and a Twitter account like *7didane.org*. Others use Youtube or Flicker to upload videos and photos like *larbi.org*. We can observe the dual-use of Twitter alongside Medium, where one writes a long piece of text on Medium and chooses to promote it by using Twitter like *eatbees.com*. We show that, focusing on the authors that moved on Twitter, the density of the graph of follower/following is higher than the density of the old corresponding citations graph: it goes from 0.16 in 2008 to 0.24 in 2018. The community aspect of the old blogosphere is conserved and even increased.

Followed by the Readers. In Fig. 3 (right), the size of each social node is correlated to the size of their community of followers or friends. For instance *7didane.org* is followed by 43,512 people on Twitter and has 141,947 friends on Facebook. In the new age of social platform, the influence of an author is usually linked with the volume of readers he can communicate with. So the internal dynamics of the blogosphere changed as well: *larbi.org* grew down as *7didane.org* rised up. We show that the diasporic characteristic of the community is conserved. Authors still speak from the outside of Morocco to both Moroccan residents and migrants. We use the netvizz app[12] to extract the country of origin of the followers of each Facebook page. As an example, *lailalalami.com* still speaks to Moroccan (24%), American (15%) and Pakistani folks (8%). In the case of a crowd-engaging medium like blogs, when a strong connection is created between an author and its readers, they may want to preserve this relation during the process of digital mutation. So, we assume that readers conserved their pseudonyms on Twitter to follow the authors they supported. As an experiment, we request for Web fragments following the template of a comment on *larbi.org*: a user name, a date and a text contents. We then extract the pseudonyms of 4177 past readers of *larbi.org* and compare them to its actual followers on Twitter. This results in a lower bound of 647 persistent readers that followed the author. They also represented a significant part of the past audience of the blog, as they wrote 26% of all the archived comments.

The Arab Spring as a Key Moment. Only 6 blogs wrote a clear farewell message before dying. But the author of *7didane.org* indicated that they discovered Twitter by following the 2009 protests in Iran[13]. We also notice that *larbi.org* first publicly mentioned Twitter by the end of 2010 during the Arab Spring and pointed out its use as a tool to organized citizens actions for the upcoming protest of February 20th, 2011 with the hash-tag #20Fev [14]. It's hard to say out of those too few examples that political mobilisations caused the mutation of blogs into social media. But we can reasonably say that the Arab

---

[12] https://apps.facebook.com/netvizz/.
[13] The message: https://frama.link/DUo84Yhx, Iran protests: https://frama.link/nZmQD_Y1.
[14] https://frama.link/-Gd44Pq3.

Spring may have been a key moment for the authors to discover the democratic possibilities of those social platforms.

5   An Ephemeral Protest Collective

The Arab Spring was in many ways influenced by an active use of social media as a mean for collective organisation [15]. In Morocco, the protests occurred early in 2011 and culminated on February 20th, 2011 when over 10.000 Moroccans demonstrated to demand democratic reforms[15]. So, we now emit the hypothesis of a community of forum members of *yabiladi.com* gathered around the events of the February 20th.

A Hub for Moroccan Migrants. Figure 1 illustrates the key role of *yabiladi.com* as an old-established place in the Moroccan e-Diasporas. Created in the late 2001, the site appeared to spread multi-support informations and to be a meeting places for the migrants living abroad. In 2002, *yabiladi.com* opened a forum section, organised in categories and threads. The conversations, there, were characterized as a mix between reactions to Moroccan and international actualities and daily life considerations: cooking, family, religion, etc.

Features of the Exploration. We define our task of exploration as finding inside the archives of *yabiladi.com* a community of users who wrote at least one message in a thread related to the February 20th. Thus, we request for Web fragments following the given ordered template: (1) a user name (2) a publication date (3) a text content. They also have to be associated to an URL containing the path *"/forum/"*. Then, we can group the fragments by category and thread, as their pattern of URL follows *"/forum/ thread_title-category_id-thread_id.html"*. We assume the remaining Web fragments to be only composed of archived forum posts. We restrict our space of exploration to the two categories: *General* and *Moroccan and Worldwide Actuality*.

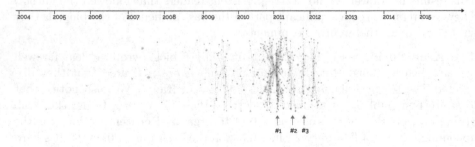

Fig. 4. Time distribution of *yabiladi.com*'s threads related to the February 20th

Revealing a Collective. We start by querying our system for a set of thread titles matching the French keywords: *"#20Fev"*, *"20 fevrier"*, etc. We manually

---

[15] https://en.wikipedia.org/wiki/Moroccan_constitutional_referendum,_2011.

validate 12 threads out of them, whether they directly deal with the organisation of the protest or react afterwards to it. We call V_0 this initial group of 12 threads, consisting of 196 messages written by a set of 94 unique users named E_0. We then select all the threads where at least 2 users of E_0 wrote a message. This new group of 343 threads is called V_1 and we can now define the graph $G = (V_1, E_0)$ as a network of threads linked by co-contributors[16]. With Fig. 4, we visualize G on a timeline (in abscissas). Red dots refer to the threads V_1 stamped by the date of their first contribution and sized by numbers of posts. Black links represent the users E_0 writing messages from one thread to another. The vertical position of each thread (in ordinate) is a fixed and arbitrary value chosen to clarify the reading of this visualisation. We find in Fig. 4 a specific moment (label #1) where the threads of G are very densely distributed. Between January and February 2011, 25% of V_1 were created. This indicates that the protest of February 20th aggregated an old established community of users that were already using the forum. We see that the pre-protest part of G (before label #1) represents a wide and sparse subgraph spread over a long period of time (from the early 2004 to 2011). In fact 62% of E_0 users wrote their first message during the pre-protest, and in particular 20% of E_0 registered to *yabiladi.com* in 2007–2008 following a huge wave of new members. They suddenly aggregate each other around label #1 and subsequent fixation points (labels #2 and #3) of the post-protest part of G. We know that the remaining 38% of E_0 contributed first and foremost to label #1 and to the rest of the *post-protest* threads. To sum up, we have two different patterns: (1) old established users converging as a group by the time of label #1, (2) new members arriving directly on *yabiladi.com* to contribute to the conversation of label #1 and taking part to the *post-protest* debates. But both parts similarly and suddenly disappeared in the early 2012.

Refine the Results. To better understand the dynamics of convergence around the protest of February 20th, we refine our comprehension of G by conducting a clustering analysis out of it using the modularity class method [2]. The 8 resulting clusters of threads[17] can be interpreted as subsequent moments of the evolution of G. Cluster #1 deals with internal debates about the functioning of the forum. Cluster #2 and #3 bundle daily-life considerations. Then Cluster #4 focus on thoughts about the Moroccan identity and comparisons between Morocco and other Maghreb countries. Suddenly, Cluster #5 witnesses the rise of a majority of threads related to the protest of February 20th after having questioned the legitimacy of the Moroccan monarchy. Cluster #6 aggregates post-protest messages. Cluster #7 deals with the political legacy of the protest, by debating about the new Moroccan constitution announced in March 2011. And finally, Cluster #8 goes back to daily life conversations. To sum up, this exploration indicates that the protest was not really prepared online. A sudden spark fired a minor part of *yabiladi.com*: 94 active users out of a total of 30,564. This wave

---

[16] Downloadable results V_1: https://frama.link/_eModem_, E_0: https://frama.link/hcxacx89.

[17] Downloadable results (as a GEXF graph file) G: https://frama.link/BZdU8CW8.

aggregated old-established members and new comers by breaking daily talks habits. The mobilization did not last in time and stopped with the reform of the Moroccan constitution. Out of the 94 users of E_0, we find that at least 26 of them created a Twitter account using the same user names[18].

6 Implication for Historical Web Studies

The development of our framework was guided by the idea that a Web site should become the object of historical studies [3]. But here, we may have reached the limits of Web archive corpora by missing a major aspect of our problematic: Web archives are intrinsically incomplete. Mostly created and designed during the early 2000's [13], Web archiving systems followed the subsequent evolutions of the Web as a medium but still fail to convey the Web as an ecosystem. The living Web is a flow of informations where various actors are organically interrelated. By contrast, the archived Web is a fixed set of discrete snapshots where records are stored apart from each other. While we were looking at the archived consequences of the Arab Spring, Web actors were already moving away from forums and blogs. The problem of extinct online collective, is less a question of disappearance than a question of transition and Web archives corpora only witness the first leap of what we call a *pivot moment of the Web*.

Pivot Moment of the Web. In the same way as the long history of writing that was punctuated by key moments (oral to written expression, invention of printing, etc.), the Web already possesses its own micro-history. We call pivot moment of the Web a period of transition between two systems, a moment when new Web uses fork from established habits and create gaps. A pivot moment arise from 3 factors: (1) the convergence at a specific time (2) between a technological leap and (3) some users sieving it. This leads the Web in new directions of development such as during the democratization of DSL in the late 1990's, the advent of smartphones and mobile Web in the 2010's or the transition from the Web 2.0 to the Web of social network as illustrated in Sects. 4 and 5.

7 Conclusion

In this paper, we proposed a framework to follow the internal dynamics of extinct online communities and conduct large scale Web archives exploration. We introduced an entity called *Web fragment*: a semantic and syntactic subset of a given archived Web page. By applying this framework to the Moroccan Web archives of the e-Diasporas Atlas, we studied the interactions between online groups, exogenous historical events and technological leap on the archived Web. In the continuity of this analysis, we will support further researches to improve the Web fragment and its multiple uses as a unit of exploration. At the border between computer sciences and digital sociology, our work opens promising questions in terms of historical Web studies. In particular, it would be interesting

---

[18] Manually counted and validated in April 2018.

to consider corpora of Web archives as records of a past ecosystem. We should address the question of mutations and transitions of Web uses regarding nearby *pivot moments*.

References

1. Ben-David, A., Amram, A., Bekkerman, R.: The colors of the national web: visual data analysis of the historical Yugoslav web domain. Int. J. Digit. Libr. **19**(1), 95–106 (2018)
2. Blondel, V.D., Guillaume, J.L., Lambiotte, R., Lefebvre, E.: Fast unfolding of communities in large networks. J. Stat. Mech.: Theory Exp. **2008**(10), P10008 (2008)
3. Brügger, N.: Website history and the website as an object of study. New Media Soc. **11**(1–2), 115–132 (2009)
4. Cai, D., Yu, S., Wen, J.R., Ma, W.Y.: VIPS: a vision-based page segmentation algorithm (2003)
5. CERN: The document that officially put the world wide web into the public domain (1993). http://cds.cern.ch/record/1164399
6. Cho, J., Garcia-Molina, H.: The evolution of the web and implications for an incremental crawler. Technical report, Stanford (1999)
7. Diminescu, D.: e-Diasporas Atlas. Explorations and Cartography of Diasporas on Digital Networks. Ed. de la Maison des Sciences de l'Homme, Paris (2012)
8. Jatowt, A., Kawai, Y., Tanaka, K.: Detecting age of page content. In: Proceedings of the 9th Annual ACM International Workshop on Web Information and Data Management, pp. 137–144. ACM (2007)
9. Kahle, B.: Preserving the internet. Sci. Am. **276**, 82–83 (1997)
10. Khouzaimi, J.: e-diasporas: Réalisation et interprétation du corpus marocain (2015)
11. Kohlschütter, C., Fankhauser, P., Nejdl, W.: Boilerplate detection using shallow text features. In: Proceedings of the Third ACM International Conference on Web Search and Data Mining, WSDM 2010, pp. 441–450. ACM, New York (2010)
12. Marchandise, S.: Le facebook des étudiants marocains. territoire relationnel et territoire des possibles. Revue européenne des migrations internationales **30**(3–4), 31–48 (2014)
13. Masanès, J.: Web Archiving. Springer, New York (2006). https://doi.org/10.1007/978-3-540-46332-0
14. Michailidou, E., Harper, S., Bechhofer, S.: Visual complexity and aesthetic perception of web pages. In: Proceedings of the 26th Annual ACM International Conference on Design of Communication, SIGDOC 2008, pp. 215–224. ACM, New York (2008)
15. Salmon, J.M.: 29 jours de révolution. Histoire du soulèvement tunisien, 17 décembre 2010–14 janvier 2011. Les Petits matins (2016)
16. Schafer, V., Thierry, B.G.: The "web of pros" in the 1990s: the professional acclimation of the world wide web in France. New Media Soc. **18**(7), 1143–1158 (2016)
17. Toyoda, M., Kitsuregawa, M.: Extracting evolution of web communities from a series of web archives. In: Proceedings of the Fourteenth ACM Conference on Hypertext and Hypermedia, Hypertext 2003, pp. 28–37 (2003)
18. UNESCO: Charter on the preservation of digital heritage (2003)

A Method for Retrieval of Tweets About Hospital Patient Experience

Julie Walters and Gobinda Chowdhury[✉]

Department of Computer and Information Sciences, Northumbria University,
Newcastle, UK
{julie.walters,gobinda.chowdhury}@northumbria.ac.uk

Abstract. Analysis of Twitter communications can capture data on hospital patient experience, and this will be more appropriate for hospital management and patient care because the data represent patients' and carers' experience about something as they happen. This paper reports on the development and testing of a semi-automatic method for retrieval of subsets of Twitter communications representing hospital patient experience on different topics and sub-topics. Twelve main topics of discussions on patient experience have been identified. Furthermore, it has been demonstrated that it is possible to retrieve tweets on most of the topics by using pre-defined search strings comprising various terms that represent a given topic.

Keywords: Twitter analysis · Social media · Patient experience
Information retrieval

1 Introduction

1.1 Hospital Patient Care

Management of patient experience and expectations is a core activity in any hospital. Capturing data and understanding individual patient experience is critical to overall patient care [1]. Previous research has highlighted the value of taking into account patients' own evaluation of their care [2]. A number of methods are used to collect data on patient experience in UK hospitals, for example,

- Through online tools like independent Care Opinion website (https://www. careopinion.org.uk/), or NHS Patient Opinion website (https://www.nhs.uk/about NHSChoices/aboutnhschoices/partners/patient-opinion/Pages/patient-opinion.aspx) that allow patients to submit their stories regarding their experience of care as a patient or service user or carer. The story they submit may be about a number of services across both health and social care. Once the story has been submitted it is moderated and published on the website. After publication the relevant staff in the care providers, commissioner or health board, regulator, patient organizations, and other local or national bodies are alerted. Staff are able to respond to the story without knowing who the author is and the author of the story can then respond to this. Changes are then made within the health service as appropriate.

© Springer Nature Switzerland AG 2018
M. Dobreva et al. (Eds.): ICADL 2018, LNCS 11279, pp. 124–135, 2018.
https://doi.org/10.1007/978-3-030-04257-8_11

- Through the NHS Choices website: The Patient and visitor information page of the Newcastle-hospitals website suggests patients and visitors submit feedback within hospitals via 'Take 2 min... Tell us what you think' boxes in public areas or alternatively, if a patient has further concerns to contact the Patient Advice Liaison Service (PALS) or if they wish to make a complaint to contact the North East NHS Independent Complaints Advocacy.
- Friends and family Test: A further mechanism for gathering feedback from patients is the Friends and Family Test, where patients are all asked the following standard question "How likely are you to recommend our ward (or service) to your friends and family if they needed similar care or treatment?" Patients can respond to this question within hospitals, online, by text or by post.
- NHS Patient Surveys: There are also a number of surveys carried out by the Care Quality Commission (CQC) [3] including surveys relating to inpatients, outpatients, emergency departments, community mental health, and maternity.

The main criticisms of current methods of feedback are the purposeful nature of the feedback and the likelihood that those people with a particular issue to raise are most likely to provide feedback of either a positive or negative nature. Interviews have received criticism for encouraging negative responses whereas surveys have been criticised for bland positive response [4].

Research shows that analysis of communications on microblogging tools like Twitter reflects 'events and trends in users' real lives because many users post tweets related to their experiences' [5]. Consequently some researchers have demonstrated how Twitter communications can be analysed to generate useful information for decision making and improving services.

1.2   Patient Experience

Patient Experience covers many different aspects of a patient's journey through the healthcare system. Research undertaken by the National Health Service [6] has identified that patients care about their experience as much as their clinical effectiveness and safety. Patient experience has been identified by the government as a high priority and many initiatives are in place to work with patients to identify their needs.

Furthermore the importance of patient experience can be understood by its significance in key hospital policy frameworks. The NHS outcomes framework is a set of indicators developed by the Department of Health to monitor the health outcomes of adults and children in England. The framework provides an overview of how the NHS is performing. Within the framework there are five domains which focus on improving health and reducing health inequalities, The fourth domain focusses on patient experience: "Ensuring that people have a positive experience of care" [7, 8]. Further to this, quality standards regarding patient experience have been established by NICE [9] to provide the NHS with clear guidance on the components of a good patient experience. The NICE guidelines developed in 2012 referred to 14 quality standards relating to patient experience which underpin the management of patient care. The quality standards provide guidance to ensure the patient experience is given due consideration in all aspects of hospital care.

Patient satisfaction measures are also increasingly used for benchmarking and accreditation purposes. Measures of patient satisfaction are considered indicative measures of service quality and quality of care. However, there is also evidence to suggest that currently the measurement of patient satisfaction and service quality is not an accurate reflection of what and how patients experience health care [10]. Furthermore, Doyle et al. [11] reviewed the evidence from 55 studies to establish the links between patient experience and clinical safety and effectiveness and concluded that patients have a role to play as partners in identifying poor and unsafe practice and help enhance effectiveness and safety.

1.3   Related Works

Twitter is a free microblogging site in which users write brief snippets of information regularly, portraying emotions, opinions, interests etc. It has developed as a platform for consumers to express their feelings and opinions on almost all aspects of customer service and has become a very popular method of communication. As of the second quarter of 2017, Twitter averaged at 328 million monthly active users, who contribute an average of 500 million tweets each day [12]. The instant portal of communication allows this huge amount of users to provide feedback and seek solutions in a public platform [13]. Communications between consumers over Twitter was described by Jansen et al. [14] as a type of electronic word-of-mouth. Due to the wide range of users from different social backgrounds, Twitter is also a good source of collecting consumer opinion, from ordinary people to professionals, organization representatives, celebrities and politicians. Thus, the tweets collected are the words of users with different interest groups and this makes it a very valuable online source of opinion.

Numerous research has taken place over the past years that aimed at developing methods and tools for extracting information from Twitter communications in different fields, including several in medicine and healthcare (see [15–27]). Many of these research have focused on developing novel tools using advanced linguistic and sentiment analysis techniques (see for example, [16, 27–31]), while others have used qualitative hybrid (a combination of quantitative and qualitative techniques for analysis of Twitter data) (see for example, [23, 32]). Again, some researchers have aimed at developing tools for capturing some specific information from Twitter such as user locations (see for example, [31, 32]).

Corley et al. [28] examined mentions of influenza on social media by text mining, and noted that it was possible to detect trends in flu. Eichstaedt et al. [34] examined the language used by individuals in social media and determined that the language used on Twitter could predict deaths from heart disease significantly better than a model combining 10 common demographic, socioeconomic, and health risk factors, including smoking, diabetes, hypertension, and obesity. Greaves and his associates [19, 20] qualitatively analysed 1000 tweets, that were sent directly to hospitals, and concluded that only a small proportion of tweets directed at hospitals discuss quality of care. Following the work of Greaves this study aims to determine a method which improves the relevance of the tweets extracted and doesn't rely on the mention of a hospital name. In contrast to previous work, which identified tweets aimed at specific hospitals

[19, 20], the purpose of this study was to initially identify aspects of patient experience irrespective of the particular hospital or hospital trust.

2 Research Aims and Methods

2.1 Aims

The overall objective of this research is to develop a simple tool that can retrieve tweets that discuss hospital patient experience on specific topics which could be of value to hospital management to take measures for improvement of patient experience. In order to achieve this objective, this research aimed to investigate:

1. How can we identify the different issues or topics that are discussed by hospital patients and carers in relation to patient experience?
2. How can we prepare a list of topics and subtopics that describe patient experience in hospitals?
3. How can we create pre-defined search strings that can retrieve sets of tweets discussing hospital patient experience on a particular topic?
4. How effective and efficient would such predefined strings be in retrieving the relevant tweets?

2.2 Methods

A number of different methods are used for analysis of tweets, e.g. (a) sentiment analysis techniques where sentiment associated with words are identified and used to categorise or analyse tweets; (b) machine learning techniques that automatically categorise tweets into some pre-defined headings or classes; (c) social network analysis that analyses characteristics of user communities participating in Twitter communications on specific topics; and (d) qualitative analysis techniques like thematic and content analysis which are based largely on manual or semi-automatic analysis [35]. In the absence of any pre-defined categories or themes to represent hospital patient experience expressed through Twitter communications, this research resorted to using a combination of quantitative (term-based search) and qualitative analysis (manual investigation) techniques to identify the key themes or topics of discussion, and thus address the first two research questions which subsequently led to address the other questions.

In the first phase, a dataset of 7321 tweets was collected, using Twitonomy, using the terms hospital and #hospital. Each tweet was examined manually to remove all retweets, news items, and duplicate tweets, non-English and marketing related tweets. This left a sample of 4360 tweets. A manual analysis of the language used in the tweets of the resulting sample was undertaken. A grounded theory approach was used to identify the "tokens" or "terms" most commonly used. After a period of testing and a number of iterations it was concluded that the tweets which included **"I"** and **"this hospital"** identified tweets which most accurately conveyed personal hospital patient experience. This supports previous research [14, 36] which has identified tweets using personal pronouns and tweets expressing personal opinion as "Personal" Tweets.

In the second phase the terms "I" and "this hospital" were used on Twitonomy in order to collect a sample of tweets each month over a period of 6 months. This produced a second dataset of 5700 tweets, the majority being personal tweets. A thematic analysis [37] was undertaken to identify the emerging topics of discussions. As there were no preconceived ideas regarding the topics which were likely to emerge from the data, a grounded theory approach [37] was deemed most appropriate. It was expected that the themes or topics would emerge as the analysis took place. A grounded theory approach was employed to classify each tweet manually. The content of each tweet in the dataset was read and examined to identify a topic. The topic headings were initially assigned considering the main purpose of the tweet recognising that many tweets could logically fall within more than one topic. For example "I hate this" would be classified as Emotion, "I hate this hospital bed" would be classified as "Hospital facilities". The set of topics was expanded until no new topics emerged. When the process was completed for the dataset, 37 significant topics relating to patient experience were identified. Further manual examination of the data identified that some the original topics were too broad and there was some significant overlap. Subsequently, after a number of iterations and testing, the topics were consolidated to 12 because some topic had to be combined because of major overlaps. A number of tweets within the original dataset were identified as not fitting into the identified topics as they were either considered to be irrelevant or to be a general observation. Irrelevant Tweets were those which were not connected to a patient in hospital, and often associated with references to high profile medical cases which are featured in the media or hospital based films or television programmes, e.g. "It totally disgusts me how this hospital treated tom Kate and Alfie, an animal would have been given better treatment". General observations included tweets which were connected to a stay in hospital but gave no insight into hospital patient experience, e.g.: "Soon as I get out this hospital, I gotta job waiting for me" or "I swear im always at this hospital". Although the refining of the topics reduced some duplication it is acknowledged that some tweets can still be classified into multiple topics. A reference set was created for future guidance on the selection and categorization of terms under each topic.

In the third phase a set of pre-defined search strings were created, with terms to represent each of the 12 main topics, that could be used to search for tweets on a specific topic. A set of tweets was collected using the terms "I" and "This hospital" for over one month, and 12 test collections were created taking the first 100 tweets from each results set where the set had more than 100 tweets. If a set had less than 100 tweets, it was ignored and the result for the following day was considered. Thus a collection 12 sets, with 100 tweet each, was built for the experiment. Each set was manually analysed and the number of tweets on each of the 12 main topics was noted. These figures were used to measure the recall of each search conducted in the following phase.

In the fourth phase, each test collection was searched with pre-defined search strings on each of the 12 topics, and the corresponding search results were noted and used to measure the recall and precision of the searches.

3 Results

3.1 Main Topics

Table 1 shows the 12 main topics (and the corresponding terms/subtopics).

Table 1. Main topics and the corresponding terms/subtopics

Topic	Terms*	No. of terms
Wanting to leave	Leave, get out, hours, go home, since, out of this hospital, out this hospital, all day, days, all night, stuck, waiting, leaving	13
Emotion	Hate, bored, love, tired, sick, hope, cry, crying, laughing, scared, anxiety, miserable, upset, don't like, disgusted, frustrated, fun, happy, hopefully, lonely	20
Friends/family	Baby, mom, family, dad, brother, sister, grandma, mum, mother, husband, cousin, mama, grandpa, granny, daughter, niece, friend, grandmother, mothers, pops	20
Hospital facilities	Bed, cold, lost, bill, smell, smells, freezing, hot, cafeteria, parking, huge, room, uncomfortable, bathroom	14
Food	Food, hungry, starving, coffee, eating, eat, lunch, breakfast, eaten, chocolate, starbucks, subway, pizza, starve, cafeteria, drink	16
Sleep	Nurse, doctor, staff	3
Staff	Sleep, sleepy, tired, nap, slept	5
Tweets by hospital staff	Job, working, work, volunteer, interview	5
Telecommunication	Wifi, phone, signal, text, tweets, charger, snapchat, texting, tweeted, "poor connection", "windows vista", computer, data, emojis	14
Specific illness	Sick, cancer, pain, disease, coughing, sicker, suicide, knee, shoulder, "back hurts", "body parts", "feel worse", "fighting for my life", "get better", "my back", A&E, aching, AH1N1, AIDS, allergic, arm, autism, blood pressure, breathing, chest, contractions, cough, diagnosed, eyes, fever, headache, kidney stones, labor, leg, liver, post-appendectomy	36
Treatment	Medicine, needle, meds, surgery, treatment, "IV line", chemo, appointment, drug	9
Entertainment	Watch, tv, Netflix, watching, mtv, Disney, ESP, film, movies, playing, ps4, speakers	12

* a cut-off point of 90 was chosen, i.e. additional terms were found and added until a total 90% of the tweets on the given topic were retrieved using all the terms together.

As Table 1 shows Twitter users use words in a variety of forms. Some occur in multiple spellings or forms e.g. mom, mama, mother, etc. Other words have the same stem, e.g. sleep, sleepy. Such variant forms of terms have not been combined just to show that variant forms of words are used in tweets; however, some terms, e.g. with the same stem, can be truncated when creating a string search. The total number of terms representing a topic (i.e. required to retrieve 90% of the tweets on the topic) varied from 3 to 37, with an average of 14. Within the "Staff" subset 90% of the original tweets which referred to staff were returned from just 3 terms: nurse, doctor and staff; however within the "Specific Illness" subset, 90% of tweets were returned from 37 terms, and yet this list may grow even bigger because some of the terms occurs only a few times.

3.2   Categorizing Tweets in the Test Collections

Each of the 12 test datasets, comprising 100 tweets each, was manually analysed to identify the number of tweets on each topic. Although, as expected, some tweets were classed under more than one topic, no new topic was found. This demonstrates that although the first test collection comprising 5700 tweets, mentioned earlier, and the 12 test collections of 100 tweets each were collected at different times, all the communications on hospital patient experience can be categorized under one or more of the 12 broad topics as mentioned in Table 1.

3.3   Pre-defined Search Strings

All the terms under each topic listed in Table 1 were combined to create a pre-defined search string for the topic. Each dataset was then searched for each topic using the pre-defined search strings and the number of hits and the number of items retrieved for each search was noted. These figures were used to calculate the recall and precision.

3.4   Retrieval Effectiveness

Tables 2 and 3 Show the recall and precision figures for each search on each of the 12 test collections.

Table 2. Measurement of recall within each dataset

Dataset	Want to Leave	Emotion	Friends /family	Hospital Facilities - other	Food	Sleep	Staff	Staff Tweet	Tele-communication	Specific Illness	Treatment	Enter-tainment
1	62%	64%	86%	57%	86%	100%	67%	80%	33%	83%	63%	50%
2	81%	54%	57%	71%	86%	60%	60%	64%	100%	0%	75%	75%
3	76%	54%	60%	54%	83%	60%	60%	80%	0%	67%	80%	0%
4	73%	61%	100%	50%	78%	50%	86%	43%	100%	0%	100%	67%
5	77%	71%	85%	50%	83%	83%	71%	67%	50%	0%	50%	67%
6	81%	59%	83%	100%	83%	75%	100%	50%	0%	50%	57%	60%
7	83%	65%	88%	50%	100%	100%	92%	100%	75%	0%	50%	67%
8	86%	74%	100%	78%	91%	100%	100%	80%	100%	0%	86%	100%
9	86%	60%	100%	59%	80%	60%	78%	63%	0%	100%	75%	75%
10	95%	80%	86%	60%	80%	75%	100%	100%	50%	50%	67%	100%
11	88%	86%	100%	71%	86%	100%	89%	78%	100%	100%	67%	50%
12	80%	72%	75%	68%	100%	100%	100%	0%	100%	0%	50%	0%
Average	81%	67%	85%	64%	86%	80%	84%	67%	59%	38%	68%	59%

Table 3. Measurement of precision of Tweets retrieved

Dataset	Want to Leave	Emotion	Friends/ family	Hospital Facilities - other	Food	Sleep	Staff	Staff Tweet	Tele-communication	Specific Illness	Treatment	Entertainment
1	59%	84%	86%	62%	60%	60%	50%	57%	100%	71%	100%	100%
2	61%	93%	62%	48%	67%	75%	50%	70%	100%	0%	75%	43%
3	89%	67%	50%	41%	56%	60%	75%	57%	0%	40%	80%	0%
4	76%	88%	63%	38%	100%	83%	55%	30%	100%	0%	100%	67%
5	77%	88%	73%	25%	63%	63%	63%	57%	100%	0%	67%	50%
6	73%	93%	91%	29%	83%	100%	33%	40%	0%	20%	80%	50%
7	81%	68%	88%	38%	75%	75%	100%	25%	60%	0%	75%	67%
8	76%	92%	50%	41%	71%	75%	100%	33%	100%	0%	67%	40%
9	83%	79%	73%	53%	67%	100%	100%	45%	0%	13%	75%	60%
10	68%	93%	86%	53%	80%	75%	100%	67%	50%	11%	80%	67%
11	71%	89%	90%	71%	86%	80%	80%	64%	100%	20%	50%	50%
12	65%	75%	75%	68%	75%	25%	90%	0%	67%	0%	80%	0%
Average	73%	84%	74%	47%	73%	73%	75%	45%	65%	29%	77%	51%

Note: Where measurement is shown as 0% there were no tweets relating to that topic within that particular dataset.

4 Discussions

Tables 2 and 3 and Fig. 1 show that the average recall was high (nearly 70%) with 80% or more for some topics. The precision figures for most of the topics were quite high with 70% or more for 7 topics. This demonstrate that it's possible to retrieve sets of useful tweets using pre-defined search strings for most of the commonly discussed topics about hospital experience. The average measurement of recall was found to be highest across all the topics within the Food topic at 86%. The level of precision was also found to be high at 73%. Perhaps unsurprisingly over 20% of the tweets were identified as emotion. The recall was found to be reasonably high within this topic and the precision was high. However, a high proportion of tweets within this topic were also attributed to other topics as patients expressed emotion relating to other factors. Tweets relating to 'friends and family' accounted for 10% of the dataset and again the recall and precision were high 85% and 74% respectively. The recall and precision of tweets associated with hospital facilities was surprisingly low at 64% and 47%. However, on further investigation this was mainly due to the use of the word bed. Although this had previously been found to be the term most frequently used when discussing hospital facilities and it was not identified as a term within another topic it was found to be used frequently within tweets relating to other topics e.g.

"Stuck in this hospital bed with this unseasoned diet 😩🍽 i can't wait to recover so i can eat what i please"

The removal of the term "bed" from the search string may significantly increase the level of precision.

Both recall and precision were low (38% and 28% respectively) for the 'Specific illness' topic. This topic also had the maximum number of terms (37). This is particularly interesting when compared to the 'Staff' topic which has the lowest number of

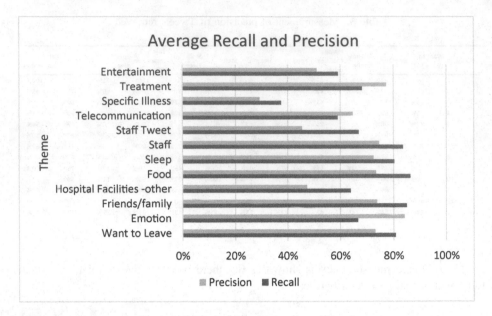

Fig. 1. Recall-precision figures for each topic

terms, and yet generated a high level of recall and precision. This suggests that the number of terms used to describe a specific illness is too high to automate and it may be more appropriate to merge with another topic such as Treatment.

The word "sick" can also fall into more than one topic. Within this study it has been classified as a term under both 'Emotion' and 'Specific Illness' which produces misleading results within the Specific Illness topic but has proved to be more accurate as a term associated with Emotion.

The level of recall and precision may also be limited in some of the topics because the number of tweets within the total dataset are very small. The subsets of tweets within the telecommunication, specific illness and entertainment topics are each less than 3% of the overall total dataset.

5 Conclusion

This study has established that the different topics discussed by hospital patients in relation to their experience can be identified by developing a method for the extraction of relevant tweets which uses search strings created from the most frequently used terms. It is noted that patients' communications can be broadly categorized into 12 topics, and they don't seem to change over a range of tweets collected at several intervals.

The range of level of recall and precision figures demonstrate the accuracy and relevance of a number of search strings created to capture discussions on specific topics. Thus the methodology has proved to be reliable for extracting tweets using the predefined search string for most of the topics that are discussed on Twitter describing patient experience. It is noted that for some topics the term sets need to be refined to remove those words which are either ambiguous or which are misleading, and hence they produce a lot of noise, and thus reduce precision.

Some topics, for example specific illness can be described by a large number of terms. Hence, it is difficult to come up with a search string that can be exhaustive enough to generate better retrieval of tweets. Further work is needed to identify more terms, if any, and to organize the terms into subcategories, e.g. in case of specific illness the type of illness may be classed under organ or disease class, which may be used to retrieve tweets on specific type of illness. It is acknowledged that further research may be needed to validate the topics and the corresponding search terms (a) using multiple sets of tweets collected at different times of the year, perhaps to see whether there are seasonal variations in terms of topics being discussed, and also (b) using other people as indexers to avoid any indexer biasness in categorizing topics under specific topics.

References

1. NHS Confederation homepage. http://www.nhsconfed.org. Accessed 15 Sept 2017
2. Yamamoto, S., Wakabayashi, K., Satoh, T., Nozaki, Y., Kando, N.: Twitter user growth analysis based on diversities in posting activities. Int. J. Web Inf. Syst. 13(4), 370–386 (2017)
3. Cqc.org.uk. Care Quality Commission (2017). http://www.cqc.org.uk/. Accessed 15 Sept 2017
4. Ahmed, F., Burt, J., Roland, M.: Measuring patient experience: concepts and methods. Patient - Patient-Centered Outcomes Res. 7(3), 235–241 (2014)
5. Al-Abri, R., Al-Balushi, A.: Patient satisfaction survey as a tool towards quality improvement. Oman Med. J. 29(1), 3–7 (2014)
6. Nhs.uk. Patient opinion - NHS Choices (2017). http://www.nhs.uk/aboutNHSChoices/aboutnhschoices/partners/patient-opinion/Pages/patient-opinion.aspx. Accessed 27 Sept 2017
7. NHS outcomes framework (2017). https://www.gov.uk/government/publications/nhs-outcomes-framework-2016-to-2017
8. Abirami, A., Askarunisa, A.: Sentiment analysis model to emphasize the impact of online reviews in healthcare industry. Online Inf. Rev. 41(4), 471–486 (2017)
9. NICE: National Institute for health and care excellence: Applying CG138 NICE patient experience in adult NHS services and QS15 NICE quality standard for patient experience in adult NHS services to complaints & the complaint process (2014). https://www.nice.org.uk/sharedlearning/applying-cg138-nice-patient-experience-in-adult-nhs-services-and-qs15-nice-quality-standard-for-patient-experience-in-adult-nhs-services-to-complaints-the-complaint-process. Accessed 12 June 2018
10. Schembri, S.: Experiencing health care service quality: through patient' eyes. Aust. Health Rev. 39(1), 109–116 (2015)
11. Doyle, C., Lennox, L., Bell, D.: A systematic review of evidence on the links between patient experience and clinical safety and effectiveness. BMJ Open 3(1). http://bmjopen.bmj.com/content/3/1/e001570. Accessed 12 June 2018

12. Statista: Number of active users 2010–2017 (2017). https://www.statista.com/statistics/282087/number-of-monthly-active-twitter-users/. Accessed 30 Sept 2017
13. Morris, M.R., Teevan, J., Panovich, K.: What do people ask their social networks, and why?: a survey study of status message Q&A behavior. In: Proceedings of the SIGCHI Conference on Human Factors in Computing Systems, pp. 1739–1748. ACM (2010)
14. Jansen, B.J., Zhang, M.M., Sobel, K., Chowdury, A.: Twitter power: tweets as electronic word of mouth. J. Am. Soc. Inf. Sci. Technol. **60**, 2169–2188 (2009)
15. Ahmed, W., Bath, P., Sbaffi, L., Demartini, G.: Measuring the effect of public health campaigns on Twitter: the case of world autism awareness D. In: Chowdhury, G., McLeod, J., Gillet, V., Willett, P. (eds.) iConference2018. LNCS, vol. 10766. Springer, Heidelberg (2018)
16. Akay, A., Dragomir, A., Erlandsson, B.E.: Network-based modelling and intelligent data mining of social media for improving care. IEEE J. Biomed. Health Inform. **19**, 210–218 (2015)
17. Farrington, C., Burt, J., Boiko, O., Campbell, J., Roland, M.: Doctors' engagements with patient experience surveys in primary and secondary care: a qualitative study. Health Expect. **20**, 385–394 (2017). https://doi.org/10.1111/hex.12465
18. Galloro, V.: Status update. Hospitals are finding ways to use the social media revolution to raise money, engage patients and connect with their communities. Modern Healthcare **41**, 6–7 (2011)
19. Greaves, F., Ramirez-Cano, D., Millett, C., Darzi, A., Donaldson, L.: Harnessing the cloud of patient experience: using social media to detect poor quality healthcare. BMJ Qual. Saf. **22**, 251–255 (2013)
20. Greaves, F., et al.: Tweets about hospital quality: a mixed methods study. BMJ Qual. Saf. **23**, 838–846 (2014)
21. Hemsley, B., Palmer, S., Balandin, S.: Tweet reach: a research protocol for using Twitter to increase information exchange in people with communication disabilities. Dev. Neurorehabilitation **17**, 84–89 (2014)
22. Kuang, S., Davison, B.: Learning word embeddings with chi-square weights for healthcare tweet classification. Appl. Sci. **7**(8), 846 (2017)
23. Lee, J.L., Decamp, M., Dredze, M., Chisolm, M.S., Berger, Z.D.: What are health-related users tweeting? A qualitative content analysis of health-related users and their messages on Twitter. J. Med. Internet Res. **16**, 122–130 (2014)
24. Misopoulos, F., Mitic, M., Kapoulas, A., Karapiperis, C.: Uncovering customer service experiences with Twitter: the case of airline industry. Manag. Decis. **52**, 705–723 (2014)
25. Scanfeld, D., Scanfeld, V., Larson, E.: Dissemination of health information through social networks: Twitter and antibiotics. Am. J. Infection Control **38**(3), 182–188 (2010)
26. Atefeh, F., Khreich, W.: A survey of techniques for event detection in Twitter. Comput. Intell. **31**(1), 132–164 (2015)
27. Giachanou, A., Harvey, M., Crestani, F.: Topic-specific stylistic variations for opinion retrieval on Twitter. In: Ferro, N., et al. (eds.) ECIR 2016. LNCS, vol. 9626, pp. 466–478. Springer, Cham (2016). https://doi.org/10.1007/978-3-319-30671-1_34
28. Corley, C.D., Cook, D.J., Mikler, A.R., Singh, K.P.: Text and structural data mining of influenza mentions in web and social media. Int. J. Environ. Res. Public Health **7**, 596–615 (2010)
29. Huang, F.L., Zhang, S.C., Zhang, J.L., Yu, G.: Multimodal learning for topic sentiment analysis in microblogging. Neurocomputing **253**, 144–153 (2017)
30. Jain, V.K., Kumar, S., Fernandes, S.L.: Extraction of emotions from multilingual text using intelligent text processing and computational linguistics. J. Comput. Sci. **21**, 316–326 (2017)

31. Inkpen, D., Liu, J., Farzindar, A., Kazemi, F., Ghazi, D.: Location detection and disambiguation from Twitter messages. J. Intell. Inf. Syst. **49**(2), 237–253 (2017)
32. Jain, A., Jain, M.: Location based Twitter opinion mining using common-sense information. Global J. Enterprise Inf. Syst. **9**(2), 28 (2017)
33. Dodd, L., Chowdhury, G., Harvey, M., Walton, G.: Information seeking behaviour of aspiring undergraduates on social media: who are they interacting with? In: Choemprayong, S., Crestani, F., Cunningham, S.J. (eds.) ICADL 2017. LNCS, vol. 10647, pp. 245–255. Springer, Cham (2017). https://doi.org/10.1007/978-3-319-70232-2_21
34. Eichstaedt, J.C., et al.: Psychological language on Twitter predicts county-level hearth disease mortality. Psychol. Sci. **26**(2), 159–169 (2015)
35. Batrinca, B., Treleaven, P.: Social media analytics: a survey of techniques, tools and platforms. AI Soc. **30**(1), 89–116 (2014)
36. Honeycutt, C., Herring, S.: Beyond microblogging: conversation and collaboration via Twitter. In: Proceedings of the 42nd Hawai International Conference on System Sciences (HICSS-42), Los Alamitos, CA. IEEE Press (2009). http://ella.slis.indiana.edu/~herring/honeycutt.herring.2009.pdf. Accessed 12 June 2018
37. Clarke, V., Braun, V.: Thematic analysis. J. Positive Psychol. **12**(3), 297–298 (2016)
38. Glaser, B.G., Strauss, A.L.: The Discovery of Grounded Theory. Aldine (1967)

Rewarding, But Not for Everyone: Interaction Acts and Perceived Post Quality on Social Q&A Sites

Sei-Ching Joanna Sin$^{(\boxtimes)}$, Chei Sian Lee, and Xinran Chen

Wee Kim Wee School of Communication and Information,
Nanyang Technological University, Singapore, Singapore
{joanna.sin,leecs}@ntu.edu.sg, chen0872@e.ntu.edu.sg

Abstract. The study analyzed 1,007 Stack Overflow posts to investigate the relationships among interaction types, user reputation, the position of a post, and perceived post quality. Interaction Process Analysis (IPA), a well-established method for studying small group interaction, was used to code the posts. The Wilcoxon rank-sum tests and multiple regression results show significant main and interaction effects. The study found that performing certain interaction acts (e.g., IPA.d: Problem of Decision, such as agrees/disagrees) can be rewarding in terms of attaining higher perceived post quality. However, not all users can reap this reward. Differential rewards based on user reputation level was observed. The implications of these findings for research and practice were discussed.

Keywords: Social question and answer · Users' interactions
Interaction Process Analysis (IPA) · Perceived post quality

1 Introduction

Social question and answer sites (SQA) such as Stack Exchange, Quora, and Yahoo! Answers are prominent sources of user-generated content. Nevertheless, many questions on SQA fail to yield suitable answers [1, 2]. This has led to considerable interest in identifying the factors that contribute to high-quality SQA posts, including message-based factors such as readability and sentiment [3, 4], as well as user-based relational factors such as social ties between question askers and answerers [5, 6]. In contrast, users' interaction within a SQA thread is seldom studied [6, 7]. This research gap is notable, as interactions between users is a core characteristic of SQA [8].

The study posits it is valuable to investigate a SQA post (i.e., a question, a comment or an answer) as an integral part of a larger conversational episode. Specifically, this in-progress work explores an overarching research question on the conversational dynamics within a SQA thread: *who performs what type of conversational interaction, when, and with what results*. On *who*, this study focused on users' reputation level [9]. On *what*, we drew on Robert Bales' Interaction Process Analysis (IPA), a well-established method for studying small group interaction [10]. On *when*, the position of a post within a SQA thread was captured, based on the timestamp of the post. On *results*, we studied the perceived quality of a post, as measured by user-generated votes [11].

© Springer Nature Switzerland AG 2018
M. Dobreva et al. (Eds.): ICADL 2018, LNCS 11279, pp. 136–141, 2018.
https://doi.org/10.1007/978-3-030-04257-8_12

The study will contribute to research and practice. Regarding research, this study builds on IPA. It can contribute towards a new line of interaction- and process-oriented SQA and information behavior research. For practice, the study identifies the interaction acts (i.e., enactment of specific types of interaction behavior) most associated with high-quality posts. This can inform the design of SQA platforms and user training.

2   Research Framework and Hypotheses

The study draws on IPA, which conceptualizes an interaction episode as a problem-solving process involving a sequence of interaction acts distributed in time and between members (p. 59) [10]. IPA studies "interaction content or process content" (p. 34) [10]. This focus makes IPA a promising method for bringing insights to SQA research, as analyses of SQA messages have mainly been done on their topics, sentiment, and textual characteristics [3, 4, 12, 13] rather than on their interaction content.

IPA includes 12 interaction categories, which are nested into higher-order categories. The current study applied the 6-category set for capturing functional problems: **IPA.a:** Problem of Communication (e.g., gives/asks for orientation information); **IPA.b:** Problem of Evaluation (e.g., gives/asks for opinions); **IPA.c:** Problem of Control (gives/asks for suggestions and directions); **IPA.d:** Problem of Decision (e.g., agrees/disagrees); **IPA.e:** Problem of Tension Reduction (e.g., shows tensions/tension release), and **IPA.f:** Problem of Reintegration (e.g., shows solidarity/antagonism).

This study is interested in the interplay among the *who* (user reputation), *what* (IPA type), *when* (position of the post), and *results* (perceived post quality). As a beginning exploration, we posed the following hypotheses:

H1:   IPA interaction type varies with the position of the post in the thread.
H2:   IPA interaction type varies with the reputation of the user.
H3:   The score of a post varies with the IPA interaction type, position of the post, and reputation of the user.
H4:   The effect of interaction type on post score differs by the reputation of the user.

3   Methods

The study sampled 1,007 posts (150 questions and their corresponding comments [$n = 654$] and answers [$n = 203$]) from Stack Overflow (SO), a prominent SQA community for programming questions. This study differs from most SQA studies in that even though IPA has been applied in studying platforms such as blogs [14] and microblogs [15], very few studies used IPA to code and analyze SQA posts [16]. Two coders coded the IPA types. Intercoder agreements were over 75%, indicating acceptable intercoder reliability. Wilcoxon rank-sum tests were used to analyze H1 and H2. A multiple regression test was used for H3 and H4. These analyses were done with R.

4   Results

The Wilcoxon tests found all six IPA types to be significantly associated with post location (Fig. 1). In summary, H1 was supported. Specifically, posts with IPA.a, IPA.b, or IPA.c tended to appear earlier in the thread than posts without those IPA types. In contrasts, posts with IPA.d, IPA.e, or IPA.f tended to appear later. Regarding H2, it was partially supported. Five out of six IPA types were significantly associated with user reputation (Fig. 2). IPA.c was the sole non-significant type ($p = .68$). Among the significant types, IPA.b (gives/asks for opinions) was the only type more likely to be posted by users with higher reputation levels. Conversely, posts with IPA.a, IPA.d, IPA.e, and IPA.f were more likely to be posted by users with lower reputation levels.

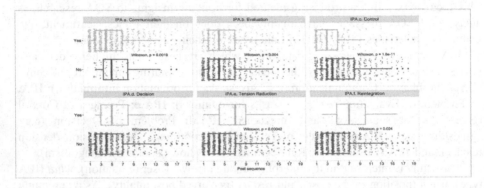

Fig. 1. IPA type and position of the post

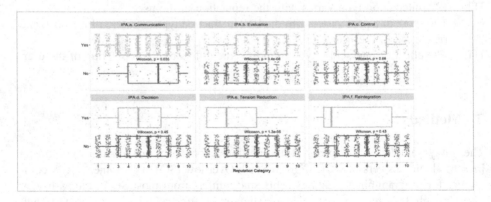

Fig. 2. IPA type and user reputation

H3 (main effects of IPA type, post position, and user reputation) and H4 (interaction effects between IPA types and user reputation) were analyzed in one multiple regression. The model accounted for the influence of SQA post type (i.e., question, answer, or comment) on post score. The overall model was significant, $F(67, 924) = 3.35$, $p < .001$, with an adjusted R^2 of 13.7%. Figure 3 shows the estimates (beta) and the significance of the variables. On main effects (H3), posts appearing later in the thread tended to have a lower score ($p = .005$). IPA.c (Problem of Control) was associated with a lower score ($p = .003$). User reputation was not significant. The main effects of the latter two were modified by two significant interaction effects discussed below.

Results on H4 (Fig. 3) showed a significant interaction between IPA.c and user reputation. Among users with the lowest reputation level, posts with IPA.c tended to receive a lower score than posts without IPA.c. In contrast, among users in five higher reputation levels, posts with IPA.c yielded a higher score. Another significant interaction effect was found between IPA.d (Problem of Decision) and user reputation. The difference was between users with the lowest and the highest reputation levels ($p = .041$). Interestingly, it is among users with the lowest reputation level where posts with IPA.d have a higher score than posts without it. Among users with the highest reputation level, posts with IPA.d ended up getting lower scores than posts without it.

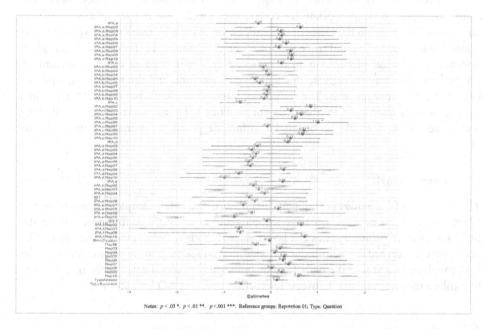

Notes: $p < .05$ *. $p < .01$ **. $p < .001$ ***. Reference groups: Reputation 01; Type. Question

Fig. 3. Multiple regression: estimates

5 Discussion

5.1 Implications

Leveraging IPA, this study found that interaction acts on SQA differed across time (H1) and user reputation levels (H2). What's more, these variables showed main (H3) and interaction effects (H4) on the perceived post quality. The significant relationships have research implications. IPA is seldom used in studying SQA [16]. Research on the interactions between IPA types and user characteristics is rarer still. The current findings provide initial evidence that IPA can be a useful framework for SQA research.

H3 and H4 not only found a significant task-oriented interaction act (IPA.c, the "Task Area" of IPA). Also found was a significant IPA.d, which belongs to IPA's "Social-Emotional Areas" [10]. Although social-emotional acts were attempted less frequently than task-oriented acts in this sample (Fig. 1), one of the former (IPA.d) still emerged significant. The implication is that affective aspects of SQA interactions still warrant attention, even when studying SQA communities that focus on factual topics.

The interaction effects between IPA types and user reputation (H4) are worth noting. The results suggest that performing certain interaction acts can be rewarding (i.e., gaining a higher post score). However, not all users can reap this reward. For example, performing a control-related act (IPA.c, ask/give suggestions) seemed to hurt the post score of users with the lowest reputation level disproportionately. Whereas, performing a decision-related act (IPA.d, agrees/disagrees) appeared to affect users with the highest reputation level more adversely. A tentative reason behind such differential rewards may be social role expectations. It is possible that SQA users view some interaction acts appropriate for certain user groups but not for others. This may affect how they vote on the posts of other users. For example, users may expect highly-reputed members to spend time on providing instrumental functions (e.g., gives information) instead of performing social-emotional acts such as offering agreement. Further research may investigate this tentative proposition and the mechanisms behind potential differential rewards. The significant interaction effects between IPA types and user reputation also have implications for broader SQA research: When conducting feature selection, it would be beneficial to include potential interaction effects in the model.

5.2 Future Work

The current study provides preliminary findings using a small sample of posts from SO. More research can be done on large samples and other SQA communities. If similar results are found, further studies can be conducted to identify in detail: What interaction act is best performed by whom during what time/stage of a SQA interaction episode. Communication and social psychology theories such as social role theory may be used to explore the mechanisms between interaction acts and SQA outcomes.

6 Conclusion

Using IPA, this study investigated the relationships among the *who* (user reputation), *what* (IPA type), *when* (position of the post), and *results* (perceived post quality) of SQA posts. IPA types were found to vary with all three variables. Notably, there were significant interaction effects between IPA types and user reputation, suggesting that interesting mechanisms are at play. Further SQA research using IPA is encouraged. Findings from this stream of research may inform the development of platform features to encourage beneficial interaction acts. They can also be used to offer personalized recommendations to users, highlighting to them what types of interaction acts are most strategical and advantageous to a successful and satisfactory SQA experience.

Acknowledgement. This work was supported by the MOE Academic Research Fund (RG58/14).

References

1. Liu, Z., Jansen, B.J.: Identifying and predicting the desire to help in social question and answering. Inf. Process. Manag. **53**, 490–504 (2017)
2. Chua, A.Y.K., Banerjee, S.: Answers or no answers: studying question answerability in Stack Overflow. J. Inf. Sci. **41**, 720–731 (2015)
3. Fu, H., Wu, S., Oh, S.: Evaluating answer quality across knowledge domains: using textual and non-textual features in social Q&A. In: Proceedings of the Association for Information Science and Technology, vol. 52, pp. 1–5 (2015)
4. Kucuktunc, O., Cambazoglu, B.B., Weber, I., Ferhatosmanoglu, H.: A large-scale sentiment analysis for Yahoo! answers. In: Proceedings of the Fifth ACM International Conference on Web Search and Data Mining, pp. 633–642. ACM, Seattle (2012)
5. Rechavi, A., Rafaeli, S.: Not all is gold that glitters: response time & satisfaction rates in Yahoo! Answers. In: 2011 IEEE Third International Conference on Privacy, Security, Risk and Trust and 2011 IEEE Third International Conference on Social Computing, pp. 904–909. IEEE Computer Society, Washington, DC (2011)
6. Liu, Z., Jansen, B.J.: Question and answering made interactive: an exploration of interactions in social Q&A. In: Proceedings of the 2013 International Conference on Social Intelligence and Technology, pp. 1–10. IEEE Computer Society, Washington, DC (2013)
7. Sin, S.-C.J., Lee, C.S., Theng, Y.-L.: Social Q&A question-and-comments interactions and outcomes: a social sequence analysis. In: Morishima, A., Rauber, A., Liew, C.L. (eds.) ICADL 2016. LNCS, vol. 10075, pp. 325–338. Springer, Cham (2016). https://doi.org/10.1007/978-3-319-49304-6_37
8. Shah, C., Oh, S., Oh, J.S.: Research agenda for social Q&A. Libr. Inf. Sci. Res. **31**, 205–209 (2009)
9. Stack Overflow: Help Center: What is reputation? How do I Earn (and Lose) it? (2018). https://stackoverflow.com/help/whats-reputation
10. Bales, R.F.: Interaction Process Analysis: A Method for the Study of Small Groups. Addison-Wesley Press, Cambridge (1951)
11. Stack Overflow: Help Center: Why is Voting Important? (2018). https://stackoverflow.com/help/why-vote
12. Shah, C., Pomerantz, J.: Evaluating and predicting answer quality in community QA. In: Proceedings of the 33rd international ACM SIGIR Conference on Research and Development in Information Retrieval, pp. 411–418. ACM, Geneva (2010)
13. Harper, F.M., Raban, D., Rafaeli, S., Konstan, J.A.: Predictors of answer quality in online Q&A sites. In: Proceedings of the SIGCHI Conference on Human Factors in Computing Systems, pp. 865–874. ACM, Florence (2008)
14. Savolainen, R.: Asking and sharing information in the blogosphere: the case of slimming blogs. Libr. Inf. Sci. Res. **33**, 73–79 (2011)
15. Lin, J.-S., Peña, J.: Are you following me? A content analysis of TV networks' brand communication on Twitter. J. Interact. Adv. **12**, 17–29 (2011)
16. Yin, Z., Peilin, W.: Interactions and user-perceived helpfulness in diet information social questions & answers. Health Inf. Libr. J. **33**, 295–307 (2016)

Towards Recommending Interesting
Content in News Archives

I-Chen Hung[1], Michael Färber[1,2], and Adam Jatowt[1(✉)]

[1] Department of Social Informatics, Kyoto University, Kyoto, Japan
ichen@db.soc.i.kyoto-u.ac.jp, michael.faerber@cs.uni-freiburg.de,
adam@dl.kuis.kyoto-u.ac.jp
[2] University of Freiburg, Freiburg im Breisgau, Germany

Abstract. Recently, many archival news article collections have been made available to wide public. However, such collections are typically large, making it difficult for users to find content they would be interested in. Furthermore, archived news articles tend to be perceived by ordinary users as having rather weak attractiveness and being obsolete or uninteresting. In this paper, we propose the task of finding interesting content from news archives and introduce two simple methods for it. Our approach recommends interesting content by comparing the information written in the past with the one from the present.

Keywords: News archive · Interestingness · Recommender systems

1 Introduction

News article archives offer rich account of events in the past and are important for humanities and social studies constituting one foundation of historical understanding [7]. Besides professionals, news archives can offer valuable content regarding our heritage also for ordinary users. However, non-professional users typically face the following issues when accessing archives. As archives are often of large size, users may quickly get disappointed especially when they do not have any precise search intent. Unstructured content and the typically unknown context of the past can easily cause confusion and boringness. Finally, the content may seem obsolete and detached from the present.

We believe that special kind of information recommendation for large size news archives could increase their utility and attractiveness for average users. The recommended information should be related to present issues yet not be obvious or inferable, and should preferably contain an element of surprise. Let us consider "ice cutter" as an example. Ordinary users might nowadays expect that *ice cutter* was a machine that cut ice into small pieces. In the past, however, especially before the widespread use of refrigerators, *ice cutter* was a person who cut ice from frozen lakes and rivers. Such content has potential to surprise non-professional readers and evoke their interest, as the contained information is

© Springer Nature Switzerland AG 2018
M. Dobreva et al. (Eds.): ICADL 2018, LNCS 11279, pp. 142–146, 2018.
https://doi.org/10.1007/978-3-030-04257-8_13

against the presumed expectation. Note that such information is not easy to be found using traditional search engines.

We propose in this paper a novel research problem which, to the best of our knowledge, has not been pursued so far: *interesting content recommendation from long-term news archives*. One of the main difficulty in finding interesting pattern or data is how to define *interestingness* properly. Geng *et al.* [4] treated interestingness as a broad concept that possibly contains features like diversity, surprisingness and so on. Silberschatz *et al.* [8] suggested that interesting information should be unexpected and actionable. Yannakakis *et al.* [10] proposed a surprise-oriented search algorithm. Unexpectedness was also considered crucial in Padmanabhan *et al.* [6] and Adamopoulos *et al.* [1]. Although there have been a few studies about how to identify content about the unexpected relationships, they focused on non-archival data such as Wikipedia or on current news [5]. Tsukuda *et al.* [9] evaluated the unexpectedness of related terms extracted from Wikipedia pages on the basis of relationships of the coordinate terms. Boldi *et al.* [2] focused on finding unexpected links in hyper-linked documents. None of the prior works however focused on archival content which has particular characteristics due to time passage.

In this paper, we propose four criteria of content interestingness in news archives: (1) *Relevance*: interesting past content should be relevant to user query and (2) *Past importance*: it should be important (not minor) in the past. (3) *Unfamiliarity*: interesting past content should be unknown to a user and (4) *Unexpectedness*: it should be unexpected or surprising to her.

In our approach we assume that users can input general queries representing their interests, and we output ranked lists of sentences considering some of the proposed criteria of archival content interestingness.

2   Approach

In our approach we divide the underlying news archive into two parts: one denoted as D_{past} and representing past documents (i.e., documents published at some period T_{past} in the past), and the other one, denoted as D_{now}, that contains documents published recently (i.e., in a recent period T_{now}) to represent information of present. Sentences from D_{past} that are relevant to user query will be ranked based on their comparison with relevant sentences in D_{now}. We propose two methods as follows:

Centroid Method. We hypothesized that interesting content should be unfamiliar and unexpected to current users. Centroid method will then rank sentences from D_{past} by their dissimilarity to the centroid vector being the average TF-IDF vector of all sentences in D_{now}. Centroid method is expected to extract relevant sentences that have less chance to be known by current users.

MRRW. The *two-layer mutually reinforced random walk* (MRRW) [3] is algorithm for computing the converged scores of nodes in a two-layer graph. We adapt the algorithm considering two time periods: T_{past} and T_{now} such that nodes in each layer represent relevant sentences in the corresponding document set. For both layers T_{now} and T_{past}, we connect nodes belonging to the same layer by calculating their similarity (cosine similarity of sentences represented by the nodes). On the other hand, a node pair consisting of nodes from different layers is connected by an edge whose weight represents the nodes' dissimilarity. MRRW process will return sentences from D_{past} that are similar to other sentences in T_{past}, yet, at the same time, are dissimilar to sentences in D_{now}. This approach is expected to reflect the *past importance* and *unfamiliarity* apart from *relevance*, since a sentence dissimilar to many sentences in T_{now} might represent novel and unfamiliar content for users.

3   Experiments

3.1   Datasets and Experimental Setup

We use the New York Times News Archive[1] which includes news articles published from 1987 to 2007. In our experiments, D_{past} contains articles published from 1987 to 1989 and D_{now} covers ones published from 2005 to 2007. Naturally, the latter part is not exactly representing the "present", and is a compromise resulting from the lack of sufficiently long datasets which would contain also recent documents. We assume that all sentences containing a query are relevant to it. We use TF-IDF and Word2vec embeddings trained on entire archive for sentence representation, and conduct experiments using 20 different queries covering equally topics from economy, politics, sports, technology and the names of geographic locations. We test **Centroid**, **TF-IDF+MRRW** and **Word2vec+MRRW** methods as well as a baseline approach based on random sentence selection **Random**.

We let 15 evaluators (6 males and 9 females in their 20s and 30s with at least bachelor level education) judge the quality of sentences. In particular, they were asked to assess the results based on *Understandability* and *Interestingness*. Evaluators needed to label the sentences by either *yes* or *no*. Before the evaluation, we extracted and pooled the top 15 returned results for each query by each tested method. Each sentence was evaluated by three evaluators, and only sentences understood by evaluators (as given by a binary *understandability* score) were considered valid. The final decision if a sentence is interesting was made based on the majority vote, i.e., if at least two evaluators gave it a score of 1.

3.2   Experimental Results

Table 1 shows the results according to Mean Reciprocal Rank (MRR) and Mean Average Precision (MAP) for 5 query categories. We could see that **Centroid** method performs quite well but the performance of methods vary between query categories. This suggests that different query categories have different best performing methods and thus one should be careful when choosing suitable recommendation approach for a given query.

---

[1]   http://www.nytimes.com/ref/membercenter/nytarchive.html.

Table 1. Performance of methods for each query category.

	MRR					MAP				
	Economy	Places	Politics	Sports	Tech	Economy	Places	Politics	Sports	Tech
Random	70.83	48.96	23.75	44.20	**70.83**	52.90	43.24	24.17	36.67	**72.68**
Centroid	**75.00**	**87.50**	**33.33**	53.57	66.67	**65.71**	**71.92**	**29.83**	53.29	59.80
TF-IDF+MRRW	70.83	**87.50**	23.61	**70.83**	10.42	51.12	69.88	28.19	**62.40**	9.51
Word2vec+MRRW	31.25	81.25	31.25	**70.83**	27.08	38.44	66.09	28.50	46.19	31.41

Random baseline has notably high precision only on *Technology* queries. Despite of weaker performance of **Word2vec+MRRW**, it still achieved high scores on *Sports* and *Places*. One possible improvement could be inputting more data for model training.

4   Conclusions and Future Work

In this paper, we propose a novel research problem of recommending interesting contents from news article archives and we describe our initial approach. Our key idea is based on data comparison across time. In future, we plan to improve the quality of results to avoid outputting trivial content or one poorly understandable due to the lack of necessary context. We will also consider other interestingness criteria that we did not explicitly include this time in our approach and time period suggestion from which interesting results can be derived.

Acknowledgments. This research was supported by MEXT grants (#17H01828; #18K19841; #18II03243)

References

1. Adamopoulos, P., Tuzhilin, A.: On unexpectedness in recommender systems: or how to better expect the unexpected. ACM TIST **5**(4), 54 (2015)
2. Boldi, P., Monti, C.: Llamafur: learning latent category matrix to find unexpected relations in Wikipedia. In: Proceedings of WebScience, pp. 218–222. ACM (2016)
3. Chen, Y.N., Metze, F.: Two-layer mutually reinforced random walk for improved multi-party meeting summarization. In: 2012 IEEE Spoken Language Technology Workshop (SLT), pp. 461–466. IEEE (2012)
4. Geng, L., Hamilton, H.J.: Interestingness measures for data mining: a survey. ACM Comput. Surv. (CSUR) **38**(3), 9 (2006)
5. Li, X., Croft, W.B.: Improving novelty detection for general topics using sentence level information patterns. In: Proceedings of the CIKM, pp. 238–247. ACM (2006)
6. Padmanabhan, B., Tuzhilin, A.: Unexpectedness as a measure of interestingness in knowledge discovery. Decis. Support Syst. **27**(3), 303–318 (1999)
7. Schwartz, J.M., Cook, T.: Archives, records, and power: the making of modern memory. Arch. Sci. **2**(1–2), 1–19 (2002)
8. Silberschatz, A., Tuzhilin, A.: What makes patterns interesting in knowledge discovery systems. IEEE TKDE **8**(6), 970–974 (1996)

9. Tsukuda, K., Ohshima, H., Yamamoto, M., Iwasaki, H., Tanaka, K.: Discovering unexpected information on the basis of popularity/unpopularity analysis of coordinate objects and their relationships. In: Proceedings of SAC, pp. 878–885. ACM (2013)
10. Yannakakis, G.N., Liapis, A.: Searching for surprise. In: Proceedings of the International Conference on Computational Creativity (2016)

A Twitter-Based Culture Visualization System by Analyzing Multilingual Geo-Tagged Tweets

Yuanyuan Wang[1]([⊠]) [iD], Panote Siriaraya[2], Yusuke Nakaoka[2], Haruka Sakata[2], Yukiko Kawai[2,3] [iD], and Toyokazu Akiyama[2]

[1] Yamaguchi University, 2-16-1 Tokiwadai, Ube, Yamaguchi 755-8611, Japan
y.wang@yamaguchi-u.ac.jp
[2] Kyoto Sangyo University, Motoyama, Kamigamo, Kita-ku, Kyoto 603-8555, Japan
spanote@gmail.com, {g1444936,g1544647,kawai,akiyama}@cc.kyoto-su.ac.jp
[3] Osaka University, 5-1 Mihogaoka, Ibaraki, Osaka 567-0047, Japan

Abstract. This paper presents a novel multilingual analysis of Twitter for exploring cultural differences. For this, we developed a Twitter-based visualization system for food culture by analyzing the differences between locations and languages in geo-tagged tweets from European countries. A key feature of the proposed system is the ability to infer similarities in food preferences between different language users in different cities even when such preferences are not explicitly shown in existing tweets.

Keywords: Multilingual Twitter analysis · Culture visualization

1 Introduction

In recent years, digital libraries have added Twitter to their lists of social media tools as a way to engage with users. An increasing number of studies have shown how data from such services could be used to better understand and visualize user behavior [1]. However, few studies in this domain have investigated how information related to cultural aspects such as similarities in language usage could be used to understand the interests and preferences of the general population. Overall, multilingual studies among Twitter users can be considered as a niche research topic [2,3].

As such, in this study, we propose a novel approach to identify and visualize the food preferences of different language users. This is done by using the linguistic properties of information in Twitter (native languages of users or languages of messages) to infer their food preferences. Our system was also designed to visualize food preferences in locations where there are few geo-tagged tweets available for a specific language user. To do so, the similarity between different language users in their food genre preferences was calculated using correlation metrics and this value was used to infer user preference.

M. Dobreva et al. (Eds.): ICADL 2018, LNCS 11279, pp. 147–150, 2018.
https://doi.org/10.1007/978-3-030-04257-8_14

2   Determining Food Venue Preferences

In order to determine the food venue preference for different language users, we calculate the venue preference evaluation score based on geo-tagged tweets. If there are few users of a language at a specific location, we consider the similarities of user food preference between that specific language user and other different language users based on Pearson's correlation to calculate the venue preference evaluation score if there are few users of a language in a specific location. For example, in an area where there are few French tweets, the evaluation score for a specific food genre could be calculated based on the similarity in food preferences between French Speakers and other language users (Spanish, Dutch, etc.). If there arc already a sufficient number of tweets in a given language, the venues are rated as follows:

$$S_{\{i,p\}} = \frac{|T \in p : l_y \in T : i \in I_t|}{|T \in p : l_y \in T|} \cdot \log \frac{|L|}{|l \in L_i|}$$

Where $|T \in p : l_y \in T : i \in I_t|$ refers to the number of tweets sent from the location p using the language l_y related to venue i, $|T \in p : l_y \in T|$ refers to the total number of venues of tweets sent from p using l_y, $|L|$ refers to the total number of languages L and $|l \in L_i|$ refers to the number of languages in i.

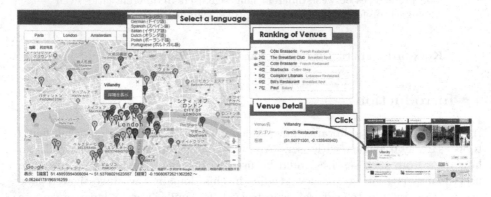

Fig. 1. The interface of our food culture visualization system.

3   Implementation and Evaluation

Geo-tagged tweets were collected for a 13 month period, during 2016/4/1 to 2017/4/30 from seven cites in Europe (London, Rome, Paris, Barcelona, Berlin, Lisbon, and Amsterdam) in seven languages (Italian, French, Spanish, German, Polish, Portuguese, and Dutch). Overall, approximately 26 million tweets and 342,992 different venues were identified. Information about the venues themselves, such as what food categories are offered, was obtained using Foursquare

API[1]. A total of 155 different food genres were detected from the tweets. When calculating similarities in food preference, the average Pearson correlation coefficient value between the different language users in their genre preferences was 0.58. On average, German language users had the highest correlation (0.65) with other language users in terms of genre preference, while Portuguese language users had the lowest overall correlation (0.46).

An interactive map-based web application was developed using PHP, JavaScript, and HTML to visualize the food preferences calculated using our approach (Fig. 1). Users could select between seven different language users and view their food venue preferences in different cities. Markers in different colors (based on different genres) are shown on the map representing the recommended food venues, and the user can check the details of the venue by clicking on a marker. An example of the top 10 food venues recommended by our system in the city of Barcelona is shown in Table 1. We confirmed that our proposed method has the ability to extract appropriate food venues by genre preferences, such as German language users, Portuguese language users, and Dutch language users in Barcelona (underlined in Table 1).

Table 1. An example of the top 10 food venues recommended in Barcelona for 3 different language users

City	Language	Top 10 food venues
Barcelona	Spanish	McDonald's in Barcelona, Pans & Company,
		Viena La Tagliatella, La Paradeta Passeig, de Grocia,
		Bracaff, Granier, Farggi, La Muscleria, Foster's Hollywood
	Italian	La Tagliatella, McDonald's in Barcelona, Granier,
		il Cafe di Roma, il Cafe di Francesco, Vivari, 100 Montaditos,
		La Paradeta Passeig de Grocia, il Cafe di Roma, Kroco Ou
	French	100 Montaditos, McDonald's in Barcelona,
		La Paradeta Passeig de Grocia, Marco Aldany, Central Cafe,
		Hard Rock Cafe Barcelona, Gran Cafe, Hidden Cafe Barcelona,
		El Tastet de la Mar, El Merendero de la Mari
	German	Pans & Company, <u>Granier</u>, <u>El Fornet d'en Rossend</u>,
		<u>100 Montaditos</u>, El Fornet, Costa Coffee, 365.cafe,
		Dehesa Santa Marta, <u>El Fornet d'en Rossend</u>,
		Restaurante Barceloneta
	Portugese	Pans & Company, Subway, Jamaica Coffee Shop, SandwiChez,
		Lizarran, <u>Farggi</u>, Taller de Tapas, <u>Camp Nou Dinner Terrasse</u>,
		Tapas24 Camp Nou, Audrey Brunch & Coffee
	Dutch	<u>Granier</u>, <u>El Fornet d'en Rossend</u>, <u>Tapas24 Camp Nou</u>,
		<u>Camp Nou Dinner Terrasse</u>,

4 Conclusion

In this work, we have proposed a Twitter-based visualization system for food culture which analyzes the differences between locations and languages in geo-

---

[1] https://developer.foursquare.com/.

tagged tweets from European countries. In situations of sparse data, the similarity between different language users in terms of their food genre preference were calculated and used to help recommend the venues.

Future work will evaluate the correlation among languages, genre preferences, and regions, and expand our approach to other types of venues apart from landmarks (e.g., library, park, etc.) in other areas (e.g., Asia and America).

Acknowledgment. The work in this paper is partially supported by SCOPE of the Ministry of Internal Affairs and Communications of Japan (#171507010), JSPS KAKENHI Grant Numbers 16H01722, 17K12686 and 17H01822.

References

1. Hu, T., Song, R., Wang, Y., Xie, X., Luo, J.: Mining shopping patterns for divergent urban regions by incorporating mobility data. In: Proceedings of CIKM 2016, pp. 569–578 (2016)
2. Pla, F., Hurtado, L.F.: Language identification of multilingual posts from Twitter: a case study. Knowl. Inf. Syst. 1–25 (2016)
3. Raghavi, K.C., Chinnakotla, M.K., Shrivastava, M.: "answer ka type kya he?": learning to classify questions in code-mixed language. In: Proceedings of WWW 2015 Companion, pp. 853–858 (2015)

Heritage and Localization

Development of Content-Based Metadata Scheme of Classical Poetry in Thai National Historical Corpus

Songphan Choemprayong[1,2,3]($\boxtimes$) (iD), Pittayawat Pittayaporn[4],
Vipas Pothipath[5], Thaneerat Jatuthasri[5], and Jinawat Kaenmuang[4]

[1] The Arc of Memory Research Unit, Chulalongkorn University, Bangkok 10330,
Thailand
songphan.c@chula.ac.th
[2] Behavioral Research and Informatics in Social Science Research Unit,
Chulalongkorn University, Bangkok 10330, Thailand
[3] Department of Library Science, Faculty of Arts, Chulalongkorn University,
Bangkok 10330, Thailand
[4] Department of Linguistics, Faculty of Arts, Chulalongkorn University,
Bangkok 10330, Thailand
[5] Department of Thai, Faculty of Arts, Chulalongkorn University,
Bangkok 10330, Thailand

Abstract. This paper addresses a conceptual framework and an application of a content-based metadata scheme of classical poetry currently deployed in the Thai National Historical Corpus (TNHC). The corpus aims to collect texts representing the Thai language from different historical periods. Applying a metadata modeling approach, the variation of classical Thai poetry is analyzed in terms of components in every verse form. The compositions of *wak*, *baat*, stanza, paragraph, and chapter are identified as main elements for the conceptual framework. For theatrical works, essential elements including <sound> and <stage> tags were also implemented. TNHC selectively applied certain standard TEI encoding elements, in XML format, to describe the content structure of the poetry. This is an early attempt to develop a metadata scheme for classical Thai poetry. There are still a number of opportunities to improve the discovery and interoperability of the collection as well as to enhance the data entry process, data management, and retrieval performance of the corpus.

Keywords: Historical corpus · Metadata scheme · Classical poetry
Thai language · TEI

1 Introduction

Historical documents carry information on how languages were used and evolved through time. Historical linguists explore dead languages, language variations, and the evolution of language through the development and analysis of historical

M. Dobreva et al. (Eds.): ICADL 2018, LNCS 11279, pp. 153–165, 2018.
https://doi.org/10.1007/978-3-030-04257-8_15

corpora. While there are a number of historical corpora in other languages, historical corpora of the Thai language are rare and scattered. The Thai National Historical Corpus (TNHC) is an initiative aiming to build a public comprehensive collection of historical texts since the formation of the state in the *Sukhothai* period to the early *Rattanakosin* period.

There were numerous challenges faced in developing a historical corpus for the Thai language, in particular due to the lack of robust tools to handle classical Thai language such as an optical character recognition system, a tokenization processor, and an automatic text classifier. Another challenge in this project is the lack of a metadata scheme to organize a wide variety of textual structures.

One of the most contesting collections in TNHC is the poetry collection. Classical Thai poetry has unique prosodic forms, a.k.a. the *chanthalak*, ruling the specific structure of meter and rhymes. There are five classical verse forms in Thai poetry: *khlong*, *chan*, *kap*, *klon*, and *rai*. Enduring for almost seven centuries, the patterns of these forms have been highly conserved until today through language education, documentation, and use. Preserving classical Thai poetry would enhance the stewardship of this authentic public knowledge.

Constructing a database to capture this sophisticated collection requires a specific metadata scheme, particularly to describe the content inside these works. While text encoding standards have been used extensively in numerous language corpora, the application of these standards is still limited to modern Thai corpora. [2] Additionally, even though there are efforts in developing metadata schemes for classical poetry in other languages, those present metadata schemes fail to accommodate unique structures and linguistic features of classical Thai poetry. It is still a great endeavor to discover common elements of poetry in different languages. A corpus collecting would definitely serve as a tool for discovery as well.

This paper reports the efforts to develop a content-level metadata scheme for a classical poetry collection in TNHC. The primary goal of this project is to establish an infrastructure to facilitate data entry, management, and analysis of the corpus. It is also expected that this paper would contribute to the interoperability of currently developed and future Thai corpora.

2   Related Works

This review section describes the current state of efforts in developing the Thai National Historical Corpus as well as initiatives related to metadata in language corpora.

2.1   Thai Corpora

Language corpora are collections of carefully selected natural language texts in electronic formats. As a representation of a language, linguists have been using corpora to study different aspects of language such as grammars, semantics, psycholinguistics, historical linguistics, sociolinguistics, dialectology, translations, and language teaching. [6] Outside the field of linguistics, a language corpus may also contribute to improve indexing and retrieving performance of a digital library. [8] It can also be used to create ontologies. [12] Computer scientists also use language corpora to develop natural language processes which are the foundation for numerous artificial intelligence (AI) applications.

There are a number of initiatives to construct Thai language corpora. [2, 12] These corpora represent different groups of the Thai language. While most of the corpora have been created privately to serve specific purposes, there are some recognized Thai corpora publicly available serving general purposes. The earlier attempt to create a public Thai corpus is ORCHID, a Thai part-of-speech (POS) tagged corpus. [17] Aiming to develop a more robust automatic POS tagger, ORCHID only represents texts in research papers in conference proceedings.

Aroonmanakun [2] later developed the Thai National Corpus (TNC) aiming to collect texts to represent modern Thai in general practice. The samples selectively include texts from a wide variety of domains and sources such as published books, journal articles, newspaper articles, brochures, and unpublished works. The samples in TNC represent standard modern Thai language. The most recent initiative to develop a public corpus is the Thai Monitor Corpus (TMC)[3] which extracted texts from publicly available social media sources. TMC represents the Thai language in a less formal style, aiming to continuously collect data on a large scale, namely about five hundred million words.

2.2   Thai National Historical Corpus

As an alternative to existing Thai corpora, the primary objective of TNHC is to represent historical Thai language from different genres and historical eras. The inclusion criteria of the data sources are texts in classical manuscripts since the *Sukhothai* period to the early *Rattanakosin* period. A group of experts in Thai literature and language carefully select a number of books, manuscripts, letters, hand-written documents, and inscriptions. [15] The selection of texts included in TNHC adapted the British National Corpus [14] and TNC's [2] criteria which concern the distribution of written texts from different domains, medium, and time.

Since most works are in the public domain, the electronic copies of selected sources are acquired from other public digital libraries or repositories. If an electronic copy could not be found elsewhere, the printed or physical copy is digitized. Since the optical character recognition systems (OCR) currently available are limited to recognizing modern characters, the digitization process heavily relies on manual input (i.e., typing). There is also the problem of the lack of supported fonts for ancient character arrangements in digitizing historical texts. Therefore, certain adjustments were applied to preserve the character arrangements closest to the original copy considering that the adjustments would not substantially weaken the retrieval performance.

In the data preparation process, TNHC adapts certain TEI header elements to describe a data source and its contextual information (for example, author's gender, domain, subject matter, and text classification). Selected elements are adjusted and utilized in accordance with the specific characteristics of the historical collection in TNHC. The document is proceeded to content-level metadata assignment which is the focus of this paper.

The last process is the text-level metadata assignment which adopts selected approaches in natural language processing, including tokenization, and pronunciation and current spelling tagging. Since the Thai language does not use punctuation to separate words, TNHC applies a two-step hybrid process to tokenize the digitized texts. First, Thai Tokenization (TLTK) [1], a tokenization system initially developed to process modern Thai language in TNC, is applied for the initial word segmentation. Since the desired tokenized unit for TNHC is a morpheme which is more appropriate for Thai historical texts, a team of linguistics scholars review and edit the results from TLTK to obtain appropriate morpheme-based word segmentation.

Since countless number of words in this historical corpus are no longer in use, providing pronunciation marks and mapping current spelling are useful for corpus users to be able to retrieve the data efficiently. Pronunciation and current spelling tagging is also administered manually by linguistics scholars. Figure 1 shows a summary of the data preparation process of TNHC.

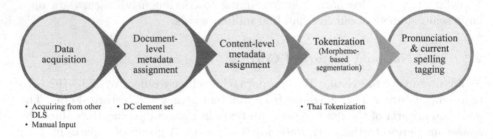

Fig. 1. Data preparation process of TNHC.

At the time of this writing, texts from twenty-two documents have been entered into TNHC, yielding approximately almost 200,000 words. It is expected that by the end of the initial project, five million words would be collected. The public interface, currently in a beta version, allows users to list and visualize the frequency of words, as well as collocate adjacent words, as shown in Fig. 2. Users are also able to search words using original spelling, current spelling, and pronunciation. Search filters are also available for certain metadata elements regarding the characteristics of data sources.

2.3   Metadata in a Language Corpus

Cultural heritage institutions have been continuously developing metadata to describe various kinds of objects in their custody. Business in almost every industry and sector also requires metadata to store numerous kinds of information

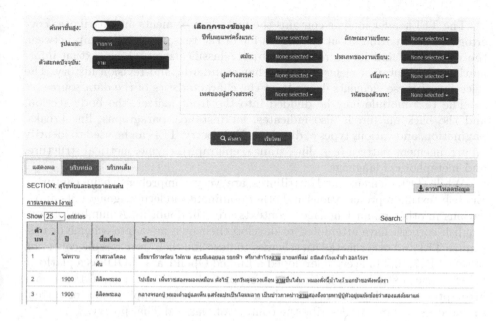

Fig. 2. TNHC search interface for public users.

valuable to them. Metadata is indeed ubiquitous in our everyday life, concerning how we describe an object or construct (i.e., an entity) in a structural manner. Developing a structured database, such as a language corpus, requires careful planning and implementation of metadata in order to store and retrieve data effectively and efficiently.

Different types of metadata serve different purposes and functions. [16] For example, descriptive metadata (e.g., title, author, and publication date) assists users in accessing and discovering resources. Administrative metadata (e.g., file type, checksum, copyright status) ensures interoperability as well as enhances stewardship of the resource. Markup languages identify content structure of the resource described such as paragraph, pagination, heading, section, list, and name. For general purposes, such description in markup languages would help with navigating the content. Additionally, this type of metadata could help linguists and language enthusiasts explore and discover different aspects of a language.

Metadata plays substantial roles in identifying and classifying these representations in a language corpus. The most prominent metadata standard in describing textual data is Text Encoding Initiative (TEI) which heavily relies on XML structure. The current version of TEI standard is TEI P5 version 3.4.0 [18]. TEI consists of modules and elements in describing an exhaustive list of properties of text. The default modules include the TEI header and the text itself.

The TEI header module contains the metadata elements and attributes covering the information about the digital file of the text, the relationship between the digital file and its source, the subject classification and contextual information, the container elements for ad-hoc standards, and revision history. The selection of these elements depends on the characteristics of the data source.

The text module may be divided into the front matter, the body section, and the back matter. It also indicates, for instance, paragraphs, line breaks, pagination, and various types of divisions. For poetry, TEI can be used to identify an arrangement pattern (e.g., line, stanza, epigraph), rhyme, metrical structure, and metaphorical language.

While TEI elements and attributes are very comprehensive in capturing English textual representations and other dominant modern languages, its applications in other minor languages' contexts are still doubtful. A number of non-English corpora have attempted to develop their own metadata scheme or customize TEI and other metadata schemes to describe their own specific collection of texts. [5,7,10] Some even developed a Linked Open Data (LOD) as a platform to exchange textual data in language corpora. [4] However, none of them have attempted to develop a metadata scheme or validate the applicability of current metadata standards to describe the content of classical Thai poetry.

3   Methods

In order to develop the metadata scheme for classical Thai poetry in TNHC, a metadata modeling technique was applied. A research team consisting of scholars from related disciplines (i.e., historical linguistics, Thai linguistics, Thai literature, information science) developed use cases of the corpus concerning both users' and administrators' requirements. Since TNHC can be used in scholarly communities as well as society at large, the development of use cases also covers requirements from linguist's and general audience's points of view.

Since classical Thai poetry has unique characteristics and entities, the structure of classical Thai poetry was analyzed as a conceptual framework of the metadata scheme. Document research was conducted to examine a set of rules, the *chanthalak*, determining the variations of rhyming pattern and meter structure of Thai poetry. The poetic texts were selected to cover all verse forms, creation time, and styles. TEI markup language, based on the XML tree structure, is adopted and customized to accommodate the complexity of classical poetry structures.

While the development of TNHC examines three levels of data structure consisting of a document level (including selected major elements across all entities in the FRBR model as well as additional elements describing authors' characteristics and works), content level (a textual structure inside an item), and a word level. This paper specifically addresses the metadata describing the content (i.e., the structure of classical Thai poetry).

4   TNHC Primary Use Cases

While there are several use cases for TNHC, this section describes primary use cases identified by the multidisciplinary research team.

Apart from facilitating specialists in Thai literature in searching for linguistic and literary elements, the data will enable them to integrate quantitative analysis into the study Thai poetry. It will also allow linguists to investigate issues related to the Thai language that had been very difficult to do, e.g. dating of historical sound changes, and prosodic and metrical structure. In addition, traditional performing artists can also search for specific elements in the texts they are working with in their projects. Moreover, the public users can use the data to assist their composition, e.g. looking for rhyming words, or famous lines.

5   General Structure of Classical Thai Poetry

This section reports the conceptual framework of this study based on the *chanthalak*. In English poetry, a line is a prosodic unit generally defined by repeating patterns marked by features such as rhyme, alliteration, and syllable-count. [13] Strictly speaking, the line in English poetry may generally correspond to the *baat* or the *wak*, which is defined differently in each verse form in the Thai tradition.

There are five major verse forms: *khlong, chan, kap, klon,* and *rai*. Each form may accommodate a certain number of sub forms. For example, *khlong* can be divided into *khlong suphap* and *khlong dan* which are different in terms of the number of syllables and rhyming patterns. The classification of *klon* is based on a variety of rules, such as the number of syllables in a *wak* (e.g., *klon hok* with six syllables and *klon paet* with eight syllables), the fixation of beginning words (e.g., *klon duk sol* and *klon sakawa*), and genre (e.g., *klon niras* detailing the traveling experience). The classification of sub verse forms is usually not mutually exclusive. Poets independently choose how the verse form is to be called. For example, *klon niras* can be arranged according to the *klon paet* structure.

To illustrate a structure of Thai poetry, the *chanthalak* of two verse forms, *klon paet* and *khlong si suphap*, is reviewed as exemplars in this section.

Klon paet is one of the sub forms of *klon suphap*. In *klon paet*, a *wak* consists of a fixed number of eight stressed syllables (seven or nine syllables are occasionally acceptable.) delimited by an end rhyme. Two *wak's* in *klon* make up one *baat*, two of which form one stanza. Figure 3 shows the structure of *klon paet*. The *chanthalak* also determines the rhyming pattern of *klon paet*. In the first rhyming pair, there are two rhyming candidates in the second *wak*. An author can only choose one position to be the rhyming syllable.

In *khlong si suphap*, on the other hand, odd-numbered and even-numbered *wak's* contain five and two syllables respectively. These long and short *wak's* make up the *baat*. Four of these seven-syllable *baat's* then make up a stanza. Notice how the number of *baat's* in a *khong si suphap* stanza is equal to the number of *wak's* in its *klon paet* counterpart, suggesting that in fact the line in

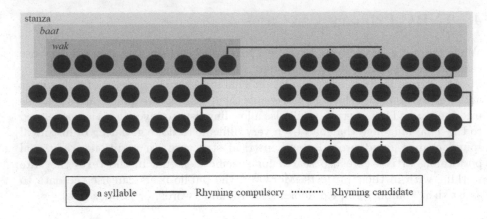

Fig. 3. The structure of *klon paet*.

a *khlong si* stanza should in fact be identified with the *baat*, rather than the *wak*. Figure 4 illustrates the requirement of *khlong si suphap* including the composition units, the rhyming pattern as well the tone marks. As a tonal language, modern Thai language consists of five tones. The rules of *khlong si suphap* also dictate which tone to be used in a specific position. Additionally, the stanza-linking rhymes are also optional for specific genres of *khlong si suphap* such as *khlong niras* (traveling experience) and *khlong supasit* (proverb).

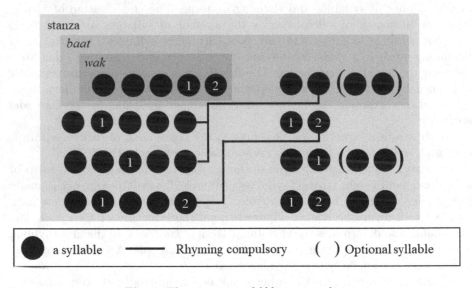

Fig. 4. The structure of *khlong si suphap*.

Although a chapter contains multiple stanzas in most verse forms, a group of stanzas together can constitute a paragraph in certain forms such as *rai*, divided by a specific punctuation mark called *fong man* (⊙). A few other punctuation marks have been found to sectionalize a group of stanzas as well.

In addition, certain forms of Thai poetry conform with Thai classical music. In a number of traditional literary and theatrical works, the poets may designate a particular song to a particular part of the work (e.g., a *baat*, a stanza, a paragraph). The verse serves as the lyrics of the song. In theatrical poetic works, authors include descriptions identifying stage setting. These supplement elements are also taken into consideration.

To preserve the structure of the original texts, a pagination tag, `<pb>`, is also included in the content level metadata of TNHC. However, it is a separate floating element since none of the structure of the texts are dependent on it. Figure 5 reveals the general structure of classical Thai poetry, based on texts collected in TNHC.

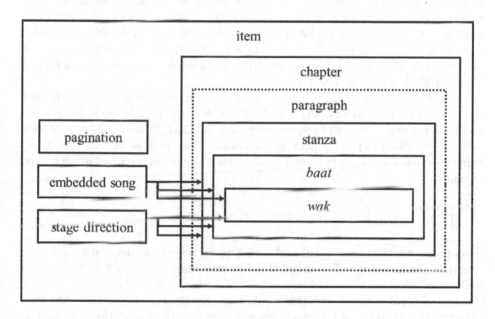

Fig. 5. The conceptual framework of classical Thai poetry.

6 TEI-Based Content-Level Metadata Scheme

Due to the complex structure of classical Thai poetry, TNHC adopted the TEI encoding scheme in the XML tree structure which is appropriate for organizing textual data in a language corpus.

For the main structure, the line, marked with the standard TEI tag `<l>`, is uniformly identified with the *baat*, regardless of the verse forms. The boundary between the two *wak's* in a *baat* is treated as a caesura, or a brief break between two phrases. In the corpus, the caesura is marked with `<caesura/>`. This decision allows poetic texts to be tagged consistently across verse forms and avoids confusions due to discrepancy between the traditional Thai and the Western terminologies. Furthermore, each stanza is considered a line group marked with the standard TEI tag `<lg>`. Each line group must be specified for its verse form by means of attribute type because some poetic texts consist of multiple verse forms. For example, *Lilit Phra Lo* consists of both *khlong* and *rai* stanzas in one paragraph. These composite paragraphs are treated as other paragraphs containing the same verse form.

For pagination, the standard tag `<pb>` is applied to mark the beginning of a page using the attribute @n to provide a page number. To identify the designated song, the standard tag `<sound>` is adopted using the attribute @type to describe the classification of a song. The standard tag `<stage>` is also implemented to describe stage direction information. Both tags are placed at the beginning of the content applied regardless of the verse unit. In addition, an optional attribute @scheme was applied as a global attribute to facilitate an identification of a source of derived classification (e.g., LCSH, *chanthalak*). Table 1 summarizes all metadata elements and selected attributes used to describe the content of classical Thai poetry in TNHC.

While certain rules following the *chanthalak* may be applied to a definite number of tags such as `<p>`, `<lg>`, and `<pb>`, the metadata scheme is designed to facilitate the explorations of pattern variations in Thai classical poetry that may not be prescribed in the traditional textbooks. Thus, instead of mandating certain rules to these elements, descriptions of these elements are in an uncontrolled manner.

7   Discussions

This paper addresses the results of an effort to develop a metadata scheme to describe the structure of classical Thai poetry which is a part of the corpus collection.

The general content structures of Thai classical poetry were examined through the analysis of the main verse forms and their variations as well as the rhyming patterns. Genre also plays a significant role in differentiating the textual structures. Thus, concerning interoperability and compatibility issues, selected elements and attributes of the TEI encoding scheme were adapted.

In terms of implementation of data entry and management, all tagging activities are done in a semi-automatic manner. Manual labeling of the content by linguists is conducted prior to an automatic conversion to a markup document. Prior to the conversion, the system validates the labeled document against the designated metadata scheme. The validated document is then imported to a relational database with n-gram index.

The current development of the metadata scheme of the classical poetry collection in TNHC primarily concerns the structure of verse forms. Nevertheless, the other highly recognized feature, the rhyme pattern, is not considered at this

Table 1. TNHC content-level metadata elements and selected attributes.

Tag	Description	Example

`<div>`	A container of a subdivision of a text. This tag is normally used to separate a chapter in Thai poetry texts.	`<div type="chapter"`
		`n="1">`
		`<sound type="naphat"`
		`scheme="CUSH">`

`<p>`	A container of a paragraph. It usually contains a group of multiple stanzas with specific punctuation marks.	`<!--...-->`
		`</sound>`
		`<stage type="business"`
		`scheme="TEI">...</stage>`

`<lg>`	A container of a stanza	`<pb n=12/>`
`<l>`	A container of a *baat*	`<p type="klon"`
`<caesura/>`	A division between *wak's*	`scheme="chanthalak">`
`<sound>`	A container of music designated to a specific part of a text.	`<lg type="stanza">` `<l type="baat" n="1">`
`<stage>`	A container of stage direction	`<!--...-->`
`<pb/>`	A mark of the beginning of a page of a paginated item	`<caesura/>` `<!--...-->`
	@facs - *(optional)* pointer to an image copy of a page	`</l>` `</lg>`
@n	*(global, optional)* a unique identifier of an element	`</p>` `</div>`
@type	*(global, option)* category of an element being described (e.g., chapter)	
@scheme	*(global, optional)* source of category used in @type attribute	

stage. Since the rhyme patterns can be mostly predictable, it is expected that a machine learning approach may come into place to help in the annotation process which would be the future development of the corpus.

Additionally, in classical Thai poetry, an author may develop or apply a prosody to a certain part of a work. Traditional Thai prosodies prescribe specific manners to manipulate sound or writing style. For instance, *bowornthodok* prosodies fix the pattern of stress of the first three syllables in every *wak* in *klon*. Some prosodies use a network structure to construct a composing and reading pattern. Generally, one prosody applies to only one verse form. Prosody information is also important for poetic enthusiasts to learn about the sound system in Thai poetry. A comprehensive analysis of prosodies of Thai poetry is further needed in order to design an appropriate metadata scheme.

Beyond describing the content, there are areas to improve in regarding the discovery and interoperability of the data in the corpus. Currently, only certain TEI header elements are used to describe documents in the corpus. While TEI header elements are compatible with ISBD, AACR2, and ANSI Z39.29, [18] a more robust metadata model for document management such as FRBR would support the analysis of language variations between different manifestations or expressions of a work. The integration between FRBR concept and TEI header has yet to be standardized [11] which is needed for further investigation.

In this early stage, the description of global attribute @type in all applicable elements, except <stage>, is not controlled, but rather indicated as in the original text. This would allow researchers to interpret patterns and relationships in an open environment. On the other hand, there is a lack of a knowledge organization system (e.g., subject headings, thesaurus, ontology) for those elements such as Thai classical music and stage direction. Therefore, the development and application of ontologies and other knowledge systems for these elements is an area to be explored for future research and requires collaborative efforts from experts in both domains.

In terms of annotating a word, the focus on a syllable of Thai poetry presents a challenge for the semantic annotation process. A multiple-syllable term can be separated between two *wak's*. Tagging only a syllable would yield an object with no semantic value. Therefore, the researcher team adjusted the tagging structure of label to consider both semantic and syntactic units. Moreover, annotations for natural language processing, such as part-of-speech tagging and name-entity recognition, would also enhance the merits of this corpus for broader applications. An efficient machine learning approach for TNHC is also in the developmental plan.

It is important to note that the development of metadata for poetry collection of TNHC heavily relies on the rules stated in the *chanthalak* textbook. However, Gedney [9] argued that there are certain well-known classic poetic works that substantially diverged from the *chanthalak*. Some obey rules not discussed in the *chanthalak*. The current metadata scheme reflects only the selective works in the corpus which may not represent a broad range of poetic patterns in Thai literary works. Collecting more diverse works is one of the main missions for this project. It would help linguists to discover constraints that have not been discussed in the *chanthalak*. Furthermore, it would also contribute to the enhancement of the data model of the corpus.

Acknowledgment. The Thai National Historical Corpus is a part of the project in celebration of HRH Princess Maha Chakri Sirindhorn's 60th birthday, organized by the Faculty of Arts, Chulalongkorn University, funded by the Maha Chakri Sirindhorn Foundation for the Faculty of Arts. The preparation of this manuscript is also partially supported by the Arc of Memory Research Unit and the Behavioral Research and Informatics in Social Science Research Unit, Chulalongkorn University. The authors would like to thank all research team members, including Pakjira Thammanutham, Karnwiruch Nuchpraharn, Santhawat Thanyawong, Wannabha Sapphasit, Naris Jereeratana, Sireemas Maspong, Thanasak Sirikhanerat, Jakrabhop Iamdanush, Ponlawat Laimanoo, Nopparut Sanah, and Phongpat Matheethammawat, for their tremendous contributions to this project.

References

1. Aroonmanakun, W.: Thai tokenization (2002). http://pioneer.chula.ac.th/~awirote/resources/thai-word-segmentation.html

2. Aroonmanakun, W.: Creating the Thai national corpus. Manusaya. J. Hum. **13**(Special Issue), 4–17 (2007)
3. Aroonmanakun, W., Nupairoj, N., Muangsin, V., Choemprayong, S.: Thai monitor corpus: challenges and contribution to Thai NLP. Vacana: J. Lang. Linguist. **6**(2), 1–16 (2018)
4. Bermúdez-Sabel, H., Curado Malta, M., Gonzalez-Blanco, E.: Towards interoperability in the European poetry community: the standardization of philological concepts. In: Gracia, J., Bond, F., McCrae, J.P., Buitelaar, P., Chiarcos, C., Hellmann, S. (eds.) LDK 2017. LNCS (LNAI), vol. 10318, pp. 156–165. Springer, Cham (2017). https://doi.org/10.1007/978-3-319-59888-8_14
5. Bibiri, A.D., Bolea, S.C., Scutelnicu, L.A., Moruz, A.M., Pistol, L., Cristea, D.: Metadata of a huge corpus of contemporary Romanian data and organization of the work. In: Proceedings of the 7th Balkan Conference on Informatics Conference, p. 35. ACM (2015)
6. Bowker, L.: Corpus linguistics is not just for linguists: considering the potential of computer-based corpus methods for library and information science research. Libr. Hi Tech **36**(2), 358–371 (2018)
7. Candela, G., Escobar, P., Navarro-Colorado, B.: In search of poetic rhythm: poetry retrieval through text and metre. In: Proceedings of the 2nd International Conference on Digital Access to Textual Cultural Heritage, pp. 53–57. ACM (2017)
8. Futrelle, R.P., Zhang, X., Sekiya, Y.: Corpus linguistics for establishing the natural language content of digital library documents. In: Adam, N.R., Bhargava, B.K., Yesha, Y. (eds.) DL 1994. LNCS, vol. 916, pp. 163–180. Springer, Heidelberg (1995). https://doi.org/10.1007/BFb0026855
9. Gedney, W.J.: Siamese verse forms in historical perspective. In: Bickner, R.J., Hartmann, J., Hudak, T.J., Peyasantiwong, P. (eds.) Center for South and Southeast Asian studies, University of Michigan, Ann Arbor, pp. 489–544 (1989)
10. González-Blanco García, E., Rodríguez, J.L.: ReMetCa: a TEI based digital repertory on medieval Spanish poetry the linked TEI: text encoding in the web In: Ciotti, F., Ciula, A. (eds.) The Linked TEI: Text Encoding in the Web. DIGILAB Sapienza University & TEI Consortium (2013)
11. Hawkins, K.S.: FRBR group 1 entities and the TEI guidelines. In: The 2008 TEI Annual Members Meeting, London (2008)
12. Imsombut, A., Kawtrakul, A.: Automatic building of an ontology on the basis of text corpora in Thai. Lang. Resour. Eval. **42**(2), 137–149 (2007). https://doi.org/10.1007/s10579-007-9045-5
13. Leech, G.N.: A Linguistic Guide to English Poetry. Routledge, London (1989)
14. Oxford Text Archive: Designing and creating the BNC. http://www.natcorp.ox.ac.uk/corpus/creating.xml
15. Pittayaporn, P., et al.: Survey and selection of texts for Thai national historical corpus. J. Thai Lang. Lit. **32**(2), 1–41 (2015). https://www.tci-thaijo.org/index.php/THlanglit/article/view/59869
16. Riley, J.: Understanding metadata: what is metadata, and what is it for?: a primer, January 2017. https://www.niso.org/publications/understanding-metadata-2017
17. Sornlertlamvanich, V., Takahashi, N., Isahara, H.: Building a Thai part-of-speech tagged corpus (ORCHID). J. Acoust. Soc. Japan **20**(3), 189–198 (1999). https://doi.org/10.1250/ast.20.189
18. TEI Consortium (ed.): TEI P5: Guidelines for electronic text encoding and interchange. 3.4.0. TEI Consortium (2018). http://www.tei-c.org/guidelines/p5/

Research Data Management by Academics and Researchers: Perceptions, Knowledge and Practices

Shaheen Majid[(⊠)], Schubert Foo, and Xue Zhang

Wee Kim Wee School of Communication and Information,
Nanyang Technological University, Singapore 637718, Singapore
{asmajid, sfoo, ZhangXue}@ntu.edu.sg

Abstract. The purpose of this study was to investigate research data management RDM) activities undertaken by academics, researchers, and research students at Nanyang Technological University Singapore. An online questionnaire was used and 241 respondents participated in this study. It was found that most of research data produced were in MS Office (text, spreadsheet, presentation) format, images, and structured statistical data. In addition to generating own research data, over one-half of the respondents were using data produced by other team members. They were storing their research data in their personal storage devices and assigning certain additional information to their files for fast and accurate retrieval. Overall, the respondents exhibited a positive attitude towards collaborative research and data sharing although a majority of them preferred data sharing with their own team members. The major concerns expressed for sharing research data were legal and ethical issues, data misuse, and misinterpretation of data. A majority of the respondents showed interest in attending research data management training. The paper suggests certain measures for promoting research data management by academics and researchers.

Keywords: Research data management · Data sharing · Data security
Singapore

1 Introduction

In recent years, proper management of research data has received tremendous attention and support. Properly managed research data provides credibility to the research process as well as enhances the integrity of its findings. Universities and research institutions all over the world are coming up with relevant policies and procedures to properly manage their research data. A crucial factor in creating a good data management culture is to familiarize all researchers, including faculty, research students, research fellows, and other individuals involved in research with the importance and procedures involved in proper research data management. The purpose of this study was to investigate research data management knowledge and practices of faculty and researchers at Nanyang Technology University Singapore.

M. Dobreva et al. (Eds.): ICADL 2018, LNCS 11279, pp. 166–178, 2018.
https://doi.org/10.1007/978-3-030-04257-8_16

2 Literature Review

With considerable increase in research activity, universities and research institutions are generating enormous amount of research data which could be in a variety for forms such as text, numerical data, qualitative data, recordings, images, machine-generated data, source codes, observations, scientific data, audio-visual transcripts, simulations, experiential data, system log files, to name a few. This 'data deluge' has forced research institutions to develop policies, procedures, infrastructures, and services to manage data, with the objective to assist researchers in creating, collecting, manipulating, analyzing, transporting, storing and preserving datasets [1]. Yoon and Schultz [2] argue that, as research is becoming more collaborative and data intensive, proper management of research data is becoming an integral component of research activity.

Properly managed research data is also necessary to make it available for consultation, verification of research claims, and for future academic and research works [3]. An important objective of research data management is to facilitate date sharing which can help benefit scholarship by reusing data to build new theories as well as to validate research by replicating it [4]. Realizing the importance of RDM, many universities and research institutions have established their data management plans to enhance their research integrity and accountability [5].

Research data management is a complex process, involving multiple activities carried out by various actors and influenced by a large set of factors [6]. Surkis and Read [7] highlight that the concept of data lifecycle is often used to help researchers understand the scope and meaning of data management. RDM involves several activities and processes to ensure that research data is properly processed, documented, stored, archived, and curated to make it readily available for access and reuse (3). Cox and Pinfield [8] explain that RDM comprises a number of different activities and processes associated with the data lifecycle, involving the design and creation of data, storage, security, preservation, retrieval, sharing, and reuse, also taking into account technical capabilities, ethical considerations, legal issues and governance frameworks.

In recent years, the importance of RDM has grown manifolds due to emphasis on data integrity and the need to reuse the gathered research data. The access and sharing of research data have been emphasized by government departments, funding agencies, and scholarly communities [5]. Many research funding agencies, conscious of the need to promote good research practices and to achieve higher value of their money, are now requiring all grant research proposals to also include a comprehensive data management plan [8]. As a result, many universities and research institutions are developing their policies and procedures for RDM to comply with the requirements of funding agencies. Similarly, several prestigious scholarly journals are now asking researchers to also submit their research data plans [9].

Despite many benefits associated with proper RDM as well as requirements of funding agencies and scholarly journals, several researchers are still not fully convinced of its utility. Although in RDM, the personal information of subjects can be anonymized, some social scientists are reluctant to share personal and confidential information of their participants as it may be considered as a breach of privacy [3]. Several researchers also express their concerns reading proper data storage, integrity, and backup procedures. Thus, there is a need that all institutions involved in RDM to properly educate their researchers about the measures taken to safeguarded their data [2].

The next logical question is who in an institution should be responsible to coordinate the RDM activities. Many feel that libraries are well suited to support RDM activities [3] as they already undertake several related activities such as developing institutional repositories, creating metadata, providing users' services, and conducting training and promotion. Yoon and Schultz [2] argue that libraries have a long history of curating and preserving information, which makes them suitable for research data management. In a 2016 report, ACRL highlights the importance of libraries in providing research data services, and developing data policies and plans [3]. Cox and Pinfield [8] note that university libraries are increasingly seen as major contributors to RDM activity, particularly in the design of research data services. However, the lack of necessary skills by librarians could be a concern. Tenopir et al. [10] report that a considerable number of librarians do not feel that they possess adequate RDM skills. It is, therefore, desirable that library and information science education programs should start teaching these skills to their students [3].

Adequate promotion and training of academics and researchers are essential for the success of a research data management program [2]. Some libraries provide one-to-one training to researchers for developing their RDM plans as well as create data management guides for them [7]. Some other libraries use training workshops, web pages, library guides, and one-to-one instruction for teaching RDM procedures [11]. Even 'data literacy' can be made a component of information literacy programs run by academic institutions [12].

Nanyang Technological University Singapore has taken several steps to implement RDM to ensure data integrity, accountability, long-term availability and sharing, and to comply with the requirements of funding agencies. Since April 2016, all new proposals for research grants are required to submit a data management plan. Similarly, all Institutional Review Board (IRB) applications need to provide information about their data management plans. NTU library runs a series of training workshops to help researchers in writing their data management plans [13].

The main objective of this study was to investigate knowledge, perceptions and practices of academics, research fellows, and research students for implementing RDM for their research projects. It is expected that findings of this study will be useful to NTU research planners and administrators to assess the preparedness of university research staff as well as to understand their perceptions and concerns of data sharing. NTU library, responsible to manage the research data repository as well as to promote RDM activities, can use these findings to review its policies, procedures, and training strategy. Similarly, other universities and research institutions in Singapore and in other countries can benefit from this study and may decide undertaking similar studies to investigate knowledge and practices of their staff.

3 Methodology

The data presented in this paper is Singapore subset of an international survey, participated by more than 30 countries. The 26-question survey was developed by a team of researchers from England, France and Turkey to collect data about 'data literacy' of academics, researchers, and research students in higher education institutions [14]. Areas covered by this online survey included demographic information of the participants, type of research data produced by them, collection and use of external research data, additional information used for describing the stored data, data sharing concerns, and training for writing data management plans.

Population of the survey comprised academic staff, researchers, and research students affiliated with Nanyang Technological University (NTU) Singapore. The study and its questionnaire were approved by the Institutional Review Board (IRB) of Nanyang Technological University through its letter IRB-2017-11-002, dated November 14, 2017. An email, with URL of the English language survey, was sent to all NTU academic staff, researchers, and research students, inviting them to participate in this study. A reminder email was sent three weeks after the launch of the survey. A total of 241 researchers participated in this study.

4 Data Analysis and Discussion

4.1 Demographics

Of the 241 respondents, 148 (61.4%) were male and 91 (37.8%) female. Two participants did not disclose their gender. A majority of the respondents (43.2%) were in the age group of 26 to 35 years, followed by 25.7% in the age group of 18 to 25 years. Another 17.0% of the respondents belonged to the age group of 36 to 45 years. The remaining 14.1% pf the respondents were older than 45 years. The distribution of respondents, based on their primary role in the university, was: 41.1% faculty, 38.6% research students, and 20.3% research fellows and research associates.

Although in the original questionnaire listed 36 popular disciplines, these were regrouped into three broad categories, i.e. science and engineering, social sciences, and humanities. As NTU was founded originally as an engineering university in 1991, the majority (69.7%) of the respondents belonged to science and engineering group. The social sciences and humanities departments in NTU were subsequently and gradually established over the last two decades, hence their representation in the survey was comparatively smaller – 22.0% respondents from social sciences and 8.3% from humanities.

4.2 Type of Research Data Produced

The respondents were asked about the type of research data generated by them. As shown in Table 1, the overall top four data types were: standard MS Office documents (81.7%), images (53.5%), structured scientific and statistical data (32.4%), and raw machine-generated data (24.9%). Respondents from all the three broad academic disciplines were heavily producing Microsoft Office documents such as text files, spreadsheets, and presentations. Participants from science and engineering disciplines were also producing images and machine-generated data. On the other hand, statistical data was mainly generated by social scientists, and images by humanities researchers.

Table 1. Type of data produced by the respondents (multiple response).

Data type	Academic disciplines			Total
	Sciences (n = 168)	S. Sciences (n = 53)	Humanities (n = 20)	(n = 241)
Standard office documents (text, spreadsheets, presentations, etc.)	136 (81.0%)	43 (81.1%)	18 (90.0%)	197 (81.7%)
Images (JPEG, GIF, TIFF, PNG, etc.)	110 (65.5%)	9 (17.0%)	10 (50.0%)	129 (53.5%)
Structured statistical data (SPSS, GIS, etc.)	39 (23.2%)	38 (71.7%)	1 (5.0%)	78 (32.4%)
Raw (machine-generated) data	56 (33.3%)	4 (7.5%)	0 (0.0%)	60 (24.9%)
Source code (scripting, Java, C, C ++, etc.)	55 (32.7%)	3 (5.7%)	0 (0.0%)	58 (24.1%)
Software applications (modelling tools, editors, compilers, etc.)	49 (29.2%)	1 (1.9%)	2 (10.0%)	52 (21.6%)
Archived data (ZIP, RAR, ZAR, etc.)	43 (25.6%)	6 (11.3%)	2 (10.0%)	51 (21.2%)
Internet and web-based data (webpages, e-mails, blogs, social network data, etc.)	31 (18.5%)	5 (9.4%)	8 (40.0%)	44 (18.3%)

The formats in which research data was generated less frequently (no shown in Table 1), included non-digital artefacts, configuration data, structured graphics, encoded text, and audio files.

4.3   Sources for Research Data

The respondents were asked how they usually get the data required for their research. A majority of the respondents were either creating their own original research data (67.2%) or acquiring it from their research team members (51.9%) (Table 2). It is understandable as researchers belonging to a particular research team are likely to work on somewhat similar topics. Another possible explanation for acquiring data from own research team members could be familiarity and reciprocity in relationship.

Respondents from social sciences (56.6%) and humanities (55.0%) were also acquiring their research data from multiple sources. It appeared that the respondents, in addition to generating their own research data, were collaborating with other research teams and individual researchers to acquire the data required for their research. It indicates a positive attitude of academics and researchers towards research data sharing.

Table 2. Sources of data acquisition (multiple response)

Data source	Academic disciplines			Total
	Sciences (n = 168)	S. Sciences (n = 53)	Humanities (n = 20)	(n = 241)
Create new data	116 (69.0%)	37 (69.8%)	9 (45.0%)	162 (67.2%)
From own research team/group at the university	99 (58.9%)	19 (35.8%)	7 (35.0%)	125 (51.9%)
From multiple known sources	66 (39.3%)	30 (56.6%)	11 (55.0%)	107 (44.4%)
From own research network (personal/professional connections)	50 (29.8%)	15 (28.3%)	9 (45.0%)	74 (30.7%)
From one known source	10 (6.0%)	6 (11.3%)	0 (0.0%)	16 (6.6%)

4.4   Required Processing for the Acquired Data

The respondents were asked about additional time and effort required to process data acquired by them from other sources. A majority (45.2%) of the respondents from science and engineering group said that they usually need only a little time to clean and prepare the acquired data (Table 3). It could be due the reason that usually data in science and engineering disciplines are more concrete and quantitative which may be comparatively easier to process and convert to a desired format. On the other hand, a majority of the respondents belonging to social sciences (49.1%) and humanities (55.0%) need to spend a lot of time and effort to make the acquired data useable. It could be due to the nature of data in social sciences and humanities which may be based on human behaviour, perceptions, preferences, attitudes, and viewpoints. Only 17.4% of the respondents, a majority of them from the sciences group, were able to use the acquired data without any problem.

Table 3. Processing required for the data acquired from other sources.

Required processing	Academic disciplines			Total
	Sciences (n = 168)	S. Sciences (n = 53)	Humanities (n = 20)	(n = 241)
With a bit of time and effort for cleaning and/or modifications	76 (45.2%)	23 (43.4%)	9 (45.0%)	108 (44.8%)
A lot of time and efforts to make it usable for the project	47 (28.0%)	26 (49.1%)	11 (55.0%)	84 (34.9%)
As it is without any problems	36 (21.4%)	4 (7.5%)	2 (10.0%)	42 (17.4%)
I do not use data from others/outside sources	37 (22.0%)	14 (26.4%)	2 (10.0%)	53 (22.0%)

4.5   Assigning Additional Information to Research Data

Assigning certain additional information to the stored data files can make their identification and retrieval fast and accurate. The respondents were asked if they usually
assign additional information to their research data files. More than 45% of the
respondents from all disciplines reported assigning 'administrative information' to their
data files (Table 4).

Table 4. Additional information assigned to research data (multiple response).

Information assigned	Academic disciplines			Total (n = 241)
	Sciences (n = 168)	S. Sciences (n = 53)	Humanities (n = 20)	
Administrative information (e.g. creator, creation date, access restrictions, etc.)	79 (47.0%)	24 (45.3%)	9 (45.0%)	112 (46.5%)
Data file description (e.g. file/data structure, field tags/descriptions, application rules, etc.)	65 (38.7%)	16 (30.2%)	6 (30.0%)	87 (36.1%)
Technical information (e.g. file format, file size, software/hardware needed to use the data, etc.)	53 (31.5%)	4 (7.5%)	4 (20.0%)	61 (25.3%)
Discovery information (e.g. creator, funding body, project title, project ID, keywords, etc.)	37 (22.0%)	12 (22.6%)	6 (30.0%)	55 (22.8%)
No, I do not assign additional information to my research data	48 (28.6%)	23 (43.4%)	7 (35.0%)	78 (32.4%)

In addition, 38.7% of science and engineering, 30.2% of social sciences, and 30.0%
of the humanities respondents, were assigning certain data file description to their
stored data. However, 32.4% of the respondents were not assigning any additional
identification information to their stored data. On the whole, only a small percentage of
the respondents were assigning additional information to their stored data, probably
due to less exposure and limited familiarity with RDM concepts.

4.6   Storage of Research Data

It was found that the first preference of an overwhelming majority (95.4%%) of the
respondents from all disciplines was to store research data in their own devices such as
personal computers, tablets, and external storage drives (Table 5). A considerable
percentage of the respondents from all the disciplines was also using cloud for their
data storage. Slightly over one-quarter of the respondents were storing their research
data in central servers or in the university repository. Probably the personal storage
devices were preferred due to ownership feeling and control, while cloud storage was
used due to its easy access from anywhere anytime.

Table 5. Preferred locations for storing research data (multiple response).

Storage type	Academic disciplines			Total
	Sciences (n = 168)	S. Sciences (n = 53)	Humanities (n = 20)	(n = 241)
Own devices (computer, tablet, external drive, etc.)	160 (95.2%)	51 (96.2%)	19 (95.0%)	230 (95.4%)
Cloud	81 (48.2%)	25 (47.2%)	10 (50.0%)	116 (48.1%)
Central servers/university repository	50 (29.8%)	8 (15.1%)	5 (25.0%)	63 (26.1%)
Outside repositories	9 (5.4%)	0 (0.0%)	2 (10.0%)	11 (4.6%)

4.7   Research Collaboration and Data Sharing

One of the objectives of research data management is to avoid duplication by promoting research collaboration and data sharing. It was found that 68.5% of the
respondents were sharing data with the members of their research teams (Table 6). This
finding is understandable as researchers belonging to the same group are likely to work
on somewhat similar topics as well as familiar with each other. In a previous finding of
this study (Table 2), 51.9% of the researchers revealed that they also use data produced
by other team members. This indicates reciprocity and a symbiotic relationship
between the surveyed academics and researchers.

Table 6. Research collaboration and data sharing (multiple response).

Collaboration and data sharing	Academic disciplines			Total
	Sciences (n = 168)	S. Sciences (n = 53)	Humanities (n = 20)	(n = 241)
Yes, with researchers in the same team	119 (70.8%)	39 (73.6%)	7 (35.0%)	165 (68.5%)
Yes, with researchers in the same university	63 (37.5%)	15 (28.3%)	4 (20.0%)	82 (34.0%)
Yes, with researchers in other institutions	53 (31.5%)	18 (34.0%)	4 (20.0%)	75 (31.1%)
No, I don't share	24 (14.3%)	7 (13.2%)	9 (45.0%)	40 (16.6%)

It was also found that 34% of the respondents were sharing research data with other
researchers within their own university, while another 31.1% were sharing data with
researchers from other institutions. A discipline based analysis revealed that a majority
of the respondents belonging to science & engineering and social sciences were sharing

their data with other researchers, while 45% of the humanities respondents admitted not sharing their data with anyone. On the whole, it emerged that a majority of the researchers had a positive attitude towards research collaboration and data sharing.

4.8 Data Sharing Behaviour

Through another question data sharing behaviour of the respondents was further explored. Overall, it was found that 51.5% of the respondents were openly sharing their research data with their team members (Table 7). Another 41.1% of the respondents said that their data is available on request. However, only 12.4% of the respondents were openly sharing their data with everyone. It appeared that, although a majority of the respondents were willing to share their research data with others, they preferred sharing either with their acquaintances or with other researchers on their specific requests. Probably these respondents, to safeguard their data, wanted to know who is using their data and for what purposes.

Table 7. Data sharing behaviour of the respondents (multiple response).

Data sharing behaviour	Academic disciplines			Total (n = 241)
	Sciences (n = 168)	S. Sciences (n = 53)	Humanities (n = 20)	
My data is openly available only to my research team	91 (54.2%)	28 (52.8%)	5 (25.0%)	124 (51.5%)
My data is available openly upon request	67 (39.9%)	26 (49.1%)	6 (30.0%)	99 (41.1%)
My data has restricted access (e.g. only parts of the dataset is accessible)	39 (23.2%)	9 (17.0%)	4 (20.0%)	52 (21.6%)
My data is openly available to everyone	22 (13.1%)	5 (9.4%)	3 (15.0%)	30 (12.4%)
My data is not available to anyone else	12 (7.1%)	9 (17.0%)	3 (15.0%)	24 (10.0%)

4.9 Data Sharing Concerns

The respondents were also asked about their concerns of sharing research data with other researchers. The major concern, expressed by 43.2% of the respondents, was the legal and ethical issues pertaining to data sharing (Table 8). Two other major concerns were 'misuse of data' (39.4%), and 'misinterpretation of data' (32.8%).

Respondents from different academic disciplines had almost similar concerns, except 40% of the humanities respondents were also concerned about the lack of appropriate policies and measures for rights protection. It appeared that, although the respondents had some concerns, their percentage was not very high, indicating their confidence in the research data management system of the University.

Table 8. Data sharing concerns (multiple response).

Data sharing concerns	Academic disciplines			Total
	Sciences (n = 168)	S. Sciences (n = 53)	Humanities (n = 20)	(n = 241)
Legal and ethical issues	70 (41.7%)	28 (52.8%)	6 (30.0%)	104 (43.2%)
Misuse of data	63 (37.5%)	28 (52.8%)	4 (20.0%)	95 (39.4%)
Misinterpretation of data	49 (29.2%)	24 (45.3%)	6 (30.0%)	79 (32.8%)
Fear of losing the scientific edge	55 (32.7%)	20 (37.7%)	1 (5.0%)	(76) 31.5%
Lack of appropriate policies and rights protection	45 (26.8%)	23 (43.4%)	8 (40.0%)	76 (31.5%)
No concerns	45 (26.8%)	6 (11.3%)	5 (25.0%)	56 (23.2%)
Lack of resources (technical, financial, personnel, etc.)	14 (8.3%)	8 (15.1%)	3 (15.0%)	25 (10.4%)

4.10   Data Management Knowledge and Applications

Several questions were asked to investigate respondents' knowledge and use of data management plans (DMP). In response to a question on the availability of DMP, 51.9% of the respondents said that such a plan exits in their University (Table 9). However, 56% of the respondents revealed that they had never used such a plan, probably because it became mandatory only in April 2016. It is possible that these respondents had not submitted any new research proposal after this date.

Another 44.4% of the respondents said that they do not have a DMP for their ongoing research project(s). However, it was a matter of concern that 61% of the respondents were either uncertain or disagree that a DMP could be helpful to researchers in managing their research data. It indicates a need to launch a rigorous awareness campaign to promote the benefits of participating in a research data management initiative.

Regarding familiarity with the concept of metadata, only 47.3% of the respondents replied in affirmative. However, an overwhelming majority (87.1%) of the surveyed participants were either uncertain or did not know if their university has prescribed a metadata for uploading their research data into the organizational data management repository. Similarly, another 90.5% of the respondents were either uncertain or did not know if their university had prescribed a standard file naming system for their data files. These findings highlight a need for more concerted efforts to adequate educate and train researchers in the University.

Table 9. Data management knowledge and applications (multiple response).

Data management knowledge and applications	Yes	Uncertain	No
Does your institution have a Data Management Plan (DMP)?	125 (51.9%)	105 (43.6%)	11 (4.6%)
Have you ever used a DMP for your research?	58 (24.1%)	48 (19.9%)	135 (56.0%)
Do you have a DMP for your current research project(s)?	66 (27.4%)	68 (28.2%)	107 (44.4%)
Do you think a DMP actually helps researchers in managing research data?	94 (39.0%)	118 (49.0%)	29 (12.0%)
Are you familiar with the term metadata?	114 (47.3%)	52 (21.6%)	75 (31.1%)
Does your university have a prescribed metadata set for uploading data to a repository?	31 (12.9%)	197 (81.7%)	13 (5.4%)
Does your university have a standard/consistent file naming system?	23 (9.5%)	151 (62.7%)	67 (27.8%)
Do you use any standard style for citing research data?	153 (63.5%)	39 (16.2%)	49 (20.3%)
Are you familiar with the concept of Digital Object Identifier (DOI)?	134 (55.6%)	40 (16.6%)	67 (27.8%)
Does your university recommend any specific guideline for citing data (e.g. APA, Harvard, etc.)?	86 (35.7%)	106 (44.0%)	49 (20.3%)

4.11 Training Participation and Interest

The respondents were asked if they have received any formal training on different aspects of research data management and also to identify areas where they would like to receive training. It was found that only a very small percentage of the respondents had attended any training on research data management (Table 10). It was worth noting that 60.2% of the respondents revealed not attending any training program.

Table 10. Training attended and needs for future training (N = 241)

S. No.	Training areas	Training received	Interest in training
1	Data Management Plan	18.7%	62.2%
2	Metadata	5.8%	57.3%
3	Consistent file naming	7.1%	42.3%
4	Version control of data sets	6.6%	43.6%
5	Data citation styles	26.1%	39.8%
6	No training received	60.2%	//////
	I am not interested in any training	//////	22.0%

For the question regarding interest to attend future training on different aspects of research data management, 62.2% of the respondents expressed their interest to learn about developing a data management plan. Another 57.3% of the respondents were interested to learn about using metadata for uploading research data in the organizational repository. There was also considerable interest in the remaining training areas. On the whole, it appeared that a majority of the respondents were not adequately trained to effectively undertake various research data management activities and were interested to learn more about them.

5 Conclusion

Proper management of research data is fast gaining popularity and momentum. Many universities are making efforts to create awareness among their faculty and researchers about the need and benefits of research data management. They are also developing policies, procedures, and infrastructure to effectively manage their research data. This study revealed that a majority of the academics and researchers at Nanyang Technological University Singapore had a positive attitude towards research collaboration and data sharing. However, they were more comfortable sharing research data with their colleagues, probably because of familiarity, inter-dependence, mutual trust, and less likelihood of data abuse. The major concerns expressed for data sharing were legal and ethical issues, data misuse, and misinterpretation of their data. The NTU library management, which is responsible to coordinate RDM activities, needs to address to these concerns through awareness campaigns and training sessions, which will motivate researchers to confidentially upload their research data.

It was also found that the respondents had only limited knowledge of and rarely undertaking various research data management activities. As now all new research funding proposals as well as IRB (Institutional Review Board) applications require a data management plan, all academics and researchers need to be aware of related policies and procedures. A majority of the respondents were mindful of this need and interested to attend relevant training. Although NTU library is regularly conducting such training sessions, rigorous promotion and schedule flexibility would be beneficial. Similarly, NTU library can consider developing an online tutorial along with quizzes which may lead to a certification in research data management (RDM) on the lines of CITI certification program [15]. In future it should become mandatory for all academics, researchers, and research students to obtain RDM certification before embarking on any research project. Similarly, library can make 'data literacy' part of its information literacy training education program. Hence, a variety of measures are needed to improve awareness about the RDM program and the benefits associated with it.

References

1. Pinfield, S., Cox, A.M., Smith, J.: Research data management and libraries: relationships, activities, drivers and influences. PLoS ONE 9(12), 1–28 (2014)
2. Yoon, A., Schultz, T.: Research data management services in academic libraries in the US. College Res. Libr. 78(7), 920–933 (2017)

3. Tripathi, M.M., Shukla, A., Sonker, S.K.: Research data management practices in university libraries. DESIDOC J. Libr. Inf. Technol. **37**(6), 417–424 (2017)
4. Poole, A.H.: How has your science data grown? Digital curation and the human factor: A critical literature review. Arch. Sci. **15**(2), 101–139 (2015)
5. Lee, D.J., Stvilia, B.: Practices of research data curation in institutional repositories: a qualitative view from repository staff. PLoS ONE **12**(3), 1–44 (2017)
6. Chiware, E., Mathe, Z.: Academic libraries' role in research data management services. South Afr. J. Libr. Inf. Sci. **81**(2), 1–10 (2015)
7. Surkis, A., Read, K.: Research data management. J. Med. Libr. Assoc. **103**(3), 154–156 (2015)
8. Cox, A.M., Pinfield, S.: Research data management and libraries: current activities and future priorities. J. Libr. Inf. Sci. **46**(4), 300 (2014)
9. Fei, Y., Deuble, R., Morgan, H.: Designing research data management services based on the research lifecycle: a consultative leadership approach. J. Aust. Libr. Information Assoc. **66**(3), 287–298 (2017)
10. Tenopir, C., Sandusky, R.J., Allard, S., Birch, B.: Research data management services in academic libraries and perceptions of librarians. Libr. Inf. Sci. Res. **36**, 84–90 (2014)
11. Morgan, A., Duffield, N., Walkley Hall, L.: Research data management support: sharing our experiences. J. Aust. Libr. Inf. Assoc. **66**(3), 299–305 (2017)
12. Javier, C.P., Marzal, M.A.: Incorporating data literacy into information literacy programs: core competencies and contents. Libri **63**(2), 123–134 (2013)
13. Nanyang Technological University. Research data management. https://blogs.ntu.edu.sg/lib-datamanagement/dmp/
14. Chowdhury, G., Walton, G., Kurbanoğlu, S., Unal, Y., Boustany, J.: Information practices for sustainability: information, data and environmental literacy. In: The Fourth European Conference on Information Literacy (ECIL), Prague, 10–13 October 2016, p. 22 (2016)
15. CITI [Collaborative Institutional Training Initiative]. CITI program: Research Ethics and Compliance Training. https://about.citiprogram.org/en/homepage/

Examining Japanese American Digital Library Collections with an Ethnographic Lens

Andrew B. Wertheimer[(✉)] and Noriko Asato

Library and Information Science Program, University of Hawai'i at Mānoa,
Honolulu, USA
{wertheim, asaton}@hawaii.edu

Abstract. This year marks the 150th anniversary of Japanese immigration to Hawai'i and the Americas. In the past two decades Japanese American history emerged as a key theme on some of the earliest digital library (DL) collections in the United States, mostly focusing on what is commonly called the "internment" or forced incarceration of 120,000 Japanese Americans during World War II. This paper looks at DLs in the United States, exploring their development, contents, and then takes a critical lens to question if it shows Japanese American agency. This approach, common in archival studies, remains rare in Library and Information Science, especially in regards to DLs. The paper also explores a community-run DL that offers a different model for consideration and further study.

Keywords: Digital Archives · Japanese Americans · *Nikkei*
Cultural heritage preservation · Ethnic identity · Japanese
Community informatics · Digital cultural memory initiatives
Cultural memory and digital heritage
Socio-technical aspects of digital libraries

1 Introduction

This paper examines Digital Libraries (DL) dealing with the Japanese American experience from an ethnographic perspective. Fetterman (2008) defines Ethnography as "the art and science of describing a group or culture;" adding, "The ethnographer enters the field with an open mind, not with an empty head." Ethnographic research, when used in sociology or anthropology, usually involves fieldwork, but for DL research, we believe this approach along with textual analysis and document analysis can be applied to attempting to critically understanding content and context of collections. This paper (1) explores one pioneering DL project in the United States related to the Japanese American experience, (2) explores what type of content this DLs presents and what perspectives it uses. We then (3) apply some social science questions focusing on Japanese American agency over their history. We are examining DLs on the Japanese American experience because many pioneering DLs and Digital Archives were based on Japanese American materials. For those unfamiliar with Japanese American history, the following section offers a brief introduction.

© Springer Nature Switzerland AG 2018
M. Dobreva et al. (Eds.): ICADL 2018, LNCS 11279, pp. 179–184, 2018.
https://doi.org/10.1007/978-3-030-04257-8_17

1.1   The Japanese American Experience in Brief

The year 2018 marks 150 years since the first immigrants left Japan to come to Hawai'i. In the decades that followed several thousand ethnic Japanese, or Nikkei, migrated to the United States, Canada, and Latin America. Like many people of color, they were initially seen by European Americans as a source of manual labor, and denied equal rights. For example, Japanese immigrants were barred from citizenship (until 1952), as well as owning land in many states. These injustices, however, paled in comparison with their World War II experience, when over 120,000 were forcibly uprooted from their homes on the West Coast and incarcerated in concentration camps. It was not until four decades later that the U.S. government finally re-examined the causes of the wartime mass incarceration. A Congressionally appointed committee found that it was the result of racism and war hysteria rather than military threat, which led to an official apology and redress payments in the 1980s. Today, Japanese Americans represent less than one percent of the U.S, population; however, their experience is quite well represented in many American DLs. Let's now examine one of the earliest collections.

One of the earliest DLs is the Japanese American Relocation Digital Archives (JARDA), which was begun in 1998, only one year following the creation of the California Digital Library (CDL), which was a pioneering DL itself. It went online in 2000 as a combined effort of several University of California campuses in coordination with the development of the CDL, and the Online Archive of California (OAC), and later as part of Calisphere. JARDA was a pilot project. The librarians and archivists were actively engaged in establishing standards for metadata description, scanning, preservation, intellectual property at the same time they curted a massive corpus including thousands of photographs, audio recordings, transcripts, letters, and reports. This can be compared with other pioneering DLs that were more like small websites featuring a few "exhibits" in order to entice visits to a physical archive. For researchers, the most useful element was the detailed Encoded Archival Description (EAD)-based finding aids to archival collections. Over time these finding aids were enriched with more digitized content. JARDA eventually drew on collections from most UC campuses and even public and private libraries and archives across the state through CDL/OAC. The majority of materials though came from two UC system libraries that had the most important Japanese American history collections. UCLA had an amazing collection that the Japanese American Citizen's League (JACL) had gathered in the early 1960s to document various aspects of Japanese American life. Although this was a rich and varied collection, UCLA did not have signed permission to digitize parts of the collection, so the original bulk of JARDA materials came from UC Berkeley's impressive collection of materials on the WWII forced relocation held by the Bancroft Library. Some of the items also were restricted because they contained confidential reports on individuals who still may have been alive; however, the majority of the collection was easy to digitize – at least from the perspective of intellectual property rights since they were created by the United States government and thus were not subject to copyright. Funding for these initial projects were received by federal and state grants related to libraries and civil rights as well as private philanthropy. The JARDA portal contains a number of online exhibits as well as teaching plans.

JARDA continued to expand, and now includes a number of rich oral history interviews, such as the Japanese American Collections gathered by Dr. Art Hansen at the California State Fullerton Center for Oral and Public History. The Cal State Collections were later digitized with funding from the National Endowment for the Humanities and the National Park Service Japanese American Confinement Sites Grants Program. There were a number of other Oral History projects, often sponsored by local JACL chapters. These oral histories became a backbone for many local Nikkei history collections, although digitizing them sometimes proved challenging as not all interviewers secured signed release forms. One problematic example of this was Sacramento's project, which had transcripts at one repository and recordings at another. Besides the oral history recordings it is important to reflect that most of the JARDA collections are about what the United States government did to Japanese Americans rather than focusing on the lived experience of Japanese Americans.

2   Analyzing a Japanese American DL Collection

For the purpose of discussing our findings, we are breaking this into a few sections. First, we will start out with a rationalization for the importance of adopting a critical ethnographic lens to apply to DLs. We will then try to answer some questions on collections, focusing on explore differences among collections.

2.1   Thinking as Professionals or Social Scientists? or Both?

Digital Librarians, like the paper-based librarians before them, are primarily practical professionals working together to develop standards, share technologies and come up with better systems. However, what we rarely do is to take a critical lens and reflect on our own professional role, our content, and consider how this impacts society. The model was set by Melvil Dewey's "Library Economy" which taught librarians to select materials based on outside expert opinion. This changed to some extent with graduate education at the University of Chicago. As Richardson (1982) shows, Chicago scholars in the 1930s imported research methods from sociology, such as surveys, along with the social science norm of objectivity. The idea of objectivity was soon combined with librarian's support for neutrality as an ethical ideal, especially during periods like the McCarthy era, when librarians were challenged to provide various perspectives. Neutrality was thus codified into the profession's code of ethics. Although this thinking came from the social sciences, it was far removed from social sciences by the 2000s when postmodernists rejected the idea that any institution or individual could be unbiased, impartial, or objective, especially when dealing with complex issues such as race, class or gender. Scholars like Pawley (1998; 2006) brought this into librarianship, asking professionals to question basic assumptions about such core concepts as what is information, and what information is privileged.

A new generation of critical library theorists pointed out how in theory and practice, being neutral basically meant seeing the world from an upper class white male perspective. Critical librarianship has been embraced by librarians working with information literacy, digital humanities, and metadata/access, but there is still limited scholarship dealing with collections, and particular ethnic DLs. For some inspiration and questions, we can look at our sister profession, archival studies. Archivists have long been engaged in the difficult struggle of applying critical theory into archival theory and practice. This new research helps archivists to examine bias in selecting and prioritizing materials, bias in archival employment, and calling for archivists to critically reflect on how we process collections, such as using approaches from anthropology fieldwork to do self-reflection notes in finding aids.

Although there is an increasing body of literature dealing with the complex issue of race in libraries and information systems, very little focuses on the Asian American experience(s). This gap is precisely what we hope to begin to begin to explore in this paper, by reflecting on DLs dealing with the Japanese American experience. So, let's start exploring our research questions.

2.2 What Kinds of Materials Are on These Japanese American DLs? Do They Represent Japanese American Agency?

We originally intended to survey DLs to discern if they reflected Japanese American life or rather they were a record of what government did to Nikkei (in other words if they were largely from the government's eyes). Unfortunately, we did not develop a way of quantifying content in terms of authorship, provenance or agency, so we were unable to answer this. However, we believe digital librarians and users should consider authorship and agency in terms of evaluating materials and reflecting if they are representative of the ethnic experience. For example, most materials about the forced relocation of Japanese Americans certainly detail how it impacted them, but were not created by them. There is a need for digital librarians as well as users of digital collections to be able to critically examine the authenticity or representation of original materials. For example, we can consider the photographs of detained Japanese Americans taken by the War Relocation Authority (WRA). In the early days of the forced relocation, these photos could not have shown Japanese American agency since their cameras were confiscated during detention. Lane Ryo Hirabayashi (2009) offers a wonderful chapter critically examining photographs by a later WRA Nikkei photographer, pointing out that even when he took photos, he did so on assignment, and others captioned his work, changed meanings and interpretations. Digital librarians need to problematize such complex documents. Clearly, even materials by Japanese Americans during that period, even outside of detention, during the war knew that their actions were on a public stage, so these materials need to be treated with critical stance rather than simply scanned and posted online. This also applies equally to prewar Japanese government records since historians have pointed out that the Foreign Ministry often ignored or misrepresented immigrant community desires (Asato 2006). The writings of the late historian and activist Ichioka (1989) and anthropologist Hirabayashi (1999) can help us to problematize such primary source materials. Although they were focusing on using them in the print era, the need to apply a critical lens becomes even more important when DLs are online and available to all.

We hope that asking such questions, such questions using ethnographic reflection can make help sensitize digital librarians when selecting collections, and reflecting on how we present these primary documents; especially when they represent an ethnic group – and even more so in cases when that group was the subject of legal or social discrimination. Digital Librarians have an important role in preserving and providing access to our cultural heritage, so it is important that it is done in a way that helps digital librarians to work ethically. Ethnographic reflection can help us to work with different communities and understand how DLs can impact people.

2.3 Need for Further Research

This paper only starts to scratch the surface of developing an ethnographic lens to the study of Japanese American DLs. Further research could include questions from other user perspectives such as exploring the information needs of Japanese Americans. Analyzing teaching materials could be a basis for evaluation. One can also explore questions related to materials that are in Japanese and English in terms of searching, OCR transcription, translation, searching, and different cultural norms. Does that added cultural capital suggest different search terms or collection emphasis? Do DLs have to be created by people who share the same ethnic experience? There also is a possibility to develop more studies on the question of online representation of Asian American experiences in DLs. How do Japanese American DL collections differ compared with other DLs representing other ethnic diasporas, such as Chinese Americans, Jewish Americans, or more recent ethnic arrivals to the U.S., like Hmong? As this paper shows, once one accepts that DLs are not neutral and should be studied critically, just as one can deconstruct literature or political text, there is no limit to the possibilities of what can be studied within the world of DLs. Perhaps the only challenging part will be to balance our theoretical inquisitiveness with the practitioners' need to be able to create systems that help professional practitioners to work with real projects.

As historians, we would also be remiss if we did not call for further research on the individual DLs themselves including oral history interviews with librarians and archivists responsible for creating these early DLs as well as the earlier archive and oral history collections that made them possible. It also should be fascinating to do a more structured research on the information needs of historians and how these have changed since Stieg's pioneering work on the area in 1981; especially how Japanese American DLs have changed historiography and research practice in the decades since.

3   Conclusion

Within a half dozen pages it is hard to summarize some of our findings regarding Japanese American DL collections. We believe that the paper highlights the possibilities of the ethnographic lens to evaluate current practices of creating ethnic DLs. These can be contrasted with community-based DLs such as Densho. The debate over setting standards for Traditional Cultural Expressions (TCEs) within ALA, SAA, IFLA, and the WIPO suggest that this will remain a contested area and that digital librarians will need a deeper cultural understanding, including ethnographic grounding in order to provide more culturally relevant collections that preserve history, but also respect how these ethnic groups are represented in the online world. Such a framework could help them to better engaged with the communities they are covering.

References

Asato, N.: Teaching Mikadoism: The Attack on Japanese Language Schools in Hawaii, California, and Washington, 1919–1927. University of Hawai'i Press, Honolulu (2006)

Fetterman, D.M.: Ethnography. In: Given, L.M. (ed.) The SAGE Encyclopedia of Qualitative Research Methods, pp. 289–292. SAGE Publications Inc., Thousand Oaks (2008). http://dx.doi.org/10.4135/9781412963909.n150

Hirabayashi, L.R.: Japanese American Resettlement Through the Lens: Hikaru Carl Iwasaki and the WRA's Photographic Section, 1943–1945. University Press of Colorado, Boulder (2009)

Hirabayashi, L.R.: Politics of Fieldwork: Research in an American Concentration Camp. University of Arizona Press, Tucson (1999)

Ichioka, Y.: Views from Within: The Japanese American Evacuation and Resettlement Study. UCLA Asian American Studies Center, Los Angeles (1989)

Pawley, C.A.: Hegemony's handmaiden? The library and information studies curriculum from a class perspective. Lib. Q. **68**, 123–144 (1998)

Pawley, C.A.: Unequal legacies: Race and multiculturalism in the LIS curriculum. Lib. Q. **76**, 149–168 (2006)

Richardson, J.V.: The Spirit of Inquiry: The Graduate Library School at Chicago, 1921-1951. American Library Association, Chicago (1982)

Stieg, M.F.: The information needs of historians. Coll. Res. Lib. **42**, 549–560 (1981)

Exploring Information Needs and Search Behaviour of Swahili Speakers in Tanzania

Joseph P. Telemala$^{(\boxtimes)}$ and Hussein Suleman

Department of Computer Science, University of Cape Town,
Cape Town 7700, South Africa
josephmasamaki@gmail.com, hussein@cs.uct.ac.za

Abstract. Studies investigating the information needs and search behaviour of Swahili speakers are rare, and this correlates with little Swahili information available online and few tools to support its access. In this study, we explored the information needs of Swahili speakers to understand their search behaviour – search language and preferences of language of information among professional and ordinary citizens. We interviewed 11 library/information experts and Swahili language specialists from Tanzania. The results indicate that Swahili speakers are increasingly searching for information from the Web. Despite the fact that many of them are not competent in English, they preferred English to Kiswahili as their search language due to the relevant results they get. They claimed, furthermore, that outdated Swahili information and scarcity of Swahili documents on the Web were other reasons for them to prefer English.

Keywords: Swahili · Tanzania · Information needs · Search behaviour
Information retrieval

1 Introduction

Though not counted as one of the human basic needs, information is yet another important need for humans; they need it for socio-economic development. The best way to deliver it is arguably through the common language of people. Kiswahili (or Swahili), the only African language among the official languages of the African Union, is the national (official) language of three East African countries: Tanzania, Kenya and Uganda; and spoken in Burundi, D. R. Congo, Malawi, Rwanda, Mozambique, Zambia, Somalia and Comoros [14]. It is estimated to have up to 100 million speakers. Thus, this population and their use of information warrants study because of the scarcity of Swahili information online. We used the case study of Tanzania because of its potential large number of speakers compared to other countries.

The survey of information needs and search behaviour from key informants presented in this paper was done with the broader aim of developing a Swahili information retrieval system. In particular, we wanted to: (1) uncover the search language preferences and the associated reasons from the people being investigated; and (2) discover the language of information preferences and reasons among professionals and citizens using opinions of the people under investigation.

M. Dobreva et al. (Eds.): ICADL 2018, LNCS 11279, pp. 185–190, 2018.
https://doi.org/10.1007/978-3-030-04257-8_18

2   Related Works

A number of works related to information needs and search behaviour exist for mobile users [2, 8, 9]; for nurses, medical doctors and physicians [3, 15]; for rural residents [7]; and for entertainment [4, 10]. However, the available literature on Swahili speakers are based on specific sectors such as agriculture [1, 5, 11]; informal sectors [6]; health [13]; and rural societies [12]. These works' foci were to identify the types and sources of information people want without paying attention to the language of information or assuming the language of information as an obvious variable. To the best of our knowledge, there is no study that analyzes the general information needs with respect to Swahili language or with the ultimate intention of developing an information retrieval system as an intervention, except for music IR [10]. Lack of comprehensive literature on the general public of Swahili speakers was the reason for us to conduct this survey.

The paper contributes threefold to the literature: (1) raising awareness on the information needs from the Web for Swahili speakers; (2) uncovering the search behaviour, based on language preferences; (3) and establishing grounded evidence of the need for building Swahili information retrieval systems.

3   Methodology

3.1   Participants

The study involved a total of 11 participants – 9 librarians/information scientists from 3 public and 2 university libraries as well as 2 Swahili specialists from the National Council of Kiswahili (*Baraza la Kiswahili la Taifa* – BAKITA, in Kiswahili). Librarians/information scientists were presumed to represent the general public of information searchers; assumed to have detailed knowledge about information and searching practice and are well-informed about their customers of information in libraries. On the other hand, Swahili specialists represented the general public of Swahili speakers.

3.2   Data Collection and Analysis

Participants were recruited through emails and phone calls and finally interviewed using Skype. The interviews were all conducted in Kiswahili, taking an average time of 25 min per participant; and recorded using a third party freeware tool called MP3 Skype Recorder. The interview schedule consisted of three major parts (see Table 1). The conversations were transcribed manually as there were no compelling tools for Swahili transcription, then translated to English. We followed a qualitative text analysis procedure, to group responses, code them and generate themes.

Table 1. Major parts of the interview schedule

Category	Variable	Measurement
Demographic information	Job title/position	Open-ended
	Work experience	Open-ended
	Previous job	Open-ended
	Relation of the previous job to the current job	Open-ended
Search behaviour	Search language	English/Kiswahili
	Reasons for the choice of such language	Open-ended
	Relevance of Swahili results	Open-ended
	Reasons for such results	Open-ended
Needs and uses of Swahili information	Swahili information needs among professionals	Open-ended
	Swahili information needs among ordinary citizens	Open-ended

4   Results and Discussion

4.1   Demographic Information

Out of the 9 librarian participants: 3 had administrative positions such as regional librarians and head of sections; 2 undertook teaching in library and information studies programs; and 4 were librarians and library officers. Meanwhile, the 2 language experts identified themselves as language investigators. Only 1 participant had less than 5 years of working experience; 5 had up to ten years; 3 had between 10 and 20 years; and the other 2 had worked for over 20 years.

4.2   Respondents Behaviour on Web Search

All the 11 participants admitted to using Web search engines in searching for information. They further unveiled that, provided the results are in the language they understand, they do not care about the language of the engine's interface. All participants except one use both English and Swahili languages in their searches for information, though admitting to prefer English to Swahili. One participant never used Kiswahili in any of his searches on the Web. The reasons for preferring English to Kiswahili, as stated by most of the participants, are that: English has *"reviewed and standard information"* [08]; it is quick to get English information that is relevant, compared to Kiswahili that results to the waste of time in searching. Kiswahili was said to be mostly used when: the context of information sought is local; searching for information not related to profession/jobs; and the searcher has difficulty with English terminology.

Participants identified the driving forces for the dynamics in the language of search as: the information need at hand; type of the task, and the information context. One participant noted that a language switch can be a search technique, *"But you can search things in English and you feel like, I can't get enough materials that I want or they are almost irrelevant, especially when the search context is in Tanzania. In that situation you simply have to switch to Kiswahili and see if you can get relevant information"* [(08)].

Findings: Web is an important source of information to many information searchers of today, and the general Swahili speaking public is interested in Web search engines. Further, searchers are typically interested in language of the results (content) and not the interface language of search engines. Both English and Swahili languages are used in searching, with users preferring English to Kiswahili, believing that English information is up to date and relevant. Context of information sought and language competence influences the search language.

4.3 Searching Using Swahili Language

3 participants were very convinced that they get relevant results when searching using Kiswahili. The remaining 7 had mixed views on the relevance of the results; some saying it depends on the precision of the query and others saying the results are insufficient, imprecise and sometimes completely irrelevant.

Scarcity of Swahili documents on the Internet was viewed as the major reason for unsatisfying results. There are a few authors in Swahili, most especially in specialized disciplines such as medicine – *"sometimes those who write don't publish their works online"* [(07)]; probably *"the authors and experts haven't seen the importance of making books in Swahili"* [(07)]. Again, *"forget about documents on the Web, look at the books for instance, when you come to our library, there are a few Swahili books as if we are not Swahili speakers"* [(07)]. Hence, searchers have very limited choices to explore. Search techniques and query formulation skills were identified as other reasons; searchers do not know what exactly they are searching for, so they create vague queries. Language proficiency of the searcher; outdated Swahili information; and searching from dedicated sources such as library directories, which have absolutely no or few Swahili documents were identified as other reasons.

Findings: Many Swahili searchers do not get relevant results or are not satisfied with the results because of: scarcity of Swahili documents on the Web; poor search techniques; language incompetence; and outdated Swahili information on the Web. Further, there are few Swahili authors on professional Swahili contents and/or they do not publish their works on the Web.

4.4 Needs and Uses of Swahili Information in the Society

Assuming they were professionals in other fields – such as accountants, medical doctors or engineers – or having attended such people, participants were asked their thoughts on whether they would need English or Swahili information in their jobs. 3 participants strongly argued that there is no place for Swahili information. The remaining 8 needed a combination of information in both languages with the preference for English information, just like the search language. Stated reasons for English information preference include the fact that professional acquired their training in English; it is hard to learn new professional terminology in Swahili for use in their searches; there is no or little scientific and professional information in Swahili as well; and English is also an official language, with lots of government documents and communications. Kiswahili information was said to be desirable when there is a need to deliver information to the public – popular science – in which a simple or indigenous language is required; and works that require writing reports in Kiswahili.

On the other hand, participants were asked their views on their requirements for Swahili information as ordinary citizens. Interestingly, none of them wanted English information! Moreover, in a multilingual country such as Tanzania, all participants perceive that Swahili information is more important and needed than English. *"If you want to verify that, look at daily English newspapers, they are very few! And the number of copies they publish is relatively small, if they print much, they will get loss"* [10].

The major reason stated by most of our participants that support the requirement of Swahili information among citizens is poor English competency, *"because of your low education and maybe many terminologies you know are in Kiswahili. So, what you do is searching for Swahili information most of the time. Your English terminology are limited"* [01].

Findings: Many professionals use both English and Swahili information, preferring English the most. Getting Swahili information for expertise practice is hard, however, it is needed by professionals in undertaking popular science and delivering services to the public. Swahili information is highly needed by ordinary citizens who are competent in Swahili.

5 Conclusions

We explored the information needs and search behaviour of Swahili speakers in Tanzania, focusing on: identifying their search language preferences and their preferences on language of information in daily use. The results indicate that the demand for Swahili information from the Web is high, most especially among the ordinary citizenry. Unfortunately, they find themselves mostly using the English language in searching for information. Relevant results are among the factors motivating them to use English. However, participants reported that many ordinary citizens are less educated with limited English vocabulary to enable them search effectively in English. Highly education Swahili speakers successfully code-switch to English to find relevant information to meet their professional needs, unlike the less formally-educated. The latter group is the focus of future work, to develop specific interventions to bridge this gap, especially in human developmental contexts.

Acknowledgements. This research was partially funded by the Hasso Plattner Institute (HPI), the National Research Foundation (NRF) of South Africa (Grant numbers: 85470 and 88209) and University of Cape Town. The authors acknowledge that opinions, findings and conclusions or recommendations expressed in this publication are that of the authors, and that the NRF accepts no liability whatsoever in this regard.

References

1. Bernard, R., et al.: Assessment of information needs of rice farmers in Tanzania; A case study of Kilombero District. Morogoro. Libr. Philos, Pract (2014)
2. Church, K., Smyth, B.: Understanding mobile information needs. In: Proceedings of the 10th International Conference on Human Computer Interaction with Mobile Devices and Services - MobileHCI 2008, p. 493 (2008)
3. Clarke, M.A., et al.: Information needs and information-seeking behaviour analysis of primary care physicians and nurses: a literature review. Health Inf. Libr. J. 30(3), 178–190 (2013)
4. Cunningham, S.J., et al.: An ethnographic study of music information seeking: implications for the design of a music digital library. In: Proceedings of the 3rd ACM/IEEE-CS Joint Conference on Digital Libraries, pp. 5–16 ACM/IEEE - CS, Houston (2003)
5. Elly, T., Silayo, E.E.: Agricultural information needs and sources of the rural farmers in Tanzania a case of Iringa rural district. Libr. Rev. 62(8/9), 547–566 (2013)
6. Ikoja-Odongo, R., Ocholla, D.N.: Informal sector entrepreneurs: the uganda experience. Libri. 54, 54–66 (2004)
7. Islam, M.S., Ahmed, S.M.Z.: The information needs and information-seeking behaviour of rural dwellers: a review of research. IFLA J. 38(2), 137–147 (2012)
8. Kassab, D., Yuan, X.: Understanding the information needs and search behaviors of mobile users. Inf. Res. 17(4), 3 p. (2012)
9. Komaki, D. et al.: How does mobile context affect people's web search behavior?: A diary study of mobile information needs and search behaviors. In: International Conference on Advanced Information Networking and Applications, AINA, pp. 245–252 (2012)
10. Lee, J.H., Downie, J.S.: Survey of music information needs, uses, and seeking behaviours: preliminary findings, pp. 441–446. Pompeu Fabra University (2004)
11. Lwoga, E.T., et al.: Information needs and information seeking behaviour of small-scale farmers in Tanzania. Innov. J. Appropr. Librariansh. Inf. Work South. Africa 40, 80–103 (2010)
12. Mtega, W.P.: Access to and usage of information among rural communities: a case study of kilosa district morogoro region in tanzania. Partnersh. - Can. J. Liebrary Inf. Pract. Res. 7(1), 1–13 (2012)
13. Pakenham-Walsh, N., Bukachi, F.: Information needs of health care workers in developing countries: a literature review with a focus on Africa. Hum. Resour. Health. 7, 30 (2009)
14. Thompson, I.: About World Languages. http://aboutworldlanguages.com/swahili
15. Younger, P.: Internet-based information-seeking behaviour amongst doctors and nurses: a short review of the literature: review article. Health Info. Libr. J. 27(1), 2–10 (2010)

Bilingual Qatar Digital Library: Benefits and Challenges

Mahmoud Sayed A. Mahmoud and Maha M. Al-Sarraj[✉]

UCL-Qatar, Qatar National Library, Doha, Qatar
{mahmoud.mahmoud.17,maha.al-sarraj.17}@ucl.ac.uk

Abstract. Large digital libraries often require designing a multilingual digital platform for their users. The multilingual access to materials still presents substantial challenges to the digital library designers. Taking the example of the Qatar Digital Library (QDL), we explore some of the tools for bilingual access and reflect on further ways of creating bilingual metadata records for QDL.

Keywords: Digitization · Case studies · Arabic · Digital libraries
National libraries · Cataloging · Indexing · Archives management
Bilingual collections

1 Background

In this work in progress paper we explore the bilingual access to digital resources in Arabic language from the Qatar Digital Library project. Qatar Digital Library launched in 2014 through a collaboration between the Qatar National Library and the British Library to provide an open access to state-of-the-art digital resources, which pertain to the rich history, heritage, and culture of Qatar including the entire Gulf region. Taking this example as a starting point we reflect of creating bilingual metadata for QDL which can be of interest to anyone dealing with bilingual access to digital libraries. English and Arabic are among the preferred languages for the development of this project. Arabic is the natural choice due to the nature of the materials and the anticipated audience of Humanities scholar based in the Gulf region while English is a preferred language due to its popularity among international users who might lack knowledge of Arabic. The bilingual nature of the resource is also mirrored in the outreach activities including social media presence via Twitter @BL Qatar Partnership, and their official blog [8].

2 Methodology

In our work we are using the theory of thesaurus-based interface design combined with the principles of rich-prospect browsing to give every user the ability of usage in their local language [1]. Exploring some of the popular current approaches to bilingual indexing, cataloging, and retrieval in digital collections, we recommends a model of creating bilingual parallel records, which combines translation by experts with the use

© Springer Nature Switzerland AG 2018
M. Dobreva et al. (Eds.): ICADL 2018, LNCS 11279, pp. 191–194, 2018.
https://doi.org/10.1007/978-3-030-04257-8_19

of controlled vocabulary and mapping for those who do not understand Arabic. More importantly, we examine the current approaches to bilingual cataloging, indexing and retrieval in QDL's digital collections based on IAMS (Integrated Archives and Manuscript System), and present examples of parallel records that combines translation with controlled vocabulary mapping as described in [6].

3   Challenges in Multilingual Digital Library Design

Creating parallel records and metadata descriptions with a combination of translation and vocabulary mapping is very important and beneficial for designing and describing digital collections presenting materials from a culture which main language is different from the popular European languages [2]. The scholarly literature explores different approaches to multilingual representation of digital collections. For example [7] focuses on the thesauri applications in three main functions of digital libraries – searching, browsing, and indexing. Shiri *et al.*, further explore thesauri use in the case of T-saurus and its application in the searching visual user interface [4]. Furthermore, Stanković *et al.* address how terminology search is applied in multilingual and bilingual thesaurus-based access to digital [5]. Based on this preliminary work, thesauri are a popular and vital tool in bilingual indexing, cataloging, and retrieving digital library platforms.

   However, all these examples come from languages other than Arabic and its specifics need to be taken into considerations when constructing bilingual digital resources in English and Arabic. In the area of digital libraries of Arabic materials additional area which had not been addressed in detail is the analysis of needs of different user segments – those proficient in Arabic and those who are interested in the culture but do not have sufficient Arabic language skills. The previous work on QDL involved representing Arabic in transliteration. This currently creates an interesting issue, how to prepare metadata of the existing digital objects which would include the proper original names and terms which had been transliterated on the earlier project stages. A new design for the Qatar Digital Library has the ambition to give users access to the present and past maps about the Gulf Region, access to handwritten documents, newspapers, and photographs among other vital historic records and this expansion of the types of digital material also requires handling the bilinguality of this collection.

   Multilingual digital libraries face complexity in data management, and confusing numbers of encoding schemes among other challenges. In fact, Diekema argues that even in a monolingual retrieval context, the synonymy as well as the lexical complexity may impact the information retrieval process [3]. As a result, these challenges impact the search process in multilingual and even in monolingual digital libraries. Stiller *et al.* describe how Europeana uses static metadata in some 31 languages combined with the choice of the preferred interface language, which is available from a drop-down menu [6]. They recommend that Europeana should avoid mixing languages in the delivery of query responses because this causes confusion to users, especially to new users, and there are multiple instances of cross-language ambiguity.

   Accordingly, the major challenge QDL faces relates to the fact that QDL project is dealing with documents dating back to 20th c., and as a result, some of the place-names may have changed. Moreover, the staff working on the project has to ensure that they do not only provide, but also adopt accurate Arabic translation of the place-names, idioms, and terms that they encounter during translation process. In doing this, QDL will have provided a reliable source of information for their users. Currently QDL ensures that its portal users can find the keywords they are searching, by mainly utilizing lists of official websites, as well as websites designed for place-names, and maps like Geonames. The retrieval of cross-language information in multilingual digital libraries requires translation. In this case, the errors which may arise during translation may affect the search of information in multilingual digital libraries. To maintain consistency in QDL Portal, QDL has a term base, that is used in referring to for phrases or words because sometimes a word or a phrase in a specific context has a different meaning from the one in the term base. Thus, it is always vital that attention is given to the context in which phrases or words occur. All these details are highlighted in the screenshots on Figs. 1 and 2.

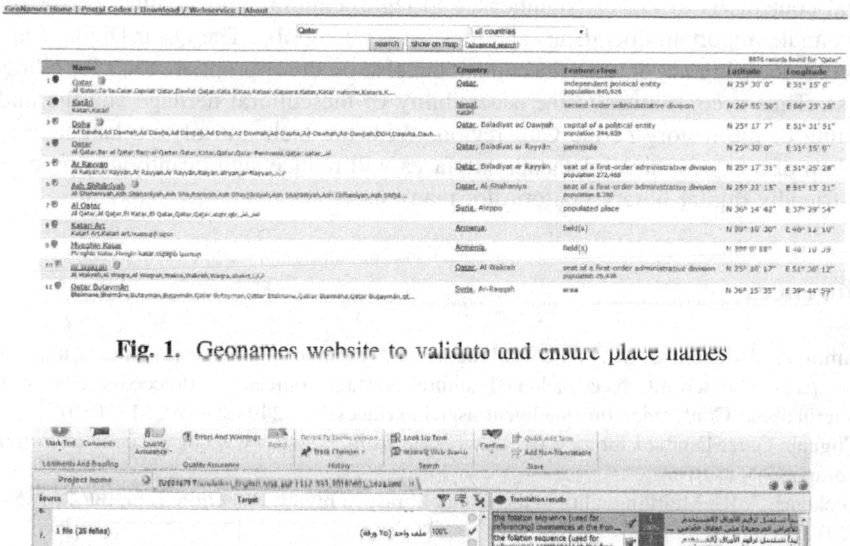

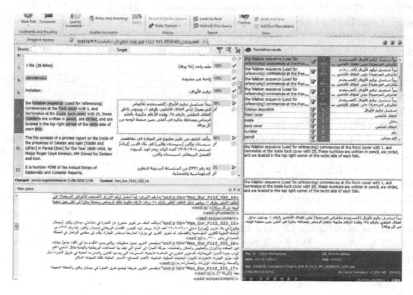

Fig. 1. Geonames website to validate and ensure place names

Fig. 2. memoQ software

4 Conclusion

QDL is currently aiming at finding further ways of presenting multilingual content, and at the same time making sure that the user experience is positive. Within QDL, the creation of multilingual metadata records is still at an early phase of development which is still ideal for a thorough planning on how to best address all these issues. Although QDL multilingual digital platform is under development, it is already facing various challenges that affect the experience of its users which require further thorough study.

Further research and development need to be undertaken more so concentrating on the development of the interface, and any problem or challenger within the interface design has to be corrected. With time, user feedback will play a key role in shaping any improvement in all the future interface versions. These improvements and adjustments will not only future QDL interface decisions, but will also lead to changes in the future conceptual framework of the entire project for even best user experiences ever.

In the contemporary world of technology, bilingual and multilingual access to digital contents is of critical significance to legal, cultural, and political personalities who handle important documents and files across the globe. The Qatar Digital Library project is focusing not only on the content but also on the appropriate tools for bilingual access. Thus it contributes to the accessibility of the cultural heritage and the understanding of the history of the Gulf region. With the inclusion of two languages, the problem of using multiple metadata interfaces will reduce significantly and promote a user-friendly digital library platform for many users.

References

1. Amin, A., Hildebrand, M., van Ossenbruggen, J., Hardman, L.: Designing a thesaurus-based comparison search interface for linked cultural heritage sources. In: Proceedings of the 15th International Conference on Intelligent user Interfaces, pp. 249–258. ACM (2010)
2. Cogapp: Qatar Digital Library (2017). Accessed from. https://www.cogapp.com/qatar-digital-library/
3. Diekema, A.R.: Multilinguality in the digital library: a review. Electron. Libr. **30**(2), 165–181 (2012)
4. Shiri, A., Ruecker, S., Doll, L., Bouchard, M., Fiorentino, C.: An evaluation of thesaurus-enhanced visual interfaces for multilingual digital libraries. In: Gradmann, S., Borri, F., Meghini, C., Schuldt, H. (eds.) TPDL 2011. LNCS, vol. 6966, pp. 236–243. Springer, Heidelberg (2011). https://doi.org/10.1007/978-3-642-24469-8_25
5. Stanković, R., Krstev, C., Vitas, D., Vulović, N., Kitanović, O.: Keyword-based search on bilingual digital libraries. In: Calì, A., Gorgan, D., Ugarte, M. (eds.) KEYSTONE 2016. LNCS, vol. 10151, pp. 112–123. Springer, Cham (2017). https://doi.org/10.1007/978-3-319-53640-8_10
6. Stiller, J., Gäde, M., Petras, V.: Multilingual access to digital libraries: the Europeana use case/Mehrsprachiger Zugang zu Digitalen Bibliotheken: Europeana/Accès multilingue aux bibliothèques numériques: Le cas d'Europeana. Inf.-Wiss. Prax. **64**(2–3), 86–95 (2013)
7. Sunny, S.K., Angadi, M.: Evaluating the effectiveness of thesauri in digital information retrieval systems. Electron. Libr. **36**(1), 55–70 (2018)
8. Untold Lives blog: http://blogs.bl.uk/untoldlives/. Accessed 26th June 2018

Digital Preservation Effort of Manuscripts Collection: Case Studies of *pustakabudaya.id* as Indonesia Heritage Digital Library

Revi Kuswara[✉]

indonesiaheritage.org, Bandung, Indonesia
revikuswara@gmail.com

Abstract. The glorious past of Indonesia culture and histories lies in the ancient manuscripts and inscriptions. Cultural heritages include rich information related social, historical and cultural. The Manuscripts & inscriptions collection are consist of various region letter with language, containing various thinking, erudition, customs and tradition with past society behavior that being nation asset value. Affected by climate, environmental and other factors, some valuable heritage information is threatened through destruction or disappearance and some is still not utilized. The development of information of technology has shown its significant role in large and fast digitization and publication. Digitization process result can store information in digital format therefore prolonging the life of the heritage items. Drafts temporary this is new get attention from certain person or group of research, especially philologist, librarians, students and public interest. *pustakabudaya.id* has initiated as one of the places to give library service and information to preserve nation culture work result for public digital access.

This article will discuss about how to collect, digitization process, storage, and online publication of manuscripts, and other cultural object in formatting of digital.

Keywords: Digitization · Digital preservation · Manuscripts · Inscriptions Cultural heritage

1 Background

Indonesia as the largest archipelago country consisting of 17.504 islands scattered across the vast archipelago has more than 300 ethnic groups with ethnic or cultural diversity owned. Manuscript and Inscriptions as one of the cultural heritage associated with the life of ethnic groups and civilizations created by our ancestors many centuries ago in the form of writing and painting with a variety of characters such as Javanese, Balinese, Sundanese, Acehnese, Batak, and so on with the style or flow certain traditional arts as outlined in various media such as on paper, palm leaves, bark, animal skins, rattan, bamboo, clay, ceramic or dluwang. Old age is likely to lead to fragile physical condition as a result of poor quality materials or media used. In addition to

© Springer Nature Switzerland AG 2018
M. Dobreva et al. (Eds.): ICADL 2018, LNCS 11279, pp. 195–200, 2018.
https://doi.org/10.1007/978-3-030-04257-8_20

storage and environmental conditions that do not fit as well as the treatment of users that can accelerate the process of frailty and physical damage to the original manuscript.

The manuscript collection is one of the mainstays of the national library which is a distinguishing feature of the library research that differentiate the function with other types of the library. Until now the national library has collection approximately 9.870 titles of the manuscripts. Most of the manuscripts are owned by the original that are not duplicated, are written for specific purposes in a very limited environment. Due to the limited number and distribution is often difficult for users who need it.

The informations can be used in manuscripts are distributed to transform into other media in various ways. Transformation effort is commonly done today is in the form of micro (microform) and digital (digital form). Both types of media as the preservation of library materials in principle aims to preserve the physical content and information. In the National Library of Indonesia there are various kinds of library materials that are classified as manuscripts in the original form or transfer media comprising:

(a) **The original of Manuscripts**

In ASEAN countries area, Indonesia has the largest collection of manuscripts stored at the National Library in various forms of handwriting contained in various media such as paper, palm leaves, dhaluang, bark, animal skins, rattan, bamboo, clay, and ceramics. The contents of manuscripts are about the story of the king, traditional ceremonies, medicine, charms, incantations repellent reinforcements and so on. To maintain the physical integrity of the manuscript was kept well in certain rooms with air conditioning appropriate to avoid damage or quickly obsolete (Fig. 1).

(b) **Printed library materials (print media)**

In addition to the original script there is also a collection of library materials in printed form that has taken over the script and transliteration. Although still not enough texts have been reproduced, but this way is quite effective in terms of preserving the text informa-

Fig. 1. Original manuscripts collection

tion is meant to be read and studied by users without the necessary tools such as the micro as well as its digital media format. Through the print media is full of information conveyed in the form of text and images can be stored into the media a better condition than the original text media.

(c) **Library of Recorded Material (electronics)**

Than through print media, manuscripts library materials can also be recorded to sound or visual recording media electronically (audio-visual). Media required to store such records, audio tapes, video discs as well as in form. For users who will use electronic aids needed to hear and see the tape library materials. Recording media in electronic form can be duplicated and disseminated to users.

Use of recording media library materials usually by way of recording the readings of translations of manuscript. There is also added to the musical instruments as a complement such as gamelan, angklung and other traditional music depending on the area where the manuscript originated.

(d) Media Library Material Transfer form Micro (Microfiche/microfilm)

Another effort to make the preservation of manuscripts is to do the transfer in the form of micro-media. The medium used is to use a sheet of black and white films that can only be read or displayed through a tool called Microfiche Reader. Through this medium of information contained in manuscript can last up to over 100 years when stored and used media with appropriate procedures. The permanent tool used is the microfiche reader. There is no change in form and function model to keep up with technology like computer hardware. So that preservation efforts by using the micro-media is the best way into the present. Not easy because of the tendency of each agency has the tools to create and display microfiche media. The need for coordination and cooperation in terms of its use.

(e) Digital Material Form

Until now the development of information technology with the Internet as a popular medium for accessing all kinds of digital information without being limited by space and time, be a good alternative for the preservation of library materials, especially for the collection of manuscripts and other library materials such as books, newspapers and maps. Compared with the forms of print media, electronic and micro in order to make the preservation of library materials for the control of the multimedia into digital form is able to package and deliver a more interesting look to replace the originals without reducing the content of the information available.

The advantages of this digital media for its users because the system can be easily and quickly disseminated globally and can provide visual information in a more interactive and communicative.

2 Digital Media as Library Material Preservation Efforts

With the development of digital technology and information currently there are several advantages to be gained by each agency to implement it. Especially for libraries, museums and archival institutions, every source of information the collection can be easily accessed by all users without any intervention done even though distance. It is undeniable that digital technology should be applied as needed. Through digital media will reduce the risk of loss of such valuable resources. So we need long-term planning and investment to make the effort.

Another advantage for users, especially academics and researchers can facilitate the process of finding the necessary resources through a range of facilities the search engines. Unlike the case when the source material in the form of printed information is still manual, there are limitations for anyone to be able to obtain it. Any institution that will conduct the transfer of digital media as an effort of maintenance sources of information and library materials will certainly face challenges and considerable risk. Especially in matters relating to finance the budget is quite large. As for the provision of support to the preparation of the formation of work teams involved. For that we need a sustained investment effort, that should be done gradually so that the load is too heavy to make it happen.

3 Workflow of Digital Preservation

Here is an illustration workflow settings that had been implemented by the National Library of Indonesia in an effort to make the process of digital preservation of library materials.

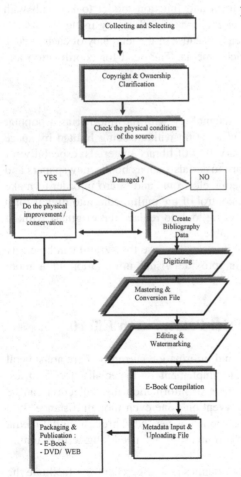

Explanation

1. Collecting and selecting the source material library materials will be made over the process of digital media. To obtain the source material library materials can be obtained from the internal and external institutions:
   a. Internal: a collection of library materials are already available at these institutions. For example, when the library resource materials library materials obtained from the central services and information.
   b. External: a collection of library materials from the environment outside of the institution e.g. museums, libraries elsewhere, private collection, or other agencies through cooperative agreements.
2. Clarify copyright and ownership of the source material library materials to be processed. When it is a public domain or the possession of the institution itself is no longer carried the written permission of the authors or publishers concerned.
3. Check the physical condition of the source material library. If there is damage or it will be bad for the

source material, if done over the media, such as when the script is done scanning the original condition would be like burning paper the influence of light radiation generated. In doing this conservation process can be carried out in collaboration with a special division to handle this.

4. Any source that has accumulated a collection of bibliographic data recordings were made in order to know the exact number and status.

5. Process over the media, such as the scanning of sheets of manuscripts and photographs in printed form or from the source slides and microfilm.

6. From the results of the transfer media or the results obtained by scanning a digital file with resolution high enough to be used as a master file. Furthermore, for purposes of editing and publication of the conversion process is carried into the appropriate file types, such as master file of the form of a TIFF or RAW format is copied into JPEG or GIF format.

7. Make the process of editing a digital file image/images, audio and video for purposes of packaging and publications. Editing done with the help of specialized applications such as Adobe Photoshop and Macromedia. Watermark provision needs to be done on each image is generated by adding a logo to a certain degree of transparency.

8. Compiling a file of each title consisting of several pages of manuscript or document that has done the editing and delivery of the watermark. Compilation format that is done can vary depending on the needs, for example in PDF format.

9. Metadata input process and upload digital files through the digital library or digital data management system. It is necessary to record any digital file collections that have been generated.

10. The process of packaging and publication of the resulting digital files into the E-Book media which can be accessed easily by its users. A common form of packaging is the use of disc media (disk) such as CD/DVD ROM which can be accessed by a stand-alone users.

4 *pustakabudaya.id* as the Indonesia Heritage of Digital Library System

The transfer media or digital preservation is done only the first step, then how the results of these efforts can be used by any user. In general, the function of this system is to facilitate the application retrieval its users to collect, manage and retrieve any digital information resources more effectively and systematically. In this case, the information relating to representation, storage, and access to resources required documentation. Within the scope of the current library and the museum has made efforts to catalog creation process (cataloging), index (indexing), acquisition, and OPAC *(Online Public Access Catalog)*, which serves to manage all sources of information and library materials owned printed.

But subsequent developments have made the effort associated with the administration and maintenance digital object itself. The need to develop a system that provides an integrated solution with the publication chain that includes the initial transfer media (digitization), the provision of indexes and metadata, collection management and user administration resources, and how to access them online via the web or through offline media available. To create a digital library system that serves as a medium for the publication of an online digital objects, must be pursued both the planning and development of technical and management.

5 Conclusion

To better preserve the cultural heritage of the nation which seeks to unify the work of libraries throughout the archipelago nation, it is necessary to conclude the following:

1. To further optimize the utilization of manuscripts by the community, especially among the younger generation there is need for awareness of the importance of conserving the nation's noble heritage by way of knowing and understanding the content of the manuscript content either through formal study and forums communities.
2. Make efforts to transfer digital media and compile to electronic book (E-Book) format, more than the text and the translation to be equally accessible in the archipelago.
3. Cooperation at the regional, national and international levels in terms of efforts to collect and save the manuscripts which is still widely spread in the community are also other sources that have been taken abroad. So it would be better if it is saved in the Museum and National Library.

References

1. Kuswara, R.: Alih Media Digital: Konsep Manajemen dan Teknis, National Library of Republic Indonesia (2008)
2. Kuswara, R.: Digital Library: Upaya Mengelola Informasi dan Pengetahuan di Era Digital, Heikelmedia (2011)
3. Dureau, J.M., Clements, D.W.G.: Principles for the Preservations and Conservations of Library Materials, The Haque, IFLA (1986)
4. Gardjito: Pendayagunaan Naskah Kuno Nusantara, National Library of Republic Indonesia (2005)

The General Data Protection Regulation (GDPR, 2016/679/EE) and the (Big) Personal Data in Cultural Institutions: Thoughts on the GDPR Compliance Process

Georgios Papaioannou[1]([⊠]) and Ioannis Sarakinos[2]

[1] University College London in Qatar, Doha, Qatar
g.papaioannou@ucl.ac.uk
[2] Athens, Greece

Abstract. This paper addresses GDPR in cultural heritage and memory institutions handling (Big) personal data. We discuss the compliance's necessity, common risk factors, needs to be taken into account, and we propose a GDPR process of phases and deliverables.

Keywords: GDPR · Heritage data · Big data

1 Introduction

The introduction of the General Data Protection Regulation (GDPR) has been a reality since the 25 May 2018, introducing rigorous obligations and big challenges. It is a new regulation centralizing all existing regulations on data protection and updating them for the digital age. As one can see at the *2018 reform of EU data protection rules* [1], organizations that process EU residents' personally identifiable information (including visitors to the EU) must ensure compliance with the rules set out in the regulation and the rights of individuals are greatly enhanced. Cultural heritage and memory institutions as handlers of (Big) personal data have (or should have) taken provision towards compliance.

2 Background

2.1 What Is Personal Data

Under the GDPR, personal data of a person include all data relating to a *living, natural person*. Specifically, personal data includes: "*Any information relating to an identified or identifiable natural person ('data subject'). An identifiable natural person is one who can be identified, directly or indirectly, in particular by reference to an identifier such as a name, an identification number, location data, an online identifier or one or more factors specific to physical, physiological, genetic, mental, economic, cultural or social identity of that natural person*" (art. 4 of the GDPR). GDPR also introduces an updated category of data, the so called "*special category of personal data*" (art. 9 of the

M. Dobreva et al. (Eds.): ICADL 2018, LNCS 11279, pp. 201–204, 2018.
https://doi.org/10.1007/978-3-030-04257-8_21

GDPR). It is an updated version of the previously, under Directive 95/46/EC, established category of "*sensitive personal data*", relating to personal data revealing racial or ethnic origin, political opinions, religious or philosophical beliefs, or trade union membership, genetic data, biometric data for the purpose of uniquely identifying a natural person, data concerning health, sex life and/or sexual orientation.

Cultural/memory organizations handle personal (Big) data, such as: name, identification number, address, telephone number, CV, social security number, genetic & biometric data, email address, employee or volunteer ID, login or physical access credentials, cookies, IP address, behavioral identifiers (e.g. geolocation), health data (e.g. disabilities, health records, treatments), opinions/preferences (e.g. political, cultural, religious, sexual and philosophical), criminal record, membership in cultural/memory organizations etc. Data relating to deceased people are regulated by national laws (GDPR Recitals 27, 158 & 160). Overall, data relating to employees, volunteers and/or visitors of a cultural/memory organization are all of GDPR interest. Processing relates to any operation or set of operations performed on personal data, whether or not by automated means (e.g. collection, recording, organization, structuring, storage, adaptation or alteration, retrieval, consultation, use, disclosure by transmission, dissemination or otherwise making available, alignment or combination, restriction, erasure or destruction). Processing for the purpose of the GDRP is everything from displaying to storing, both electronically and/or in physical form. Posting or displaying a photo of a natural person is also a processing activity.

2.2 The Necessity to Comply

Organizations in the area of cultural heritage and memory institutions are affected [2, 3], since they hold and generate (Big) personal data in need of processing and GDPR compliance [4]. As such, cultural and memory institutions need to comply with GDPR's main objective, i.e. to ensure that personal data are collected, processed and transferred lawfully. There have been attempts towards some guidelines to this end. An example is that of Shone [5] for cultural organizations in the UK belonging to the Association of Independent Museums. Also, the Network of European Museum Organisations (NEMO) prepared an one-hour webinar [6, 7]. There are also training sessions [8] and services addressed to cultural sector [9].

3 The GDPR Compliance Process

3.1 Common Risks Factors and Needs

Risk factors relate to (a) employees', visitors', volunteers', customers' and vendors' data collection, processing and storage processes, (b) personal data flows with third parties (partners, outsourcers, etc.), (c) paper-based records, and (d) sensitive personal data (e.g. employees', members' and friends' health and financial data, etc.) handling.

Cultural and memory organizations need to review and update the following: (a) *Marketing & Fundraising* activities. Direct marketing can only be done if one of the six lawful bases under Art. 6 of the GDPR apply. These are *consent, contract, legal obligation, vital interests, public tasks,* and *legitimate interests,* with consent and legitimate interests being the most regular ones. (b) *Amend their Code of Ethics, Collection and Privacy policies-notices* in order to be GDPR compliant, especially in regards to the information towards living, natural persons (visitors, employees, vendors etc.). (c) *Maintenance and display of collections* must be done lawfully. This should mean that collections in display must fall under at least one of the aforementioned six lawful bases. If this type of activity may be considered as "filing system" under the GDPR, special provisions must apply. (d) *Keeping documentation of collections* in a safe, secure and well organized environment. The same applies to *personal data storage* of employees, volunteers, object creators and/or third parties, whether in physical or electronic form. (e) *Transferring of items and the personal data of their creators* observing GDPR. Except from the agreement signed, consent needs to be sought by the creators. (f) *Archiving* process should be subject to technical and organizational measures which are in place in order to ensure, in particular, the principle of data minimization. (g) *Profiling of donors* must be coupled with the right of donors to request from the institution to refrain from screening activities as a way of selecting them. (h) *CCTV & Voice recording.* Appropriate notifications and documentations must be prepared and put in place for the lawful processing of data created through their use. (i) *Friends/Membership groups.* Museum and/or galleries tend to have membership and/or Friends groups, either as part of the institution or as separate entities. Individual consent to share and use personal data must be secured.

3.2 Phase-to-Phase Compliance Guide and Deliverables

The above must be achieved through a process called *GDPR compliance process.*

Phase 1 – Appointing a team of experts in the fields of legal, IT and Security, to perform the GDPR compliance process. Team's characteristics: knowledge on data laws, privacy laws, operations and specifics of cultural/memory organizations.

Phase 2 – Project setup and raising awareness within the cultural/memory organization (staff, employees and members of the board) on key GDPR aspects, requirements and needs. Deliverable: GDPR organization-specific education materials.

Phase 3 – Identification of personal data that the cultural/memory organization holds. This is usually done through a file called "Data Processing Activity Register" (art. 30 of the GDPR). Basically, the appointed team, assisted by each department of the cultural/memory organization ("Data Privacy Champions"), will review, identify and register what personal data each department holds, how, for how long, why etc. Deliverable: Data Processing Activity Register.

Phase 4 – Assessment of current GDPR compliance, i.e. assess current maturity levels against GDPR's requirements, understand risks, identify compliance gaps. Deliverables: Assessment summary and the Data Privacy Impact Assessment report (DPIA). DPIA is necessary in high risk cases, e.g. use of CCTV cameras.

Phase 5 – Addressing identified gaps and proposing actions. Deliverable: Measured compliance steps, identified gaps and proposed remediation actions.

Phase 6 – Implementation. The appointment of a Data Protection Officer (DPO) is advised, fulfilling GDPR compliance tasks and sustainability on a service contract.

4   A Concluding Remark

GDPR presents a great opportunity for cultural institutions to revise and improve the ways they handle (Big) personal data and information, develop competitive advantage and, ultimately, contribute towards creating personal data protection culture for the community in general. It is an opportunity that should not be missed.

References

1. 2018 reform of EU data protection rules. Official website of the European Commission, 16 July 2018. https://ec.europa.eu/commission/priorities/justice-and-fundamental-rights/data-protection/2018-reform-eu-data-protection-rules_en. Accessed 22 Sept 2018
2. White, B.: General Data Protection Regulation 2018 – Ready? Set? Go?. Cultural Heritage Institutions Privacy Alliance (CHIPA), 24 May 2018. https://www.privacyalliance.co.uk/2018/03/24/general-data-protection-regulation-2018-ready-set-go/. Accessed 17 July 2018
3. MGS blog: Don't Panic! 4 things to do now before GDPR [Blog post]. Museums Galleries Scotland Blog, 4 April 2018. http://www.mgsblog.org/connect/dont-panic-4-things-now-gdpr/. Accessed 16 July 2018
4. Zarsky, T.Z.: Incompatible: the GDPR in the age of big data. Seaton Hall Law Rev. **47**, 995–1020 (2017)
5. Shone, H.: Success Guide. Successfully managing privacy and data regulations in small museums. Association of Independent Museums (AIM), Ludlow (2017). https://www.aim-museums.co.uk/wp-content/uploads/2017/10/SG-9.pdf. Accessed 16 July 2018
6. NEMO: What Museums Need to Know to Comply with the New General Data Protection Regulation (GDPR), 02 February 2018. https://www.ne-mo.org/news/article/nemo/what-museums-need-to-know-to-comply-with-the-new-general-data-protection-regulation-gdpr.html
7. M+H Advisor: Advisor FREE Webinar GDPR – and what you need to know – The Resources, 30 November 2017. https://advisor.museumsandheritage.com/news/advisor-webinar-general-data-protection-regulation-need-know/
8. Korn, N.: Museums and their GDPR data protection obligations [Blog post], 22 May 2018. https://naomikorn.com/2018/05/22/museums-and-their-gdpr-data-protection-obligations/. Accessed 16 July 2018
9. Sutton, M.M., Ingram, H.: Data Protection and Art & Cultural Heritage, Collyer Bristol Law Firm website, 11 January 2018. https://www.collyerbristow.com/item/2156-data-protection-and-art-cultural-heritage. Accessed 16 July 2018

A Recommender System in Ukiyo-e Digital Archives for Japanese Art Novices

Jiayun Wang[1]([⊠]), Biligsaikhan Batjargal[2], Akira Maeda[3],
and Kyoji Kawagoe[3]

[1] Graduate School of Information Science and Engineering,
Ritsumeikan University, Kusatsu, Japan
gr0278vx@ed.ritsumei.ac.jp
[2] Kinugasa Research Organization, Ritsumeikan University, Kyoto, Japan
[3] College of Information Science and Engineering, Ritsumeikan University,
Kusatsu, Japan

Abstract. In the past decades, many digital archives are developed for storing cultural materials such as arts and books. Art Research Center (ARC) at Ritsumeikan University has developed digital archives for various Japanese ancient cultural materials. The ARC digital archive preserves a large amount of Ukiyo-e artworks. In this paper, we propose a recommender system that is suitable for the ARC Ukiyo-e digital archive, to help the users obtaining the interested Ukiyo-e artworks conveniently. The recommender algorithm is based on the user log data, which is easy to obtain and represents the user behaviors. The proposed method is named CARC, which uses restricted Boltzmann machine (RBM) for collaborative filtering to initialize the recommendation list, and then uses content-based filtering (CBF) for generating more explicit recommendation list. The proposed recommender system is effective to extract the pattern of users' behaviors and construct the recommendation list that fits the taste of users.

Keywords: Digital archive · Recommender system · Japanese cultural heritage Neural network · Restricted Boltzmann machine

1 Introduction and Related Works

The artwork Ukiyo-e is regarded as a traditional art that reflects the history of Japan. To preserve it, in recent years, Ukiyo-e prints are digitized and preserved in some digital archives, such as Ritsumeikan ARC (Art Research Center) Ukiyo-e Portal Database Search System (hereinafter referred to as ARC database) [1]. The existing search systems in digital archives of Ukiyo-e can be divided into two categories: (i) provide keyword search service; (ii) provide image search service. These ways of information retrieval can fulfill some of the users' needs, only when the users know exactly what they want and how to find the contents. However, for the general users who are unacquainted of keywords or images, it is difficult to find the interested Ukiyo-e by using existing search services.

© Springer Nature Switzerland AG 2018
M. Dobreva et al. (Eds.): ICADL 2018, LNCS 11279, pp. 205–209, 2018.
https://doi.org/10.1007/978-3-030-04257-8_22

Considering the increase of interest-driven users coming to use digital archives, we propose an RS (recommender system) to solve the problem described above. An RS filters out redundant information, as well as predicts interesting contents for the current user. This research focuses on the issue of developing recommendation algorithms of ARC Database.

To support the usage of those multimedia materials in digital archives, some interest-based applications are proposed. Bohnert et al. [2] proposed a keyword-based approach for predicting the interesting exhibits out from all the museum exhibits, to help museum visitors select personally interesting exhibits to view.

Recently, machine learning methods have achieved good results on the issue of predicting user preferences. Liang et al. [3] have developed a probabilistic rating auto-encoder to perform unsupervised feature learning and generate latent user feature profiles from a large-scale user-item rating data.

This research is the continuous work of our previous research [4], which indicates the effectiveness of applying restricted Boltzmann machine on the current issue.

2 Motivation and Problem Description

The current search system equipped on the ARC database mainly target experts but not the general users. However, there is also a potentially high need that users want to browse the ARC database for some general contents by interests.

The problems that exist in developing a recommendation algorithm can be described as below:

(i)   The sparseness problem in most of the RSs also exist in the ARC database. The amount of viewed contents is very few.
(ii) The data about user preference is insufficient. In this database, general users cannot sign up or log in to save their liked contents. Comments or ratings of Ukiyo-e prints are also absent.
(iii) Cold-start problem exists in this issue because of the lack of the user profile.

3 Proposed Method

3.1 Concept

To solve the problems that are indicated in the previous section, we propose a method named CARC (CBF After RBM for CF) combined by (i) RBM (restricted Boltzmann machine) for CF (collaborative filtering); and (ii) CBF (content-based filtering). The details of these two methods will be described later. We proposed a prototype of this method in a previous research [4]. The previous methods are to multiply the results of RBM and CBF to obtain the final prediction. In this paper, the improved method is proposed to calculate the CBF similarity by using the prediction results of RBM. Also, we propose a framework of the RS.

3.2 Framework of the Recommender System

In this system, some manually selected Ukiyo-e prints are shown to the user in advance. Then, the system will find the similar prints to what the user chooses. The proposed RS interacts with the user by asking the user's interests and making the recommendation. The recommendation made by the system is calculated by the CARC method.

3.3 Restricted Boltzmann Machine and Content-Based Filtering

RBM is a two-layer neural network consisting of a visible layer and a hidden layer [5]. It learns the probability distributions of training data and reconstructs the test data by the learned probability distributions, which is proved to effectively extract features on sparse dataset. Figure 1 describes the training data and learning procedure of the RBM in our system.

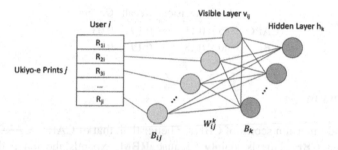

Fig. 1. The input of RBM is the view-frequency (R_{ij}) of users to the Ukiyo-e prints. The number of nodes in visible layer equals the number of the Ukiyo-e prints. The number of hidden layer nodes is set as 100. The number of the hidden layer has influence on the prediction of RMB, but we do not discuss it here, 100 is a often selected number. The RBM model can finally learn the probability distribution by updating the weights W_{ij}^k and biases B_{ij}, B_k.

We use CBF [6] to generate recommendations based on the categories of Ukiyo-e prints. If a user likes a certain print, the system will recommend the prints with similar categories. RBM makes recommendation based on the log data. It can be regarded as a model that learns all the users' behavior. Therefore, personality is not considered in RBM. We propose CBF to adjust the recommendation list to be personalized, because CBF makes recommendation by finding similar items of user interests (the selected prints).

4 Experiment

4.1 Dataset

The dataset includes the log data of 3,290 distinct IP addresses (it is viewed as distinct users) for 2,739 Ukiyo-e prints. Our previous study finds that, in this issue, the larger the training data is, the lower the MAE is. Since MAE leads to better result, we set the training data as a relatively large proportion, and the test data in RBM are used to calculate CBF value in the next step, we should ensure there is enough test data. Finally, we set the training/test proportion as 3,000 records for training, and 290 records for prediction.

4.2 Results

We use mean absolute error (MAE), precision score, recall score and coverage to measure the recommendation method. Here, the precision and recall are calculated at top 10.

We compare the proposed CARC method with conventional content-based filtering (Table 1).

Table 1. Comparison of CARC and CBF on four metrics

	MAE	Precision	Recall	Coverage
CARC	0.35	0.11	0.19	0.03
CBF	0.20	0.18	0.19	0.01

5 Conclusion

The MAE and precision scores of CBF are better than that of CARC. CARC has better coverage than CBF. This is mainly because RBM expands the range that can be recommended.

In the previous research, we found only using RBM method can predict whether a user likes a certain item, but cannot predict the ranking. In this paper, we proposed to add CBF to the RBM method to rank the recommendations, that will be useful in RS when providing users with the recommendation candidates. The method proposed in this paper has expanded the scope of recommendations a lot, but the quality of recommendation has not improved significantly. We will do further research on improving the recommendation quality in the future, by filtering the appropriate recommendations based on this research.

References

1. http://www.dh-jac.net/db/nishikie-e/search_portal.php?enter=portal
2. Bohnert, F., Zukerman, I.: Using keyword-based approaches to adaptively predict interest in museum exhibits. In: Nicholson, A., Li, X. (eds.) AI 2009. LNCS, vol. 5866, pp. 656–665. Springer, Heidelberg (2009). https://doi.org/10.1007/978-3-642-10439-8_66
3. Liang, H., Baldwin, T.: A probabilistic rating auto-encoder for personalized recommender systems. In: Information and Knowledge Management, pp. 1863–1866 (2015)
4. Jiayun, W., Kawagoe, K.: Ancient Japanese painting recommendation for non-Japanese novices. DEIM Forum (2018)

5. Zhang, S., Yao, L., Sun, A.: Deep learning based recommender system: a survey and new perspectives. arXiv preprint arXiv:1707.07435 (2017)
6. Pazzani, M.J.: A framework for collaborative, content-based and demographic filtering. Artif. Intell. Rev. **13**(5–6), 393–408 (1999)

User Experience

Tertiary Students' Preferences for Library Search Results Pages on a Mobile Device

Nicholas Vanderschantz(✉) ⒾⒹ, Claire Timpany ⒾⒹ, and Chun Feng

University of Waikato, Hamilton, New Zealand
{vtwoz,ctimpany}@waikato.ac.nz,
cf37@students.waikato.ac.nz

Abstract. Technology advancements and availability will result in library catalogues becoming more regularly accessed on small screen mobile devices in coming years with academics and students likely to be amongst the earliest adopters. There remain numerous unanswered questions regarding how to design library catalogues which offer effective library search on mobile devices. This broad research area requires the attention of HCI, design, and reading researchers alike. This paper begins to address the user needs of library patrons when searching for books on a mobile device. Recommendations for mobile library catalogue design and further research is provided.

Keywords: Book search · Digital library use · Library catalogue design
Mobile interface design

1 Introduction

Tertiary students frequently search for printed books and eBooks both within the physical library as well as outside that library. These book searches are typically conducted using a digital library catalogue with a range of large screen and small screen technologies. The design of library catalogue interfaces will impact user success as well as user preference and therefore we suggest there is a need to investigate how tertiary students are searching for and using books during their educational pursuits.

This paper expands on the work reported in Hinze et al. (2017) where we discussed the user habits and preferences of tertiary library patrons. Here we discuss our further investigation into the design of library search interfaces presented on mobile devices. A case study of present library catalogues and bookshop systems was used to inform the design of mobile interface prototypes. These prototypes were then used by students at two universities during an observed task study. Through this investigation we have identified mobile library catalogue features that impact user preferences.

2 Related Work

The work related to this investigation concerns the searching and browsing of digital libraries on mobile devices. The correlation of searching and browsing is discussed in the literature, for example Vemuri et al. (2006) identify that browsing and searching are

© Springer Nature Switzerland AG 2018
M. Dobreva et al. (Eds.): ICADL 2018, LNCS 11279, pp. 213–226, 2018.
https://doi.org/10.1007/978-3-030-04257-8_23

fundamentally different activities, but argue that both fulfil important roles. Early work reported that browsing the surrounding shelves for books related to a user's search is a common serendipitous technique (Morse 1971) used by information seekers in physical libraries (Bates 1989). More recently Cooper and Prager (2000) suggested that electronic retrieval of information may hinder these serendipitous opportunities and thus researchers (i.e. Su 2005) suggest interface design metaphors such as the bookshelf metaphor may support serendipity in digital environments.

With increased prevalence of digital information seeking on small screen devices investigations of the use and usability of mobile digital library interfaces have begun. Liu et al. (2015) analysed mobile services provided by academic libraries of 100 universities. Wu et al. (2018) considered the use of library interfaces across multiple devices. Paterson et al. (2011) studied student attitudes towards mobile library services while our related study (Vanderschantz et al. 2018) reviewed interface preferences of students for libraries.

The remainder of this section briefly outlines the pertinent literature regarding choosing books and the display of search results.

2.1 Choosing Books

Hinze et al. (2012) note that when choosing books from physical and digital libraries, book-seekers typically follow a process that involves four main steps. We expand their description of these steps slightly and describe to include digital book selection, while their original description discussed physical books: (1) identifying books of interest via the catalogue or on the shelf, (2) retrieving those books physically or digitally, (3) selecting the books which best meet the book-seekers needs and finally (4) accessing the content within the book. These steps are similar to those summarised in a study by McKay et al. (2012a) when looking at eBook selection in an academic library. They found that when people borrow or choose books from digital or physical libraries, their behaviour could be divided into three steps; gathering or collecting data to identify potential books, examining each book and evaluating relevance, then borrowing the books related to their information needs. Ross (2000) investigated choosing books for leisure reading rather than academic library search. That research suggests that when choosing books the process must include five relevant elements: reader's desired reading experience; alerts for new books available; the elements of a book that match the readers desired reading experience; the books clues to the reading experience that it offers; and the cost to the reader to get access to the book.

2.2 Display of Search Results

Shneiderman et al. (2000) suggest that central to the work of digital library researchers is the need to assist readers to find the resources they are looking for in a catalogue and arguably within a text. This requires investigation of how to design an overview of the information within the library or catalogue, how to create interfaces that users find intuitive, and usable, and how to effectively display search results for users.

The search results page (SRP) is crucial for information seekers during book seeking and browsing. The SRP provides book information, lists of options, as well as bibliographic data, all of which will assist the user in making an informed decision. Mi and Weng (2008) identified 10 important considerations for displaying the results of a book search that were often omitted from the interface or search result displays that they surveyed, including; item availability, book covers, intuitive navigation between results lists and individual records, and the ability to browse related results by call number.

There are few studies which have been conducted to understand preferences for the design of library interfaces. In one study, Merčun and Žumer (2008) compared six library catalogues and found that none provided the same range of benefits included in the Amazon search interface. They concluded that the best interfaces provided features such as relevance ranking, faceted navigation, and supported browsing in their search results. Vanderschantz et al. (2015) also conducted a paper prototype study investigating design preferences for personal eBook libraries on mobile devices. The results of their study found that visual display of the book cover, book content, metadata, and book-related information all influenced reader preferences regarding the visual presentation of the interface.

3   Case Study

In 2017 an audit of the catalogue interfaces for six university libraries, two city libraries, three book retail websites, and one eBook catalogue was conducted to identify common interface features. A single keyword search for the term "design" was undertaken in each interface, from which an audit of the search results pages (SRPs) and the book result pages (BRPs) of each of the 12 interfaces was conducted. The interfaces were reviewed on both a desktop computer screen and a tablet device with negligible visual difference. We identified and classified the SRPs into four common design metaphors.

The two universities in China used the Text/Title metaphor, which listed search results in a numbered or ordered list with very little or no visual display of supporting information. Date, author, and publisher information was supplied by one of these two interfaces, while only date information was supplied in the second interface.

The three universities in NZ and the single university in the UK used interfaces with the Title/Cover metaphor in a list view. A small book cover was positioned with the book title in a numbered or ordered list format. All instances of the Title/Cover metaphor also comprised bibliographic information including authors, dates, and publisher information. When a cover was not available in the system a generic icon was used that depicted if the item was a book, article, or another form of resource in the catalogue.

One public library, and the Google Books interface used the Intro/Summary metaphor. This interface presented typical bibliographic information as well as summary or introductory information related to the book or article. Visual information in the form of a book cover was also present for both interfaces.

The Large Cover metaphor was identified for the three book retail websites audited. There was emphasis on the presentation of the cover of the book as a focal point resulting in pages that were presented as a list with fewer entries visible on a single screen without scrolling. To combat this, two of the three interfaces presented result entries in a grid pattern rather than a vertical list. All three of these interfaces included the book title and author as textual information alongside the large cover image. Only one of the Large Cover interfaces contained publisher information in the grid formatted list results and a different Large Cover interface included date information in a vertical list.

All of the interfaces audited used a vertical scroll and paged presentation of the results. The formatting for all of the library interfaces was a vertical list. Visual separation was created by negative space, background colours in a zebra striping, or a horizontal rule between entries. The bookstore catalogues were the only interfaces to present information in a grid view. It was not uncommon for cover information to be missing and for interfaces to contain no visual information in the SRPs. The amount of bibliographic information displayed by the different interfaces and within the identified categories was inconsistent and appeared to depend greatly on software developers rather than on user requirements or needs. All interfaces moved from an SRP to a single BRP when an item was selected from the search results list.

The findings of this case study were used to inform prototype design of test material for the research discussed in the following sections.

4 Material Design

To develop testing material for this study a typical design process was followed Lawson (2006) explains that there is no single definition for what a design process is, but suggests that a design process involves the exploration of a range of potential solutions based on the problem that needs to be solved and the knowledge available. These potential solutions are refined to a point where they provide a solution to that problem. The process that was followed for this research was such that the design team first investigated and defined the problem, second developed initial design ideations, third developed and evolved the design ideations, and fourth iterated this process before settling on solutions to test. The findings of the visual audit of library and book retail interfaces along with findings derived from the related work were used to guide and develop the design of interface and interaction metaphors that could be tested as SRPs. Four central design metaphors were identified. A selection of the wireframe ideations for SRP designs are shown in Fig. 1 and described in the following section.

4.1 Initial Design Ideations

Figure 1, SRP ① is based on the very traditional vertical list format with a supporting book cover and metadata. We identified this design metaphor in the case study in both the Title/Cover and the Large Cover categories. The book cover metaphor is important to assist with searching as it provides a visual reference for recognition (Mi and Weng 2008) and was found by McKay et al. (2012a, b) to influence length of use and loan times for eBooks. The information to be included in this type of SRP would be book title, author, publication date, and book location with either a small or large book cover as a supporting visual.

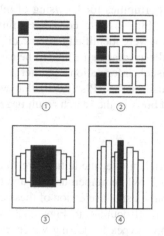

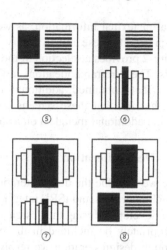

Fig. 1. Library SRP Interface Concepts (see Sect. 4.1)

Fig. 2. Library SRP Interface Concepts (see Sect. 4.2)

Figure 1, SRP ② is based on the horizontal grid format with a supporting book cover and metadata. This SRP metaphor allows for less metadata and supporting information than SRP ① due to the grid spacing that is available. In the case study we were able to identify that it was typical for title and author information to be presented, but not always in its entirety. A small or large cover graphic would support the textual information depending on the size of the grid cells implemented.

Figure 1, SRP ③ extends book cover use identified in the case study and incorporates the related work of Vanderschantz et al. (2015) who investigated the use of a cover-flow metaphor in library interfaces. This SRP does not easily allow for display of metadata that is not held on the cover of the book.

Figure 1, SRP ④ also extends the work of Vanderschantz et al. (2015) who investigated the use of spines in digital library interfaces. This SRP does not easily allow for display of metadata that is not held on the spine of the book and contains a similar amount of information to that of the Title/Text interfaces identified in our case study.

4.2 Developing and Evolving the Design Ideations

Here we describe the design work undertaken to develop and evolve the initial SRP interfaces illustrated in Fig. 1. Traditionally the design of a library search result interface assumes a single transition from a search results page (SRP) to a book result page (BRP). That is to say, once a book or item is selected within a list, the search result page is replaced with a single book result page. This study is concerned with interfaces on a touch screen mobile device, therefore modern transitional screens typical of mobile device apps form a part of the design space for this problem. To investigate how transitional screens might extend the presentation of metadata, and visual or textual information, as well as provide opportunities for browsing of related search results these initial library SRP wireframes (Fig. 1) were considered further. Figure 2 provides a selection of the enhancements that were identified for these original SRPs. The wireframe ideations in Fig. 2 were hypothesized as being able to be used as SRPs that contained additional metadata and visual information. Further it was hypothesized that these screens could serve as transitional SRP's (tSRP) that would provide additional metadata on a single user tap of a book in the search result page list.

4.3   Design Iteration

Here we describe the design iteration that was undertaken after the initial investigation of SRP interfaces and tSRP interfaces in Figs. 1 and 2. While numerous SRP and tSRP were developed during the design ideation process only a small selection of these could appropriately be included in the initial user study (and detailed in Figs. 1, 2, & 3). Through design iteration we resolved eight study prototypes for testing which can be divided into two equal groups. These prototypes included four apps that contained only an SRP, and a resulting BRP (labelled A1, A2, A3, A4). A second group of apps included an SRP, a resulting tSRP, and a resulting BRP. These prototypes were developed to extend prototypes A1—A4 and were labelled B1, B2, B3, B4.

Figure 3 shows design ideations for the SRPs (top) and corresponding tSRPs (bottom) used in the study reported here. For example, Fig. 3 SRP ① was used in our study for both prototype A1 and B1 with tSRP ⓐ being used in prototype B1. Equally, Fig. 3 SRP ② is used for both A2 and B2, with tSRP ⓑ being used in B2 etc.

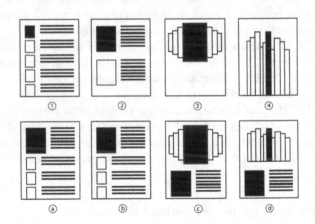

Fig. 3. Library SRP (top row) & tSRP (bottom row) Interface Concepts

4.4   Solutions to Test

Here we describe the design development that was undertaken to produce eight interactive interfaces that were able to be used in testing. The wireframe interfaces illustrated in Fig. 3 were refined and implemented as design solutions with Fig. 4 illustrating the design solution resolved on for prototype A1 and prototype B1.

The prototypes that were developed for user testing incorporated realistic book covers, metadata, and related visual information. The prototypes were deployed as dynamic interactive mobile apps on an Android mobile tablet device.

Given the space we present in Fig. 4 only the screens developed for prototypes A1 and B1. The green line in Fig. 4 illustrates the user flow for prototype A1, while the blue line illustrates the user flow for prototype B1. On the left of Fig. 4 is the search page used for every prototype in the study. When a search for the word "design" was fired using this left-hand screen (Fig. 4), the user was presented with the top middle screen when they were using either prototype A1 or B1 (see Fig. 3 SRP ①). In prototype A1 if the user selected the top book, they would be presented with the far-right screen, a BRP. In prototype B1, should the user select the top book on the SRP (top middle of Fig. 4) they would be presented with the tSRP (bottom middle of Fig. 4 and see Fig. 3 tSRP ⓐ). Should the user select the top book again using the tSRP, they would be presented with the far-right BRP.

Fig. 4. Library SRP & tSRP Interface Designs for prototype A1 and B1 (Color figure online)

5 Method

An observed task user study and guided interview were conducted with participants on two university campuses. The studies were conducted by a single researcher at one university in New Zealand and one university in China, typically inside or within the immediate vicinity of the university's library. Our researcher is fluent in both English and Chinese. Both libraries contained printed and digital documents in both English and Chinese, amongst other languages. Participants at the NZ university typically undertook their studies in English, while participants from the Chinese university might be taught in either English or Chinese.

The sample of 75 participants included 37 males and 38 females. 60 participants were surveyed at the NZ university and 15 at the university in China. A cross section of both undergraduate and postgraduate students at both universities agreed to participate.

As per the institution's ethical approval, all participants received a verbal explanation of the study and completed a signed informed consent.

Participants were allowed as much time to explore and interact with the library search interfaces as each required. These interfaces were displayed on a Nexus7 ASUS tablet, a 200 mm tall by 114 mm wide by 8.65 mm thick device. No tuition was given for the use of these interfaces. Following the users' exploration of all eight of the prototypes the researcher conducted a guided interview to investigate the preferences and choices made by the participants. Field notes and interview recordings were made by the researcher by hand and were later manually coded and analysed.

6   Results

The results presented here from our observations and interviews give insight into the reading and search habits of our participants as well as their preferences for the visual designs that were tested. The results of the interview questions posed to participants regarding their current reading and library search behavior are discussed more fully in (Vanderschantz et al. 2018) – but will be referred to throughout this section to support the findings of the visual design preferences for search result pages.

6.1   Perceived Importance of Interface Elements

Importance of Related Books. 74 of 75 participants stated it was important when searching in a library interface that books relating to the topic of their current search be presented to them (Vanderschantz et al. 2018). Among these 74 participants, 57 thought related books would help them to find out what they want, 13 people thought it could give them more information for their search, and the remaining four participants believed related books provided further choices to assist with their search. The only participant, who thought related books were not important in the library search interface, explained "it gives too much information, and is not helpful for … searching".

Importance of Book Descriptions. Participants were asked if the book description was important in the library search page. 71 of the 75 participants thought the book description was important. Among these 71 participants, 43 thought the book description could make choosing between books easier. 15 people thought that the description could clarify information they needed about the book to inform the decision to select or not select a specific book. 13 expected that the book description would provide additional related information during search to help identify topics and features of the books returned by the search.

Importance of Book Covers. Including the book cover on a library search page was considered to be important for 72/75 participants (Vanderschantz et al. 2018). Among these 72 participants, 36 thought the book cover would make the book that they searched easy to find on the shelf. 15 assumed that the book cover could help them to decide if the book contains the information they are looking for. 11 participants thought it could give them more information, and the remaining ten participants believed the book cover improves the aesthetics of the interface, making it look "more interesting".

Importance of Book Spines. 43 participants considered the book spine important in the library search interfaces. 37 thought the book spine would help them to find the particular book that they would want to loan or read, and the other six participants thought it could give them clear information about the books available in the area of their search. From the 32 participants who thought the book spine was not important in the library search interface, 30 of them thought it was not likely to be helpful for the speed or accuracy of their searching, two of them described the book spines as hard to read, with P15 noting "too many choices, which does not help in searching for a book".

6.2   Preference for the Design of Library Interfaces

18 participants identified prototype B1 as their first choice and 16 participants chose A1. These two prototypes contained the same initial search results page, a traditional list view with a small supporting cover image for each list entry. B1 had a tertiary SRP with a larger cover image and some further metadata given when a search result was selected. A2 and B2 still rated relatively highly by participants with 13 and 7 partic- ipants respectively choosing these two prototypes as their preferred prototypes (Fig. 5).

Taken together, the results for these four prototypes show the significance of the book cover when paired with metadata in a list view. This is reinforced by the qual- itative feedback gained through the interviews. The most often given reason for choosing a preferred prototype was that the interface was considered easy for finding books (57%). For example, when selecting NF A1 as their preferred prototype all 16 participants described this interface as easy. Eleven of the 18 participants who selected B1 and four of the 16 participants who selected A1 specifically detailed the information (metadata) given in the interface as "useful" and "helpful" to them while searching.

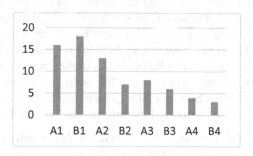

Fig. 5. Participant preference of library search prototype (n = 75)

Perceived Most Useful Prototype for Searching. In the previous questions partici- pants described their preference without any parameters, we next asked participants which prototype they found most useful for searching for a specific book. Similar to their preference for prototype, when asked specifically about the prototype that was most useful to them for searching, 18 participants considered B1, 14 participants A1, 11 participants A2 and six participants B2, as the most useful interface for their searching (Fig. 6).

36% of the participants reported that their chosen interface gave clear information. Participant P9 explained that "I like the second page of B1, it shows me accurate information when I clicked on one book, and this is very helpful". While another participant P23 stated "the information in A1 is clear and enough" presumably suggesting that they are able to make a decision about a book without the additional metadata that is provided by the tertiary SRP provided by B1.

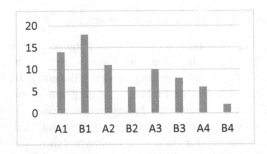

Fig. 6. Participant preference of library search prototype for searching for a specific book (n = 75)

Perceived Most Useful Prototype for Browsing. Participants were asked which prototype they found most useful for browsing for a book. Differing from the answers given when asked about preference during search, when asked about browsing, greater numbers of participants preferred prototype A2. A2 provided users with less visible search results on a screen before scrolling was required yet provided more metadata per list entry than A1 provided. The second most often chosen prototype for browsing was B1 chosen by 18 participants. B1 provided more results on the initial search results page with limited metadata while the tertiary SRP for B1 provided additional metadata for the selected book while retaining further books in the list for consideration (Fig. 7).

The most common reason given was that the interface provided clear information when browsing books (63%). Sixteen of the 19 participants who selected A2 and 10/18 participants who selected B1 discussed the information provided as useful to them.

Perceived Most Useful Interface for Providing Information When Browsing Books. Participants were asked in which example they find the level of information most useful for browsing. 19 participants chose A1, 17 participants B1. 16 chose A2 and 8 chose B2. 54% of the participants described their choice of prototype as providing clear information while 31% of the respondents believed the prototype they chose provided the right amount of information to be highly efficient for searching.

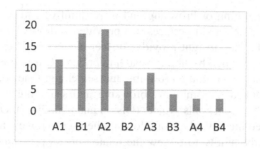

Fig. 7. Participant preference of library search prototype for browsing books (n = 75)

Perceived Most Useful for Decision Making. Participants were asked in which prototype they find the level of information most useful for making a decision. Participants tended to choose prototypes A1 and B1, 20 participants preferring B1 while 18 participants chose A1. Participants reported their interface of choice provided sufficient information for decision making or was efficient for browsing and searching.

Most Intuitive Transition from Screen to Screen During Navigation. When a user tapped one of the four results entries in prototypes A1, A2, A3 or A4 they were presented with a book result page, however, when the user tapped a result in B1, B2, B3, or B4 they were presented with a tertiary search results page (as shown in Fig. 4). 41 of the participants chose an interface that provided a tertiary search results page compared to 34 participants who chose an interface that did not provide a tertiary search results page before a book result page (Fig. 8).

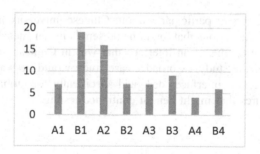

Fig. 8. Participant preference of library search prototype for intuitive navigation (n = 75)

7 Discussion

The 75 participants in this study browsed and borrowed from physical libraries regularly (Vanderschantz et al. 2018). The interactive prototypes that this study asked them to compare allowed us to assess the user preference for the display of search results and the importance of related books on user's preferences during their use of the systems. The somewhat traditional interface result list metaphor was preferred by participants in this study for all of the variables that we tested. Participants reported that these lists proved useful for searching or browsing and were intuitive and efficient interfaces to use. Participants often selected interfaces that provided additional information in either the SRP or the tSRP. This insight provides further evidence of the importance of the broader information provided by library search interfaces. Our implementation of tSRP provided opportunities to combine browsing and searching. One solution identified in the literature that looked at combining browsing and searching to meet information seeking needs was the ScentTrails project (Olston and Chi, 2003). Our implementation of tSRP also provided the advantage of allowing the user to review a greater amount of metadata yet retain the ability to review the related books presented by the interface. This is likely akin to reviewing the back of a book or book metadata in the stacks of a physical library as identified by Hinze et al. (2012). The identified usefulness of tSRP by our participants supports the premise of Mi & Weng (2008) that intuitive navigation between results lists and individual records is important.

The often-given reasons for participants preferences regarding the design of our prototypes were ease of book identification, clarity of information, assistance with book choice, and intuitiveness of the interaction and user experience. The metadata features most discussed as important by our participants were book cover, book title, author information, publication date, and blurb information. It has been reported widely that book covers effect user selection in physical libraries (Reutzel and Gali 1998; Hinze et al. 2012; McKay et al. 2012a,b; Stelmaszewska and Blandford 2004) and bookshops (Buchanan and McKay 2011). These preferences reinforce the findings of McKay et al. 2012a,b who noted that users read-time and tendency to abandon a book was influenced by inconsistencies present in the interface relating to metadata as well as cover presentation. Similar to our study, Vanderschantz et al. (2015) reported that users preferred an interface that displayed both a book cover and supporting bibliographic information.

The smaller numbers of participants at our Chinese university limits the ability to statistically analyse interactions that might be present between sites. Equally, this study did not allow for the testing of an interface that was in Chinese and how this might impact the results of the study. A broader case-study would be warranted to identify and examine instances of interfaces designed specifically for mobile screens and the metaphors and features that might benefit continued testing.

8   Conclusion

This paper explored interface and information presentation for library catalogues and digital libraries used by tertiary students. We executed an audit of existing library catalogue and bookshop interfaces to understand how best to develop the design of test material for our study reported here. Six university libraries, two city libraries, one eBook catalogue, and three book retail websites were reviewed. From the resulting set of design metaphors identified we created eight interactive digital prototypes for library search interfaces that were included in a user study with 75 participants at a university in NZ and a university in China. We conclude that across the range of identified design metaphors presently implemented by the library catalogues audited, the interfaces do not meet the needs or preferences of tertiary library catalogue users on mobile devices.

In analysing the interviews, we identified that most participants reported a preference for an interface that comprised book covers coupled with good quality bibliographic metadata. We recommend interfaces be designed to include the following information (in priority order); cover, title, author, publication date, publication information, library location information, as well as a book description. The interviews revealed that an interface that required the user to tap for additional information before proceeding to a traditional book result page was not seen as a hindrance to users. Therefore, if providing less information in an initial search result page will allow for presentation of a greater number of results on a screen, it is advised that a tertiary search result page be implemented with this additional metadata that is valued by the users.

References

Bates, M.J.: The design of browsing and berrypicking techniques for the online search interface. Online Rev. **13**(5), 407–424 (1989)

Buchanan, G., McKay, D.: In the bookshop: examining popular search strategies. In: Proceedings of the 11th Annual International ACM/IEEE Joint Conference on Digital Libraries, pp. 269–278. ACM (2011)

Cooper, J.W., Prager, J.M.: Anti-serendipity: finding useless documents and similar documents. In: Spragu, R.H. (ed.), Proceedings of the 33rd Annual Hawaii International Conference on System Sciences, Maui, Hawaii. IEEE Computer Society, Piscataway, NJ (2000)

Hinze, A., McKay, D., Vanderschantz, N., Timpany, C., Cunningham, S.J.: Book selection behavior in the physical library: Implications for ebook collections. In: Proceedings of the 12th ACM/IEEE-CS joint conference on Digital Libraries, pp. 305–314. ACM, New York, NY (2012)

Hinze, A., Vanderschantz, N., Timpany, C., Saravani, S.-J., Cunningham, S.J., Wilkinson, C.: Use of mobile apps for teaching and research – implications for digital literacy. In: Choemprayong, S., Crestani, F., Cunningham, S.J. (eds.) ICADL 2017. LNCS, vol. 10647, pp. 173–184. Springer, Cham (2017). https://doi.org/10.1007/978-3-319-70232-2_15

Lawson, B.: How Designers Think the Design Process Demystified, 4th edn. Elsevier/Architectural, Oxford; Burlington, MA (2006)

Liu, Y.Q., Briggs, S.: A library in the palm of your hand: mobile services in top 100 university libraries. Inf. Technol. Libr. **34**(2), 133–146 (2015)

McKay, D., Hinze, A., Heese, R., Vanderschantz, N., Timpany, C., Cunningham, S.J.: An exploration of ebook selection behavior in academic library collections. In: Zaphiris, P., Buchanan, G., Rasmussen, E., Loizides, F. (eds.) TPDL 2012. LNCS, vol. 7489, pp. 13–24. Springer, Heidelberg (2012a). https://doi.org/10.1007/978-3-642-33290-6_2

McKay, D., Buchanan, G., Vanderschantz, N., Timpany, C., Cunningham, S.J., Hinze, A.: Judging a book by its cover: interface elements that affect reader selection of ebooks. In: Proceedings of the 24th Australian Computer-Human Interaction Conference. ACM, New York, NY, US (2012b)

Merčun, T., Žumer, M.: New generation of catalogues for the new generation of users: a comparison of six library catalogues. Program **42**(3), 243–261 (2008)

Mi, J., Weng, C.: Revitalizing the library OPAC: interface, searching, and display challenges. Inf. Technol. Libr. **27**(1), 5–22 (2008)

Morse, P.M.: On browsing: the use of search theory in the search for information, Bulletin of the Operations Research Society of America, Supplement, vol. 19, p. 1 (1971)

Olston, C., Chi, E.H.: ScentTrails: integrating browsing and searching on the web. ACM Trans. Comput.-Hum. Interact. **10**(3), 177–197 (2003)

Paterson, L., Low, B.: Student attitudes towards mobile library services for smartphones. Libr. Hi Tech **29**(3), 412–423 (2011)

Reutzel, D., Gali, K.: The art of children's book selection: a labyrinth explored. Read. Psychol. **19**(1), 3–50 (1998)

Ross, C.S.: Making choices: what readers say about choosing books to read for pleasure. Acquis. Libr. **13**(25), 5–21 (2000)

Shneiderman, B., Feldman, D., Rose, A., Grau, X.F.: Visualizing digital library search results with categorical and hierarchical axes. In: Proceedings of the fifth ACM conference on Digital libraries, pp. 57–66. ACM, New York, NY (2000)

Stelmaszewska, H., Blandford, A.: From physical to digital: a case study of computer scientists' behaviour in physical libraries. Int. J. Digit. Libr. **4**(2), 82–92 (2004)

Su, S.: Desirable search features of web-based scholarly e-book systems. Electron. Libr. **23**(1), 64–71 (2005)

Vanderschantz, N., Timpany, C., Hinze, A.: Design exploration of ebook interfaces for personal digital libraries on tablet devices. In: Proceedings of the 15th New Zealand Conference on Human-Computer Interaction, pp. 21–30. ACM (2015)

Vanderschantz, N., Timpany, C., Feng, C.: A snapshot of reading, searching, and browsing preferences of tertiary students. In: Proceedings of the 31st British Computer Society Human Computer Interaction Conference. BCS (2018)

Vemuri, N.S., Torres, R.D.S., Fox, E.A., Fan, W., Shen, R.: Exploring digital libraries: integrating browsing, searching, and visualization. In: Proceedings of the 6th ACM/IEEE-CS Joint Conference on Digital Libraries, Digital Libraries 2006, JCDL 2006, pp. 1–10. IEEE (2006)

Wu, D., Liang, S., Bi, R.: Characterizing queries in cross-device OPAC search: a large-scale log study. Library Hi Tech **36**(3), 482–497 (2018)

Book Recommendation
Beyond the Usual Suspects
Embedding Book Plots Together
with Place and Time Information

Julian Risch[✉], Samuele Garda, and Ralf Krestel

Hasso Plattner Institute, University of Potsdam, Prof.-Dr.-Helmert-Str. 2-3, 14482
Potsdam, Germany
{julian.risch,samuele.garda,ralf.krestel}@hpi.de

Abstract. Content-based recommendation of books and other media is
usually based on semantic similarity measures. While metadata can be
compared easily, measuring the semantic similarity of narrative literature
is challenging. Keyword-based approaches are biased to retrieve books of
the same series or do not retrieve any results at all in sparser libraries. We
propose to represent plots with dense vectors to foster semantic search
for similar plots even if they do not have any words in common. Further,
we propose to embed plots, places, and times in the same embedding
space. Thereby, we allow arithmetics on these aspects. For example, a
book with a similar plot but set in a different, user-specified place can
be retrieved. We evaluate our findings on a set of 16,000 book synopses
that spans literature from 500 years and 200 genres and compare our
approach to a keyword-based baseline.

Keywords: Recommender systems · Text mining
Document embedding

1 Recommending Books Beyond the Usual Suspects

When users want to find a new book to read they typically trust best-seller lists
or their favorite author. While this approach is easy to implement, the user will
never discover serendipitous results or find hidden gems. We argue that users
want to read books similar to those they enjoyed to read in the past. However,
beyond the usual suspects, such as books of their favorite author, it is hard to
find books with similar plots. Further, for more difficult searches with a lower
recall base (i.e. fewer relevant books in the corpus) and increased data sparsity
(only few information given for the existing books), there are no usual suspects.
For this reason, we consider a recommendation task where the goal is to suggest
similar books for a given example book. This task is typical in the scenario
of users who just provided an initial book review, for example, at an online
shopping platform. The task can also be interpreted as a search, where a user
specifies an exemplar query. In that case, the query is an example of the books

© Springer Nature Switzerland AG 2018
M. Dobreva et al. (Eds.): ICADL 2018, LNCS 11279, pp. 227–239, 2018.
https://doi.org/10.1007/978-3-030-04257-8_24

that the user is interested in. Central to both, book similarity searches and book recommendation tasks, is the way that similarity of books is defined.

Based on metadata information, books of the same author or the same genre can be recommended. However, assessing the semantic similarity of book plots goes beyond metadata comparison and comes with several challenges. Often times, recommender systems have no access to the full text of books, but only to synopses or abstracts. While a synopsis summarizes the entire plot line, an abstract tells only parts of the story and aims to motivate potential readers to buy the book. Besides these challenges, naive keyword-based similarity measures have two major disadvantages with regards to data sparsity: (1) books with similar plot but different wording cannot be found and (2) shorter book synopses reduce the chance of finding any similar books. Further, recommendations by a keyword-based approach are biased towards books of the same series, because they use the same words for, e.g., main characters. However, if a user searches for such books, there is no point in a semantic similarity search. The same results could also be retrieved with a metadata search for other books of the same author. To foster serendipity, a similarity measure for books that aims at retrieval and recommendation tasks should consider semantic similarity of the actual content: the plots, rather than metadata. To compare semantic similarity of different plots, an abstract representation of plots is needed. Even the full text description of two semantically similar books might not have many words in common. With shorter text descriptions (abstracts and synopses) this challenge of data sparsity gets even more difficult.

In this work, we propose a content-based recommender system that recommends similar books beyond books with the same keywords. Further, we allow users to specify aspects of requested similarity, but also of allowed dissimilarity. To this end, we define three aspects that can be searched for: plot, place, and time. We choose these aspects because plot, setting (place and time), and characters compose the three main elements of fiction. We neglect similarity of characters across books for two reasons. First, searches for the exact same character can be performed with keyword searches for their name. Typically such searches lead to books of the same author. Second, to find a similar (but not the same) character, the entire plot needs to be considered and the comparison of plots is already covered.

By embedding plot, place, and time in the same space we enable similarity searches based on these aspects. Further, we allow to search for book plots that are mixtures of two given book plots. To this end, we average embeddings of the two given book plots. The book whose plot embedding is closest to the calculated average is a mix of the two given plots. In addition, we enable arithmetics with books: Users can subtract and add places and times to book plots. As an example, a user might have read a crime story that is set in Greece at the time of 1900 and would like to read a similar crime story, but which is set in Portugal in 2018. Our approach enables such searches, because there is a representation for *Greece, Portugal, 1900, 2018,* and also for the given book's plot. From the vector for the given book, we can subtract the vectors for *Greece* and *1900* and add the vectors for *Portugal* and *2018*. The book that is closest to the result of the former calculation is recommended to the user.

We evaluate our recommendations in comparison to a bag-of-words (BoW) baseline and use the distance in the embedding space as a semantic similarity measure. To evaluate the semantic similarity of book synopses, we use the path distance between synsets (sets of one or more synonyms) in WordNet. Further, we evaluate arithmetics in the embedding space and give examples how this new way of book search retrieves relevant and surprising results—beyond the usual suspects. Our implementation of the embedding and the recommender system is open-sourced and published together with the used datasets online[1]. Our contributions are summarized as:

1. an algorithm to embed book plots, places, and times in the same space;
2. a recommender system based on arithmetics in this space;
3. experiments that compare a BoW approach and our approach at a recommendation task showing an increased WordNet similarity score by 7%.

2   Related Work

Relevance aspects for book search requests have been identified by Koolen et al. [7] based on previous work by Reuter [15]: Accessibility, content, engagement, familiarity, known-item, metadata, novelty, and socio-cultural background. With our book recommendation approach, we target the familiarity aspect of relevance, where books similar to known books shall be retrieved. However, for ease of use, familiarity relevance can be reduced to metadata relevance. To this end, the similarity measure for books is reduced to meta data only. As a result, only books by the same author or of the same year of publication are retrieved. Similarity of book titles could still be considered as metadata similarity. However, a comparison of titles becomes challenging if it focuses on semantic similarity. Latard et al. analyze how a search engine could profit from semantic similarity of keywords. However, their approach relies on semantic lexicons (WordNet, VerbNet). Due to limitations of these lexicons with regard to multi-word keywords, they are able to identify correct categories for only 22% of the articles [8]. In contrast, our unsupervised, embedding-based approach does not rely on any lexicons or encyclopedia to identify semantically similar words.

The idea of a semantic web has been extended to a web of books, which could connect logical concepts, figures, tables, and references in a semantic graph [6]. It is an open research question how rich semantic graphs can be automatically extracted from books to facilitate semantic searches. One approach to improve search in digital libraries of scientific publications is to generate additional metadata by applying topic models [11]. Depending on the domain, the scientific objective, used dataset, software, etc., can be extracted and clustered to facilitate semantic search. Similarly, Charalampous and Knoth classify document types to enrich meta data for improved search and recommendation results [5].

---

[1] https://hpi.de/naumann/projects/repeatability/text-mining.html.

Bogers and Petras compare tags and controlled vocabularies (CV) at book searches with different information needs [3]. They find that tags and controlled vocabularies complement each other: CV work better if the search request is about a certain mood or reading experience. In contrast, tags work better for content-based search requests and for known-item searches. The authors also find that complex information needs in book search cannot be handled with tags or controlled vocabularies. They conclude that topical information in books needs other representations [4]. With our work, we propose such a representation in the form of an embedding space for plots, places, and times.

Another field of application for latent similarity measures are domains that use different words to describe similar concepts. For example, cross-collection topic models can reveal latent similarity of patents and scientific papers even if they do not have any words in common [16]. While a document's topic distribution is also a dense representation, our approach uses embeddings as document representations. Word embeddings have become a standard way to encode words for various downstream applications of natural language processing. However, how to obtain an embedding of a full document is still a topic of ongoing research. A naive way is to average all the vectors of all words in a document [17]. However, learning a dense vector representation for a document with paragraph2vec significantly outperforms word vector averaging as well as BoW approaches at information retrieval tasks [9]. A specific task of book recommendation is narrative-driven recommendation, where the users' interests are given as a narrative description [2]. In this work, we consider the plots of books that the user liked as a narrative description of interests.

3   Embedding Plots, Places, and Times in the Same Space

We propose to represent books as a composition of their plot, place, and time in the same embedding space. More specifically, each plot, each place, and each time is represented as a dense vector in the same 300-dimensional space. Further, each book is represented as the sum of its plot, place, and time in the same space. Our approach allows arithmetics in this space, so that the difference of two books can be interpreted with respect to plot, place, and time. This approach extends the idea of Mikolov et al. [13] from arithmetics on word embeddings to document embeddings and abstract concepts, such as plot embeddings. The similarity of two plots is calculated as the cosine similarity of their vector representations. Figure 1 visualizes a book A and a book B, which are composed of similar plots but different places. We can make use of this composition in the following way: When a user searches for a book that is similar to book B, we can recommend book A, because it has a similar plot. Moreover, when the user chooses a particular place, our approach recommends books with similar plots that are set at the specified place. In Fig. 1, we search for a book that has a similar plot as book B and is not set in France but in Japan.

The basis of our embedding space are pre-trained word embeddings. We make use of the 300-dimensional *Wikipedia 2014 + Gigaword 5* embeddings

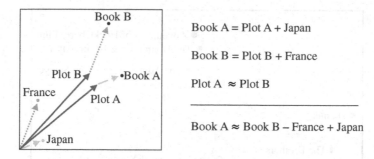

Book A = Plot A + Japan

Book B = Plot B + France

Plot A ≈ Plot B

_____

Book A ≈ Book B – France + Japan

Fig. 1. Our embedding space allows to perform arithmetics on books, their plots, places, and times. Book A and B have a similar plot but are set at different places.

published[2] by Pennington et al. [14]. Based on these word embeddings and the paragraph2vec approach by Le and Mikolov [9], we calculate document embeddings. Instead of considering all words of a book's synopsis for a book's embedding, we split the synopsis into three parts and generate three separate embeddings. We generate an embedding (1) for the set of words that describe the plot's place, (2) for the set of words that describe the plot's time, and (3) for all other words, which describe the plot independently of its place and time. The book itself is represented as the sum of these three representations.

3.1   Plot Representation

Given a book's synopsis, we apply named entity recognition to separate words that describe place or time. This separation allows us to consider only words that describe neither place nor time for the plot representation. Besides time and place terms, we also remove English stop words, which are not useful in discriminating individual plots. We generate a dense vector representation with paragraph2vec from the remaining words. Figure 2 shows a segment of a 2D-projection of the plot embedding space. Examples that we discuss are highlighted in black, others are grayed out. The vector space visualizations in this paper have been generated based on tensorflow's projector[3] and t-SNE dimensionality reduction [10]. For example, the two adventurous books *Adventures of Huckleberry Finn* and *The Adventures of Tom Sawyer* have similar plots and are close to each other. Further, the plots of *The Brothers Karamazov, Pride and Prejudice, The Sorrows of Young Werther,* and *Hamlet* have unfulfilled love and revenge with elements from tragedies and crime stories in common.

Interestingly, we can mix book plots by averaging their vector representations. In this scenario, a user provides two books as examples. These books can be of different genres. If we lookup the vector representations of the two books' plots in our embedding space, we can calculate their mean vector. This vector

---

[2] nlp.stanford.edu/projects/glove/.
[3] projector.tensorflow.org/.

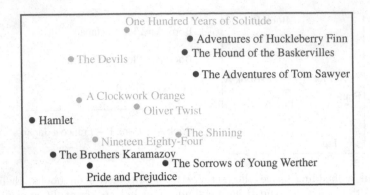

Fig. 2. Books with similar plot are closer to each other in the embedding space.

represents a mixture of the two books' plots. If we retrieve a book that has a plot vector close to that mean vector, we can recommend interesting mixtures. For example, mixing a crime fiction with a romance novel, we retrieve romantic suspense novels.

3.2   Place Representation

Besides the plot itself, we extract where the plot takes place. With named entity recognition, we extract names of politically or geographically defined locations, such as countries or cities. We lookup the word vector of each mentioned place from pre-trained word embeddings and average all such vectors to obtain an embedding of the book's place. Figure 3 shows a segment of a 2D-projection of the place embedding space. Close neighbors of *Portugal* are *Lisbon*, *Spain*, and *Catalonia*. Presumably because of the frequent term *United Kingdom*, the word *Kingdom* itself is close to *England* and *Britain*. African countries are closer to each other in the embedding space than to European countries. Based on these embeddings, our recommendation approach derives that two books are set in semantically similar places if one is set somewhere in Portugal and the other is specifically set in the Portuguese city Lisbon.

3.3   Time Representation

We extract also time information from book synopses with named entity recognition. For documents that contain no time information explicitly, we propose a different approach to estimate the time the book's plot is set in. To this end, we leverage an external knowledge base: Wikipedia. Every year has its own Wikipedia page[4], which describes important events in this year and also lists births and deaths of public figures. We analyze all these pages and index words that are specific to a subset of years. For example *Apollo 13* occurs only in the

---

[4] en.wikipedia.org/wiki/List_of_years.

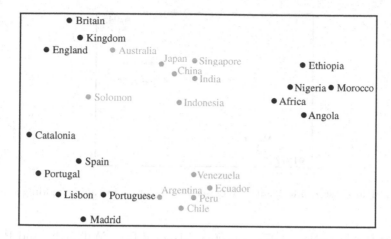

Fig. 3. Geographically close locations are closer to each other in the embedding space.

page for the year 1970, the year of the mission in the Apollo space program. *Portuguese Republic* occurs first in 1910, matching the proclamation of the first Portuguese Republic. Further, *Berlin Wall* first occurs in the page for 1961 and occurs for the last time in the page for 1990, which exactly matches the time frame from its construction to destruction. We train a naive Bayes classifier on the set of Wikipedia page texts and their corresponding years. As a consequence, given a text document as an input, such as a Wikipedia page, but also a book's synopses, we can predict a year. According to the training data, this year is likely to be mentioned together with the words in the input document.

Figure 4 shows a segment of a 2D-projection of the time embedding space. Although the years 1918 and 1945 are not consecutive, they are very close in the embedding space. Probably, this is because the two years mark the ends of World War I and II. The semantic similarity of the two years matches the idea of our recommendation approach: A user, who read a book that is set in 1945 might also want to read a book that is set in 1918, because of the similarity of the historic events at that time. As expected, years with a short time distance in between are also close in the embedding space, such as 1898, 1900, and 1912 or 1812, 1820, and 1821.

4   Experiments

With our experiments, we want to evaluate the semantic similarity of a given book and books recommended by our approach. This similarity is difficult to evaluate without a large user study among users, who are familiar with a large number of books. To still be able to evaluate our approach, we propose an automatic evaluation and further provide anecdotal evidence with examples. We consider a book synopses dataset[5] by Bamman and Smith [1]. The dataset

---

[5] www.cs.cmu.edu/~dbamman/booksummaries.html.

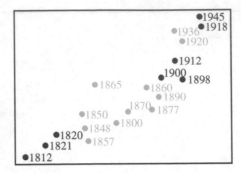

Fig. 4. Time-wise similar years are closer to each other in the embedding space.

describes 16,559 books by 4715 authors extracted from Wikipedia and Project Gutenberg, along with aligned metadata from Freebase, including book author, title, and genre. Most of these books have been published between 1950 and 2000. 500 books are from the 19th century or older. Each synopsis contains about 430 words and after stop word removal about 260 words remain. Figure 5 visualizes the variety of the dataset with histograms for genre and publication year.

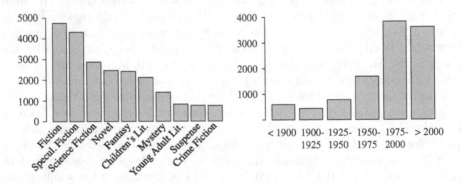

Fig. 5. The distribution of publication years and top 10 genres (out of 227) in the book dataset. Multiple genres can be assigned to the same book.

4.1 Evaluation Metric

The used metric is only an approximation of how users would judge semantic similarity of books. To automatically calculate the semantic similarity of an input book and each recommended book, we make use of WordNet[6]. To extend this metric from semantic similarity of pairs of words to pairs of full synopses, we follow the approach of Mihalcea et al. [12]. For each noun, verb, adjective, and

---

[6] wordnet.princeton.edu/.

adverb, we retrieve its synset (a set of one or more synonyms) from WordNet. For each synset, we identify the most similar synset from the other book and add its similarity score to the overall book similarity score. The synset similarity score is a path-based score in the range 0 to 1. It is based on the shortest path that connects the synsets in the is-a (hypernym/hyponym) taxonomy. Finally, the book similarity score is the average of all maximum synset similarity scores. Because synset similarity is not a symmetric measure, we define the similarity of two book synopses A and B as:

$$(\text{synset\_sim}(A, B) + \text{synset\_sim}(B, A))/2.$$

4.2 Embedding-Based Recommendation

The task of the following experiment is to recommend 10 books for a given input book. As a baseline to compare with, we implement a BoW approach. In particular, we implement a K-nearest-neighbor approach that is based on tf-idf weighted BoW representations of each document. To show that our approach improves on this baseline, we compare recommendations of the baseline against a combined approach of the baseline and our embedding-based approach. The BoW approach is supposed to make good recommendations if there is another book in the dataset with similar wording. However, we assume that our embedding-based approach excels if there are no such books in the dataset—or if they are considered non-relevant because such books are usual suspects. Therefore, if a recommendation of the BoW approach has only few words in common with the input book, we replace this recommendation by one of our embedding-based recommendations in the combined approach.

For a set of 50 randomly sampled books, both, the baseline approach and our combined approach, make 10 ranked recommendations each. As a result, the average score of the first recommendation is 0.467 for the BoW approach compared to 0.501 for our proposed approach (7% improvement). For the first 10 recommendations the score is 0.454 for BoW compared to 0.478 for our embedding-based approach. Our approach improves the semantic similarity of the input book and the top recommendations compared to a BoW baseline.

4.3 Plot Representation

To evaluate the dense vector representation of plots, we consider mixed book plots. For the following experiment, we sampled 10 pairs of books of genre *Crime Fiction* and *Romance Novel*. For each pair, we predict 5 recommendations with our embedding-based approach. The BoW baseline is not able to mix book plots.

Given the romance novel *Waking the Dead* and the crime fiction *Bones to Ashes* as input books, the fiction *Sons of Fortune* is the third-closest neighbor to the average vector of their plot embeddings. In *Sons of Fortune,* there are two twin brothers who fall in love with the same girl. Moreover, one of them is a lawyer and defends the other one on the charge of murder. A second example is the mix of the romance novel *A Passage to India* and the mystery, suspense, crime fiction *2nd Chance*. The closest book to their averaged plot embeddings is *Houseboy*. This book is both a love story and a crime story, but no genre information is designated in the dataset. Therefore, another application of our approach could be to automatically assign genres to books without any labels. In our dataset, 3718 books do not have any genre assigned.

4.4 Place Representation

The following experiment examines how place embeddings affect book recommendations. Given the embedding of the book *Oliver Twist*, we subtract the embedding of its places and add the place embedding for *China*. The resulting vector's closest neighbor is the book *Spilled Water*, which is set in China. Further, both books, *Oliver Twist* and *Spilled Water* are about an orphan who is forced to work. Our approach correctly recommends a book with a similar plot that is set at a user-specified place. The average WordNet semantic similarity of the first 5 recommendations is very similar for our approach (0.561) and a BoW baseline (0.563). Our approach has the advantage that the place can be user-specified. Another input example is the book *Nineteen Eighty-Four*. If we search for books with similar plot but specify the location as *China,* our approach recommends *When the People Fell*. The latter is a science fiction story about the colonization of Venus by a future Chinese government. Although the location is not as requested, the recommendation is interesting because of the connection to China. Further, both books are about obedience to authority and therefore have similar plot. Given the book *The Whiskey Rebels* and adding the vector for *Italy,* our approach recommends *Wings of the Falcon,* which is set in Italy. Both books are about rebelling against power.

4.5 Time Representation

Besides the place of a book's plot, users can specify its time. As input, we consider *A Farewell to Arms* by Hemingway, which is about a soldier in World War I. The first recommendation of our approach, if we add the vector for *1944,* is *The Wolf's Hour*. This book has a similar plot, but is set in World War II. Another example is *Adventures of Huckleberry Finn,* which is about the adventures of a child around 1850. If we add the vector for *1960,* the first recommendation is *Summer of Night*. This book is about children's adventures set in 1960s. The book *Matari* can be described as a love story set in Japan in 1800. If we add the vector for *2000,* one recommendation is *.hack//Zero,* which is science fiction with a love story set in Japan and another is *Manga Kenkanryu,* which is set in Japan in the year 2002. Although we request a specific year, not all recommendations mention exactly *2000,* but very close years, such as *2002*. Our approach correctly derives that a plot set in 2002 is time-wise similar to a plot set in 2000.

4.6 Movie Recommendation as a Similar Task

To show that our approach is applicable to other data, we run additional experiments for the similar task of movie recommendation. Similar to the book dataset, we extracted a movie dataset from Wikipedia pages and published it online together with the sourcecode. It contains 6456 movie descriptions from the years 2000 to 2016. Each movie is described by about 1340 words. Figure 6 visualizes a segment of a 2D-projection of the movie plot embedding space. *Star Trek* and *Star Wars* both are about space adventures and are therefore located close to each other. Interestingly, *The Ring* and *The Lord of the Rings* are separated from each other, although the titles have the word *Ring* in common. Indeed, the plots of the two movies are very different and while a ring is centric to the story of *The Lord of the Rings*, *Ring* has only a symbolic meaning in *The Ring*. A keyword-based approach would assume that both movies are similar, because a word in their titles overlaps. However, in the embedding space, *The Ring* is close to *Harry Potter and the Philosopher's Stone,* which makes sense because both movies are about a child with supernatural or magical power.

Similar to the experiments on the book dataset, we compare WordNet similarity scores of a BoW baseline with our combined, embedding-based approach. For 50 movies, the average score of the first recommendation is 0.547 for the BoW approach compared to 0.566 for our proposed approach. For the first 10 recommendations the score is 0.540 for BoW compared to 0.562. The improved semantic similarity of recommendations and the input document shows that our approach is applicable to other data beyond books.

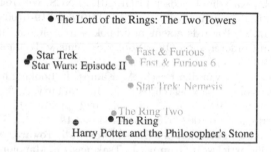

Fig. 6. Movies with similar plot are closer to each other in the embedding space.

5 Conclusions and Future Work

We proposed to embed book plots and their setting in the same space. In this space, we can do arithmetics to express book searches and to extend recommendations beyond the usual suspects. In contrast to a BoW baseline, our embedding-based approach is able to retrieve similar books that do not have any words in common. We find that embeddings achieve semantically more similar recommendations on datasets of books and movies. The semantic similarity of book synopses is evaluated based on the path distance between synsets (sets of one or more synonyms) in WordNet. Last but not least, we allow users to specify place and time when they search for books with similar plot.

Future Work could improve the extraction of place and time information or could add more aspects. For example, for crime stories the murder weapon could be extracted and represented in the same embedding space. Another idea is to use hierarchical embeddings for places and times. Thereby, the hierarchical relationship of *21st century* and *2018* or *Asia* and *Japan* could be represented. A detailed user study could evaluate how users interact with and search in the proposed embedding space and how satisfying our recommendations are.

References

1. Bamman, D., Smith, N.A.: New alignment methods for discriminative book summarization. arXiv:1305.1319 (2013)
2. Bogers, T., Koolen, M.: Defining and supporting narrative-driven recommendation. In: Proceedings of the Confernece on Recommender Systems (RecSys), pp. 238–242. ACM (2017)
3. Bogers, T., Petras, V.: An in-depth analysis of tags and controlled metadata for book search. In: iConference, vol. 2, pp. 15–30 (2017)
4. Bogers, T., Petras, V.: Supporting book search: a comprehensive comparison of tags vs. controlled vocabulary metadata. Data Inf. Manag. 1, 17–34 (2017)
5. Charalampous, A., Knoth, P.: Classifying document types to enhance search and recommendations in digital libraries. In: Kamps, J., Tsakonas, G., Manolopoulos, Y., Iliadis, L., Karydis, I. (eds.) TPDL 2017. LNCS, vol. 10450, pp. 181–192. Springer, Cham (2017). https://doi.org/10.1007/978-3-319-67008-9_15
6. Khusro, S., Ullah, I.: Towards a semantic book search engine. In: Proceedings of the International Conference on Open Source Systems & Technologies (ICOSST), pp. 106–113 (2016)
7. Koolen, M., Bogers, T., van den Bosch, A., Kamps, J.: Looking for books in social media: an analysis of complex search requests. In: Hanbury, A., Kazai, G., Rauber, A., Fuhr, N. (eds.) ECIR 2015. LNCS, vol. 9022, pp. 184–196. Springer, Cham (2015). https://doi.org/10.1007/978-3-319-16354-3_19
8. Latard, B., Weber, J., Forestier, G., Hassenforder, M.: Towards a semantic search engine for scientific articles. In: Kamps, J., Tsakonas, G., Manolopoulos, Y., Iliadis, L., Karydis, I. (eds.) TPDL 2017. LNCS, vol. 10450, pp. 608–611. Springer, Cham (2017). https://doi.org/10.1007/978-3-319-67008-9_54
9. Le, Q., Mikolov, T.: Distributed representations of sentences and documents. In: Proceedings of the International Conference on Machine Learning (ICML), pp. 1188–1196. JMLR (2014)
10. van der Maaten, L., Hinton, G.: Visualizing data using t-SNE. J. Mach. Learn. Res. 9, 2579–2605 (2008)
11. Mesbah, S., Fragkeskos, K., Lofi, C., Bozzon, A., Houben, G.-J.: Facet embeddings for explorative analytics in digital libraries. In: Kamps, J., Tsakonas, G., Manolopoulos, Y., Iliadis, L., Karydis, I. (eds.) TPDL 2017. LNCS, vol. 10450, pp. 86–99. Springer, Cham (2017). https://doi.org/10.1007/978-3-319-67008-9_8
12. Mihalcea, R., Corley, C., Strapparava, C., et al.: Corpus-based and knowledge-based measures of text semantic similarity. AAAI 6, 775–780 (2006)
13. Mikolov, T., Yih, W.t., Zweig, G.: Linguistic regularities in continuous space word representations. In: Proceedings of the Conference of the North American Chapter of the ACL (NAACL), pp. 746–751. ACL (2013)

14. Pennington, J., Socher, R., Manning, C.D.: Glove: global vectors for word representation. In: Proceedings of the Conference on Empirical Methods in Natural Language Processing (EMNLP), pp. 1532–1543 (2014)
15. Reuter, K.: Assessing aesthetic relevance: children's book selection in a digital library. J. Assoc. Inf. Sci. Technol. (JAIST) **58**(12), 1745–1763 (2007)
16. Risch, J., Krestel, R.: What should i cite? Cross-collection reference recommendation of patents and papers. In: Kamps, J., Tsakonas, G., Manolopoulos, Y., Iliadis, L., Karydis, I. (eds.) TPDL 2017. LNCS, vol. 10450, pp. 40–46. Springer, Cham (2017). https://doi.org/10.1007/978-3-319-67008-9_4
17. Socher, R., et al.: Recursive deep models for semantic compositionality over a sentiment TreeBank. In: Proceedings of the Conference on Empirical Methods in Natural Language Processing (EMNLP), pp. 1631–1642. ACL (2013)

Users' Responses to Privacy Issues with the Connected Information Ecologies Created by Fitness Trackers

Zablon Pingo$^{(\boxtimes)}$ ⓘ and Bhuva Narayan ⓘ

University of Technology Sydney, Sydney, Australia
{zablon.pingo, bhuva.narayan}@uts.edu.au

Abstract. With increased innovation and adoption of digital technologies in our everyday life for various purposes, media, privacy experts, advocates, scholars and researchers have noted and raised privacy and security concerns associated with the misuse of personal information from digital technologies. These technologies enable collection, processing and re-purposing of personal information for various purposes by commercial and interested entities. This paper presents a privacy awareness perspective in an attempt to understand how people respond to privacy concerns while using activity tracking devices and applications, loyalty cards and related data sharing within various information ecologies. The research used a constructivist paradigm; we interviewed twenty-one users of activity trackers and loyalty cards to understand their privacy practices. Results show that privacy is a flexible concept which is a result of users' negotiation between the benefits and the harms of disclosing personal information.

Keywords: Activity trackers · Fitness trackers · Privacy · Privacy awareness
Informational privacy · Contextual integrity

1 Introduction

Digital services and infrastructure are increasingly beneficial to consumers everyday life; however, scholars, researchers, experts and journalists have raised significant privacy concerns across the digital technologies [1–3], which threaten to deprive consumer benefits through profiling, surveillance [4–7] dataveillance [8], personality profiling for targeted marketing and other purposes [9]. The consequences of these practices are associated with bias in information access [10], social and economic inequality, self-harm, financial loss, hidden influence and manipulation, price discrimination, and censorship among others [6, 11]. These growing privacy concerns and risks arise from service providers' misuse of data, processing, and repurposing from multiple sources not limited to search engines, social media, loyalty systems, and consumer Internet-connected devices like fitness trackers, among other digital technologies [12, 13]. The ever-increasing privacy risks require users of information technologies to have some level of awareness and privacy protection strategies.

© Springer Nature Switzerland AG 2018
M. Dobreva et al. (Eds.): ICADL 2018, LNCS 11279, pp. 240–255, 2018.
https://doi.org/10.1007/978-3-030-04257-8_25

To understand and protect consumers' privacy on digital technologies, most studies take legal and information systems approaches [14, 15] but not much is known from users' experiences, perceptions and responses towards the efforts of managing information flows in activity trackers. Privacy protection in the current information age depend on a range of mechanisms including: improving security of the technologies through securing the systems, public policy and individuals awareness to the privacy concerns to determine the risks of sharing such information openly online or to organisations without a good understanding of the surrounding practices [13]. Privacy awareness is essential to compliment the existing mechanisms of ensuring individuals have some understanding and recognition of how information is tracked, used and potentially misused in online environments, for individuals to take appropriate measures to protect themselves [16]; individuals need to evaluate their information sharing practices, and understand how the data they produce is used, shared and loses its private nature [17].

While most of the privacy studies evaluate technical aspects of privacy and security of the fitness devices and the applications [15, 18, 19], this study provides a qualitative perspective of users' everyday privacy practices while using devices and related synergies created around them. This paper adds to the privacy literature by providing accounts of how consumers respond to privacy issues raised in popular everyday technologies; in this case fitness trackers, and loyalty card systems which have created complex information ecologies that collect and open up personal information to third party organisations [20]. Information ecologies in this context refers to the interconnected nature of socially produced data as a result of human activities popularly known as "social big data". For example, Coles Supermarkets in Australia have introduced synergies where consumers can link their loyalty cards with fitness tracking devices, and since the company also sells insurance, it has implications for potential device and data linkages [21].

The study attempts to answer the research question: How do people manage privacy in regard to the connected information ecologies created through the use of activity trackers and loyalty cards systems in everyday life? What strategies do people deploy to protect their privacy when using fitness trackers and the information ecologies around them?

2 Research Context

In the current data-driven economies there are apparent negative impact to individuals occasioned by use of personal information by data brokers, without the subject's knowledge or understanding, consequently violating individuals' rights to privacy [6, 22]. Informational privacy has become important due to the increased exposures and associated risks in digital technologies [12, 13, 23] making it an important aspect worth exploring from multiple perspectives including understanding how people respond to privacy concerns. Scholars have explained people's privacy attitudes, perceptions and behaviours with findings indicating a discrepancy between behaviour and perception, which is popularly referred to as privacy paradox [24].

While most privacy research takes legal and information system approaches, this research presents a human-centred perspective of users' privacy management practices through consumers' experiences and practices in digital technologies. It is important to understand how individuals take appropriate measures to protect their privacy rather than relying on normative practices to privacy protections. Thus privacy awareness is presented here not as a way of "setting rules and enforcing them" [25] but as a way of exploring how users understand and use a series of strategies to protect informational privacy in various digital technologies.

3 Privacy in the Context of Interconnected Information Ecologies

With the increased use of Internet-connected devices, privacy has become an important concept debated and regulated across the world through national and international laws. Hence, understanding users' privacy concerns and awareness in the current information age, where activity trackers and loyalty systems are ubiquitous, is important. This is because these digital technologies increasingly require information subjects and recipients to manage informational privacy in individual and organisational contexts. The technologies enhance connection and production of data and also enable information to get out of the envisaged contexts and boundaries, which can be considered as a breach of privacy [26].

Generally, data subjects or users of the technologies are required to determine appropriateness of information to be shared, while the recipients or organisations or data holders are expected to use the information in accordance with their intended purposes. The privacy as contextual integrity framework provides an important lens to evaluate how different parties manage this information flow. Since privacy is a socially negotiated and constructed phenomena in social processes, Nissenbaum argues that individuals should understand and have the means to manage informational privacy within their social and economic contexts [26]. Nissenbaum [27] further posits that most spheres of life are guided by "norms of information flow" in the sense that not "anything goes." To ensure privacy of individuals is protected, personal information within information ecologies should flow appropriately in accordance to [these] information norms" [28].

3.1 Personal Activity Trackers, Lifelogging, and Related Data Practices

Consumers use a variety of devices to capture and archive everyday life activities in a process referred to as lifelogging [29]. The self-tracking/lifelogging devices dominating the current consumer market are personal activity trackers or fitness tracking devices and applications. The activity trackers or fitness trackers are electronic devices characterised by the following features: worn on users' body, use accelerometer, altimeters, or sensors to track a wearer's movements and biometric, and uploads activity data to online applications [30].

The devices and applications are used for the purposes of keeping track of fitness and health through monitoring body activities and workouts such as sleep patterns, daily steps, floors climbed, intense activities (like swimming, cycling, resting time), calculating fitness-related measures, calories burned, quality of sleep, cardiovascular workouts etc. [15]. These wearable devices collect various kinds of information including data on bodily functions and physical activities (sport activities, sexual activity, travel), medical symptoms (headache, pain, allergies), spatial data (location, time, what you see) consumption data (alcohol, nicotine, caffeine, water, drug, etc.), mental health data (mood, stress, alertness), and physiological statistics [31].

Additionally, during the device set-up, users provide demographics including: gender, age, identity (photo, name, biometric data), and relational data (email, phone number). Once one starts to use the devices, personal health information or health activity data is collected, including heart rate, body mass index or BMI, weight, sleep data, calories burned, GPS locational data, dietary logs, etc. [15, 32]. The gadgets also synchronise wirelessly with other devices to provide additional information such as: text notification, calls, caller ID, and music control, and they are also compatible with third party applications and other mobile gadgets [15].

Researchers note that these self-monitoring practices are motivated by the need for recording things for one's own use and for memory purposes [33] and the practices are now commonly referred as quantified-self for the purposes of monitoring body fitness or health [34, 35]. Lupton [35] notes that while the users purchase the devices for personal use, the data is managed on proprietary platforms or databases which are involved in the data politics [36, 37]. This raises fundamental concerns and questions of how to maintain users' data privacy [35]. The data produced by these devices have become of interest in the current big data discussions and data politics, given the new business synergies created around them such as the example of Coles retail stores and insurance companies in Australia [21, 35, 38]. These self tracking technologies and practices have risks as well as benefits given their pervasive nature to capture contextual data in a continuous manner and the use the data for health research and management purposes [35, 39, 40]. The expanding body of data capturing presents a wealth of resources for data analytics, especially behaviour analysis for targeted marketing among others opportunities [6]. Lupton further notes the positive side of the use of data captured from these sensor equipped devices can potentially offer solutions to improve efficiency in safety, wealth generation and resource management in various sectors especially health, education, environment [36] and development of smart cities.

Whilst this data can be beneficial to users, the lifelogged information is sensitive [33], and hence prone to privacy breaches [15] and misuse beyond the users' knowledge. Researchers argue that digital technologies are increasingly used as a monitoring tool and as disciplinary tools to regulate human behaviour by exerting power over individuals through collection of data and profiling [41]. For example, the wearable devices can be used to investigate user activities, travel and driving behaviours of individual's and predict individual lifestyle characteristics [42] and so on.

3.2 Privacy and Security Concerns in Activity Trackers

Neff and Nafus [37] note that privacy and security challenges in activity tracking devices are technical ones; others are demonstrating this through compromising selected popular consumer activity trackers [43, 44]. These products also provide a range of features for users to control their information sharing with other applications like social networks [45] and the ability to share data with other people and to third parties for personalised programs [15].

Additionally, the Symantec security experts note that most trackers can easily be turned into surveillance tools by unauthorised third parties given the ability to track the location of people [31, 37]. A study of communication between activity tracker and online web servers also identified critical vulnerabilities which can compromise users' privacy and security [44, 46]. Similar experiments confirmed the security vulnerability of the popular fitness trackers (Garmin, Fitbit, Xiaomi, Misfit, Polar). possible illegal access to device servers and manipulation of the data [18]. In an experimental study on Fitbit and Lose it!, applications, researchers found users can permit third party apps to access data from their devices including calendars, camera, contacts, locations, microphone, phone, sensors, SMS, storage) and other metadata which is unknown to the users of the applications [15].

The fact is that service providers hold a great amount of data about people around the world, including medical devices connected to the Internet, with an ability to transmit data from data subjects. For example, pacemakers that capture and send cardiac rhythmic data to manufacturers' data warehouse and doctors for patient monitoring purposes, while the data producers/data subjects have limited access to their data, demonstrates a lack of control by the individuals [47]. This was demonstrated by Hugo Campos, a user of medical device- implantable cardioverter-defibrillator (ICD) who tracked his body fitness activities using an activity tracker, but had to file a court case to compel the ICD manufacturer to give him access to his own data; he was the data subject but did not have access to it [48]. Campos' [48] experience of denial to access or lack of control to the data produced from his heart monitoring while doctors had full unrestricted access to the information demonstrate data holders' immense power over the restricting access to these form of data although the data is about users' own body [48]. This incident forced Campos to sue the manufacturer of the devices after being informed that the data generated from ICD was "proprietary data" [49]. This example indicates how the data produced from IoT devices are implicated in data politics and legal battles over the ownership of data, which openly indicates that the data belongs to third parties and not to the device users or the data subjects [48]. Fixing the security and privacy issues raised in the big data and Internet of Things era is complex, and needs both technical solutions, legal alignments with the challenges, and users' awareness [15, 45, 50].

3.3 Third Party and Other Activity Trackers

Fitness tracking devices and apps also have third party applications which users can connect their devices or data to for other additional services [15]. For example, a user of Fitbit application or device can allow or deny access to Fitbit data access by the third party who also have their own privacy policies. Some of the data, which can be accessed include: sleep data, food, water logs, activity and exercise, and weight, which users may knowingly or unknowingly understand what terms are tied to such linking of the data and what third parties put the data into which use. The applications include Lose it! and Strava [15]. The applications collect data from phones and fitness trackers and allow users to share the routines with friends and followers, on social media, which sometimes may pose security risks to the users due to the ability to locate individual routine or physical location. In addition the fitness devices, applications can be linked to other applications and systems where consumers are presented with incentives to share personal information in-exchange for services or reduced insurance premiums [21, 51], as presented in Fig. 1.

4 Research Design

The research design was guided by the objectives of the study to understand users of activity trackers and loyalty card systems and privacy perceptions, and how they manage personal information in the applications. Thus in this study we were interested in understanding users privacy awareness and protection practices, with the increasing use of the devices and application for self- monitoring, health monitoring and sharing of the data for other services.

For participants to be eligible to participate in this study, they fulfilled the following criteria: were 18 years or older and must have been using at least one of the activity tracking devices and using a membership card or loyalty card. The participants were invited to participate in the study through social media messages, university listserves, bulletin-board flyers and through word of mouth. The participants were between the age of 19 to 52 years old with 12 females and 9 males. All the participants were actively using a variety of fitness tracking devices and popular loyalty cards within Australia as referred in the Table 1.

The research used a qualitative approach through face-to-face interviews to get insights on how participants' experience and manage their information and data privacy according to their preferences. The use of semi-structured interviews offered a flexible opportunity for the interviewees to answer the questions [52]. Twenty-one participants from Sydney Australia were interviewed between November 2017 and December 2017 in forty-five to one-hour-long interviews. The names of the participants have been anonymised through the use of pseudonyms to ensure the privacy of the participants.

The interviews were audio-recorded, transcribed for analysis and later coded in NVivo for thematic analysis. The NVivo was used to collate related themes and for finding patterns within the data to facilitate the analysis [53]. Although the study was informed by the contextual integrity theory of privacy [26] we used thematic analysis to identify all the patterns emerging from the interview data. The interviews were guided by the overarching questions of how people manage personal information flows across the synergies created through activity trackers, users' privacy concerns, and behaviour toward affordances that link data across organisations or third parties. Finally the participants were also asked about the use of privacy settings within the activity tracking application and their awareness of the privacy policies of the respective services.

Table 1. Participant Demographics

Participants (Pseudonyms)	Gender M	F	Age range	Activity tracker Type	Loyalty card
Kelly		X	30–39	Fitbit	X
Vera		X	20–29	Fitbit	X
Marcello	X		20–29	Garmin	X
Deepak	X		20–29	Garmin	X
John	X		40–49	Fitbit	X
Elaine		X	20–29	Fitbit	X
Molly		X	30–39	Fitbit HR2	X
Dolly		X	20–29	Fitbit	X
Janet		X	30–39	Fitbit	X
Sue		X	20–29	Fitbit, Apple watch	X
Harry	X		20–29	Fitbit	X
Teresa		X	40–49	Fitbit	X
Michael	X		40–49	Fitbit	X
Evelyn		X	40–49	Fitbit	X
Ivan			40–49	Fitbit	X
Lillian		X	20–29	Garmin, Fitbit	X
Pauline		X	40–49	Garmin	X
Julie			40–49	Fitbit	X
Daniels	X		10–19	Xiaomi, Apple watch	X
Joe	X		20–29	Fitbit, apple watch	X
Andrew	X		50–59	TomTom	X

5   Findings and Discussion

The data analysis identified participants' informational privacy preferences and management practices in their everyday-use of the activity trackers and possible connections with the loyalty cards and to other additional applications. Various themes emerged during the analysis process, including: appropriateness of information shared in particular platforms, information avoidance and privacy policies, managing data sharing practices including locational data, which are all presented below.

5.1   A Negotiating Attitude Toward Determining Information Sharing

Normative notions of privacy management require users of digital technologies to assess the risks of providing or disclosing personal information on online platforms or to organisations versus concealing the information. Since the personal information collected through these devices and applications represent a person's identity and everyday-life activities, misuse of this information might have possible privacy implications.

Such privacy concerns compel users to take precautionary measures to limit the amount of information when signing-up or sharing across applications. The interviewees were asked about their responses to linking fitness data with other applications or services and were presented with scenarios such as the existing retail store program in Fig. 1, which allows consumers to link loyalty cards systems, activity trackers and insurance providers in exchange for benefits. The program provides a means for users of the devices to link the fitness tracker data and loyalty cards and share the data to an insurance provider in exchange for points or reduced insurance premiums.

Fig. 1. Flybys loyalty system connects with activity tracker and insurance provider [21]

While the majority of participants considered the information in fitness trackers as sensitive and uncomfortable to share due to privacy concerns, twenty of the participants were also willing to share or link the devices in return for tangible benefits. This can be attributed to consumers' motivation to satisfy their immediate needs while considering privacy as a distant concern ("why would anyone be interested in me") with possible minimal impact ("I have nothing to hide") compared to the benefits derived from the use of the technologies or making such connections that allows organisations to link and use the derived data.

The finding corroborates prior research, which indicated that users of various digital technologies are willing to share most form of data for instant monetary gratification [54, 55]. These responses are partly associated with peoples' perception of this information as something that only exists in a virtual world that is less likely to impact on their real life; this may have an influence on consumers' behaviours towards making such trade-off decisions [56]. For example, although our research participant Julie was concerned about how the fitness data might be used against her due to concerns about her health status, she was willing to make such a trade-off for instant monetary in exchange for sharing fitness information:

> "If actually sharing my information was going reduce my premiums I absolutely do it, but I don't know that would be the case. It might actually take my information and go while you're overweight. Therefore we're going to increase your premiums. I think for me the insurance companies will be happy that someone who's is overweight as me with my family history both my parents are overweight as well that I'm actually exercising as much as I am"

Due to perceived economic effects, individuals are likely to share data with such connected synergies by making a quick cost-benefits analysis; as Julie further explained:

> "I don't know I mean it's a tricky situation because in one sense I'm really healthy because I'm exercising a lot. But honestly at the moment I am so poor maybe I would, just because if reduces my premiums then I would."

Other participants also indicated similar sentiments of readiness to link their loyalty cards and fitness data for monetary benefits:

> "I am open to doing that, because it reduces cost, for minimal effort on my part. Reduced privacy for at least some money."

While participants considered the information from their fitness trackers as sensitive health data and uncomfortable to share, only one participant had extreme concerns towards the sharing and connecting of fitness trackers and loyalty cards with insurance companies, or participating in such reward schemes. For example, one respondent said:

> "I'm very wary of giving more information to my insurance and I wouldn't want to do is. it can quickly be used against me or use for the wrong purpose. And once it's given that I don't have any control of how this will be used whatever is a good intent. I guess I am somehow very conservative person and I don't want my insurance to know what I'm. Why I'm Running. How many times I'm running. How is my heartbeat going, maybe it's my conspiracy theory thing but yeah I'll think it could easily then be used for reviewing maybe terms and conditions of my insurance and I wouldn't want that."

Amongst all the participants only one participant was unwilling to share or link the devices and share personal data from the activity tracker for any benefits. The findings demonstrate the vulnerability of users towards the trade-off of health/personal data for instant benefits while ignoring their privacy concerns arising from the use of the data.

The activity tracker applications also provide a means for users to share their fitness data on social media like Twitter, Facebook and other third party applications. The majority of participants indicated a lack of interest in sharing their fitness data on social media with the exception of a few who indicated that they had posted the fitness data on social media to share their achievement while training for some up coming marathon events.

The willingness of consumers to make such trade-offs in sharing information across contextual boundaries and also to make a considered and rationalised decision when deciding to share their data while knowing possible future risks is in line with findings from earlier research [54] which indicated that people have adopted an "it depends attitude" when it comes to sharing personal information for economic benefits, although privacy experts and researchers raise the possibility of misuse under such trade-offs because users hardly have time to understand all the terms and conditions of such services.

5.2   Controlling Locational Data in Activity Tracking Applications

For the Internet-connected and GPS-enabled activity tracker devices, it is difficult for consumers to control locational data due to covert and technical transmissions of locational data. Also when users set-up the activity trackers they provide personal information, which includes name of the place, users personal information (name, e-mail address, age and any characteristic that is unique to a person) and locational information: spatial (coordinates) and also temporal information (non-real time and real time) [57]. The locational information disclosure in the activity tracker applications is both technical and voluntarily shared with third parties and service providers. For example, the fitness tracker applications permit users to share locational information in the device applications [18] with other users or on social media, thus individuals have some form of control to decide whether to disclose, or not use the locational feature. One participant indicated that they have connected the fitness application to another third party application (Strava) to map distance and route used etc.; however, due to security concerns about people being able to locate her home, she disconnected and deleted the application:

> "I'm very concerned with some applications they know already where I am through my mobile phone not just Fitbit. Yeah there was this app - Strava I used, but I stopped because it knows my location like home. So if I'm doing a run it will know that I'm always stopping in one area and I'll know that that's my base and therefore that was my home. So I stopped using that."

To control the flow of locational information, participants indicated continual effort and attempts to limit access by deactivating locational features on their smartphones or applications and avoiding using the location features in fitness application or avoiding using automatic uploads of the data to their social media platforms like Facebook or Twitter. For example, Pauline explained why and how she limits access to location information for privacy reasons:

> "I want to limit my exposure of my personal information as much as possible. I don't use my location on my phone or fitness trackers because I don't want people out there to know where I'm located. So only when I'm desperate and I need to go somewhere, I use Google Maps, then I put my location on and then as soon as I finish up takeoff my location."

Teresa also explained that she always denies access to location while using smartphone applications, and only activates location service in the applications when necessary:

> "I don't like sharing my location for every application. Just [that] I have a bad feeling about being monitored, about people knowing exactly where I am and I just it's just does not sit comfortably with me."

Majority of the participants were highly concerned about locational privacy concerns especially in disclosing their home addresses and their real-time location for security reasons. Most of the participants indicated they enabled the location functionality when using some applications on their smartphones applications. While protection of location privacy takes multiple perspectives, the findings indicate users of the applications actively deploy necessary measures within their means to maintain their locational privacy by controlling the locational information sharing in devices and applications.

5.3   Complexity in Managing Personal Data

Social media applications provide privacy settings to limit access to personal information by an unintended audience or unauthorised individuals. The activity tracker devices and applications equally provide privacy settings to enable users to limit the type of information that should be accessible to other fitness applications.

However, in this study, the users expressed their lack of complete control over the personal data in devices since they are Internet-connected devices and due to the complexity of the interconnected technologies. The participants pointed out that while the fitness applications provide new opportunities for personal use, they equally pose unknown risks to users. For example, one participant reflected on the challenges of understanding how to balance between the "new opportunities of using the digital technologies and managing the privacy risks". The participants pointed out:

> "...given the options in a very clear simple way to manage my own privacy then I would really like to have that because at the moment it's quite cryptic sometimes and it's all hidden somewhere and it's like if we're looking at one app but then we don't know where and how far it's linked to all the different devices and all. So it's not just the app it's the devices and it's other people's devices and then it's always linking a lot of different things thinking other people's devices my devices my time, my location. So how much I can control that I don't know because it's so new it might also with new opportunities or new threats as well that we may not be aware of especially malicious ones."

The fitness tracker applications provide privacy settings to enable users to control personal demographics (birthday, height, weight) and statistical information on calorie intake and calories burned, sleep, distance walked, steps taken, floors climbed etc., and post graphs and posts within the application and social media platforms. The application allows users to customise the settings with three options to make the personal information private, public or share it with friends within the networks or to social networking sites.

In many of these fitness applications, users can form groups in the application and share fitness information and make comments on other users' profiles just like on social media or social networking sites. None of the participants indicated having used or customised the privacy settings. This could be attributed to most participants having no interest in sharing the data in their respective social media even though it is possible to avail opportunities to share the data/information. The privacy settings feature requires effort and some form of privacy literacy to understand how they function, in order to meaningfully use them to safeguard the informational privacy of oneself and others.

5.4   Information Avoidance, Privacy Policies and Privacy Management

All the twenty-one participants did not read the privacy policies before using or signing up for the fitness and loyalty cards systems. While the privacy policies are presented as main tools to negotiate and inform users of digital technologies on how the information is collected, processed and used by the service providers, participants indicated they never read them because of the information overload they present. The participants explained:

> "I kind of start reading that and then; I think nobody actually reads all of that, everyone just clicks. I agree, and that's all. It's too much information and it's boring." (Elaine)

> "It's a bit time consuming and no one can actually read it. If you get privacy statement, you just click agree and move on to the next step" (Deepak)

Information behaviour researchers explain that people deployed information avoidance as a coping mechanism to deal with cognitive dissonance and information overload [58]. Thus, with the negotiated nature of privacy, and on account of the legalese presented in privacy policies, a kind of cognitive dissonance is triggered, compelling users to take a passive role in consuming the technology without making an effort to understand the consequences of such behaviour for their informational privacy. The participants' behaviour reflects lack self-determination in privacy negotiation. For example, Julie said:

> "I am lazy with privacy policies, because it's too long and I think that makes me very loose with my privacy."

Similarly, other participants noted that privacy policies present constraints due to a lack of choices, saying that the conditions were rigid in the way consumers have to agree to the terms as presented. Teresa explained that she superficially glances at the privacy policies and finally agrees anyway, since the alternative is to forgo the use of the product or application altogether which is not an option at that particular moment:

> "I read them in a very superficial way and sometimes I don't read because I figured that if you want to use the devices or application you have to agree with the policy. If you don't agree with the policy don't use the device use some other mechanism." (Teresa)

> "I know everyone should read that, but…it's just like maybe I don't really care if they're going to share my names with somebody, or my email, or something like that because it's not too personal information. If it would be more serious information like my bank account, or something like that, yeah, I would definitely read all of that. But because it's only my name, date of birth and how much I weigh, it's not that serious." (Vera)

The continual avoidance to use privacy policies calls for new ways to enhance their use either through active measures such as stringent data protection regulation by privacy regulators to compel service providers to address the complexities, and for the users to equally negotiate or understand the synergies around the data collected from the devices and applications. For example, privacy researchers have increasingly advocated for improvements to the mode of presentation and transparency through simplification of the language and fonts and the provision of choices of opting-in or opting-out that clearly indicate the how the collection, processing, transferring or sharing of personal information is done [59].

While privacy is presumed as a fundamental right, users of digital technologies have limited control or lack the means to exercise that right due to the limited options. Additionally, people give consent to the terms of service without reading them, which indicates vulnerability due to a lack of understanding of how the data is used by third parties or service providers. To address the constraints in the privacy policies, new mechanisms have emerged to advocate for improvement of privacy policies and terms of services with organisations and researchers dedicating themselves to monitoring [60] technological corporations, and advocating the provision of consumer-friendly privacy policies in an effort to support general public awareness. These approaches are deliberate attempts to enhance transparency and openness in protecting users' information privacy and also enhance privacy awareness among the users. This may foster usability of the policies rather than having them serve purely legal functions, rather than as negotiation and informing tools of how the data is collected, processed and used, in a clear, simple-to-understand language.

6 Conclusion

This study examined users of activity trackers and loyalty cards to understand their privacy awareness and use and sharing of data. Past research on mobile-device fitness applications suggest the use of the "Inform, Alert, Mitigate" method to enhance users' privacy awareness in applications to ensure users have control on how the information is collected and used [61]. Although this method is effective in giving some degree of privacy and data control to users, the business synergies created around data may by-pass these controls.

The study findings show individuals use a variety of methods in an attempt to protect their data and locational privacy; however, the practices are not consistent due to users' attitudes toward the trade-off of data for benefits. While the study findings indicate user awareness of privacy concerns associated with sharing information in digital technologies, they also point to a vulnerability due to the willingness to share data in exchange for benefits without understanding the terms of services. The readiness to share personal information with third parties and service providers without reading or understanding the terms of service call for more transparency in the way service providers inform how they collect, process, transfer and use personal information. This will ensure the usability of the information in a beneficial way by users and also enhance consumers' trust in service providers and related entities.

Additionally, the continued reluctance by users to read privacy policies indicates a vulnerability for users, and hence service providers need to be open on how they preserve the contextual integrity of the data they collect intentionally or inadvertently, and how they handle the information flows, with the protection of consumers in mind.

As indicated in the literature, researchers have raised privacy and security concerns related to activity trackers, and therefore it is important for users to understand the vulnerabilities they are exposed to while using these applications and devices. Users' knowledge, skills and awareness of privacy issues is integral to the contextual integrity of the information and data that and service providers collect. Therefore, they should also take the responsibility to educate users and provide an enabling environment for users to manage their personal information and privacy according to their expectations.

References

1. Solove, D.J., Schwartz, P.M.: Consumer Privacy and Data Protection. Wolters Kluwer, New York (2014)
2. Christl, W., Kopp, K., Riechert, P.U.: Corporate Surveillance in Everyday Life. Crackedlabs (2017)
3. Rosenblat, A., Kneese, T., Boyd, D.: Networked employment discrimination. Open Society Foundations' Future of Work Commissioned Research Papers (2014). https://papers.ssrn.com/sol3/papers.cfm?abstract_id=2543507
4. Solove, D.J.: A taxonomy of privacy. Univ. Pennsylvania Law Rev. **154**, 477–564 (2006)
5. Kitchin, R.: The Data Revolution: Big Data, Open Data, Data Infrastructures and Their Consequences. Sage, Los Angeles (2014)
6. Haynes, D., Robinson, L.: Defining user risk in social networking services. Aslib J. Inf. Manag. **67**, 94–115 (2015)
7. Lyon, D.: Surveillance, power and everyday life. In: Kalantzis-Cope, P., Gherab-Martín, K. (eds.) Emerging Digital Spaces in Contemporary Society, pp. 107–120. Palgrave Macmillan, London (2010)
8. Clarke, R.: Introduction to dataveillance and information privacy, and definitions of terms (1999). http://www.rogerclarke.com/DV/Intro.html
9. Lambiotte, R., Kosinski, M.: Tracking the digital footprints of personality. Proc. IEEE **102**, 1934–1939 (2014)
10. Pariser, E.: The Filter Bubble: How the New Personalized Web is Changing What We Read and How We Think. Penguin, New York (2011)
11. Acquisti, A., Brandimarte, L., Loewenstein, G.: Privacy and human behavior in the age of information. Science **347**, 509–514 (2015)
12. Christl, W., Kopp, K., Riechert, P.U.: How companies use personal information against people: automated disadvantage, personalized persuasion, and the societal ramifications of the commercial use of personal information. Cracked Labs (2017)
13. Correia, J., Compeau, D.: Information Privacy Awareness (IPA): a review of the use, definition and measurement of IPA. In: Proceedings of the 50th Hawaii International Conference on System Sciences, Hawaii (2017)
14. Svantesson, D., Clarke, R.: A best practice model for e-consumer protection. Comput. Law Secur. Rev. **26**, 31–37 (2010)
15. Torre, I., Sanchez, O.R., Koceva, F., Adorni, G.: Supporting users to take informed decisions on privacy settings of personal devices. Pers. Ubiquit. Comput. **22**, 1–20 (2017)
16. Rotman, D.: Are you looking at me? Social media and privacy literacy. In: 4th iSchool Conference, Chapel Hill, USA (2009). http://hdl.handle.net/2142/15339
17. Givens, C.L.: Information Privacy Fundamentals for Librarians and Information Professionals. Rowman & Littlefield, Lanham (2015)
18. Fereidooni, H., Frassetto, T., Miettinen, M., Sadeghi, A.-R., Conti, M.: Fitness trackers: fit for health but unfit for security and privacy. In: 2017 IEEE/ACM Connected Health Applications, Systems and Engineering Technologies (CHASE), pp. 19–24. IEEE, Philadelphia (2017). https://ieeexplore.ieee.org/document/8010569/
19. Clausing, E., Schiefer, M., Morgenstern, U.: Internet of Things: Security Evaluation of nine Fitness Trackers. AV TEST, The Independent IT-Security institute, Magdeburg (2015). https://www.av-test.org/fileadmin/pdf/avtest_2015-06_fitness_tracker_english.pdf
20. Ajunwa, I., Crawford, K., Ford, J.S.: Health and big data: an ethical framework for health information collection by corporate wellness programs. J. Law Med. Ethics **44**, 474–480 (2016)

21. Flybys: Small Steps, Big Impact. The Path to a Healthier Lifestyle Starts with Just One Step (2016). https://www.flybuys.com.au/collect#/partners/fitbit
22. Crawford, K., Schultz, J.: Big data and due process: toward a framework to redress predictive privacy harms. Boston Coll. Law Rev. **55**, 39–92 (2014)
23. Floridi, L.: Four challenges for a theory of informational privacy. Ethics Inf. Technol. **8**, 109–119 (2006)
24. Barnes, S.B.: A privacy paradox: social networking in the United States. First Mon. **11**(9) (2006)
25. Palen, L., Dourish, P.: Unpacking privacy for a networked world. In: SIGCHI Conference on Human Factors in Computing Systems, pp. 129–136 (2003). https://dl.acm.org/citation.cfm?id=642635
26. Nissenbaum, H.: Privacy in Context. Stanford University Press, Stanford (2009)
27. Nissenbaum, H.: Privacy as contextual integrity. Washington Law Rev. **79**, 119 (2004)
28. Barocas, S., Nissenbaum, H.: Big data's end run around anonymity and consent. In: Julia, L., Victoria, S., Stefan, B., Helen, N. (eds.) Privacy, Big Data, and the Public Good: Frameworks for Engagement, vol. 1, pp. 44–75. Cambridge University Press, New York (2014)
29. Sellen, A.J., Whittaker, S.: Beyond total capture: a constructive critique of lifelogging. Commun. ACM **53**, 70–77 (2010). https://dl.acm.org/citation.cfm?id=1735243
30. Hoy, M.B.: Personal activity trackers and the quantified self. Med. Ref. Serv. Q. **35**, 94–100 (2016)
31. Barcena, M.B., Wueest, C., Lau, H.: How Safe is Your Quantified Self? Symantec, Mountain View (2014)
32. Christovich, M.M.: Why should we care what fitbit shares-a proposed statutory solution to protect sensative personal fitness information. Hast. Commun. Entertain. Law J. **38**, 91 (2016)
33. Rawassizadeh, R.: Towards sharing life-log information with society. Behav. Inf. Technol. **31**, 1057–1067 (2012)
34. Wolf, G.: Know thyself: tracking every facet of life, from sleep to mood to pain. Wired (2009). https://www.wired.com/2009/06/lbnp-knowthyself/
35. Lupton, D.: The Quantified Self. Polity Press, Malden (2016)
36. Lupton, D.: Digital Sociology. Routledge, London (2015)
37. Neff, G., Nafus, D.: The Self-tracking. MIT Press, Cambridge (2016)
38. Lupton, D.: You are your data: self-tracking practices and concepts of data. In: Selke, S. (ed.) Lifelogging, pp. 61–79. Springer, Wiesbaden (2014). https://doi.org/10.1007/978-3-658-13137-1_4
39. Lo, B.P., Ip, H., Yang, G.-Z.: Transforming health care: body sensor networks, wearables, and the Internet of Things. IEEE Pulse **7**, 4–8 (2016). https://ieeexplore.ieee.org/document/7387856/
40. United States Federal Trade Commission: Internet of things: privacy and security in a connected world (2015). https://www.hsdl.org/?view&did=805589
41. Foucault, M.: Discipline and Punishment: The Birth of the Prison. Vintage, New York (1977). (Ed. by Alan Scheridan)
42. Doherty, A.R., et al.: Passively recognising human activities through lifelogging. Comput. Hum. Behav. **27**, 1948–1958 (2011)
43. Lewis, S.J.: Assessment of the privacy and security of smart toys marketed to children. Top10VPN (2017). https://www.top10vpn.com/wp-content/uploads/2018/02/Top10VPN-smart-toys-safety-report.pdf

44. Rahman, M., Carbunar, B., Banik, M.: Fit and vulnerable: attacks and defenses for a health monitoring device. https://www.ieee-security.org/TC/SP2013/posters/Mahmudur_Rahman. pdf

45. Zhou, W., Piramuthu, S.: Security/privacy of wearable fitness tracking IoT devices. In: 9th Iberian Conference on Information Systems and Technologies (CISTI): IEEE, pp. 1–5. IEEE (2014). https://ieeexplore.ieee.org/document/6877073/

46. Boam, E., Webb, J.: Qualified self going beyond quantification. Designmind (2014). https:// designmind.frogdesign.com/2014/05/qualified-self-going-beyond-quantification/

47. Michael, K.: Implantable medical device tells all: uberveillance gets to the heart of the matter. IEEE Consum. Electron. Mag. 6, 107–115 (2017). ieeexplore.ieee. org/document/8048728/

48. Campos, H.: Fighting for the right to open his heart data: Hugo Campos at TEDxCambridge 2011 (2011). https://youtu.be/oro19-l5M8k

49. Hinckley, D.: This big brother/big data business goes way beyond apple and the FBI. Huffpost (2016). https://www.huffingtonpost.com/david-hinckley/this-big-brotherbig-data_ b_9292744.html

50. World Economic Forum: Rethinking Personal Data: Strengthening Trust (2012). http:// www3.weforum.org/docs/WEF_RethinkingPersonalData_ANewLens_Report_2014.pdf

51. Pingo, Z., Narayan, B.: When personal data becomes open data: an exploration of lifelogging, user privacy, and implications for privacy literacy. In: Morishima, A., Rauber, A., Liew, C.L. (eds.) ICADL 2016. LNCS, vol. 10075, pp. 3–9. Springer, Cham (2016). https://doi.org/10.1007/978-3-319-49304-6_1

52. Bryman, A.: Social Research Methods. Oxford University Press, Oxford (2015)

53. Bazeley, P.: Qualitative Analysis with NVivo. Sage, London (2007)

54. Rainie, L., Duggan, M.: Privacy and Information Sharing. Pew Research Center (2015). http://www.pewinternet.org/2016/01/14/2016/Privacy-and-Information Sharing/

55. Acquisti, A.: Privacy in electronic commerce and the economics of immediate gratification. In: Proceedings of the 5th ACM Conference on Electronic Commerce, pp. 21–29. ACM (2004). https://dl.acm.org/citation.cfm?id=988777

56. Bandara, R., Fernando, M., Akter, S.: Is the privacy paradox a matter of psychological distance? An exploratory study of the privacy paradox from a construal level theory perspective. In: Proceedings of the 51st Hawaii International Conference on System Sciences, Hawaii (2018). https://scholars.uow.edu.au/display/publication116721

57. Wernke, M., Skvortsov, P., Dürr, F., Rothermel, K.: A classification of location privacy attacks and approaches. Pers. Ubiquit. Comput. 18, 163–175 (2014)

58. Case, D.O., Given, L.M.: Looking for Information: A Survey of Research on Information Seeking, Needs, and Behavior. Academic Press, San Diego (2017)

59. Briedis, M., Webb, J., Fraser, M.: Improving the Communication of Privacy Information for Consumers. Australian Communications Consumer Action Network (2016)

60. Terms of Service Didnt Read: "I have read and agree to the Terms" is the biggest lie on the web. We aim to fix that (2017). https://tosdr.org/blog/tosdr-in-action-i-have-read-and-agree. html

61. Tailor, N., He, Y., Wagner, I.: POSTER: design ideas for privacy-aware user interfaces for mobile devices. In: Proceedings of the 9th ACM Conference on Security & Privacy in Wireless and Mobile Networks, pp. 219–220. ACM, Darmstadt (2016). https://doi.org/10. 1145/2939918.2942420

Multiple Level Enhancement of Children's Picture Books with Augmented Reality

Nicholas Vanderschantz$^{(\boxtimes)}$ (iD), Annika Hinze (iD),
and Aysha AL-Hashami

University of Waikato, Hamilton, New Zealand
{vtwoz,hinze}@waikato.ac.nz,
asshal@students.waikato.ac.nz

Abstract. This paper reports a case study on using Augmented Reality (AR) in children's books. in which we explored the use of various types of interactions at different levels. An AR enhanced 2-page spread is developed to explore interactivity in printed books. We describe the design process and the insights gained into the requirements for AR enhancement of children's books.

Keywords: Augmented reality · Children's books · Interaction model
Reading

1 Introduction

In this paper, we report on our case study into the opportunities of using Augmented Reality (AR) enhancement to printed children's picture books. The AR elements were developed by a design team following an established design process to identify the problem, hypothesize initial design ideations, iterate and develop design solutions. The paper focusses on the design decisions, reports on the proof-of-concept implementation, and discusses insights, however we do not discuss technical implementation of the AR.

2 Related Work

It is well established that children may benefit from picture books through the consumption of both words and pictures (Bloom 2002). We previously studied interactive children's books (Timpany and Vanderschantz 2012), identifying two types of interaction, physical interactions and intellectual interactions. Most interactive books feature either physical interaction or intellectual interaction, but few books cater for both forms of interaction (Timpany and Vanderschantz 2013).

Presently eBooks provide video, audio and interactive elements and some enhance engagement with the storyline through user in-book and out-of-book tasks. eBooks offer the opportunity for enhanced engagement with the storyline in ways that printed books cannot, yet this affordance has not been fully explored (Itzkovitch 2012).

© Springer Nature Switzerland AG 2018
M. Dobreva et al. (Eds.): ICADL 2018, LNCS 11279, pp. 256–260, 2018.
https://doi.org/10.1007/978-3-030-04257-8_26

The potential of Augmented Reality integration on mobile devices has matured in recent years. AR has been explored for educational use (cf. Huang, Li and Fong 2016) and AR books may assist children (cf. Yilmaz, Kucuk and Goktas 2017) and parents during shared reading of children's books (cf. Cheng and Tsai 2014).

3   Design Thinking

We summarize here our design considerations for the AR application:

Focus on Objects Mentioned in the Story Text. The objects to animate in the AR view were decided to be those that were mentioned or described in the text of the story. The decision for each object depended on whether it was a primary object in the story or not. For example, the text in our example page explicitly mentions the panda, so it should be animated and pop-up when scanning the page. On the other hand, the tree is not mentioned in the text, and therefore was not animated.

Determining Objects to be Made Visible or Animated. While a number of inanimate objects can easily be shown on a page, fewer objects can be included in animations to avoid crowding on the phone screen. Having fewer animated objects was also deemed positive with regard to directing a child's attention and ensuring single focus.

Division of the Target Images. Each animation target must be unique and easy to recognize by the camera. It was decided not to encode any specific order for the animated objects to pop-up on the screen (but rather leave the selection to the reader).

Interaction Types for Different Elements. It was decided to assign different types of interactions to the objects and to make these dependent on the element and the target reactions. We used both visual animations (appearing objects, movement) and sound animations (animal sounds, spoken text).

Camera Level and Distance. While children may hold the camera closer to the page when scanning the image, parents may trial different distances to the page to explore various levels. We decided to therefore make the required level of the camera flexible in order to suit different users. Integration of varied physical and intellectual interactivity was achieved through the unique use of multi-level targeting afforded by allowing different camera distances. Camera angle also needed to be considered to ensure correct identification of images irrespective of device orientation.

4   Material Design

We used the children's book *Hannah's Favorite Place* (Fiona Mason 2015), a book written, illustrated, and developed as a traditional printed picture book, as well as an adaptive printed picture book (Wright 2015), see example pages in Fig. 1.

Fig. 1. Illustrations of the tradition (L) and physically enhanced (R) book.

4.1 Image Target

For this investigation, we selected a single spread (i.e., two pages) showing one of Hannah's favorite places: the zoo. The text on this spread reads: "Her auntie took Hannah on trips to the zoo; they'd look at the pandas, the chimps and birds too" with a supporting illustration, some of which is mentioned in the text (see Fig. 2).

The image target that was used for the AR enhancement converted some of the page elements into objects to be displayed in AR mode. Figure 3 shows the image target that was used in this project. This image target is similar to the spread found in the original version of the *Hannah's favorite place*, however some elements were initially hidden. Figure 2 shows the image as it first appears to a reader, while Fig. 3 shows all animated objects. It can be seen that the following objects are initially hidden: the bird flying in front of the cat, the banana that the chimp was holding, as well as the drawing of the other chimp. These elements are discoverable through the use of AR interactions. Experiments were conducted to test all the possibilities of holding the camera by either the children or adults. We decided to divide the image into three levels as shown in Fig. 3. The application has three levels of AR interactivity. These levels depend on how close the camera is when scanning the target. In each level, different animated objects aim to support both enjoinment and learning.

Level 1 (Purple Frame in Fig. 3 - Playful Interactions): The user holds the camera close to the image target so the camera scans one object at a time (thus, there are six image targets in this level). In this level, the camera is closer to each object (assuming children will hold the phone). At this level, all objects were animated individually. A user can view and explore six primary objects (i.e. Hannah and her auntie, two pandas, two chimps, birds and a cat) on the target page. Each object will pop-up individually. Additionally, sounds will be played, such as screaming chimps when one of the chimps is being shown in the AR view. Figure 4 is a screenshot of the mobile app that shows an object from level one.

Level 2 (Red Frame in Fig. 3 - Simple Educational Interactions): The user holds the camera slightly further away from the image target so the camera can scan about one-third of the spread, i.e. two objects at a time. At this level, there are two image targets, and different objects appear in each part of the page. This level is educational but in a fun way aiming to assist children to learn how to spell words and recognize the related object of that name. As shown in the phone screen in Fig. 5, this level introduces words and arrows that point to existing objects in the target page.

Level 3 (Yellow Frame in Fig. 3 - Playful and Educational Interactions): The user holds the camera furthest away from the image target so the camera can scan the whole spread at one time. There is only one image target to be discovered. This level was implemented to target both the enjoyment and learning aspects. Children can explore new objects in this level, which are the bees that appear only at this level. Moreover, in level three the story text was played in the background, i.e. the children can hear a person reading the text for them. Introducing new objects in this level could increase the excitement of the children and motivate them to hear the attached audio.

Fig. 2. Spread from *Hannah's Favorite Place* (Fiona Mason 2015).

Fig. 3. The three levels of the image target.

Fig. 4. An object that appears in level one.

Fig. 5. Shows the word and arrows that appear in level two.

5   Conclusions and Recommendations

The aim of our project was to develop an AR application for a children's picture book that explored the potential to engage both physical and intellectual interactions. We used three levels of interactivity to provide a variety of interactions and engagement opportunities. Our application combines fun and learning aspects at different camera levels. We engage the user in a range of physical and intellectual interactions through different types of animation and user interaction with the page. We used sounds, animated objects, as well as appearing and disappearing objects which we believe will draw children's attention and delight. Revealing objects like the banana and the bird in the application aims to increase children's engagement. Adding new objects (such as bees and additional text) in the augmented animations attempts to encourage children to explore the target page further. Using a number of enhancements in the AR version of the book should appeal to children's sense of curiosity, encouraging children to compare the two versions of the book (physical book and AR application), and afford opportunities to explore the book in more detail and through multiple sittings.

Further exploration of the possibilities of AR enhanced picture books at multiple interaction levels is warranted through user studies and development of further testing material. We extend this paper with reporting of insights from an initial expert walk-through of this system in our related working paper (Vanderschantz et al. 2018).

References

Bloom, P.: How Children Learn the Meanings of Words. MIT Press, Cambridge (2002)

Cheng, K.-H., Tsai, C.-C.: Children and parents reading of an augmented reality picture book: analyses of behavioral patterns and cognitive attainment. Comput. Educ. **72**, 302–312 (2014)

Huang, Y., Li, H., Fong, R.: Using augmented reality in early art education: a case study in Hong Kong kindergarten. Early Child Dev. Care **186**(6), 879–894 (2016)

Itzkovitch, A.: Interactive eBook Apps: The Reinvention of Reading and Interactivity (2012). http://uxmag.com/articles/interactive-ebook-apps-the-reinvention-of-reading-andinteractivity

Mason, F.: Hannah's Favorite Place. Unpublished draft (2015)

Timpany, C., Vanderschantz, N.: A categorisation structure for interactive children's books. Int. J. Book **9**, 97–110 (2012)

Timpany, C., Vanderschantz, N.: Using a categorisation structure to understand interaction in children's books. Int. J. Book. **10**, 29–44 (2013)

Yilmaz, R.M., Kucuk, S., Goktas, Y.: Are augmented reality picture books magic or real for preschool children aged five to six. Br. J. Educ. Technol. **48**(3), 824–841 (2017)

Wright, K.: A comparison of children's books: picture books versus physically and intellectually adaptive children's books. Unpublished Master's Thesis, University of Waikato, New Zealand (2015)

Vanderschantz, N., Hinze, A., Al-Hashami, A.: Using augmented reality to enhance children's books. Computer Science Working Papers 02/2018, Department of Computer Science, The University of Waikato, Hamilton, New Zealand (2018)

A Visual Content Analysis of Thai Government's Census Infographics

Somsak Sriborisutsakul(✉) ⓘ, Sorakom Dissamana ⓘ,
and Saowapha Limwichitr ⓘ

Chulalongkorn University, Bangkok, Thailand
somsak.sr@chula.ac.th

Abstract. This paper reports an approach to visual content analysis and findings of the initial phase of developing the coding sheet for analyzing government infographics in Thailand. It sought to examine story topics and visual displays appeared in census infographics at the outset. All 108 infographics from the National Statistical Office (NSO) website were chosen to be studied. There were two expert coders responsible for a pilot coding. The first expert was designated to analyze the contents, and another coder was assigned to identify narrative visualization used in the census infographics. Overall, the preliminary findings reveal that the NSO focused on the creation of static infographics in which their contents, together with the static visuals, represented census data in a single page. Although the NSO static infographics were the most common format found for its visual communication, further studies are required to examine different kinds of infographics generated by other Thai government agencies dealing with varied information other than census data.

Keywords: Infographics · Visual communication · Census data

1 Introduction

Every year the National Statistical Office (NSO) of Thailand has been assigning its staff to gather data from hundreds of fieldworks. As the amount of survey data collected increases, the NSO has produced its infographics, since 2014, to help Thai people in general as well as other groups of stakeholders at all levels to conveniently access to its official statistics or census data. It is believed that these infographics can be used to make the audience understand key information as well as insights derived from the census data, to quickly communicate official messages regarding public policies, to simplify the presentation of large amounts of census data, and to monitor changes in statistical aspects over time [1]. In the current Thai context, there are no guidelines regarding what kinds of data visualization (e.g. graphics, tables, charts, maps and pictograms) can be used to concisely illustrate and present the government data in form of infographics while keeping the reader in mind. Without such guidelines, the NSO's practices today in its census infographics creation seem to fall into the trap of visual communication, for example, information overload, excessive graphics, distracting texts, misleading scales, and inconsistent presentation.

© Springer Nature Switzerland AG 2018
M. Dobreva et al. (Eds.): ICADL 2018, LNCS 11279, pp. 261–264, 2018.
https://doi.org/10.1007/978-3-030-04257-8_27

Many census infographics have been published on the NSO's website for five years. It is believed that they are a useful means of government communication with great potential for making census data more accessible to the general public, but empirical evidence for this belief is not easy to find. To fill this void, the purpose of the current study was to explore characteristics for contents of the NSO infographics, and to determine visual displays appearing in these census infographics.

2 Background and Related Work

Government communication in the digital age have been moving in a more sophisticated direction that requires citizens to accept high levels of public data collection and use so that government agencies could communicate and market to them more effectively. As a tool of data visualizations, infographics become popular in the government sector for disseminating huge amount of census and survey data to the masses.

2.1 Gathering Census Data in Thailand

According to the 2016 Global Open Data Index, Thailand is number 51 globally in making sure its citizens have open access to government held data. The area of national statistics ranks the second category with 85% score among the 15 categories in terms of its open license, open and machine-readable format, downloadability, public availability, and free access at any cost even though Thailand's key national statistics on demographic and economic indicators remain to be not up-to-date [2]. National statistics collected by the NSO are some of the most important data available to users of Thai government's information, as it is applicable to a wide range of purposes. Some examples of the NSO's census and survey include population and housing, agriculture, business and industry, information and communication technology, natural resources and environment, and so on. Most census data is available in multiple formats, printed publications, electronic documents, numeric files, datasets, and – a newly released medium – infographics [3].

2.2 Communicating Census Data Through Infographics

Census infographics generally are a combination between narrative texts and visual displays of statistical results which allow government communicators to disseminate key census data in an attractive way to both general public and policy makers. There are three basic components of creating census infographics — contents, visuals, and promoting infographic use, but the last component is beyond the scope of this paper. Contents of census infographics may be topics, facts, messages or stories that the graphic, numeric and textual are intended to convey. The contents are usually specified in titles of each infographic. For visual parts, they consist of charts, maps, tables, icons, and pictures supporting the contents of census infographics so that the audiences can quickly summarize census and survey data. To our knowledge, previous research in the area of census infographic design for government communication is quite limited. There has been a usability research on the effectiveness of census infographics, emanating from the U.S. Census Bureau [4]. Thus, this preliminary study aimed to contribute towards the advancement of the area of the study by applying a visual content analysis to examine census infographics in the different context, i.e. in a Thai setting.

3 Methods

All 108 census infographics published on the NSO website in May 2018 were chosen to be studied for this visual content analysis. Each of them was analyzed independently by two expert coders to do a pilot coding. The first expert was assigned to identify and group the contents of the infographics into 21 different categories of story topics. Meanwhile, the second expert coded the visual displays appearing in the infographics with regard to Segel and Heer's genres of narrative visualization [5]. All the contents and visuals were coded into an Excel spreadsheet and then calculated for analysis. The frequencies and percentage occurrences for the contents and visuals were also used in this visual content analysis.

4 Results

4.1 Contents of Infographics

The story topics of 108 census infographics were mostly about labour statistics (30, 27.78%), demography population and housing (12, 11.11%), and revenue and household expenditure as well as health statistics (10, 9.26%).

4.2 Visual Displays of Infographics

Form
Regarding visual forms of elements in 108 census infographics, graphs (e.g. line charts and bar charts) are the most popular elements. Among all the visuals studied, 39% of them had graphs. The categories with the next highest number of elements are illustrations (38%) and maps (12%).

Highlighting
The NSO always uses highlighting techniques to draw audiences' attention to specific areas on its infographics by augmenting them with distinctive features. It was found that the most common highlighting technique used in the infographics are colors (40%), zooming (36%) and different font sizes (24%), respectively.

Ordering
In terms of ordering that arranges the path audiences take through an infographic, random access is the most popular way of ordering (98%). This means that there is no suggested path at all on most census infographics. Only 2% of them were found to offer the path prescribed by the NSO producer (linear).

Messaging

The ways in which most census infographics communicate with observations and commentary to audiences are their titles (47%). They work like a headline at the top and create viewers' first impression. Other messaging tactics used in many infographics are the insertion of data sources or references (29%) at the end of the NSO infographics and the provision of summaries (24%) in form of short and hierarchical texts to support the visual contents.

5   Conclusions

The present study shows that the census infographics produced by the NSO in specific or by a Thai government agency in general, have relied on the classic creation for print consumption in documents, i.e. computer-generated posters. Their visual displays are classified into a kind of static infographics. They totally lack interaction with viewers. This static form of the NSO's infographic design may be better suited to terms like 'info-posters' [6] not 'infographics'. Also, their contents only convey statistics and survey data from the NSO's perspective without a broader audience's participation. The preliminary findings of this study are a start to understanding the use of info-graphics for government communication in the Thai context to foster audience engagement. As visual communication is gaining more significance in the public sector, more research is needed to study innovative means of communication [7]. Therefore, a further step, based on existing results, would be to analyze infographics created by other Thai government agencies that represent different kinds of information beyond census data.

References

1. National Statistical Office of Thailand: About us. http://www.nso.go.th/sites/2014en/Pages/aboutus/aboutus.aspx
2. Communicating With Census Data: Storytelling. https://www.census.gov/content/dam/Census/library/working-papers/2017/demo/communicating-with-census-data-storytelling.pdf
3. Stowers, G.: The Use of Data Visualization in Government. http://www.businessofgovernment.org/sites/default/files/The%20Use%20of%20Visualization%20in%20Government.pdf
4. Gareau, M., Keegan, R., Wang, L.: An exploration of the effectiveness of infographics in contrast to text documents for visualizing census data: what works? In: Yamamoto, S. (ed.) HIMI 2015. LNCS, vol. 9172, pp. 161–171. Springer, Cham (2015). https://doi.org/10.1007/978-3-319-20612-7_16
5. Segel, E., Heer, J.: Narrative visualization: telling stories with data. IEEE Trans. Vis. Comput. Graph. **16**, 1139–1148 (2010)
6. Kirk, A.: Data Visualisation: A Handbook for Data Driven Design. SAGE, Atlanta (2016)
7. Bohman, S.: Data visualization: an untapped potential for political participation and civic engagement. In: Kő, A., Francesconi, E. (eds.) EGOVIS 2015. LNCS, vol. 9265, pp. 302–315. Springer, Cham (2015). https://doi.org/10.1007/978-3-319-22389-6_22

Digital Library Technology

BitView: Using Blockchain Technology to Validate and Diffuse Global Usage Data for Academic Publications

Camillo Lamanna[1]([✉]) [iD] and Manfredi La Manna[2] [iD]

[1] University of Sydney, Sydney, NSW 2006, Australia
clam5986@uni.sydney.edu.au
[2] University of St Andrews, St Andrews, UK

Abstract. We suggest that blockchain technology could be used to underpin a validated, reliable, and transparent usage metric for research outputs. Previous attempts to create online usage metrics have been unsuccessful largely because it has been difficult to co-ordinate agreement between all parties on the rules of data collection and the distribution of the workload of data synthesis and dissemination. Blockchain technology can be utilized to bypass this co-ordination problem. We propose the creation of a bibliometric blockchain (called BitView) which forms a decentralized ledger of the online usage of scholarly research outputs. By means of a worked example, we demonstrate how this blockchain could ensure that all parties adhere to the same rules of data collection, and that the workload of data synthesis is distributed equitably. Moreover, we outline how public-private key cryptography could ensure that users' data remains private while librarians, academics, publishers, and research funders retain open access to all the data they require. It is concluded that a usage metric underpinned by blockchain technology may lead to a richer and healthier ecosystem in which publishers and academics are incentivized to widen access to their research.

Keywords: Bibliometrics · Blockchain · Usage factor

1 Introduction

In this paper, we suggest that blockchain technology could be used to underpin a validated, reliable, and transparent usage metric for research outputs. The argument proceeds in four steps. In Sect. 2, we outline the reasons why previous attempts to create usage metrics have been unsuccessful; in particular, we note that is has been difficult to co-ordinate agreement between different stakeholders (ranging from global publishing houses to local institutional repositories) with regard both to data standardization and to the correct distribution of the necessary workload. Collating, cleaning, and disseminating usage data – it has been assumed – is expensive and no single body, understandably, wished to undertake this financial and technical responsibility.

In Sect. 3, we suggest that blockchain technology could be utilized to bypass the workload distribution problem outlined in the preceding section. By analogy to the

M. Dobreva et al. (Eds.): ICADL 2018, LNCS 11279, pp. 267–277, 2018.
https://doi.org/10.1007/978-3-030-04257-8_28

most well-known application of blockchain (Bitcoin), we suggest that each usage (i.e. online view or download) of digital content increments the 'value' of that object's digital object identifier (DOI) by one. Just as each financial transaction is validated by the nodes on the Bitcoin blockchain, each usage event is validated by agreed standards on the proposed bibliometric blockchain. We maintain that this application of blockchain would be a simple, efficient, and decentralized mechanism by which the 'work' of measuring and validating online usage would be efficiently distributed between stakeholders. Moreover, we outline how public-private key cryptography could be used to ensure that: (i) individual users' online activity remains secure; (ii) there would be free, open access to online usage statistics; (iii) publishers and institutional repositories (PIRs) would have an unencrypted log of the usage of their own digital content; (iv) libraries would be able to measure quickly and easily their usage of different publications.

We conclude that a robust online usage metric, facilitated by blockchain technology, would provide granular information and hitherto hidden insights about the temporal and spatial map of the usage of research outputs. Among other things, this could help assess 'impact' as defined by research assessment exercises. Indeed, a transparent and validated online usage metric may help to restructure the incentives of authors, readers, and PIRs – promoting accessibility and reducing paywalls. This, in turn, may lead to a substantial increase in the percentage of research content that is openly accessible. Thus, the bibliometric blockchain may help create a healthier ecosystem for scholarly communication.

2   Challenges Facing Journal Metrics

The Journal Impact Factor (JIF) has become increasingly unpopular in recent years. Many argue that it is overly reductive: there is no substitute for reading a journal in order to ascertain the quality of the material within [1]. Some claim that it is unsound, and that the simple measure may be manipulated by certain editorial practices [2–4]. Others identify it as outdated, and suggest journals be ranked by editorial efficiency and the quality of the review process [5].

With this growing unrest, a burgeoning industry has developed to create new metrics of scholarly impact. The Eigenfactor has been founded upon the principle that not all citations are equal, and uses more involved mathematics in order to weight citations from highly-cited journals above a citation from an academic orphan [6]. CiteScore tweaks the formula of the JIF in order, its creators claim, to make it less vulnerable to calculating journal editors [7]. Altmetrics promise a more holistic approach, incorporating data from Facebook, Twitter and a host of other sources into its score [8].

The JIF and many emerging competitors rely on the premise that a citation (or its social media equivalent: a 'Like' or retweet) is the closest available proxy to the far less tangible quality of being rigorous, original, and relevant. This was understandable in the 1950s when the JIF was created – citations were the only measurable proxy and inevitably therefore also the best; but this is no longer the case [9].

In the past two decades, as the new citation-based metrics have multiplied in number, there has also been a growing interest in measuring "usage" – typically understood to mean HTML or PDF downloads of an article [10–12]. The mid-2000s saw a number of attempts to add usage data to the arsenal of metrics available to quantify scholarly communication. In the United States, one group proposed the 'usage impact factor' [13]; in the United Kingdom, another group developed the 'usage factor' [14, 15] – however, standardizing the way in which these data were collected across repositories proved challenging. In order to ensure "consistent, credible, and comparable" standards when collating usage data, the non-profit organization Counting Online Usage of Networked Electronic Resources, known as Project COUNTER, was set up and released its first code of practice in 2003 [16]. COUNTER standards ensure that compliant publisher and institutional repositories are consistent in their counting of double-clicks, web robot hits, federated search activity, and so on [17].

In the UK, in 2011, the final report of the PIRUS project devised the following model for the aggregation and dissemination of journal usage data across publishers and institutional repositories:

> a full-text entry is downloaded → a log entry is created and passed to a "central clearing house" (CCH) → CCH filters the log entries by COUNTER rules → CCH disseminates usage statistics [18]

However, there was no willing candidate for the role of the CCH: "PIRUS proposed the establishment of a global central clearing house, ... [but] the majority of publishers were not yet, largely for economic reasons, ready to implement or participate in such a service" [19]. In response to financial reticence on the part of publishers and to the difficulties of creating a global CCH, PIRUS became IRUS-UK, which functions now as an aggregator of usage data from UK institutional repositories [20]. However, the goal of aggregating global usage data from publishers has yet to be achieved.

This is a clear instance of market failure. On the demand side, there is a demonstrable need for reliable usage data: both from publishers keen to record and publicize the global usage of articles published in their journals, and from research institutions and funding bodies keen to measure the (non-citation-based) impact of publications. On the supply side, views and download data are collected by a multiplicity of individual PIRs and are ready to be harvested on a global scale. We surmise that the root cause of this failure is a misalignment of incentives: commercial publishers are inclined to distrust a mechanism that attaches value to post-prints (an open access entity) at the expense of citations (attached to published articles – a private commodity).

3   BitView

We suggest that the problem of a creating a global central clearing house could be bypassed by using blockchain technology. Blockchain is "an open, distributed ledger that can record transactions between two parties efficiently and in a verifiable and permanent way" [21]. The most well-known application of blockchain technology is Bitcoin, a decentralized digital currency which uses blockchain to record transactions on a public ledger.

For our proposed implementation, the core intuition is that an online view can be seen as a transfer of one unit of "view-currency" from the viewer to the unique DOI of the viewed material. The privacy of the viewer is maintained using cryptographic techniques to ensure that only the PIR through which the viewer accessed the output has access to their identifying data. The proposed implementation would take the form of a consortium blockchain. In a consortium blockchain, a predefined group of nodes can write on the ledger of transactions, and wider group can read the ledger; in the case of BitView, these predefined nodes would be recognized PIRs, and they alone would be able to submit data to the blockchain, while any online user would have access to read the ledger. This is as opposed to a public blockchain, such as Bitcoin, where any user can become a node which both reads and writes to the blockchain.

A worked example may help elucidate the mechanics of the implementation (see Table 1).

The key points from Table 1 are that (i) viewers will maintain their privacy insofar as their identity is secured cryptographically when using online resources; (ii) researchers, funding bodies, publishers, institutional repositories, and librarians can all interrogate the blockchain directly to ascertain the relevant usage data, without needing to go back and forth between different parties (i.e. when librarians collate usage reports from different publishers); (iii) the blockchain automatically cross-checks that COUNTER rules are applied correctly.

As each view increments the "currency" value of the DOI by one, we suggest calling the proposed blockchain 'BitView'.

3.1   The Immediate Benefits of BitView

Broadly speaking, the benefits of using blockchain technology to keep a decentralized record of validated usage data can be divided into three categories

The first advantage is that BitView would be inexpensive to run. Each step of the blockchain process (collating view transactions; submitting these to other nodes; validating, encrypting and cross-validating the data; and incorporating the finalized block into the blockchain) is automated, and therefore requires no time-consuming human input.[1] With regard to storage requirements, it is worth noting that the Bitcoin blockchain (which has processed 300 million transactions at the time of writing and records almost 10 years of data) can be stored on a modern smartphone. Therefore, the BitView blockchain will be more accessible to smaller PIRs (which do not have the resources necessary to implement COUNTER). Finally, BitView would be inexpensive to update. Currently, when the COUNTER Code of Practice is updated, this requires a

---

[1] Some readers may be aware that Bitcoin is highly resource-intensive – according to some estimates consuming as much electricity as the country of New Zealand. This is because, being a public blockchain, "miners" are required to perform computationally expensive cryptographic calculations in order to provide "proof-of-work". By using a consortium blockchain model, BitView has no miners nor the requirement to provide proof-of-work, and therefore its energy requirements will be very modest.

Table 1. BitView blockchain overview.

Step	Overview	Example
1	A viewer accesses an output via a PIR	Joe Bloggs accesses an article from the Journal of Bloggometrics via the SciBlog Repository
2	The PIR logs this access in a standardized format: (user, institution, DOI, timestamp, access_type, download_type)	SciBlog records the following on a local server: (j.bloggs, Blogg College, 10.1000/blo00000001, 1/1/2019 12:00:00, restricted, PDF)
3	The PIR keeps a record of all such accesses in a one hour period. If a user is logged-in then their user credentials are recorded, otherwise their IP address is recorded.	The local SciBlog record contains one hour of usage data: (j.bloggs, Blogg College, 10.1000/blo00000001, 1/1/2019 12:00:00, restricted, PDF) … (1.1.128.192, Unknown, 10.1000/blog00015, 1/1/2019 12:59:59, open_access, HTML)[1]
4	Every hour, each PIR submits its transaction record to the blockchain for scrutiny	SciBlog submits its usage data to the blockchain along with its public key: 3048 0241 00C9 18FA SciBlog deletes its log on the local server and begins recording the next hour of data
5	A randomly-selected node collates all the submitted transaction records and applies the COUNTER rules	Double-counted entries will be removed, as will accesses from known web bots
6	A different randomly-selected node cross-checks that the COUNTER rules have been applied correctly – if compliant, the new block is encrypted and added to the chain	The SciBlog public key is used to encrypt the user data on its transaction record: (502D 6772 333C 9F8B, Blogg College, 10.1000/blog00000001, 1/1/2019 12:00:01, restricted, PDF) In this way, there is no user-identifiable data on the blockchain record.
7	A **researcher** or **funding body** can search the blockchain to see how a particular output is being accessed	The author of a particular DOI can search the public blockchain record for their article (e.g. 10.1000/blog00000001). This will return both the total validated 'view-count' and, as all accesses are time-stamped, a log of when each use-activity took place.
8	A **publisher** or **institutional repository** can search the blockchain to see how its own outputs are being accessed; they can also	An employee of SciBlog searches "10.1000/blog" – this returns all entries where the Journal of Bloggometrics has been accessed. Recall that in Step 6, SciBlog's public key was used to encrypt the user's details. SciBlog (and only SciBlog) can now use its *private* key to decrypt this data, giv-

9	access data about which users are utilizing their resources A **librarian** can search the blockchain to see how much usage a particular journal receives through their institutional access	ing: (j.bloggs, Blogg College, 10.1000/blo00000001, 1/1/2019 12:00:00, restricted, PDF) Jack Jones, who works for Bloggs College, searches the public blockchain for "Bloggs College" AND "10.1000/blog"; this returns all entries where a user from Bloggs College has accessed the Journal of Bloggometrics.

lengthy transition period of up to four years for PIRs to become compliant with the new reporting rules [22]. BitView, conversely, could be updated with a simple single upgrade.

Secondly, the blockchain offers complete transparency. Critics of usage metrics have argued that "validating a journal's usage factor is both technically and feasibly impossible for a journal editor" insofar as they would need to "request the original transaction log file from a publisher and have the ability to extract the relevant data, apply COUNTER's Code of Practice, and perform the appropriate calculations on the data" [23]. Using the proposed system, the community of blockchain nodes ensures that COUNTER's Code of Practice has been adhered to. Whereas COUNTER compliance is currently subject to regular, expensive, time-intensive audit, with BitView, COUNTER compliance would be ensured by the BitView nodes in an automated fashion. It should be recalled, however, that this transparency does not come at the cost of privacy: cryptography can be used to ensure that both individual users and institutions do not have any identifiable data visible on the blockchain.

Thirdly, we suggest that BitView usage data will be more robust. According to recent estimates, the majority of website views come from non-human users: bots, spiders, crawlers [24]. Much of this activity is legitimate and useful: Google's bots ultimately allow us to search the web. However, much of it is not. In addition to benign bots, online repositories are frequently subject to scraping attacks where automated processes attempt to collect all available articles, databases, video resources, and so on [25]. Thus, in order for usage data to be in any way useful, the signal of human users must be extracted from this noise. A global blockchain consortium offers one of the most effective solutions to this problem. A decentralized network of nodes allows for a greater ability to identify irregularities in usage. Each new block will be generated from the collated online usage data submitted by *all* PIRs in the network in the past hour: therefore, the system will be able to identify in real-time if a particular IP address or a certain online resource is over-represented in the data (i.e. because a new web scraper or bot is active). Currently, with data being collated and sent in to a central clearing house on a monthly basis, such real-time data analysis is not possible and therefore anomaly detection is cruder. Moreover, the decentralized method of recording online usage will create a virtuous circle in data validation – more nodes allow for greater processing power and greater proportional capture of online activity, this in turn allows for more complete data collection and robust data cleaning as outlined above, which in turn increases the value of joining the blockchain consortium to other PIRs; if they join and become nodes, the circle completes another turn.

3.2   Some Objections

First of all, some may be skeptical of adopting technology associated with cryptocurrencies in order to log the usage of scholarly online material. Against this, the utility of blockchains are increasingly being recognized by mainstream businesses and governmental organizations – with applications found from American healthcare to Estonian elections, from Swiss re-insurers to Ghanaian land registries [26–29]. It is foreseeable, therefore, that the popular understanding of blockchain will shift to understand it as a core technology of the online and real world. The BitView blockchain is not a lawless band of extra-legal entities, but something more prosaic: a tightly-regulated network of nodes maintaining a secure ledger of links between viewers and DOIs.

Secondly, it may be argued that using blockchain is an over-engineered solution to the problem of collating usage data. In response to this, we maintain that it is only through using blockchain that three key challenges of recording online scholarly activity can be solved: (i) the identity of users needs to be visible to those whose own repositories are being accessed, but not to others; (ii) PIRs must be able to protect their data while making it publicly available; (iii) PIRs must cross-validate one another's usage data without sharing identifiable data publicly. By encrypting viewer-identifying data, using private-public key cryptography to protect the identity of publishers, and using automated technology to cross validate the application of COUNTER rules, we submit that the BitView consortium blockchain is an efficient solution to the asymmetrical needs of privacy on the one hand and transparency and accessibility on the other.

Finally, some may argue that it will be impossible to ensure that online usage data are sufficiently accurate to be of use. This, of course, is an objection to the overall enterprise of measuring online usage, and not one specific to the use of the blockchain. Arguments for and against this point of view have already been made elsewhere [30–32]. However, it is worth recalling that the BitView blockchain will allow for robust and verifiable filtering of non-human online activity. Moreover, by creating a publicly-interrogable ledger of online views, we posit that interested researchers will use this rich and open-access dataset to devise novel and competing view-metrics, much as has been done already for citation data. For example, supposing that the data show a significant variation in online viewing practices across academic disciplines, it would be possible to generate field-weighted view statistics in order to standardize view data across academic fields. However, this example is somewhat superficial compared to what the blockchain could reveal: interested researchers would have access to a hitherto unavailable detailed global picture of academic view-activity. This could highlight how academic interest in certain fields moves across time and space and how information disseminates and dissipates. The 'black' repository of online articles Sci-Hub recently released the map of online downloads from its archive over a six-month period [33]. This map, however, offers only a fraction of the insights available of a dataset that captures COUNTER-compliant global PIR online usage.

3.3   The Downstream Benefits of BitView

How would the blockchain of accurate usage data affect the field of scholarly communication? In our view, the most significant benefits of BitView will ultimately depend on the changes in behavior by both authors and readers that it will trigger. Under the current system, the archiving of published articles is largely dependent on individual inclination and the customs of different disciplines. Whereas for a particle physicist placing post-prints on ArXiv is typically a matter of course, in most other disciplines the extent of archiving in institutional repositories is very patchy, with large swathes of published material being available only behind a paywall.

The reasons for the widespread reluctance to post post-prints are easy to identify: once a paper has been accepted for publication, the author rightly feels that the main objective has been achieved. A marker has been placed on the research landscape that will be preserved by the publisher in a form suitable for garnering citations, which, in conjunction with the prestige of the journal, constitute the acknowledged currency of academic recognition and esteem. The incentive to archive a post-print in a repository is rather weak: even assuming that the open access availability of a post-print increases the volume of views, the link from a post-print view to the citation of the published article is tenuous and in many cases impossible because of paywalls.

The incentive to post post-prints would be radically changed if views had a direct impact on the academic value of published research and were not regarded merely as an indirect means to increase citations. This, of course, would require the collection, verification, and diffusion of reliable data on views which can then be summarized in robust metrics. But this is precisely what BitView can provide. Even in countries where there is no centralized impact-based system of research funding (as provided, for example, by Research Excellence Framework in the UK), authors will want to add academic value to their published research by ensuring that data of views of their post-prints are validated by internationally-agreed protocols (such as COUNTER). As soon as views count, the counting of views matters. Authors will find that it is in their own interest to archive their post-prints in their institutional repository (IR) so that view-currency funds accrue to their own view-account. Moreover, the importance of online views will incentivize IRs to join the blockchain if they have not already done so. It is difficult to underestimate the benefits of a simple recording mechanism (as provided by BitView) whereby for every published article there is at least one freely accessible post-print counterpart. The Holy Grail of universal open access to academic publications has so far eluded the efforts of many individuals and organizations concerned about the inefficient dissemination of knowledge that is inevitably implicit in the proprietary nature of articles published in for-fee access journals. In addition to this, the paywall barriers to the dissemination of knowledge perpetuate research inequalities: the best-funded institutions have access to the greatest body of research on which to draw, placing them at an inherent and unfair advantage over the institutions that do not have the same resources. In this way, the status quo is perpetuated and reinforced.

It is easy to see that the availability of BitView will also change viewing behavior. Whereas under the current chaotic and unregulated mechanism for viewing post-prints (and published articles) views do not constitute a valid currency for academic recognition, under BitView instead viewers will have the opportunity of checking that their views-currency is well spent. By accessing research material through a BitView-compliant repository, viewers not only will be assured that the view data are properly recorded and assigned to authors, but they will be also directly responsible for their privacy settings and therefore will have the opportunity to increase the value of their view data. This last point requires some explanation: during the first stage of implementation, we expect BitView to provide accurate, verified, but basic data on views – essentially the number of hits per period of time. But we envisage also a second stage in which BitView-compliant repositories will respond to the demand by both authors and academic institutions (University promotion and tenure committees, grant-giving bodies, and especially public and private organizations desirous to use robust non-citation-based impact metrics for the allocation of research funding, etc.) to provide more granular data on views. For example, researchers publishing articles on geographically-relevant matters (e.g., malaria in sub-Saharan Africa) may wish to know the location of their viewers, as it would add a completely new dimension of "impact" to the number of citations of their papers. Repositories would then offer a menu of privacy settings to viewers, ranging from (default) total anonymity to location (continent, country, region, city) to personal details (e.g., academic status/location).

Three virtuous circles would propel the diffusion of knowledge: in a BitView world *trusted* repositories would guarantee transparency as well as safeguarding individual privacy, thereby making views data both reliable and valuable. At the same time *concerned* authors keen to maximize the 'usage factor' of their work (i.e. maximize the number of views and downloads it receives across platforms) would have a strong incentive to deposit their post-prints in BitView-compliant institutional repositories, and finally *responsible* viewers would play a role in enriching views-impact data. The end-result of this interaction would be a substantial increase in the availability of open-access accurate versions (i.e., post-prints) of published, proprietary, articles.

4   Conclusion

In conclusion, we argue that this use of blockchain can solve a fundamental problem in creating a transparent network of PIRs – it allows the creation of a ledger of downloads that is simultaneously public (and therefore all nodes in the blockchain can agree that the COUNTER rules have been applied correctly) and private (with the usage statistics of each individual PIR available only to them via their private key). It creates a decentralized record of global data where the (very modest) computational and data storage workload can be equitably distributed across PIRs. Finally, and most importantly, it would allow the development of robust data regarding the usage of material online. With validated and accepted criteria for demonstrating that all views are being treated alike, we envisage that it will finally be possible to standardize usage metrics, which will then gain currency in benchmarking research outputs. This will create a publishing ecosystem which incentivizes authors and publishers to widen access to their outputs, encourages readers to share their viewing habits wisely, and allows everybody to understand better the temporal and spatial spread of scholarly communication.

References

1. Seglen, P.O.: Why the impact factor of journals should not be used for evaluating research. Br. Med. J. **314**(7079), 498–502 (1997)
2. The PLoS Medicine Editors. The impact factor game. PLoS Med. **3**(6), e291 (2006)
3. Arnold, D.A., Fowler, K.K.: Nefarious numbers. Not. Am. Math. Soc. **58**, 434–437 (2011)
4. Martin, B.R.: Editors' JIF-boosting stratagems – which are appropriate and which not? Res. Policy **45**(1), 1–7 (2016)
5. Vanclay, J.: Impact factor: outdated artefact or stepping-stone to journal certification? Scientometrics **32**(2), 211–238 (2012)
6. Bergstrom, C.T.: Eigenfactor: measuring the value and prestige of scholarly journals. College Res. Libr. News **68**(5), 314–316 (2007)
7. Zijlstra, H., McCullough, R.: CiteScore: A New Metric to Help You Track Journal Performance and Make Decisions (2016). https://www.elsevier.com/editors-update/story/journal-metrics/citescore-a-new-metric-to-help-you-choose-the-right-journal
8. Trueger, N.S., Thoma, B., Hsu, C.H., Sullivan, S., Peters, L., Lin, M.: The altmetric score: a new measure for article-level dissemination and impact. Ann. Emerg. Med. **66**(5), 549–553 (2015)
9. Lindsey, D.: Using citation counts as a measure of quality in science: measuring what's measurable rather than what's valid. Scientometrics **15**(3–4), 189–203 (1989)
10. Bollen, J., Van de Sompel, H., Smith, J.A., Luce, R.: Toward alternative metrics of journal impact: a comparison of download and citation data. Inf. Process. Manag. **41**(6), 1419–1440 (2005)
11. Kurtz, M.J., Bollen, J.: Usage bibliometrics. Annu. Rev. Inf. Sci. Technol. **44**(1), 1–64 (2012)
12. Glänzel, W., Gorraiz, J.: Usage metrics versus altmetrics: confusing terminology? Scientometrics **102**(3), 2161–2164 (2015)
13. Bollen, J., Van de Sompel, H.: Usage impact factor: the effects of sample characteristics on usage-based impact metrics. J. Assoc. Inf. Sci. Technol. **59**(1), 136–149 (2008)
14. Pesch, O.: Usage factor for journals: a new measure for scholarly impact. Ser. Libr. **63**(3–4), 261–268 (2012)
15. Shepherd, P.: Altmetrics, PIRUS and usage factor. Insights **26**(3), 305–310 (2013)
16. Fleming-May, R.A., Grogg, J.E.: Standards, tools, and other products. Libr. Technol. Rep. **46**(6), 11–16 (2012)
17. Project COUNTER: The COUNTER Code of Practice for e-Resources: Release 4 (2012). https://www.projectcounter.org/wp-content/uploads/2016/01/COPR4.pdf
18. Shepherd, P., Needham, P.: PIRUS2: Final Report (2011). http://www.cranfieldlibrary.cranfield.ac.uk/pirus2/
19. MacIntyre, R., Alcock, J., Needham, P., Lambert, J.: Measuring the usage of repositories via a national standards-based aggregation service: IRUS-UK. In: Schmidt, B., Dobreva, M. (eds.) New Avenues for Electronic Publishing in the Age of Infinite Collections and Citizen Science: Scale, Openness and Trust: Proceedings of the 19th International Conference on Electronic Publishing, pp. 83–92. IOS Press, Amsterdam, Netherlands (2015)

20. Needham, P., Stone, G.: IRUS-UK: making scholarly statistics count in UK repositories. Insights 25(3), 262–266 (2012)
21. Iansiti, M., Lakhani, K.R.: Truth about Blockchain. Harv. Bus. Rev. 95, 118–127 (2017)
22. Project COUNTER: Transition Timeline (2017). https://www.projectcounter.org/wp-content/uploads/2017/07/transition-timeline-005-1.pdf
23. Davis, P.: The Journal Usage Factor—Think Locally, Act Locally (2011). http://scholarlykitchen.sspnet.org/2011/09/29/journal-usage-factor-think-locally-act-locally/
24. Zeifman, I.: Bot Traffic Report 2016 (2016). https://www.incapsula.com/blog/bot-traffic-report-2016.html
25. Foster, Z.: Academia.edu, personal communication (2018)
26. Orcutt, M.: Who Will Build the Health-Care Blockchain? MIT Technology Review, September 2017. https://www.technologyreview.com/s/608821/who-will-build-the-health-care-blockchain/
27. Heller, N.: Estonia, the Digital Republic, New Yorker, 18–25 December 2017. https://www.newyorker.com/magazine/2017/12/18/estonia-the-digital-republic
28. Lerner, M.: Blockchain Technology Breaks Through. Business Insurance, 7 March 2017. http://www.businessinsurance.com/article/20170703/NEWS06/912314245/Blockchain-technology-breaks-through-to-the-insurance-industry
29. Ayemoba, A.: Africa's First Multinational Blockchain Land Registry to be Launched in Kenya and Ghana. Africa Business Communities, December 2017. https://africabusinesscommunities.com/news/africa%E2%80%99s-first-multinational-blockchain-land-registry-to-be-launched-in-kenya-and-ghana/
30. Luther, L.: White paper on electronic journal usage statistics. Ser. Libr. 41(2), 119–148 (2001)
31. Peters, T.A.: What's the use? The value of e-Resource usage statistics. New Libr. World 103 (1–2), 39–47 (2002)
32. McDowell, N., Gorman, G.E.: The relevance of vendors' usage statistics in academic library e-resource management: a New Zealand study. Aust. Acad. Res. Libr. 35(4), 322–344 (2004)
33. Bohannon, J.: Who's Downloading Pirated Papers? Everyone. Science, 28 April 2016. http://www.sciencemag.org/news/2016/04/whos-downloading-pirated-papers-everyone

Adaptive Edit-Distance and Regression Approach for Post-OCR Text Correction

Thi-Tuyet-Hai Nguyen[1(✉)], Mickael Coustaty[1], Antoine Doucet[1],
Adam Jatowt[2], and Nhu-Van Nguyen[1]

[1] L3i, University of La Rochelle, La Rochelle, France
{hai.nguyen,mickael.coustaty,antoine.doucet,
nhu-van.nguyen}@univ-lr.fr
[2] Department of Social Informatics, Kyoto University, Kyoto, Japan
adam@dl.kuis.kyoto-u.ac.jp

Abstract. Post-processing is a crucial step in improving the performance of OCR process. In this paper, we present a novel approach which explores a modified way of candidate generating and candidate scoring at character level as well as word level. These features are combined with some important features suggested by related work for ranking candidates in a regression model. The experimental results show that our approach has comparable results with the top performing approaches in the Post-OCR text correction competition ICDAR 2017.

Keywords: Post-OCR processing · Noisy channel · Language model Regression model

1 Introduction

Born-analog documents still contain massive knowledge which is valuable to our society. For the purpose of preservation and easier accessibility, a lot of efforts have been devoted to optical character recognition (OCR) systems to transform paper-based documents into digital form. However, poor physical quality of documents and limitations of text recognition techniques result in the low performance of OCR systems. Erroneous OCR-generated texts not only prevent users from retrieving relevant information but also cause reading difficulties. Post-processing is the last activity in OCR pipeline, attempting to detect and correct OCR errors.

Diverse approaches have been conducted for OCR post-processing. They can be divided into three main categories: manual error correction, dictionary-based error correction and context-based error correction [2].

The first type lets humans manually review and correct OCR-ed texts. It requires continuous manual intervention. Therefore, it is not only costly but also time-consuming and error-prone.

This work has been supported by the European Union's Horizon 2020 research and innovation programme under grant 770299 (NewsEye).

The second type uses a lookup dictionary to search for misspelled words and correct them automatically [17]. This kind of approach is easy to implement and use, however, it is unable to correct errors due to their grammatical and semantic contexts.

Finally, the context-based approach type is proposed to eliminate the disadvantages mentioned above. Most solutions of this type make use of the noisy channel model and statistical language model. Some approaches apply machine translation techniques which translate OCR output into corrected text in the same language. Some others combine different features in a prediction model to avoid bias and select a more accurate candidate from a pool of candidates.

The OCR post-processing consists of two parts: error detection and error correction. In this paper, we focus on the second part with the given list of known error positions. Our approach explores the noisy channel model, language model as well as other features for generating and ranking candidates using machine learning techniques. The evaluation results show that our method reaches comparable performance to the best performing teams in the English monograph dataset of the Post-OCR text correction competition ICDAR 2017 [4].

The remainder of this paper is organized as follows. In Sect. 2, we describe previous works related to OCR post-processing. Section 3 gives the detailed description of our approach. The experimental results are shown and discussed in Sect. 4. Finally, we give some conclusions in Sect. 5.

2 Related Work

The post-processing model detects and corrects misspellings of both non-words and real-words in the OCR-ed text. The literature of this research field contains a rich family of models, especially with the context-based type.

The dictionary-based type tries to correct misspelled words in isolation and does not take the context other nearby errors into consideration [17]. This type is simple to implement, but it cannot deal with real-word errors.

The context-based type considers grammatical and semantic contexts of errors and is more promising to correct such real-word errors. Most of the techniques of this type rely on noisy channel and language model. The others explore different machine learning techniques to suggest correct candidates.

Tong et al. [20] explored multiple features, including character n-grams, confusion probabilities, and word bi-gram language model to fix errors. Using some features similar to the ones in Tong et al., WFST-PostOCR approach (the participant in the Post-OCR text correction competition) [4] applied the probabilistic character error model and language model. However, these models were compiled into weighted finite-state edit transducers (WFST). The best token sequence was the best path of WFST. This team achieved the third rank with 28% improvement, which confirmed the importance of error model and language model in correcting erroneous OCR-ed text.

Other promising approaches of competition, including Multi-Modular Domain-Tailored (MMDT), Character Level Attention Model (CLAM), Character-based Statistical and Neural Machine Translation (Char-SMT/NMT), are based on machine translation techniques.

MMDT [18] approach combined many modules from word level (Original words, Spell checker, Compounder, Word splitter, Text-Internal Vocabulary) to sentence level (Statistical Machine Translation) for candidate suggestion. Then, the decision module of Moses decoder [13] was used to rank candidates. In our opinion, Text-Internal Vocabulary function, which suggests high-frequency words in OCR-ed text as correction of errors with a small distance, easily leads to bias.

Two other competition approaches (Char-SMT/NMT, CLAM) rely on character based machine translation technique. There are however some limits of machine translation at character level. Character-level models enable to produce non-words which may be close to the reference. It is necessary to ensure that words generated by a character-level model should be valid words before ranking and suggesting them as relevant candidates. Tiedemann [19] suggested to include a string similarity measure as feature function. Furthermore, Afli et al. [1] demonstrated that machine translation at word level is better than at character level.

Other approaches applied a regression model in candidate ranking. Kissos et al. [12] extracted six features to train a linear regressor, including confusion probability with a single edition, unigram frequency, context feature (backward bi-gram frequency, forward bi-gram frequency), term frequency in the OCR-ed text, and word confidence. In our opinion, the unigram frequency feature is not a good feature because it does not take run-on errors into account, for example, for the error "doubtfud.of" the possible correct candidate is "doubtfull of" which is bi-gram instead of unigram. In addition, similar to internal vocabulary feature of MMDT, term frequency feature also easily causes bias. Furthermore, this approach did not consider an important feature used in real-word error correction [10], which is the similarity between error and candidate.

Mei et al. [15] also suggested to rank candidates using a predictive model. They extracted six features of each candidate. Besides word n-gram and candidate frequency features, they paid attention to string similarity which is missing from Kissos' approach. However, they ignored another important feature (confusion probability) which is used in several successful post-processing approaches [6, 12, 14, 20].

Our method belongs to the context-based approach type. We propose to make use of confusion probability obtained from the noisy channel model of multiple editions (instead of single edition), and context probability given by language model. Then, these two features and some essential features suggested by related works [12, 15] are used to train a regression model. The experimental results show that our multi-modular approach is comparable to the ones of the teams participating in the Post-OCR text correction competition ICDAR 2017.

3 Regression Approach for Post-OCR Text Correction

We explore all information related to error from characters constituting error to context words surrounding error to suggest correct candidates. Our approach is divided into three steps: candidate generating and weighting relying on an adaptive edit-distance, candidate scoring using language model and candidate ranking based on a regression model. Details of each step are discussed in the following subsections.

3.1 Candidate Generating and Weighting Based on an Adaptive Edit-Distance (Step 1)

In the first step, we generate candidates based on the character candidate graph which can deal with run-on and split-word errors. We then score such candidates using a modified confusion probability.

Candidate Generating: A string can be generated from the other string by edit operations of three edition types (deletion, insertion, or substitution). Therefore, we create the character candidate graph based on a "seed" word (an OCR error) with three corresponding node types (deletion, insertion, or substitution). Then we use this graph to generate candidates by one or more edit operations. More specifically, if two characters are generated from one "seed" character, this is a deletion node; otherwise, if one character is generated from two adjacent "seed" characters, it is an insertion node. In case that one character is substituted by one "seed" character, we have a substitution node.

Training dataset reveals that insertion and deletion caused by two adjacent characters are more common than those caused by three or more adjacent characters, therefore in this paper, we limit to two adjacent characters.

After graph construction, Breadth First Search (BFS) with some heuristic tuned from training dataset (maximum length of candidates, minimum confusion probability) is used to deal with the complexity.

The example graph is shown in Fig. 1. If "ar.d" is an OCR error, all "seed" characters 'a', 'r', '.', and 'd' are denoted as yellow nodes. High frequency substitution characters of 'a', 'r', '.', and 'd' are 'e', 'n', ',' and 'l', respectively, which are denoted as green nodes. Two adjacent characters 'r', '.' can be combined to generate the character insertion node 'n' denoted as a red node; one "seed" character 'd' can be divided into two characters "il" denoted as a blue node. One possible candidate of the error "ar.d" in Fig. 1 is "and" which is generated from substitution node 'a', insertion node 'n', and substitution node 'd'.

By using the character candidate graph, our approach can deal with two difficult error types, which are split-word errors (for instance, "appointed" is recognized as "ap pointed") and run-on errors (for example, "doubtfull of" is recognized as "doubtfud. of"). However, there are some limitations in quality control of too many candidates generated by one run-on error. Therefore, this paper only allows a punctuation and a digit be substituted by the space.

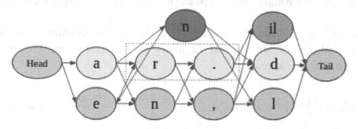

Fig. 1. Example of character candidate graph (Color figure online)

Candidate Weighting: The conditional probability $pr(x|w)$ of the given source word w recognized by the OCR software as the string x (also known as confusion probability of source word and OCR string) can be estimated by the confusion probabilities of the characters in x assuming that character recognition in OCR is an independent process [20].

Let $x_{1,i}$ be the first i characters of OCR string x and let $w_{1,j}$ be the first j characters of source string w. We define $pr(x_{1,i}|w_{1,j})$ to be the conditional probability that the substring $w_{1,j}$ is recognized as substring $x_{1,i}$ by the OCR process. $pr(x_{1,i}|w_{1,j})$ can be calculated as below:

$$pr(x_{1,i}|w_{1,j}) = \max \begin{cases} pr(x_{1,i}|w_{1,j-1}) * pr(del(w_j)) \\ pr(x_{1,i-1}|w_{1,j}) * pr(ins(x_i)) \\ pr(x_{1,i-1}|w_{1,j-1}) * pr(sub(x_i|w_j)) \end{cases} \tag{1}$$

In typical formula, the insertion, deletion conditioned on the previous character are computed as follows [5].

$$pr(del(w_j)) = \frac{del[w_{j-1}w_j]}{count[w_{j-1}w_j]}, \quad \text{if deletion} \tag{2}$$

$$pr(ins(x_i)) = \frac{ins[w_{j-1}x_i]}{count[w_{j-1}]}, \quad \text{if insertion} \tag{3}$$

$$pr(sub(x_1|w_j)) = \frac{sub[x_i, w_j]}{count[w_j]}, \quad \text{if substitution} \tag{4}$$

where $del[w_{j-1}w_j]$ is a number of times that the source characters $w_{j-1}w_j$ were recognized as w_{j-1} in the training set; $ins[w_{j-1}x_i]$ is a number of times that w_{j-1} was recognized as $w_{j-1}x_i$; $sub[x_i, w_j]$ is a number of times that w_j was recognized as x_i. These equations reveal that in order to calculate the confusion probability of insertion and deletion, there must be the same previous character.

Because erroneous OCR characters frequently appear together, two or more error characters can be recognized as one different correct character, or one character can be recognized as different correct characters [11]. It means that the insertion, deletion can depend on the different previous character instead of the same previous one. For example, "li" can be wrongly recognized as 'h', 'm' can be wrongly recognized as 'in', etc.

As a result, we propose to calculate the probability of deletion and insertion by using the probability of substitution of many characters by one character or one character by many characters.

$$pr(del(w_j)) = pr(sub(x_{i-1}|w_{j-1}w_j)) = \frac{sub[x_{i-1}, w_{j-1}w_j]}{count[w_{j-1}w_j]}, \quad \text{if deletion} \tag{5}$$

$$pr(ins(x_i)) = pr\big(sub(x_{i-1}x_i|w_{j-1})\big) = \frac{sub[x_{i-1}x_i, w_{j-1}]}{count[w_{j-1}]}, \quad \text{if insertion} \quad (6)$$

For instance, the correction is "and", and the error is "ar.d". In this case, the correct letter 'n' is recognized as the error characters "r.". It is similar to insertion error type except that it does not have the same previous character, so we cannot apply the typical formula of insertion Eq. 3 directly. Typical approach (denoted as typical-prob. in experiments) uses the substitution formula twice to calculate that confusion probability:

$$pr(\text{'ar.d'}|\text{'and'}) = pr(sub(\text{'a'}|\text{'a'})) * pr(sub(\text{'r'}|\text{'n'}))$$
$$*pr(sub(\text{'.'}|\text{''})) * pr(sub(\text{'d'}|\text{'d'}))$$

Our approach (denoted as modified-prob. in experiments) applies the substitution formula once:

$$pr(\text{'ar.d'}|\text{'and'}) = pr(sub(\text{'a'}|\text{'a'})) * pr(sub(\text{'r.'}|\text{'n'})) * pr(sub(\text{'d'}|\text{'d'}))$$

Our proposal also affects on creating the character confusion matrix. In particular, if one character (c) is recognized as two characters which are different from character (c), it is insertion. If two characters $(c1, c2)$ as recognized as one character which is different from characters $(c1, c2)$, it is deletion. Otherwise, it is substitution.

3.2 Candidate Scoring Using Language Model (Step 2)

After generating and weighting candidates at character level, in the second step, we utilize context information to score candidates of each OCR error.

Similar to some approaches of the context-based type, we consider the typical statistical language model (SLM) to deal with this problem. Moreover, we also explore the state-of-the-art recurrent neural network based language model (RNN-LM) [16] to compare two types of language models in context of erroneous OCR-ed text. SLM and LSTM are trained on the same training dataset used in "One Billion Word Language Model Benchmark" of Chelba et al. [3]. Each candidate is weighted according to the probability of trigram in SLM or that of predicting next word in RNN-LM.

In terms of SLM, the weight of each candidate is a sum of probabilities of three trigrams related to that candidate. For example, we have a phrase "yield to thbse who are", and two candidates {"those", "there"}, of the error "thbse". The weight of each candidate is calculated as follows:

$$weight_1(\text{"those"}) = pr(\text{"yield to those"}) + pr(\text{"to those who"})$$
$$+ pr(\text{"those who are"})$$
$$weight_1(\text{"there"}) = pr(\text{"yield to there"}) + pr(\text{"to there who"})$$
$$+ pr(\text{"there who are"})$$

For constructing RNN-LM, we apply one of the most common type of RNN - Long Short Term Memory (LSTM) [8]. The weight of each candidate is a sum of probabilities of predicting the next word related to that candidate. More specifically, LSTM needs a seed which is a context to predict a next word. The candidate can appear in the context (seed) or be the next word.

To compare with trigram language model, we keep the total length of the seed and the next word to be three. For instance, we have the same phrase with SLM "yield to thbse who are" with the same error candidate {"those", "there"} of the error "thbse", the weight of each candidate is computed as below:

$$weight_2(\text{"those"}) = pr(seed = \text{"yield to"}, next-word = \text{"those"})$$
$$+ pr(seed = \text{"to those"}, next-word = \text{"who"})$$
$$+ pr(seed = \text{"those who"}, next-word = \text{"are"})$$
$$weight_2(\text{"there"}) = pr(seed = \text{"yield to"}, next-word = \text{"there"})$$
$$+ pr(seed = \text{"to there"}, next-word = \text{"who"})$$
$$+ pr(seed = \text{"there who"}, next-word = \text{"are"})$$

3.3 Candidate Ranking Based on a Regression Model (Step 3)

After generating candidates and weighting them at character level and word level in two previous steps, this step reuses these features and some complementary features to predict the confidence of each candidate becoming a correction by a regression model. Then such confidence is used for candidate ranking. This step consists of two parts: feature extraction and candidate ranking.

Feature Extraction. Four important features used in our approach are selected and modified from a set of features of two related works [12, 15]. The first feature is "Probability of 3-length sequences related to errors" is the modified version of context feature, suggested by both of the related works; in terms of [12], this feature is "backward/forward bigram frequency"; in terms of [15], this is "exact/relax-context popularity". The second feature is "Probability of n-gram candidate", which is the general version of "unigram frequency" of two related works. Two last important features are features missing from each related work.

As analyzed in Sect. 2, "similarity feature" is an important feature used in real-word correction, which is ignored by [12]. Similarly, "confusion probability" is successfully used in several post-processing approaches, but is ignored by [15]. As to other features, we cannot use them because of different reasons. In fact, due to lack of information from the dataset, "word confidence" is ignored. We also remove the feature which is a part of other features, for example, "lexicon existence", which is included in "unigram frequency" feature. In addition, we refuse features that easily lead to bias such as "term frequency in OCR-ed text".

Let w_c be a candidate, C be a set of all candidates, and w_e be an OCR error. The details of each feature score are described in this section.

Probability of 3-Length Sequences Related to Errors: This feature is the normalized weight of step 2 mentioned in Sect. 3.2.

$$score(w_c, w_e) = \frac{weight_2(w_c)}{\sum\limits_{w'_c \in C} weight_2(w'_c)} \tag{7}$$

Probability of n-Gram Candidate: Candidate can be a single word or a sequence of multiple words, it means that candidate is word n-gram. Instead of using the frequency of candidate and accepting 0 value if candidate is not in the training data, we use the probability of candidate in word n-gram model which already applied smoothing techniques for solving sparsity problem. This feature is the normalized probability of candidate in word n-gram model.

$$score(w_c, w_e) = \frac{pr(w_c)}{\sum\limits_{w'_c \in C} pr(w'_c)} \tag{8}$$

Longest Common Subsequence (LCS) is an alternative in qualifying the similarity between two strings. Islam *et al.* [9] proposed two variations of LCS, including Normalized Longest Common Subsequence (NLCS) and Normalized Maximal Consecutive Longest Common Subsequence (NMCLCS).

NLCS considers the length of both the shorter and the longer string for normalization, as follows:

$$NLCS(w_c, w_e) = \frac{2 * len(LCS(w_c, w_e))^2}{len(w_c) + len(w_e)} \tag{9}$$

MCLCS requires the consecutive common subsequence. There are three variations of MCLCS with additional conditions. $MCLCS_1$ and $MCLCS_n$ use substrings beginning at the first and the n-th character, respectively; $MCLCS_z$ only considers substrings ending at the last character.

$$NMCLCS_i(w_c, w_e) = \frac{2 * len(MCLCS_i(w_c, w_e))^2}{len(w_c) + len(w_e)} \tag{10}$$

where $MCLCS_i$ can be $MCLCS_1$, $MCLCS_n$ or $MCLCS_z$.

Confusion Probability: This feature is the normalized weight of step 1 in Sect. 3.1:

$$score(w_c, w_e) = \frac{weight_1(w_c)}{\sum\limits_{w'_c \in C} weight_1(w'_c)} \tag{11}$$

Candidate Ranking. A regression model is used for scoring candidates. For training and testing a regressor, if a candidate is a correction, its feature vector is labeled as 1. Otherwise, the feature vector is labeled as 0. Candidate with the highest confidence is suggested as the correction.

However, correcting run-on errors often produces irrelevant candidates which cause a big difference between corrected word and ground truth one. For example, post-processing tries to find the most suitable candidate from a dictionary for a run-on error "where loan", and suggests the top candidate such as "helios" which is totally different from the GT "where I can". Therefore, the final filter based on the edit distance between error and its top candidate decides whether use the top candidate or keep the error.

4 Experiments

In this section, we first describe details of the dataset and metric used in the evaluation. Then we analyze the performance of our approach in comparison with the results of the teams taking part in the competition.

4.1 Evaluation Dataset

The English monograph dataset of the ICDAR 2017 Post-OCR text correction competition [4] with 666 training documents and 41 testing documents is used for evaluating our approach. These documents are selected from digital collections of the National Library of France (BnF) and the British Library (BL). The corresponding GT has been extracted from BnF's internal projects and can be obtained through the competition's homepage[1].

4.2 Evaluation Metric

We use the average Levenshtein distances as the evaluation metric, same as used in the Post-OCR text correction competition ICDAR 2017 [4]. The metric can be viewed as the modified version of character error rate, which considers the confidence of each candidate to be the correction in case that there are many candidates of one error.

$$avgDistance = \frac{\sum_{i=1}^{n} weight_i * distance(candidate_i, correctWord_i)}{N} \quad (12)$$

where $weight_i$ is the confidence of $candidate_i$ to be the correct word, n is a number of OCR errors, and N is a total number of characters in reference.

This official metric of the competition is intended to take into account partial improvement, even when the word correction is not fully matching the GT.

The improvement percentage is calculated based on the comparison of the original distance (the distance between the OCR output and GT) and the corrected distance (the distance between the corrected output and GT).

---

[1] https://sites.google.com/view/icdar2017-postcorrectionocr/, last visited on 28 June 2018.

4.3   Evaluation Results

By combining two ways of calculating step 1's weight and two ways of calculating step 2's weight, we consider four approaches in total: "typical-prob.SLM", "modified-prob. SLM", "typical-prob.LSTM" and "modified-prob.LSTM". The overall performance of our approaches is shown in Table 1.

In terms of performance of step 1, as mentioned in Sect. 3.1, our approach of calculating the confusion probability considered the common way in which erroneous characters appear, therefore our suggestion "modified-prob." strongly outperforms the typical approach "typical-prob." even with different techniques of step 2 (SLM or LSTM).

As to the performance of step 2, in erroneous OCR-ed context, SLM has slightly better performance than LSTM, with about 1.8% of relative increase of improvement in case of "typical-prob." and 2.4% in case of "modified-prob".

Regarding the performance of step 3, experimental results show that gradient boosting regression model [7] on top of decision trees with the least square loss function outperforms other regression models.

Among 10 participants of the correction task in the Post-OCR text correction ICDAR 2017, only six teams can improve the distance with GT, and other teams almost deteriorate documents. These final results confirmed the difficulty of post-processing step to deal with the noisy OCR output and the uncleaned GT.

Our best regression model ("modified-prob.SLM") obtains higher performance than 9 teams. It should be emphasized that our approach is better than the multi-modular approach of statistical machine translation approach and spelling checker (MMDT) and the neural machine translation approach applied on post-OCR problem (CLAM), with around 51% and 4.1% relative increase, respectively. Although our result is still lower than the one of the best-performing participant (Char-SMT/NMT), it is unfair to compare our multi-modular approach with the ensemble one. While our solution uses only one best regression model to score candidates, Char-SMT/NMT trained several models of both statistical and neural machine translation, and then combined the top candidates generated from such models.

Table 1. Overall performance scores over English monograph dataset of the Post-OCR text correction ICDAR 2017 with top 4 competition teams.

Approach	Improvement (%)
Baselines	
Char-SMT/NMT	**43**
CLAM	29
WFST-PostOCR	28
MMDT [18]	20
Proposed methods	
modified-prob.SLM	**30.2**
modified-prob.LSTM	29.5
typical-prob.SLM	22.4
typical-prob.LSTM	22

In addition, if we recommend top 3, top 6 candidates for each error, the best improvement percentage of our best approach "modified-prob.SLM" is 40.5% and 42.8%, respectively. It should be clear that the best improvement percentage is calculated based on the original distance and the best corrected distance (the distance of the most relevant candidate among the top n candidates with the GT word). In other words, in semi-automatic mode, our multi-modular approach can suggest correct candidates with the comparable performance with the ensemble approach of the winner Char-SMT/NMT.

5 Conclusion

In this paper, we explored a modified method of generating and calculating the confusion probability, which has better performance than the standard edit distance method. When we compare the performance of SLM and LSTM in erroneous OCR-ed contexts, the experiments show that SLM is slightly better than LSTM in terms of 3-length sequence. Finally, by extracting important features suggested in two previous works and using a regression model for candidate ranking, our best approach is comparative with approaches in ICDAR2017 Competition on Post-OCR Text Correction though it still under-performs the ensemble approach of machine translation techniques.

References

1. Afli, H., Barrault, L., Schwenk, H.: OCR error correction using statistical machine translation. Int. J. Comput. Linguist. Appl. **7**, 175–191 (2016)
2. Bassil, Y., Alwani, M.: OCR post-processing error correction algorithm using Google online spelling suggestion. arXiv preprint arXiv:1204.0191 (2012)
3. Chelba, C., et al.: One billion word benchmark for measuring progress in statistical language modeling (2013)
4. Chiron, G., Doucet, A., Coustaty, M., Moreux, J.P.: ICDAR2017 competition on post-OCR text correction. In: 2017 14th IAPR International Conference on Document Analysis and Recognition, ICDAR, vol. 1, pp. 1423–1428. IEEE (2017)
5. Church, K.W., Gale, W.A.: Probability scoring for spelling correction. Stat. Comput. **1**(2), 93–103 (1991)
6. Evershed, J., Fitch, K.: Correcting noisy OCR: context beats confusion. In: Proceedings of the First International Conference on Digital Access to Textual Cultural Heritage, pp. 45–51. ACM (2014)
7. Friedman, J.H.: Greedy function approximation: a gradient boosting machine. Ann. Stat. 1189–1232 (2001)
8. Hochreiter, S., Schmidhuber, J.: Long short-term memory. Neural Comput. **9**(8), 1735–1780 (1997)
9. Islam, A., Inkpen, D.: Semantic text similarity using corpus-based word similarity and string similarity. ACM Trans. Knowl. Discov. Data **2**, 10 (2008)
10. Islam, A., Inkpen, D.: Real-word spelling correction using Google Web IT 3-grams. In: Proceedings of the 2009 Conference on Empirical Methods in Natural Language Processing, vol. 3, pp. 1241–1249 (2009)

11. Jones, M.A., Story, G.A., Ballard, B.W.: Integrating multiple knowledge sources in a Bayesian OCR post-processor. In: International Journal on Document Analysis and Recognition, p. 925–933 (1991)
12. Kissos, I., Dershowitz, N.: OCR error correction using character correction and feature-based word classification. In: 2016 12th IAPR Workshop on Document Analysis Systems, DAS, pp. 198–203. IEEE (2016)
13. Koehn, P., et al.: Moses: open source toolkit for statistical machine translation (2007)
14. Llobet, R., Navarro-Cerdan, J.R., Perez-Cortes, J.C., Arlandis, J.: Efficient OCR post-processing combining language, hypothesis and error models. In: Hancock, E.R., Wilson, R. C., Windeatt, T., Ulusoy, I., Escolano, F. (eds.) SSPR/SPR 2010. LNCS, vol. 6218, pp. 728–737. Springer, Heidelberg (2010). https://doi.org/10.1007/978-3-642-14980-1_72
15. Mei, J., Islam, A., Wu, Y., Moh'd, A., Milios, E.E.: Statistical learning for OCR text correction. arXiv preprint arXiv:1611.06950 (2016)
16. Mikolov, T., Karafiát, M., Burget, L., Černocký, J., Khudanpur, S.: Recurrent neural network based language model. In: Eleventh Annual Conference of the International Speech Communication Association (2010)
17. Niwa, H., Kayashima, K.: Postprocessing for character recognition using keyword information
18. Schulz, S., Kuhn, J.: Multi-modular domain-tailored OCR post-correction. In: Proceedings of the 2017 Conference on Empirical Methods in Natural Language Processing, pp. 2716–2726 (2017)
19. Tiedemann, J.: Character-based pivot translation for under-resourced languages and domains. In: Proceedings of the 13th Conference of the European Chapter of the Association for Computational Linguistics, pp. 141–151 (2012)
20. Tong, X., Evans, D.A.: A statistical approach to automatic OCR error correction in context. In: Fourth Workshop on Very Large Corpora (1996)

Performance Comparison of Ad-Hoc Retrieval Models over Full-Text vs. Titles of Documents

Ahmed Saleh[1,2]([✉]), Tilman Beck[1], Lukas Galke[1,2], and Ansgar Scherp[1,3]

[1] Kiel University, Kiel, Germany
[2] ZBW – Leibniz Information Centre for Economics, Kiel, Germany
a.saleh@zbw.eu
[3] University of Stirling, Stirling, UK

Abstract. While there are many studies on information retrieval models using full-text, there are presently no comparison studies of full-text retrieval vs. retrieval only over the titles of documents. On the one hand, the full-text of documents like scientific papers is not always available due to, e.g., copyright policies of academic publishers. On the other hand, conducting a search based on titles alone has strong limitations. Titles are short and therefore may not contain enough information to yield satisfactory search results. In this paper, we compare different retrieval models regarding their search performance on the full-text vs. only titles of documents. We use different datasets, including the three digital library datasets: EconBiz, IREON, and PubMed. The results show that it is possible to build effective title-based retrieval models that provide competitive results comparable to full-text retrieval. The difference between the average evaluation results of the best title-based retrieval models is only 3% less than those of the best full-text-based retrieval models.

Keywords: Information retrieval · Learning to rank · Deep Learning

1 Introduction

Using only titles has shown to be effective for document classification [1] and top-k recommendations [2]. This motivates us to investigate the possibility of building effective retrieval models based only on documents' titles. According to Croft et al. [3], there are four main categories of ranking models: (1) set theoretic models or Boolean models, (2) vector space models (e.g., TF-IDF), (3) probabilistic models (e.g., BM25), and (4) feature-based retrieval (e.g., L2R). Furthermore, there are recent advances in Deep Learning that provide neural network models capable of capturing the semantics of words. We employ representative examples of retrieval models from these categories and compare them regarding their performance over full-text vs. title. For this purpose, we utilize five datasets, out of which three are obtained from digital libraries: PubMed,

© Springer Nature Switzerland AG 2018
M. Dobreva et al. (Eds.): ICADL 2018, LNCS 11279, pp. 290–303, 2018.
https://doi.org/10.1007/978-3-030-04257-8_30

Econbiz and IREON, and two standard test collections [4]: NTCIR-2 and TREC Disks 4&5.

From the different categories of ranking models, the learning-to-rank model (L2R) outperforms other title-based statistical ranking models. The L2R model only requires a small set of features, which is automatically determined by a correlation-based feature selection method applied on a large set of established IR retrieval features. The average evaluation results over all datasets showed that the best full-text-based retrieval models outperform the best title-based retrieval models by only 3%. Thus, based on our results, we can state that it is possible, given certain constraints, to build an effective titles-based information retrieval model that provides competitive results compared to a retrieval model operating on full-text.

The remainder of the paper is organized as follows: In Sect. 2, we review the state of the art in the field. The considered retrieval models for our study from the four categories are presented in Sect. 3. The evaluation approach is described in Sect. 4 and the results are reported in Sect. 5. Section 6 discusses the results, before we conclude.

2   Related Studies

There have been a number of retrieval models that specifically attempted to model the structure of documents, including the division of content into title, body, etc. However, to the best of our knowledge, there are no recent studies that use state-of-the-art retrieval techniques to compare ad-hoc retrieval over titles with ad-hoc retrieval over full-text. In this section, we provide a brief account of prior work related to our comparison. Subsequently, we present in detail in Sect. 3 the retrieval models that have been selected for our comparison study.

Using logo text has shown to be more efficient for documents retrieval tasks [5]. The authors showed that Keywords can be searched more quickly than title material. The addition of keywords to titles increases search time by 12%, while the addition of digests increases it by 20%.

In the domain of biomedical literature, Lin compared full-text retrieval with abstract retrieval [6]. Lin used the MEDLINE test collection and two ranking models: BM25 and a modified TF-IDF. The results show that full-text search outperforms abstracts-only search. Hemminger et al. [7] compared full-text retrieval with retrieval based on the metadata provided by the PubMed database, using gene names as queries. In their work, metadata comprise of titles and abstracts. Hemminger et al. concluded that full-text searches yield better results. However, the authors acknowledge that their study is limited on account of the fact that searching by gene name may not be representative of general biomedical literature searches. Furthermore, the authors used only an exact matching retrieval model to search for a small number of gene names in their study. They suggested extending their work by conducting a similar analysis in other domains. In this paper, we use five datasets from different domains and retrieval models from different IR categories in order to compare the full-text vs. title searches.

3   Compared Retrieval Models

Overall, we ensure that we cover well the four dominant categories of retrieval models [3]. We start by discussing the vector space and probabilistic models. Subsequently, we present learning to rank models. Finally, we present the deep neural networks models.

Vector Space and Probabilistic Models. As a baseline, we employ the vector space model TF-IDF [8]. TF represents the frequency of occurrence of a term, while the IDF factor of a term is inversely proportional to the number of documents in which the term appears. This means the fewer the term appears in the corpus, the higher the IDF factor and vice versa.

As a concept-based models, we employ the TF-IDF extensions, CF-IDF [9] and HCF-IDF [2]. CF-IDF is an extension of TF-IDF that counts concepts instead of terms. Concepts are terms from a controlled vocabulary (e.g. the term "Financial crisis" in the economics thesaurus (See footnote 1)). HCF-IDF [2] is an extension to CF-IDF that considers the hierarchical structure of concepts. The algorithm uses spreading activation and gives less weight to the more general concepts in the hierarchy.

Another retrieval model which utilizes the IDF weighting for ranking the documents is BM25. BM25 has been used as a baseline in TREC Web track [5,6]. It is a combination of BM11 and BM15 scaled by a scaling factor b. BM25CT is an extension to BM25 which uses a combination of terms and concepts that appears.

Learning to Rank (L2R) Models. Learning to Rank (L2R) is a family of machine learning techniques that aim at optimizing a loss function regarding a ranking of items. It has been successfully applied in the past for different IR tasks. Chen et al. [10] proposed a learning to rank approach for finding non-factoid answers in an answer sentence retrieval task. They used a combination of Explicit Semantic Analysis (ESA), Word2Vec [11] as semantic text representations, and Metzler and Kanungo's features (MK). Chen et al. showed that the combination of the semantic features and the MK feature set provides better ranking results than ranking based on MK feature set.

L2R consists of a set of supervised ranking models that are trained with a set of numerical feature vectors in order to retrieve the top-k relevant documents in response to a user's query. The feature vectors are calculated using the content of the documents and/or the queries. L2R models are generally categorized in pointwise, pairwise, and listwise approaches depending on the way the model performs the optimization task [12]. Pointwise is the category of L2R models where a relevancy degree is generated for every single document regardless of the other documents in the results list of the query. In contrast, the loss function of pairwise approaches considers only one pair of documents at a time. Finally, in the listwise L2R models, the input consists of the entire list of documents associated with a query and the output consists of a ranked list of documents for each query. As a pairwise approach, we use RankNet [13], LambdaMart [14], and RankBoost [15]. Finally, for listwise L2R we use AdaRank [16], Coordinate Ascent [17], and ListNet [18].

Deep Learning Models. The recent resurgence of neural networks has also affected the Information Retrieval community. Zhang et al. [19] provided a detailed survey to illustrate the rough evolution of Neural IR research and word embedding approaches to IR. For web search, Huang et al. [20] propose a series of deep structured semantic models (DSSM). The most successful instance of the model uses a multilayer feed-forward neural network to map both the query and the title of a webpage to a common low-dimensional vector space. The similarity between the query-document pairs is computed using cosine similarity. The main novelty is the usage of word-hashing, which dramatically reduces the vocabulary size without neglecting too much information. The reduction in vocabulary size allows the neural network to learn effectively from a large amount of available labeled data. DSSM is composed of four different layers. The first layer is the input layer. It contains the word sequences of the document and the user query. The second layer transforms the word sequences into sub-word units to reduce the large amount of vocabulary size. Subsequently, the sub-word units are used as input for a feed-forward neural network. In order to determine the relevancy of a document, cosine similarity between the query and the documents is computed on the output layer. The documents are ranked with respect to their similarity scores. As an extension to the DSSM model, Shen et al. [21] enhance on that by replacing the feed-forward neural network with a convolutional neural network. Afterwards, they introduced convolutional neural networks with max-pooling in the DSSM architecture (C-DSSM) [22]. The convolutional layer and max-pooling layer are utilized to identify keywords and concepts, in both the query and the document, and project them into a lower-dimensional semantic layer. C-DSSM is claimed to be state-of-the-art in retrieval performance [21].

4 Evaluation

In order to evaluate the effectiveness of title-based retrieval vs. a full-text retrieval, we use five datasets, which are described in Sect. 4.1. In Sect. 4.2, we present our evaluation procedures and parameters. In Sect. 4.3, we explain how we apply the correlation-based feature selection algorithm to sample a subset of features for L2R models. In Sect. 4.4, we present the metric used for evaluating the retrieval results.

4.1 Datasets

We use labeled datasets which have a full-text and a title. This enables a direct and fair comparison of retrieval performances over the two forms of content. The datasets fall under two categories: (1) standard IR datasets and (2) digital library datasets.

Standard IR Datasets. For the standard IR datasets, a document is given a binary classification as either relevant or non-relevant. This decision is referred to as the gold standard or relevance judgments. We used the following two standard IR datasets, namely NTCIR-2 and TREC 4&5, which provide a set of topics and human relevance judgments. Table 1 presents an overview of the datasets characteristics.

Table 1. Overview of the datasets characteristics. |avg| denotes the average number of documents and queries

	NTCIR-2	TREC 4& 5	EconBiz	IREON	PubMed	|avg|
# of documents	322,059	507,011	288,344	27,575	646,655	**358,329**
# of queries	66,729	72,270	6,204	7,912	28,470	**36,317**

(1) *NTCIR-2:* The dataset consists of 49 search topics and 322,059 documents' abstracts. We use the search topics as queries. The documents were extracted from the NACSIS Academic Conference Paper Database, collected between 1997–1999, and NACSIS Grant-in-Aid scientific research database, collected between 1988–1997. The documents are from electronics, chemistry, physical sciences, and clinical reports. We use a combination of the titles and abstracts to make up for the missing full-texts. Furthermore, the dataset includes relevance judgments of 66,729 query-document pairs.

(2) *TREC 4&5:* consists of 507,011 English documents from various newspaper or newswire sources (Financial Times, Foreign Broadcast Information Service, Los Angeles Times) and government proceedings (Congressional Record, Federal Register) collected between 1998 and 1994. For our investigation, all data items needed to have a full-text and a title. When examining the files, around 50 thousand documents were missing one of these elements. These documents are mainly from the Federal Register and Los Angeles Times and thus were ignored for our experiments. TREC provides human annotated relevance judgments for some query-document pairs. We use TREC-6 ad-hoc qrels in our experiments. TREC-6 ad-hoc qrels consists of 50 topics and relevance judgments of 72,270 query/document pairs.

Datasets of Digital Libraries. In case of the digital library datasets, a hierarchical domain-specific thesaurus that provides topics (or concepts) of the libraries' domain is usually included. Furthermore, many of the digital library documents are manually annotated, by domain experts, with at least one of these concepts. Thus, in our evaluation of the digital library datasets, we consider the document as relevant to a concept if and only if it is annotated with the corresponding concept.

We use the following three digital library datasets Econbiz, IREON, and PubMed which come with a hierarchical thesaurus. This thesaurus provides topics on economic, political, and medical subjects.

(3) *EconBiz:* ZBW, the world's largest economics library, is running a search portal, called EconBiz, for economics' scientific publications. From EconBiz, we obtain 1 million URLs of open access scientific publications and generate a dataset of 288,344 full-text English publications. As user queries, we use the economics thesaurus (STW). The economics thesaurus provides 6,204 economics subjects, i.e., concepts in economics. The thesaurus is developed and maintained by an editorial board of domain experts at ZBW – Leibniz information centre for economics. In this dataset, 203,851 documents are annotated with at least one thesaurus concept.

(4) *IREON:* The German information network 'International Relations and Area Studies' provides us with a dataset of 27,575 full-text politics publications in English. The dataset also contains a politics thesaurus (FIV) with 7,912 political English subjects. Again, the thesaurus subjects are used as queries in our experiments. In this dataset, 3,936 documents are annotated with at least one thesaurus concept.

(5) *PubMed:* PubMed consists of around 27 million citations for biomedical literature from MEDLINE, life science journals, and online books. Some of the citations include links to full-text content from PubMed Central and publisher websites. From PubMed central, we obtained 646,655 full-text open-access English articles. PubMed is provided by the US national library of medicine. As queries, we use the medical terms from the Medical Subject Headings (MeSH) thesaurus. MeSH consists of 28,470 subjects. In this dataset, 506,802 documents are annotated with at least one thesaurus concept.

4.2   Experimental Procedure

In order to compare the retrieval performance over titles versus full-text, we implemented the retrieval models described in Sect. 3. The retrieval models generate a ranked list of documents for each query-document pair. In order to evaluate the performance of the retrieval models, we compare the ranked list with the gold standard (see Sect. 4.4). The procedures for evaluating the standard IR datasets is slightly different from the one of the digital library datasets. In the case of the standard IR datasets, where the human relevance judgments are provided, we generate the lists of the *top-20* documents using the full-text and titles retrieval models, respectively. Afterwards, the lists are compared to the relevance judgments provided as gold standard. Whereas with the digital library datasets, the items of the ranked list are considered as relevant if and only if the search query is included in the document annotations, i.e., binary decision whether a certain annotation that we have queried for is provided with the document's gold standard, or not.

In order to generate the evaluation results for **vector space models and probabilistic retrieval models**, tokenization, stop words removal, and porter stemming are applied. As described in Sect. 3, the concept-based approaches HCF-IDF and CF-IDF utilize the concepts from STW, FIV, and MeSH, and BM25CT utilize a vector union of the terms and concept features.

Table 2. Overview of the L2R features

MK set [23]	Sentence length, Exact match, Term overlap, Synonym overlap, Language Model with Dirichlet smoothing
Modified letor [24]	Covered query term number, IDF, Sum/Min/Max/Mean/Variance of TF, Sum/Min/Max/Mean/Variance of length normalized TF, Sum/Min/Max/Mean/Variance of TF-IDF, Language model absolute discounting smoothing, Language model with Bayesian smoothing using Dirichlet priors, Language model with jelinek-mercer smoothing
Ranking model features	TF-IDF, BM25, CF-IDF, HCF-IDF, Word2Vec [10]

For the **L2R models**, following the suggestions of Qin et al. [25] and Minka et al. [26], the documents are sampled in the following way. First, we use BM25 on titles and full-texts to rank all the documents with respect to each query, and then the top 1,000 documents for each query are selected for feature extraction. Subsequently, we extract 29 features for each of the query-document pairs (see details on feature selection in Sect. 4.3). Therefore, we obtain two feature files, one for the titles and one for the full-texts, for each dataset. We utilize these files together with the gold standard to train the six L2R models selected in Sect. 3. The LambdaMART model is trained using 1,000 trees with 10 leaves per tree. The learning rate is set to 0.1 and 256 threshold candidates for tree splitting was used. The minimum number of samples for a leaf was set to 1. Early stopping is applied, if there was no improvement for 100 consecutive rounds. The RankNet model is trained using 100 training epochs, one hidden layer, and 10 hidden nodes. The learning rate was set to 0.00005. For the RankBoost model, we use 300 training epochs and 10 threshold candidates. AdaRank is trained in 500 rounds with a learning tolerance of 0.002. The number of epochs for the ListNet model is 1,500 and the learning rate is set to 0.00001. In the case of Coordinate Ascent, we apply 5 random restarts and 25 search iterations per dimension. The performance tolerance is set to 0.001. No regularization was used. In order to ensure that we obtain optimal L2R models that do not over or under-fit, we applied the bias-variance tradeoff method [27].

Finally, we generate the evaluation results for the **semantic models** DSSM and CDSSM. A trained model, with a click-through dataset of 30 million query/clicked-title pairs from Microsoft is used to determine the semantic cosine similarity between each query-document pair in our datasets. Based on the similarity scores, the top twenty documents are passed to the evaluation metric (described in Sect. 4.4).

4.3   Feature Selection for L2R Models

A good IR system can retrieve the most important documents in a fast and scalable way using only a limited amount of information about the query and documents. The information is contained in the features of both document and query and therefore a good set of features has to be found. The aim of the feature selection is to find a meaningful subset of features which can still produce sound results. Given a large number of different IR features, we want to find those features which cover diverse information and still contribute the most to the retrieval of the most important documents.

In line with previous literatures [23,24], we use a set of 29 features (see Table 2) to train our models. The features are the Metzler and Kanungo (MK) [23] set, modified LETOR [24], semantic, and statistical features. The original MK feature set used six features for the query-based summarization task. Due to the difference to our task (comparing query and title), we ignore the sentence location feature because the titles usually consist only of one sentence. Regarding the features Term Overlap and Synonym Overlap, we remove stop-words and perform porter stemming on the queries and titles. The Term Overlap is the fraction of query terms that occur in the document (titles or full-text), while the Synonyms Overlap is the fraction of query terms that either occur or have a synonym in the document. We utilize NLTK (See footnote 1) to generate synonyms. For the LETOR feature set, we ignore all web-related features (e.g. Sitemap term propagation). The language model parameters are taken from the original work. Additionally, we use the vector representation of words (Word2Vec) to compute the similarity between a query-document pair and use it as an L2R feature. For this purpose, we use Google News, the pre-trained distributional model [28], and gensim framework to generate the similarity scores [29]. Regarding the language model features, we use an Elasticsearch (See footnote 1) full-text index to generate them. Moreover, we use the scores of the ranking models (BM25, CF-IDF, and HCF-IDF) as L2R features.

We further investigate the possibility of sampling a meaningful subset of features that decreases the error rate of the ranking models. For this purpose, we apply a correlation-based feature selection algorithm (CFS) [30] on each dataset and content modality, i.e., separately for full-text and title. The CFS algorithm computes a score for a subset S of the 29 features containing k features using the following equation (denoted as $score_{CFS}(S)$ in [30]): $score_{CFS(S)} = \frac{k \cdot \overline{r_{gf}}}{\sqrt{k+k(k-1)\overline{r_{ff}}}}$ where $\overline{r_{gf}}$ is the average gold standard(g)-feature correlation and $\overline{r_{ff}}$ represents the average inter-correlation between the features. The formula denotes higher scores to the subsets which have a low 'feature-feature' correlations and high 'gold standard-feature' correlations.

We calculated $score_{CFS}(S)$ for all feature subsets of sizes $|S| = \{1, \dots, 29\}$, which equals $2^{29} - 1 = 536, 870, 911$ possible subsets, for each dataset and configuration (full-texts or titles). The best feature sets, in terms of their $score_{CFS}(S)$, are reported in Table 3. We utilize these features in our learning-to-rank models. The results are presented in Table 4.

The CFS results showed that some features, such as BM25, contribute the most to the results. This is consistent with that of Qin et al. [24], who found that using BM25 as a feature in L2R models improves the overall performance of the L2R models.

Table 3. Best feature subsets (BFS) based on the CFS approach. # is the number of features in the corresponding BFS

Dataset	Content	Best Feature Subset (BFS)	#	$score_{CFS(BFS)}$
NTCIR-2	Full-text	BM25, Exact match	2	0.20
	Titles	BM25, Exact match	2	0.15
TREC	Full-text	BM25, Exact match, Sum of length normalized TF	3	0.28
	Titles	BM25, Language model with Dirichlet smoothing, Minimum of TF-IDF, Term overlap, Word2vec	5	0.13
Econbiz	Full-text	Language model with absolute discounting smoothing, Language model with Bayesian smoothing using Dirichlet priors, Min TF-IDF, Var TF-IDF	4	0.41
	Titles	BM25, Exact match, Language model, Synonym overlap, Term overlap, Covered query term number, Max TF-IDF, Mean length norm TF, Mean TF, Mean TF-IDF, Min length norm TF, Min TF, Min TF-IDF, Sum length norm TF, Sum TF, Sum TFIDF	16	0.71
Politics	Full-text	Language model with Dirichlet smoothing, Language model with absolute discounting smoothing, Language model with Jelinek-Mercer smoothing, Max TF-IDF, Mean TF-IDF, Min TF-IDF, Sum TF, Sum TF-IDF, Var TF-IDF	9	0.41
	Titles	BM25	1	0.54
PubMed	Full-text	Language model with Jelinek-Mercer smoothing, Mean TF-IDF	2	0.46
	Titles	Language model with absolute discounting smoothing, IDF	2	0.44

4.4 Evaluation Metric

We evaluate the retrieval results using normalized discounted cumulative gain ($nDCG$). We assume that users do not look beyond two pages of 10 results. Thus, we limited our evaluation to the top 20 results. The metric $nDCG$ compares the top-20 documents (DCG), with the gold standard and is computed as follows:
$nDCG@k = \frac{DCG@k}{IDCG@k}$, where $DCG@k = rel(1) + \sum_{i=2}^{k} \frac{rel(i)}{\log(i)}$ D is a set of documents, $rel(d)$ is a function that returns one if the document is rated relevant, otherwise zero, and $IDCG_k$ is the optimal ranking.

5   Results

In this section, we present the results of the titles vs. full-text retrieval comparison. We observe that the retrieval over titles yields a close nDCG@20 values, or even higher metric values in case of the NTCIR-2. Table 4 presents the performance of the title- and full-text-based ranking models on all datasets.

Table 4. Average nDCG@20 scores using full-text (FT) vs. titles (T) over the five datasets. The L2R results are calculated using the full feature set (FFS) and the best feature subset (BFS).

Family	IR Method	NTCIR-2		TREC		EconBiz		IREON		PubMed	
		T	FT	T	FT	T	FT	T	FT	T	FT
VSM	TF-IDF	0.19	0.18	0.21	0.39	0.26	0.22	0.661	0.36	0.80	0.54
	CF-IDF	0.05	0.05	0.12	0.13	0.13	0.19	0.44	0.32	0.66	0.49
	HCF-IDF	0.23	0.24	0.10	0.12	0.25	0.20	0.659	0.37	0.80	0.54
PM	BM25	0.24	0.32	**0.23**	**0.41**	0.25	0.20	0.662	0.37	0.80	0.55
	BM25CT	0.24	0.31	0.20	0.405	0.27	0.19	0.660	0.37	**0.81**	0.56
L2R-FFS	LambdaMART	0.25	0.30	0.22	0.39	**0.67**	0.68	0.83	0.69	0.67	0.67
	RankNet	0.28	0.29	0.13	0.10	0.28	0.10	0.20	0.21	0.30	0.30
	RankBoost	0.26	0.32	0.21	0.34	0.52	0.69	0.80	0.59	0.70	0.79
	AdaRank	0.21	0.31	0.19	0.22	0.50	0.67	0.79	0.65	0.56	0.52
	ListNet	0.21	0.24	0.15	0.07	0.28	0.10	0.20	0.20	0.30	0.30
	Coord. Ascent	0.29	0.33	0.22	0.39	0.57	**0.80**	**0.95**	**0.77**	**0.81**	**0.80**
SM	DSSM	**0.33**	0.26	0.18	0.23	0.29	0.33	0.41	0.39	0.34	0.33
	C-DSSM	0.32	0.32	0.18	0.20	0.29	0.34	0.42	0.44	0.32	0.35
L2R-BFS	LambdaMART	0.20	0.15	0.16	0.33	0.56	0.63	0.70	0.65	0.42	0.65
	RankNet	0.28	0.25	0.05	0.046	0.28	0.10	0.26	0.41	0.59	0.63
	RankBoost	0.26	0.37	0.13	0.30	0.52	0.10	0.80	0.47	0.30	0.72
	AdaRank	0.29	**0.37**	0.18	0.37	0.48	0.49	0.94	0.61	0.59	0.70
	ListNet	0.29	**0.37**	0.19	0.37	0.28	0.28	0.94	0.41	0.39	0.49
	Coord. Ascent	0.29	**0.37**	0.18	0.38	0.53	0.10	0.94	0.69	0.59	0.78

For the NTCIR-2 dataset, we observe that the learning to rank model, Coordinate Ascent, with the full set of 29 features attained the $nDCG@20$ value of 0.33, which is 0.01 higher than C-DSSM and BM25 on full-text retrieval. The same metric value of 0.33 has also been attained from the titles retrieval using the DSSM model. Having reduced the features to the best feature set, BM25 and exact matching, coordinate ascent performance slightly improved on full-text retrieval (0.37). However, the titles retrieval of the same model remained at the same value (0.29).

In the case of the TREC dataset, we observe that BM25 achieved the best results on full-text and titles retrieval. BM25 attains a nDCG of 0.41 on full-text compared to 0.23 on titles. The L2R methods, LambdaMart, and Coordinate Ascent using the full feature set and the best feature set attained close results to BM25 on both full-text and titles.

Considering the evaluation results for the EconBiz dataset, we used the STW concepts as queries. We observe that the retrieval over full-text yields higher nDCG metric values. The best title-based retrieval model, LambdaMART, attains a nDCG of 0.67 compared to 0.80 of Coordinate Ascent on full-text.

For IREON and PubMed, we used the FIV and MeSH concepts as queries. The titles retrieval was competitive with the full-text retrieval. In both datasets, Coordinate Ascent achieved the best retrieval results. On titles, Coordinate Ascent attained nDCG values of 0.95 and 0.81. These values are 18% and 1% higher than the best full-text retrieval models, respectively.

6   Discussion

The results show that a title-based retrieval over large document corpora is possible. For four of our five datasets, we obtained nDCG@20 scores that are similar or even better than the scores obtained from the best retrieval models over full-text. Figure 1 visualizes the nDCG scores of the best performing retrieval methods for each individual dataset. Below, we discuss the key insights for each dataset.

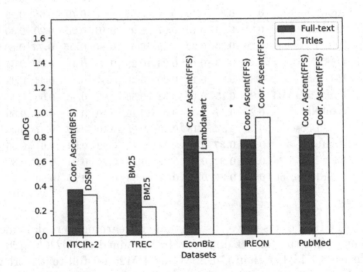

Fig. 1. Average nDCG@20 of the best performing retrieval models

For NTCIR-2, the best title-based retrieval model DSSM attained the same nDCG metric value as the second best full-text-based retrieval model Coordinate Ascent. In order to generate the L2R results, we used 29 features including Word2Vec and MK feature sets. Applying the CFS method resulted in generating BM25 and the number of exact matches as the best feature subsets. By using solely those two features, the best L2R method on full-text, Coordinate Ascent, gained 4% in terms of nDCG. NTCIR-2 was the only dataset, in which DSSM achieves the best title-based retrieval results. Our study conforms with Cohen et al. [31], who showed that DSSM performs poorly on a traditional dataset for ad-hoc retrieval and argue that the word-hashing method discards too much information.

For the TREC and EconBiz datasets, the titles retrieval results were not competitive with those of full-text retrieval. The nDCG values of the best full-text-based models on TREC and EconBiz were 18%, and 13% better than the best titles-based models datasets respectively.

For the IREON and PubMed datasets, the retrieval over titles results in consistently higher metric values in terms of nDCG.

Aggregating the best nDCG values over all datasets and configurations, the best titles-based retrieval models attain a value of 0.60, whereas the best full-text retrieval models attain a mean score of 0.63 (3% relative improvement). Therefore, we believe that title-based retrieval can be considered providing competitive results comparable with the full-text-based retrieval.

One may consider it as a limitation of our study that thesauri concepts STW, FIV, and MeSH are used for retrieving the results from the digital library datasets EconBiz, IREON, and PubMed, respectively. Considering that these thesauri concepts belong to the same domain as their corresponding datasets, one can consider that finding matching documents is easier. However, the concepts are purposefully chosen as queries as they often resemble topics that users of the scientific digital libraries actually search for.

Reproducibility. All the code for reproducing the experiments is publicly available as bitbucket repository[1].

7 Conclusions

We conducted a study to compare title-based with full-text-based ad-hoc retrieval. For this purpose, different retrieval models of different families (probabilistic models, vector space, learning to rank models and semantic models) were compared. We used five datasets, out of which three datasets are obtained from digital libraries: Econbiz, PubMed and IREON, and two standard test collections. Overall, our experiments show that title-based ad-hoc retrieval models can provide close, and sometimes even better, results compared to the full-text ad-hoc retrieval.

Acknowledgement. This work was supported by the EU's Horizon 2020 programme under grant agreement H2020-693092 MOVING.

---

[1] https://bitbucket.org/a_saleh/icadl2018.

References

1. Galke, L., Mai, F., Schelten, A., Brunsch, D., Scherp, A.: Using titles vs. full-text as source for automated semantic document annotation. In: International Conference on Knowledge Capture (K-CAP), May 2017
2. Nishioka, C., Scherp, A.: Profiling vs. time vs. content: what does matter for top-k publication recommendation based on twitter profiles? In: 2016 IEEE/ACM Joint Conference on Digital Libraries (JCDL), pp. 171–180. IEEE (2016)
3. Croft, W.B., Metzler, D., Strohman, T.: Search Engines: Information Retrieval in Practice, vol. 283. Addison-Wesley, Reading (2010)
4. Christopher, D.M., Prabhakar, R., Hinrich, S.: Introduction to Information Retrieval, vol. 151, p. 177 (2008)
5. Barker, F.H., Veal, D.C., Wyatt, B.K.: Comparative efficiency of searching titles, abstracts, and index terms in a free-text data base. J. Doc. **28**(1), 22–36 (1972)
6. Lin, J.: Is searching full text more effective than searching abstracts? BMC Bioinform. **10**(1), 46 (2009)
7. Hemminger, B.M., Saelim, B., Sullivan, P.F., Vision, T.J.: Comparison of full-text searching to metadata searching for genes in two biomedical literature cohorts. J. Am. Soc. Inf. Sci. Technol. **58**(14), 2341–2352 (2007)
8. Salton, G., Wong, A., Yang, C.S.: A vector space model for automatic indexing. Commun. ACM **18**(11), 613–620 (1975)
9. Goossen, F., IJntema, W., Frasincar, F., Hogenboom, F., Kaymak, U.: News personalization using the CF-IDF semantic recommender. In: The International Conference on Web Intelligence, Mining and Semantics. ACM (2011)
10. Chen, R.C., Spina, D., Croft, W.B., Sanderson, M., Scholer, F.: Harnessing semantics for answer sentence retrieval. In: Workshop on Exploiting Semantic Annotations in Information Retrieval, pp. 21–27. ACM (2015)
11. Mikolov, T., Sutskever, I., Chen, K., Corrado, G.S., Dean, J.: Distributed representations of words and phrases and their compositionality. In: Burges, C.J.C., Bottou, L., Welling, M., Ghahramani, Z., Weinberger, K.Q. (eds.) Advances in Neural Information Processing Systems, vol. 26, pp. 3111–3119. Curran Associates, Inc. (2013)
12. Liu, T.Y.: Learning to rank for information retrieval. Found. Trends Inf. Retr. **3**(3), 225–331 (2009)
13. Burges, C., et al.: Learning to rank using gradient descent. In: Proceedings of the 22nd International Conference on Machine Learning, pp. 89–96. ACM (2005)
14. Wu, Q., Burges, C.J., Svore, K.M., Gao, J.: Adapting boosting for information retrieval measures. Inf. Retr. **13**(3), 254–270 (2010)
15. Freund, Y., Iyer, R., Schapire, R.E., Singer, Y.: An efficient boosting algorithm for combining preferences. J. Mach. Learn. Res. **4**, 933–969 (2003)
16. Xu, J., Li, H.: AdaRank: a boosting algorithm for information retrieval. In: The Annual International ACM SIGIR Conference on Research and Development in Information Retrieval, pp. 391–398. ACM (2007)
17. Metzler, D., Croft, W.B.: Linear feature-based models for information retrieval. Inf. Retr. **10**(3), 257–274 (2007)
18. Cao, Z., Qin, T., Liu, T.Y., Tsai, M.F., Li, H.: Learning to rank: from pairwise approach to listwise approach. In: The 24th International Conference on Machine Learning, pp. 129–136. ACM (2007)
19. Zhang, Y., et al.: Neural information retrieval: a literature review. arXiv preprint arXiv:1611.06792 (2016)

20. Huang, P.S., He, X., Gao, J., Deng, L., Acero, A., Heck, L.: Learning deep structured semantic models for web search using clickthrough data. In: International
Conference on Information and Knowledge Management (2013)
21. Shen, Y., He, X., Gao, J., Deng, L., Mesnil, G.: Learning semantic representations using convolutional neural networks for web search. In: The International
Conference on World Wide Web, pp. 373–374. ACM (2014)
22. Shen, Y., He, X., Gao, J., Deng, L., Mesnil, G.: A latent semantic model with
convolutional-pooling structure for information retrieval. In: The International
Conference on Information and Knowledge Management. ACM (2014)
23. Metzler, D., Kanungo, T.: Machine learned sentence selection strategies for query-
biased summarization. In: SIGIR Learning to Rank Workshop (2008)
24. Qin, T., Liu, T.Y.: Introducing LETOR 4.0 Datasets. CoRR (2013)
25. Qin, T., Liu, T.Y., Xu, J., Li, H.: How to make LETOR more useful and reliable.
In: SIGIR Workshop on Learning to Rank for Information Retrieval (2008)
26. Minka, T., Robertson, S.: Selection bias in the LETOR datasets. In: SIGIR Workshop on Learning to Rank for Information Retrieval, pp. 48–51. Citeseer (2008)
27. Fortmann-Roe, S.: Understanding the bias-variance tradeoff (2012)
28. Mikolov, T., Chen, K., Corrado, G., Dean, J.: Efficient estimation of word representations in vector space. arXiv preprint arXiv:1301.3781 (2013)
29. Rehurek, R., Sojka, P.: Software framework for topic modelling with large corpora.
In: The LREC Workshop on New Challenges for NLP Frameworks (2010)
30. Hall, M.A.: Correlation-based feature selection of discrete and numeric class
machine learning (2000)
31. Cohen, D., Ai, Q., Croft, W.B.: Adaptability of neural networks on varying granularity IR tasks. arXiv preprint arXiv:1606.07565 (2016)

Acquiring Metadata to Support Biographies
of Museum Artefacts

Can Zhao[1]([📧]) [iD], Michael B. Twidale[2] [iD], and David M. Nichols[1] [iD]

[1] Department of Computer Science, University of Waikato,
Hamilton 3240, New Zealand
cz93@students.waikato.ac.nz,
david.nichols@waikato.ac.nz
[2] School of Information Sciences, University of Illinois at Urbana-Champaign,
Champaign, IL 61820, USA
twidale@illinois.edu

Abstract. Museum collections are primarily experienced in physical museums. Metadata and linked data have the potential to support new models of interaction with heritage objects outside museums. Object biographies are a conceptual lens through which to view object metadata. We explore the concept of object biography through an interview-based study of selected artefacts from local New Zealand museums. We discuss how the nature of this metadata can support new object-centric interaction in the wider environment.

Keywords: Metadata · Museum · Object biography

1 Introduction

Museum collections have challenging metadata requirements due to the unique nature of the artefacts to be described. Available metadata impacts in-museum display, participation in the linked data of the semantic web and potential new interaction models.

Previous studies have shown that heritage objects with insufficient display and interpretation can be ignored during on-site visits [21], they can be curated into personal collections online (either before or after on-site visits) but abandoned thereafter [19]. Heritage objects can often be seen as isolated in physical museums [10].

Ciolfi [4] argues that a variety of technological platforms and their applications have largely reproduced one restricted "model of engagement with heritage" that features a curator or guide offering a sole institutional voice to visitors. We share this desire for an expanded view of heritage and for exploring interactions and participation that convey heritage beyond museums. Metadata and linked data have the *potential* to support interaction with heritage objects outside museums but current inhibitory issues lie in the quality, quantity and dispersal of published artefact metadata and linked data [2, 7].

We see *object biography* as one approach to inform a richer representation of, and thus interaction with, heritage artefacts. Being an established, as well as a recognised concept in archaeology and museum studies [21, 24], this biographical approach seeks to uncover the relationships between people and objects via life histories of an object or

M. Dobreva et al. (Eds.): ICADL 2018, LNCS 11279, pp. 304–315, 2018.
https://doi.org/10.1007/978-3-030-04257-8_31

assemblage [10, 14, 15]. Artefacts accumulate and transform meanings and values from the moment they come into existence: the significance of an artefact is based in its connection to people and events. When consideration is given to these life moments of an object, their social contexts and consequences, "little is left out" [10].

In this paper, we describe a small exploratory study designed to investigate object biographies for selected artefacts from local New Zealand museums. The discussion considers the implications for supporting new models of artefact-centric interaction with collections.

2 Background

Heritage artefacts are commonly viewed as static items preserved inside physical museums. The motivation for the present study is an interest in exploring the relationship between the provision of object metadata and interactions outside museums. We aim to embed heritage artefacts into a general audience's everyday lives—where and when they are—via technologies that better create an ambient appreciation of place and integration into history. This perspective motivates an exploration of what is needed in an artefact record to support people in such engaged communities.

Creating heritage object metadata can be a difficult and laborious task. Unlike books and other similar items, heritage objects are not often self-documenting: metadata is not easily derivable directly from a heritage object itself. Except for some details such as dimensions, most metadata must be derived by practiced analysis and careful scholarship. Consequently, there is a very clear long tail with a few 'star' artefacts having rich metadata and most having minimalist sparse metadata. However, metadata aimed at supporting traditional descriptive uses is not necessarily biographical in form or detail.

Among heritage linked data publishing initiatives, some work has been undertaken into computational human biographies for historical or digital humanities investigation (see [9, 13, 16]). For example, one approach that explicitly models time and space for medieval and Renaissance manuscripts has an expectation of generalising the outcome to all types of artefacts [3]. Several classes relating to an object biography—manuscript, actor, time and location at regional, national and international levels—are used for description [3]. These approaches suggest that representations of heritage objects can be explored via examining object-people relationships [10]. For example, Pye suggests framing this issue as: "what it [the object] means to people now" [22].

The reported quality, quantity and dispersal issues are currently featured in library, archive and museum (LAM)-provided artefact metadata. Applications facilitating the general audience's interaction with heritage information outside the institutions primarily use their resources, either directly or for producing new assets. By borrowing three categories—education, exhibition enhancement and reconstruction—proposed for elucidating the purpose of heritage applications [1], we summarise the characteristics of six applications that used heritage resources outside of physical institutions (Table 1). The selected applications cover all of the three primary purpose categories. There is a strong focus on photographic and video resources: which inherently locate attention to a particular place and time. An architectural focus is common in these applications, and in other tours, as it naturally fits with walking in urban areas. Other resources are typically customised especially for the specific application. In general, these types of applications do not integrate complementary artefacts from local museums: we suggest that this is due to the lack of appropriate biographical metadata for those items.

Table 1. Summary of six applications that use heritage resources outside physical institutions.

Application	Primary purpose category	Tour focus	Tour type	Heritage resource used
CityViewAR [12, 18]	Reconstruction	Architecture (Buildings collapsed in earthquakes)	Flexible	Heritage photographs of architecture, objects
Explore [20]	Exhibition enhancement	Life stories of objects (Seasonal stories at Seurasaari Island)	Flexible	Images and videos with text descriptions
Public houses, Private lives: Excavating Christchurch's colonial hotels from Heritage Trails [11]	Education	Life stories of objects (Objects used during the stay of European settlers at hotels)	Fixed	Heritage photographs of architecture, images of objects
Mobile app of *Representing Reformation* [17]	Exhibition enhancement	Life stories of objects (Thetford Priory site)	Fixed	Images and 3D models of architecture, images of sites
Svevo tour [8]	Exhibition enhancement	Life stories of a person (Italo Svevo)	Flexible	Heritage photographs, images of manuscripts, images and 3D models of objects, radio and concert recordings, movies
Walk1916 [6]	Reconstruction	Life stories of an event (Easter Rising)	Flexible	Heritage photographs of sites

However, the observed focus of museums on the objects in their physical collections may also be related to existing practice. Chen and Marty [5] have noted the risk that museums are inclined to apply exhibit design approaches solely to think about the user in the life of the museum, but not to also think about the museum in the life of the user. A museum website or online collection can be accessed from home, but novel applications can bring museum resources into our lives; making us aware of cultural connections in our immediate vicinity. Just as more commercial apps try to make us aware of nearby shopping opportunities. Placing the museum into the lives of users means 'exporting' the artefacts into the wider environment (both physical and digital).

Vassilakis et al. [23] claim that "we need to give "life" to the cultural heritage in order for it to become active and support the delivery of rich experiences" and that existing descriptive metadata does not support such new access models. The examples in [23] focus on in-museum experiences where objects present themselves differently based on the proximity of other objects (in the context of travelling exhibitions). Objects should be able to 'answer' the question "where have I traveled" [23]: although it is not clear if that extends to the biographical sense that we have adopted.

Enabling artefacts to have a presence beyond the walls of the museum is one way to place museums in the life of their users and this can only be achieved digitally. Embracing the concept of object biography is one mechanism for structuring metadata to enable object-centric interactions. Current object metadata has not been created with this application in mind and so we need to explore specific biographical capture.

3 Study Design

To explore whether, and how, employing a biographical approach could contribute to acquiring and understanding heritage artefact metadata, we designed a three-phased qualitative study that involved selecting objects, interviewing key informants and collecting structured descriptive metadata. The key informants (participants) were recruited by word of mouth and using snowball sampling from three related groups: LAM professionals, heritage experts and enthusiastic amateurs. One practical benefit of working with these loosely defined groups was to expand the otherwise limited pool of potential participants. More importantly, participants with diverse backgrounds would help us explore possibilities in the "multiple communities that heritage engages" [4].

At the beginning of each session, we requested the participant to select two to four artefacts using six criteria: the artefacts should be travelled, studied by the participant, related to each other, presented in the institution's or participant's work, enquired of, or received feedback, from the public, as well as being varied in classification. Some flexibility was allowed so that not all criteria had to be met.

Once the selections were confirmed, a semi-structured interview was conducted with audio and video recording. The interview concentrated on acquiring artefact metadata via questioning the participant's experience with the artefacts, getting *direct* and *relevant locations* marked on maps, then asking for the participant's view of the artefacts' information that a general audience could find interesting, valuable information that they were eager to convey, as well as communication between the participant and audiences based on the artefacts. We used non-digital resources comprised of board game pieces, cut cardboard pieces, sticky notes, A3-sized maps printed from OpenStreetMap and pens to mark the locations where each artefact has been (i.e. direct), and to where it is relevant with the associated time and context (see Fig. 1).

Two pilot studies were run by separately focusing on academic visits and personally collected artefacts. After revising the study protocol, five sessions were conducted with the interviews lasting for 5.75 hours in total. The participants included one enthusiastic amateur who donated artefacts to museum (P1), one librarian (P2) and three museum professionals (P3, P4 and P5). P3 and P5 were based at council-funded or operated institutions, whilst P4 was affiliated to their local museum, where volunteers from the community played an active role in operation. P1's interview was completed in a usability lab, and the remainder were performed in the respective institutions.

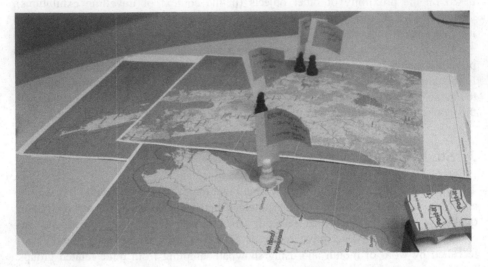

Fig. 1. Physical maps and markers used in a location marking activity

Table 2. The selected objects for the study.

Object No.	Object
S1 incl. O1 – O3	3 uniform patches
O4	Official photo of Air Training Corps (ATC) Flying Scholarship
S2 incl. O5 – O7	3 photos of ATC Flying Scholarship cadets
S3 incl. O8 – O11	4 pieces of ATC course documentation
S4 incl. O12 – O14	3 photos of cadet in uniform
O15	Jansson map
O16	Stokes map
O17	Printing Press – 'Excelsior'
O18	Wedding Dress – Bodice and Skirt
S5 incl. O19 – O22	4 pieces of Buckland China
S6 incl. O23 – O25	3 illuminated manuscripts
S7 incl. O26 – O30	5 wooden patterns for moulding mine machinery wheels
O31	Camera
S8 incl. O32 – O33	Cup and Plate
S9 incl. O34 – O35	2 pamphlets – *Maori Settlement of the Waikato District*

4   Results

The participants selected 35 single objects: they were presented in the study sessions (and listed in Table 2) as 6 individual objects and 9 sets of objects that consist of the other 29 pieces. Individual objects and sets of objects are respectively numbered from O1 to O35 and from S1 to S9. The existing structured descriptive metadata (the *existing metadata*) of 12 single objects—O16, O17, O18, O19 to O22 of S5, O31, O32 and O33 of S8, as well as O34 and O35 of S9—was gathered. The other 23 pieces did not have any structured descriptive metadata digitised by 4 July 2018: S1, O4, S2, S3 and S4 were recently donated to museum; O15 was rediscovered in 2017 and not catalogued; S6 and S7 also had no digitised structured information. The new metadata of all the selected objects were acquired verbally from the interviews (the *acquired metadata*). The verbal data was transcribed and then coded in NVivo 12. Both sets of metadata were interpreted through an object biography lens.

4.1   Two Sets of Metadata and Their Extents

In the existing metadata, that associated with O16 primarily described a facsimile edition of *Discoveries in Australia* in MARC standards[1], as O16 was attached to the book. O17, O18, S5, O31, S8 and S9 were recorded in compliance with Spectrum format[2]. For S5 and S9, the existing metadata were at the set level. O32 and O33, both part of S8, however had been individually recorded with the same *Acquisition Notes*.

The acquired metadata were free-flowing, narrative and thus less scholarly. They revealed their relatedness to seven types of biographies: the biographies of selected objects, "typical life" of the similar objects [14], related places, related time periods, related persons, other objects associated with the related persons, other intangible items associated with the related persons.

Employing object biography as a conceptual tool enabled the comparison shown in Table 3 of the extent and certainty (see Sect. 4.2) between the two sets of metadata across three object life stages—being made (*Made*), being exchanged, used or owned (*Exchanged*) and being collected (*Collected*)—informed by [14]. Six metadata property categories: location, time, person, event, value and meaning and context were abbreviated as *L, T, P, E, V* and *C*. Hyphens (-) symbolise no existing metadata. Black circles represent metadata values that were certain, whereas white circles represent uncertainty. Blank cells indicate no existing metadata and no metadata was acquired.

The details from the existing metadata and the acquired metadata were predominately given multiple labels from the six property categories. For example, one of the *Provenance Notes* of O17's existing metadata contained "… [a] Maori newspaper called 'Te Paki o Te Matariki' … was also published at the Parliament from 1891 to 1902, reputedly by this press, but it would seem to be too small for the pages." The implication was that there were events examining and cataloguing the use of O17 in a museum practice context. The related metadata acquired from P3 included some extra

---

[1]   https://www.loc.gov/marc/.

[2]   https://collectionstrust.org.uk/spectrum/.

details: "… I know that [O17] is not likely to have been used for the newspaper and is more likely to have been maybe a notice or used for that kind of publication. "… [I]t would only have been a single sheet from this printing press, so we need to have an example of that and we don't have any here at the museum."

The acquired metadata overall covered a greater extent than the existing metadata, even with the differing amounts of existing detail. The information of the objects across their lives was difficult to derive from the existing metadata, particularly for the first and second life stages. The acquired metadata bridged some of the gaps with more details that embraced a higher level of uncertainties.

4.2 Detail, Certainty, Spatial and Temporal Granularity

The detail of the metadata varied among the artefacts or sets of artefacts from being "[f]ully catalogued" to being produced using limited resources. The existing metadata were machine-readable in principle, yet the catalogued details that were biographical and potentially useful for enabling access to artefacts in wider environment commonly existed in free-text form as descriptions and notes, very occasionally with uncertainties (e.g. one of O17's *Provenance Notes* in Sect. 4.1).

The acquired metadata yielded a considerable amount of details of each artefact/set of artefacts. The participants were willing to supply uncertain information that was either rarely catalogued or not included in the existing metadata. The amounts of uncertain information therefore markedly increased in the acquired metadata. Among the spatial and temporal details that were certain, some were clearly not fine-grained.

One observation was that raising the mutual relationships between the certainties or uncertainties in one selected object/set of objects and the uncertainties or certainties in the similar objects or the objects associated with the related persons was spontaneous and sometimes connected with the reasoning behind the information. P1 recalled the production of O3 of S1: "Because this shop [that did monograms] was literally across the road from the barracks we were in … and we'd seen people going out with patches and so I just went: 'Why don't we get one?'. I'm guessing there were probably other [cadets who took the] courses that did the same thing, I'd never seen one. So, in that sense I thought 'what's the rarity value?', put it on display." The location, value and context of O15's second life stage, as well as time, person and event across its second and third stages involved uncertainty. The reason was the purchase and acquisition events of O15 were associated by P2 with a deceased person and were "impossible to confirm": "It just is a very strong feeling on my part that that is what [they] did, because our careers overlapped and [they] would do this … We have a lot of good maps because of [them], so I think this is one of those."

The supplied spatial and temporal granularity was another recurring theme. The grain-size of the location properties frequently stayed at city or town level, whilst that of the time properties varied from within months to two decades. P5 explained how S8 saved their donor's life: "… [T]hey were used during World War I. "We're not exactly sure where [the related person] was, at what point in time, but it's believed that he was drinking, and the bullet came through. … [T]hat hit the cup and [plate] instead of him."

Table 3. The extent and certainty of the existing and acquired metadata.

Object No.	Existing metadata divided by different life stages																		Acquired metadata divided by different life stages																	
	Made						Exchanged						Collected						Made						Exchanged						Collected					
	L	T	P	E	V	C	L	T	P	E	V	C	L	T	P	E	V	C	L	T	P	E	V	C	L	T	P	E	V	C	L	T	P	E	V	C
S1 incl. O1 – O3	-	-	-	-	-	-	-	-	-	-	-	-	-	-	-	-	-	-	●	●	●	●	●	●	●	●	●	●	●	●	●	●	●	●	●	●
O4	-	-	-	-	-	-	-	-	-	-	-	-	-	-	-	-	-	-	●	●	●	●		●	●	●	●	●	●	●	●	●	●	●	●	●
S2 incl. O5 – O7	-	-	-	-	-	-	-	-	-	-	-	-	-	-	-	-	-	-	●	●	●	●		●	●	●	●	●	●	●	●	●	●	●	●	●
S3 incl. O8 – O11	-	-	-	-	-	-	-	-	-	-	-	-	-	-	-	-	-	-							●	●	●	●	●	●	●	●	●	●	●	●
S4 incl. O12 – O14	-	-	-	-	-	-	-	-	-	-	-	-	-	-	-	-	-	-	○	○	○	●	○		○						●	●	●	●	●	●
O15	-	-	-	-	-	-	-	-	-	-	-	-	-	-	-	-	-	-	●	●	●	●	●	●	○	○	○	○	○	○	●	○	○	●	●	●
O16	●	●	●	●						●	●		●						●	●	●	●	●	●	●	●	●	●	●		●	●	●	●	●	●
O17	●	●	●	●	●		●	●	○	○	○	○	●	●	●	●		●	●	●	●	●	●	●	○	●	●	○	○	●	●	●	●	●	○	●
O18		●		●		●	●	●	●		●	●	●	●		●		●	●		○		○		●	●	●	●	●	●	●	●	●	●	●	●
S5 incl. O19 – O22	●	●	●	●		●	●	●	●	●	●	●	●	●	●	●		●	●	●	●	●	●	●	○	●	●	○	●	○	●	●	●	●	●	●
S6 incl. O23 – O25	-	-	-	-	-	-	-	-	-	-	-	-	-	-	-	-	-	-	○		○				●	●	●	○	○	●	●		●	○	○	●	●
S7 incl. O26 – O30	-	-	-	-	-	-	-	-	-	-	-	-	-	-	-	-	-	-	●			●			●	●	○		○		●	●	●	●	●	●	●
O31				●	●			●				●												●	●	●	●	●	●	●	●	●	●	●	●	●
S8 incl. O32 – O33			●	●	●	●		●			●			●					○	●	●	●	●	●	●	●	●	●	●	●	●	●	●	●	●	●
S9 incl. O34 – O35	●	●	●	●				●			●			●					●	●	●	○	○	●	○	○					●	●	●	●	●	●

4.3 Interesting Takeaway Points

Artefact metadata that a general audience might find interesting and that the participants wanted an audience to take away were acquired.

A pattern was that the interesting and valued takeaway points of the metadata were strengthened by the intersections of the biographies (i.e. the seven types of biographies identified in Sect. 4.1), both factual and imaginary. The audiences made meanings via intersecting their own biographies—one sub-type under the biography of related persons—with other types of perceived biographies (e.g., "people putting themselves in the shoes of people in that time and thinking about that", said P3). The pattern was captured from the acquired metadata including those of O3 of S1, O15, O17 and S8. One example was a part of S6's (i.e. three illuminated manuscripts "for retiring local personalities") metadata offered by P4:

"... A lot of them haven't survived because they've been poorly stored ... and then people can't see the value. ... I think it depicts an era where your service to a business, organisation or whatever, was valued.

"... I say it compares [with medieval illustrated manuscripts] because the artwork is similar but now that's been done with pen, ... It makes you think, doesn't it?

"... [A lady] said to me this is a medieval skill. I was thrilled ... I said: 'Yes, it is a medieval skill.' She said: 'I didn't realise that in modern times that that skill had carried through.' ... She was just blown away that the museum had gone to the trouble of raising money, finding a conservator and getting them [restored] in such high quality."

5   Discussion

The acquired metadata has the potential of being transformed into biographical metadata and, therefore, supporting novel interactions with heritage artefacts. The following section discusses the knowledge gained from the study for creating biographical metadata and new scenarios of accessing heritage artefacts.

5.1   Creating Object Biographies

The notion of object biography was used in this study as:

- A conceptual tool for designing the metadata acquisition method, analysing and understanding the existing and acquired metadata
- A potential structure of the acquired metadata.

The method was successful in establishing the viability of metadata acquisition for biographies of the selected objects, however, time constraints meant that some follow-up would be needed to produce complete descriptions suitable for implementation. The method might also only work with a relative small number of objects, the present focus is nevertheless on quality over quantity. For some artefacts and for some participants, an acquisition tool could possibly be used on location or remotely with digital mapping services. Future prototyping could help participants with temporal and spatial granularity as providing metadata for a novel visitor interaction may well be too abstract.

The biography of an artefact should comprise "a reasonable number of actual life histories" [15], though it does not have to tell "a neat linear life story" when the evidence is lacking [14]. Together with the captured biographical intersections that were perceived as interesting, this understanding offers an implication of biographically structuring the acquired details of the selected artefacts.

The mutual relationships between the certainties/uncertainties in one object and the uncertainties/certainties in the similar objects or the objects associated with the related persons, signifies alternative approaches for representing uncertainty that could in turn lead to new user experiences. Additionally, the rich stories of the wooden patterns of S7 might extend to other industrial artefacts in the region with a mining context. The acquired details could be a resource for creating the biographies of the similar artefacts with insufficient records [14, 15].

5.2   Using Object Biographies to Create New Access Models

An object can die and be reborn as it joins in and departs from relationship spheres [14]. By adopting this biographical viewpoint to cope with the jumps and idleness that an object experienced, we could assist a user to not only appreciate the object's remembered past, but also connect with the object's co-created present in their life [5, 19].

Vassilakis et al. [23] suggested shifting the viewpoint of a collection to an artefact and allowing the artefact to 'present' itself to visitors. We aim to extend that approach by allowing the artefacts to be present across the external environment. We have seen that the participants can express biographical metadata about the objects in their collections and this potentially enables these new forms of access.

The implication of a user expressing interest (by whatever means) in an object is that their interest is *spread* to the biographical trail of that object across time and space. This transfer of user interest enables new scenarios of use that can take objects outside museums and place them into their geographical context, for example:

> *Jane is visiting a foreign country. She uses an audio tour guide to access enhanced descriptions of selected objects during a museum visit. Later in her trip she visits a different town and her mobile device notifies her that several of those objects had been present in this town. Her device offers to customise a tour of the relevant locations in chronological order and suggests other related objects in the local museum.*

Conversely, user location histories can be used for in-museum recommendation: where the recent biography of the visitor intersects with the biographies of the artefacts.

6 Conclusion

The potential of object biographies to enable new forms of context-rich interactions is constrained by the available metadata. Artefact records typically do not contain the type or detail of machine-readable metadata needed to support the projection of objects from physical museums to the wider environment. Although a small scale, exploratory study, we believe we have shown the potential of our approach as a method to gather object biography metadata. Participants seemed to find the study enjoyable with relatively low effort: which is important if we are to ask busy people with expertise to share insights. The acquired metadata was somewhat different from the existing metadata:

- More extensive, narrative and less scholarly
- More mutually informed uncertain and certain information among the artefacts
- More focus on biographically intersected topics that would be of interest to a visitor
- Less consistent as to the level of detail, spatial and temporal granularity.

As such, although we refer to the information obtained as artefact metadata, it has many features more in common with the kinds of information provided on interpretive displays next to artefacts in exhibits, than to the fields in an artefact collections database. The main contributions of this paper are:

- To adapt the object biography as a conceptual tool to support new forms of context-dependent interaction with museum artefacts
- The description of a metadata acquisition technique tailored for object biographies
- To report that metadata acquired via this method has properties which seem promising for creating engaging user experiences.

We note that these initial findings are derived from a small focused sample and we aim to expand our set of artefacts as the ideas are implemented in a mobile application.

Acknowledgements. We would like to thank the participants, notably those from local heritage institutions.

References

1. Bekele, M.K., Pierdicca, R., Frontoni, E., Malinverni, E.S., Gain, J.: A survey of augmented, virtual, and mixed reality for cultural heritage. J. Comput. Cult. Herit. **11**(2), 1–36 (2018). https://doi.org/10.1145/3145534
2. Both, J., de Hooge, D., IJff, R., Inel, O., de Boer, V., Aroyo, L.: Linking Dutch World War II cultural heritage collections with events extracted by machines and crowds. In: CEUR Workshop Proceedings, vol. 2063. (2017). http://ceur-ws.org/Vol-2063/events-paper3.pdf
3. Burrows, T., Hyvönen, E., Ransom, L., Wijsman, H.: Mapping manuscript migrations: digging into data for the history and provenance of medieval and renaissance manuscripts. Manuscr. Stud.: J. Schoenberg Inst. Manuscr. Studies **3**(1), 249–252 (2018). https://doi.org/10.1353/mns.2018.0012
4. Ciolfi, L.: Can digital interactions support new dialogue around heritage? Interactions **25**(2), 24–25 (2018). https://doi.org/10.1145/3181368
5. Chen, H.L., Marty, P.F.: The digital museum in the life of the user. Proc. Am. Soc. Inf. Sci. Technol. **42**(1) (2005). https://doi.org/10.1002/meet.1450420132
6. Cushing, A.L., Cowan, B.R.: Walk 1916: exploring non-research user access to and use of digital surrogates via a mobile walking tour app. J. Doc. **73**(5), 917–933 (2017). https://doi.org/10.1108/JD-03-2017-0031
7. Dijkshoorn, C., et al.: The Rijksmuseum collection as linked data. Semant. Web **9**(2), 221–230 (2018). https://doi.org/10.3233/SW-170257
8. Fenu, C., Pittarello, F.: Svevo tour: The design and the experimentation of an augmented reality application for engaging visitors of a literary museum. Int. J. Hum. Comput. Stud. **114**, 20–35 (2018). https://doi.org/10.1016/j.ijhcs.2018.01.009
9. Fokkens, A., et al.: BiographyNet: extracting relations between people and events. In: Bernád, Á.Z., Gruber, C., Kaiser, M. (eds.) Europa baut auf Biographien: Aspekte, Bausteine, Normen und Standards für eine europäische Biographik, pp. 193–224. New Academic Press, Wien (2017)
10. Gosden, C., Marshall, Y.: The cultural biography of objects. World Archaeol. **31**(2), 169–178 (1999). https://doi.org/10.1080/00438243.1999.9980439
11. Heritage New Zealand: Heritage Trails. https://play.google.com/store/apps/details?id=com.mytoursapp.android.app592
12. HIT Lab NZ: CityViewAR. https://www.hitlabnz.org/index.php/products/cityviewar/
13. Hyvönen, E., Leskinen, P., Tamper, M., Tuominen, J., Keravuori, K.: Semantic national biography of Finland. In: CEUR Workshop Proceedings, vol. 2084, pp. 372–385 (2018). http://ceur-ws.org/Vol-2084/short12.pdf
14. Joy, J.: Reinvigorating object biography: reproducing the drama of object lives. World Archaeol. **41**(4), 540–556 (2009). https://doi.org/10.1080/00438240903345530
15. Kopytoff, I.: The cultural biography of things: commoditisation as process. In: Appadurai, A. (ed.) The Social Life of Things: Commodities in Cultural Perspective, pp. 64–91. Cambridge University Press, Cambridge (1986)
16. Larson, R.: Bringing lives to light: biography in context. Final report of Electronic Cultural Atlas Initiative, University of California, Berkeley (2010). https://www.ischool.berkeley.edu/events/2010/bringing-lives-light-biography-project
17. Law, E.L.-C.: Augmenting the experience of a museum visit with a geo-located AR app for an associated archaeological site. In: Vermeeren, A., Calvi, L., Sabiescu, A. (eds.) Museum Experience Design. SSCC, pp. 205–224. Springer, Cham (2018). https://doi.org/10.1007/978-3-319-58550-5_10

18. Lee, G.A., Dünser, A., Kim, S., Billinghurst, M.: CityViewAR: a mobile outdoor AR application for city visualization. In: IEEE International Symposium on Mixed and Augmented Reality 2012 Arts, Media, and Humanities Proceedings, pp. 57–64. IEEE, New York (2012). https://doi.org/10.1109/ismar-amh.2012.6483989

19. Marty, P.F.: My lost museum: user expectations and motivations for creating personal digital collections on museum websites. Libr. Inf. Sci. Res. 33(3), 211–219 (2011). https://doi.org/10.1016/j.lisr.2010.11.003

20. McGookin, D., Tahiroǎlu, K., Vaittinen, T., Kytö, M., Monastero, B., Vasquez, J.C.: Exploring seasonality in mobile cultural heritage. In: Proceedings of the 2017 CHI Conference on Human Factors in Computing Systems, pp. 6101–6105. ACM, New York (2017). https://doi.org/10.1145/3025453.3025803

21. Monti, F., Keene, S.: Museums and Silent Objects: Designing Effective Exhibitions. Ashgate Publishing, Farnham (2013)

22. Pye, E.: Challenges of conservation: working objects. Sci. Mus. Group J. 6 (2016). https://doi.org/10.15180/160608

23. Vassilakis, C., Poulopoulos, V., Antoniou, A., Wallace, M., Lepouras, G., Nores, M.L.: exhiSTORY: smart exhibits that tell their own stories. Futur. Gener. Comput. Syst. 81, 542–556 (2018). https://doi.org/10.1016/j.future.2017.10.038

24. Webley, L., Adams, S.: Material genealogies: bronze moulds and their castings in later Bronze Age Britain. Proc. Prehist. Soc. 82, 323–340 (2016). https://doi.org/10.1017/ppr.2016.8

Mining the Context of Citations in Scientific Publications

Saeed-Ul Hassan[1](✉) (iD), Sehrish Iqbal[1] (iD), Mubashir Imran[2] (iD),
Naif Radi Aljohani[3] (iD), and Raheel Nawaz[4] (iD)

[1] Information Technology University, Ferozepur Road, Lahore, Pakistan
saeed-ul-hassan@itu.edu.pk
[2] The University of Queensland, St Lucia, QLD 4072, Australia
[3] King Abdulaziz University, Al-Malae'b St, Jeddah, Saudi Arabia
[4] Manchester Metropolitan University, Manchester M15 6BH, UK

Abstract. Recent advancements in information retrieval systems significantly rely on the context-based features and semantic matching techniques to provide relevant information to users from ever-growing digital libraries. Scientific communities seek to understand the implications of research, its importance and its applicability for future research directions. To mine this information, absolute citations merely fail to measure the importance of scientific literature, as a citation may have a specific context in full text. Thus, a comprehensive contextual understanding of cited references is necessary. For this purpose, numerous techniques have been proposed that tap the power of artificial intelligence models to detect important or incidental (non-important) citations in full text scholarly publications. In this paper, we compare and build upon on four state-of-the-art models that detect important citations using 450 manually annotated citations by experts - randomly selected from 20,527 papers from the Association for Computational Linguistics corpus. Of the total 64 unique features proposed by the four selected state-of-the-art models, the top 29 were chosen using the Extra-Trees classifier. These were then fed it to our supervised machine learning based models: Random Forest (RF) and Support Vector Machine. The RF model outperforms existing selected systems by more than 10%, with 89% precision-recall curve. Finally, we qualitatively assessed important and non-important citations by employing and self-organizing maps. Overall, our research work supports information retrieval algorithms that detect and fetch scientific articles on the basis of both qualitative and quantitative indices in scholarly big data.

Keywords: Citation context analysis · Influential citations · Machine learning
Self-organizing maps

1 Introduction

The measure of impact generated by scientific literature is often accounted by the citations it received [1], Based on absolute citation counts, numerous bibliometric measures (such as H-Index, G-index, and SNIP etc.) have been introduced over the years. Whilst, such measures reflect upon different quantitative aspects of a scholarly

© Springer Nature Switzerland AG 2018
M. Dobreva et al. (Eds.): ICADL 2018, LNCS 11279, pp. 316–322, 2018.
https://doi.org/10.1007/978-3-030-04257-8_32

literature impacts. It has been disputed whether these measures also provide insights regarding the impact, the cited work had within a scientific literature? To address this issue, it is suggested to look into the qualitative aspects of a citation.

Moravcsik and Murugesan [2], deconstructed citations identified in scientific literature into four dimensions; (a) Conceptual Use or Operational Use (was some theory used as support or some technical method/equation adopted); (b) Evolutionary or Juxtapositional (cited work is base or alternate); (c) Organic or Perfunctory (does the citing work explain certain point or is it just a general acknowledgement); and (d) Confirmative vs. Negational (does the citation claim correctness or dispute). The study shows that a major portion (40% cited articles) were general acknowledgements. This reinforces the importance of citation context. Numerous studies discuss the issue of identifying the importance of citations using supervised machine learning techniques applying contextual and quantitative features [3–5]. The algorithms and techniques to approach a certain research problem, as well as the writing style of the author [6], contribute greatly in making an article influential. The number of citations received by scientific literature often accounts for their quantitative impact, but not all citations can be considered equal. Thus, to understand the influence of cited work in citing work, categorizing citations into levels of importance and incidental class is essential.

In this paper, we aim to address the problem of classifying cited work as important or incidental. The followings are the contributions of our paper: At first, we compare four state-of-the-art citation classification techniques using the dataset downloaded from ACL Anthology corpus[1] of 20,527 publications. Further, we present 29 features that outperform existing state-of-the-art techniques by extracting top features from all four selected techniques. Finally, we qualitatively analyze the distinction between important and non-important citations by employing self-organizing maps.

2 Literature Review

A citation context is essentially the text surrounding reference markers. Conventionally, citation analysis has been used to measure the quality of articles in scholarly literature, hence the tracking of citations plays a vital role. It has been argued by Valenzuela [4] that all citations are not equally important, therefore, classification is needed to distinguish the important ones from the unimportant. Xu et al. [7] proposed a citation classification technique by using three classes: functional, ambiguous and perfunctory. They used heterogeneous set of features for classification i.e. cue patterns, positional features, network-based features and structural features to measure the relationship between the author and the article. According to their results combining these features is a challenging task but individually their features perform well. Citation analysis has been used widely to detect scientific collaboration patterns, observing knowledge graphs, impact measurement etc.

Cohan and Goharian [8] addressed the problem of inaccurate citation context extraction, they presented a framework for the automatic summary of research articles

---

[1] http://www.aclweb.org/anthology/.

by using the context of citations. The framework is consisted of three parts: (a) to find context of citation (b) identify features of the citation context (c) and generating a summary of citation contexts. A new study of multiple in-text references (MIR) with respect to their position in the article and syntactic context has been proposed by Bornmann et al. [9]. They used a dataset of 80,000 research articles for analyzing two characteristics: (a) the position of the MIR in rhetorical structure of article and (b) the total number of references in context that make a MIR. Presence of MIR implies the presence of features i.e. topic, keywords and methods common to work cited in aggregated of in-text reference.

3   Data and Methodology

We obtained data from the data corpses of Association for Computational Linguistics (ACL) containing 20,527 articles that are publicly available. These articles contained 106,509 citations. Within these citations 450 unique citations were randomly chosen and labeled as important or unimportant/incidental by a group of field experts [4]. This labeling was further authenticated by a group of experts in the field of computational linguistics. Out of these 14.6% of the citations were considered important by the experts while the rest were marked as unimportant.

3.1   Citation Classification Models

In this section, we define the data extraction, select state-of-the-art supervised machine learning model [1, 3–5] and construction of our supervised and unsupervised models.

Teufel Model. Teufel et al. [3] recommended a technique to categorize the citation function automatically by extracting sets of features i.e. (shallow and linguistically inspired features, part-of-speech-based recognition and finite grammar using string). Each feature is classified into four categories, namely; weakness, comparison, sentiments and neutral. These features are further categorized as weak, positive or neutral. Using the supervised classification model, an accuracy of 83% was attained.

Amjad Model. Amjad et al. [1] used Teufel et al. [3] work and proposed different context-level and polarity–level features for; (a) reference tagging (b) reference grouping and (c) non-syntactic reference removal and polity. For categorizing citations SVM (kernel = linear, c = 1.0) with 10-folds cross-validation was used for context identification and attained a precision of 92% on a recall of 76.4%. For citation purpose classifications 70.5% accuracy has been attained.

Valenzuela Model. Valenzuela et al. [4] argued that we cannot categorize citations as being of equal importance. Hence, they proposed a citation categorization mechanism into important and non-important class. For this purpose, they mined 12 new features mostly related to the nature of the reference and the section in which it is cited. They constructed a supervised classification model with SVM (kernel = RBF) and RF. Both classifiers attained an encouraging area under the curve (AUC) of 80%.

Hassan Model. Hassan et al. [5] extended Valenzuela's et al. [4] work and presented 13 features categorized into three groups; context-based features; cue word-based features; and textual features. They constructed a model with five classifiers, namely Random Forest, SVM, KNN, Decision Tree and Naïve Bayes. RF outperforms other classifiers, with an AUC of 91%.

Hassan_29 Model. By combining the features of all models [1, 3–5], there are a total 64 features. To extract the best features, we employed the Extra-Trees classifier proposed by Geurts et al. [10], that divide the complete selection of data at each step and randomly picks a decision boundary. Finally, we elected all 29 features that had an Extra-Trees classifier score greater than 1%. We named our machine learning model as 'Hassan_29'.

Deployed Unsupervised Models. To obtain a better understanding of the data we devised unsupervised approaches. This helps us to better visualize how our data set and each distinct feature point contained within it behaves. The unsupervised approach used Self Organizing Maps (SOM). This study employed a 10×10 (neurons) SOM on Hassan_29 to observe the behavior of cited literature.

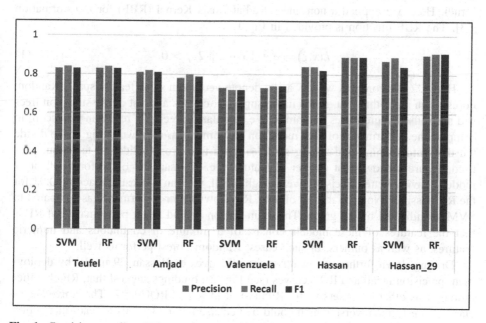

Fig. 1. Precision, recall and F1 score computed by SVM and RF on four state of the art models and newly proposed Hassan_29 model.

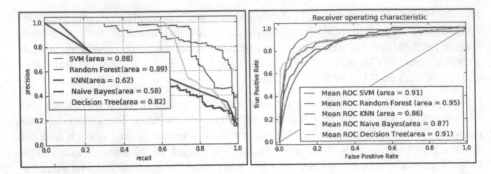

Fig. 2. (left) Precision recall curve and (right) ROC curves for Hassan_29 model using SVM, RF, KNN, Naïve Bayes and decision tree classifiers.

3.2   Experimental Settings and Results

We compared the performance of features extracted using four state-of-the-art techniques and 'Hassan_29' features by training models on SVM [11] and RF [12]. The SVM finds the best boundaries of the outputs by converting data using a specific kernel. Here, we applied a non-linear Radial Basis Kernel (RBF) for transformation [13]. The RBF function is provided in Eq. 1.

$$k(x, z) = e^{-\gamma} \| x - z \| 2, \gamma > 0 \tag{1}$$

Here $e^{-\gamma}$ is a constant, while x and z denote vectors in some feature space. Random Forest is an algorithm that, as the name suggests, creates a forest of classification trees and splits the feature nodes randomly. We calculated precision, recall and F1-score to compare the performance of each model on the same dataset shown in Fig. 1. To divide the data into training and testing samples three-fold cross validation technique was used. Figure 1 shows that our set of features i.e. 'Hassan_29' outperforms all other models, having better precision over a high recall, with an f-measure reaching 0.91 for the RF classifier. Note, on this set of data, RF shows better performance as compared to SVM as indicated by the graph. The main reason behind better performance of RF is that the features of these models consist of a mixture of continuous and numeric features, as well as outliers. In such cases, Random Forest performs well.

Drilling down further, we evaluate the effectives of Hassan_29 model by deployment precision recall and ROC curves (see Fig. 2). Findings suggest that, RF classifier outperforms other classifiers with PR curve of 89% and ROC 95%. The Naïve Bayes classifier performed worst, which could be because the model fails to learn interaction among the features as our dataset is relatively small.

For better data visualization and a qualitative understanding of features, we apply SOM to reduce the data dimension to 2D.

Figure 3 (left) represents a heat map of SOM neurons. The background represents the average distance map of the weight, where lighter color (white) represents greater distance (lesser weight), while dark color (black) represents lesser distance (greater weight). The green and red marker represents each class from the dataset and their

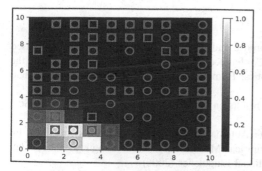 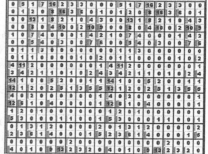

Fig. 3. (left) heat map of SOM classifying important (green box)/incidental (red circle) citations and (right) density of citations mapped on each neuron. Top row (green) of each cell represents important while bottom (red) row represents incidental (Color figure online).

position corresponds to the neuron on which they are classified. Figure 3 (right) represents the mapping of each citation to a certain neuron. Positive classes form independent tight large clusters, with many neurons (e.g. at (1,4), (2,4)), however non-important class performed better creating large independent cluster at adjacent neurons. This makes it is easier to identify non-important citations as compared to important.

4   Concluding Remarks

We have compared and build upon four state-of-the-art models that address the problem of classifying citations into important and non-important groups. We have shown that our machine-learning model, with top 29 features, outperforms all existing state-of-the-art models. In addition, we found that qualitative assessment helps better understand the feature set being examined. A potential limitation of this study is the adoption of the definitions that as such came with the dataset [4, 14]. In future studies, other definitions and features could be explored, such as stylometric features from fulltext [6].

Overall, our proposed technique contributes to Bibliometric Enhanced Information Retrieval system by increasing query search capabilities of search engines. Moreover, citation classification can be used to qualitatively measure the impact of publications in our growing scholarly big data and in the behavioral analysis of scientific domains. Finally, this study can help to improve citation-based full text summarization techniques.

Note that the data and the code used in this paper can be downloaded from the following URL: https://github.com/slab-itu/citation_context_icadl_2018.

References

1. Abu-Jbara, A., Ezra, J., Radev, D.: Purpose and polarity of citation: towards NLP-based bibliometrics. In: Proceedings of the Conference of the North American Chapter of the Association for Computational Linguistics: Human Language Technologies, pp. 596–606 (2013)
2. Moravcsik, M.J., Murugesan, P.: Some results on the function and quality of citations. Soc. Stud. Sci. **5**(1), 86–92 (1975)
3. Teufel, S., Siddharthan, A., Tidhar, D.: Automatic classification of citation function. In: Proceedings of the Conference on Empirical Methods in Natural Language Processing, pp. 103–110. Association for Computational Linguistics (2006)
4. Valenzuela, M., Ha, V., Etzioni, O.: Identifying meaningful citations. In: AAAI Workshop: Scholarly Big Data (2015)
5. Hassan, S.U., Safder, I., Akram, A., Kamiran, F.: A novel machine-learning approach to measuring scientific knowledge flows using citation context analysis. Scientometrics **116**(2), 973–996 (2018)
6. Hassan, S.U., Imran, M., Iftikhar, T., Safder, I., Shabbir, M.: Deep stylometry and lexical & syntactic features based author attribution on PLoS digital repository. In: Choemprayong, S., Crestani, F., Cunningham, S. (eds.) Digital Libraries: Data, Information, and Knowledge for Digital Lives. LNCS, vol. 10647, pp. 119–127. Springer, Cham (2017). https://doi.org/10.1007/978-3-319-70232-2_10
7. Zhu, X., Turney, P., Lemire, D., Vellino, A.: Measuring academic influence: not all citations are equal. J. Assoc. Inf. Sci. Technol. **66**(2), 408–427 (2015)
8. Cohan, A., Goharian, N.: Scientific document summarization via citation contextualization and scientific discourse. Int. J. Digit. Libr. **19**(2-3), 287–303 (2018)
9. Bornmann, L., Haunschild, R., Hug, S.E.: Visualizing the context of citations referencing papers published by Eugene Garfield: a new type of keyword co-occurrence analysis. Scientometrics **114**(2), 427–437 (2018)
10. Geurts, P., Ernst, D., Wehenkel, L.: Extremely randomized trees. Mach. Learn. **63**(1), 3–42 (2006)
11. Auria, L., Moro, R.A.: Support vector machines (SVM) as a technique for solvency analysis. Technical report, Deutsche Bundesbank, Hannover; German Institute for Economic Research, Berlin (2008)
12. Breiman, L.: Random forests. Mach. Learn. **45**(1), 5–32 (2001)
13. Cao, H., Naito, T., Ninomiya, Y.: Approximate RBF kernel SVM and its applications in pedestrian classification. In: The 1st International Workshop on Machine Learning for Vision-based Motion Analysis-MLVMA (2008)
14. Hassan, S.U., Akram, A., Haddawy, P.: Identifying important citations using contextual information from full text. In: ACM/IEEE Joint Conference on Digital Libraries (JCDL), pp. 1–8. IEEE (2017)

A Metadata Extractor for Books
in a Digital Library

Sk. Simran Akhtar[1], Debarshi Kumar Sanyal[2(✉)], Samiran Chattopadhyay[1],
Plaban Kumar Bhowmick[2], and Partha Pratim Das[2]

[1] Jadavpur University, Kolkata 700098, West Bengal, India
sksimranakhtar@gmail.com, samiranc@it.jusl.ac.in
[2] Indian Institute of Technology Kharagpur, Kharagpur 721302, West Bengal, India
debarshisanyal@gmail.com, plaban@cet.iitkgp.ernet.in,
ppd@cse.iitkgp.ernet.in

Abstract. Books form a significant part of the National Digital Library
of India (NDLI). However, extracting metadata from these books is difficult owing to variations in style, graphic fonts, and use of background
images. This paper presents a lightweight tool to automatically extract
metadata from academic books. We also describe results of a preliminary
evaluation of our tool on school books indexed in NDLI.

Keywords: Metadata extraction · Digital Library · Rule-based system

1 Introduction

The National Digital Library of India (NDLI)[1] is being developed to provide
immersive learning experience to learners of all disciplines. Books form a prominent part of NDLI. In many cases, title and other metadata are drawn as pictures
to make them more attractive. This makes automated extraction of metadata
difficult. Rule-based (e.g., [1]) and learning-based algorithms (e.g., [2,5,7]) have
been used to parse research papers and citations. There are works on extraction
of titles from book covers ([3,4,8]) but we could not find open source metadata
extractors for books. Their rarity is perhaps attributable to the wide variety in
appearance of book cover and front matter. We needed a tool to extract metadata from books, especially, school books available in NDLI. In this work-in-
progress paper, we present a lightweight tool[2] that uses spatial cues and regular
expressions to extract metadata from books and output them according to NDLI
schema.

2 System Description

NDLI metadata schema for books comprise Dublin Core (DC) and Learning
Resource Metadata Initiative (LRMI) attributes. DC attributes include title,

---

[1] https://ndl.iitkgp.ac.in.
[2] Code available at https://github.com/dksanyal/Metadata-Extractor-for-Books.

© Springer Nature Switzerland AG 2018
M. Dobreva et al. (Eds.): ICADL 2018, LNCS 11279, pp. 323–327, 2018.
https://doi.org/10.1007/978-3-030-04257-8_33

description (or abstract), contributors (editor and illustrator), table of contents, identifier (ISBN), and copyright year among others. LRMI attributes pertain to educational framework (for example, *Central Board of Secondary Education*, India), education level (for example, class II in the given academic framework), and the like. Given the front matter of a book as a PDF file, we convert it to XML using `pdftohtml`[3]. Spatial cues (i.e., position of the text) and a dictionary of hand-crafted regular expressions are used to extract the desired metadata from the XML file. In particular, the contents of the first non-blank page is initially assumed to be the title. Then we filter out lines that match patterns like `Class\s*[IVX]+` and `Supplementary.*Class\s*[IVX]+` as abstract, keeping the remainder as title. The education level is formed from the numerals after `Class` in abstract. Editor is identified by the keyword `Editor`. Illustrator names generally occur against `Illustrations` or `Cover, Layout and Illustrations` or similar phrases. The table of contents is located by presence of `[(contents)(table of contents)(theme)(what is inside this book)(foreword)]`. For ISBN, we look for the string `ISBN` followed by numerals while for copyright year, we look for `[(copyright)©(all rights reserved)]+.*\d{4}`. Above pattern searches are done ignoring case. The output is post-processed to correct spelling errors. We use the web service ACT-DL[4] [6] to produce Dewey Decimal Classification (DDC) from title, abstract, and table of contents. We call this sequence of operations the *basic flow*.

Unfortunately, sometimes title extraction fails completely. This turns out to be due to use of images for titles. So, if it is found that the title is an empty string, the PDF file is directed to an *alternate flow*: it converts the file to a TIFF image using `ImageMagick`[5], then converts each page to hOCR format using the optical character recognition (OCR) tool `Tesseract`[6] (legacy mode, no LSTM). These hOCR files are then processed by basic flow to extract title. Abstract and education level are extracted if abstract from basic flow was empty, too. DDC is regenerated. Figure 1 shows an example where the alternate flow succeeds.

3   Evaluation

The thrust of NDLI being on educational resources, we tested our tool on a corpus of 115 NCERT[7] school books (test cases) spanning multiple disciplines and education levels. These books undergo periodic revision in contents but their layout does not change much. We measure precision P, recall R and $F1$-score *for each metadata attribute* (e.g., title).

---

[3] https://sourceforge.net/projects/pdftohtml/.
[4] http://act-dl.base-search.net/api.
[5] https://www.imagemagick.org/.
[6] https://github.com/tesseract-ocr.
[7] National Council of Educational Research and Training (NCERT) is an autonomous organization set up in 1961 by the Government of India.

dc.title: "raindrops Book 2 special Series"
dc.description.abstract: "Textbook in English for Class II"
dc.source: "NCERT"
dc.source.uri: "http://www.ncert.nic.in/"
dc.identifier.isbn: "9789350071663"
dc.date.copyright: "2011"
dc.contributor.editor: "Uppal,Shveta|Kumar,Hemant"
dc.contributor.illustrator: "Jabin,Seema"
dc.description.toc:
    1.: ACTION SONG (POEM) :   "1"
    2.: OUR DAY :   "3"
    3.: MY FAMILY :   "8"
    4.: WHATS GOING ON? :   "13"
    5.: MOHAN, THE POTTER :   "18"
    6.: RAIN IN SUMMER (POEM) :   "22"
    7.: MY VILLAGE :   "24"
    8.: THE WORK PEOPLE DO :   "32"
    9.: WORK (POEM) :   "38"
    10.: OUR NATIONAL SYMBOLS :   "40"
    11.: THE FESTIVALS OF INDIA :   "43"
    12.: THE MONKEY AND THE ELEPHANT: "50"
    13.: GOING TO THE FAIR :   "54"
    14.: COLOURS (POEM) :   "57"
    15.: SIKKIM Let's Practise :   "61"
dc.subject.ddc:
    level1:
        300:                         "Social sciences"
        800:                         "Literature"

Fig. 1. Left figure shows part of metadata generated for the middle book. Includes: ``dc.title": ``raindrops book 2 special series", ``dc.description. abstract": ``textbook in English for class II", ⋯. Title extraction for the middle book fails in basic flow but succeeds in alternate flow. But alternate flow fails for the cover on the right.

Metadata attribute of a book may be single-valued (e.g., ISBN) or multi-valued (e.g., editors of a book). For a metadata attribute, we define $P = \frac{1}{N^*} \sum_{\substack{i=1 \\ |Y_i|>0}}^{N} \frac{|X_i \cap Y_i|}{|Y_i|}$ and $R = \frac{1}{N} \sum_{i=1}^{N} \frac{|X_i \cap Y_i|}{|X_i|}$ where X_i is the set of manually-annotated gold standard values of the attribute for test case i, Y_i is the set of extracted values (possibly empty) of the attribute for test case i, N is the number of test cases where the attribute is present, and N^* is the number of test cases for each of which at least one value of the attribute is extracted (i.e., $N^* = |\{i : |Y_i| > 0\}|$). Recollect $F1 = 2PR/(P+R)$. When members of X_i and Y_i are strings (i.e., for title, abstract, editor, illustrator), we measure *overlap* in 2 ways. The first is *exact* match of the strings. The second is an *approximate* match where we compute the normalized Levenshtein distance (NLD) between an extracted string and a golden string. If the distance is no more than 0.1, we classify them as a matched pair. The performance of the basic flow is captured in Fig. 2. Precision and recall for title and abstract when using NLD are higher than those in exact match, indicating errors in text extraction. The alternate flow boosts the performance moderately through OCR, as shown in Fig. 3. For exact match, the average recall for title, abstract, education level, and DDC increases from 0.772 to 0.8 while the overall average $(P, R, F1)$ change from $(0.901, 0.852, 0.876)$ to $(0.901, 0.865, 0.883)$. Regular expressions prove quite effective in our case mainly because the books are from the same publisher and hence, share similarity in format; most errors occur in text detection and recognition, and DDC class assignment.

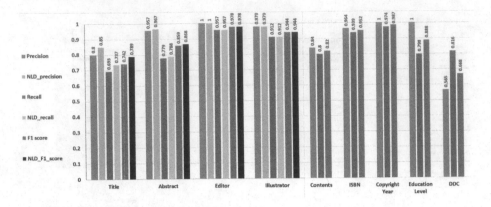

Fig. 2. Overall performance of metadata extractor on NCERT books in basic flow only. NLD stands for normalized Levenshtein distance.

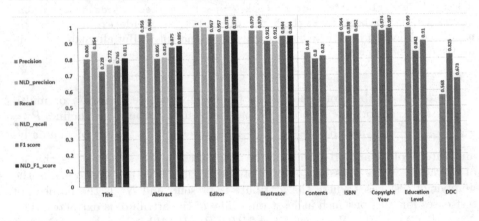

Fig. 3. Overall performance of metadata extractor on NCERT books in basic flow augmented with alternate flow. Improved extraction is observed for title, abstract, education level (except for a slight fall in its precision), and DDC.

4   Conclusion and Future Work

We presented a tool that extracts metadata from digital books with high $F1$-score. In future, we aim to improve the performance with advanced image processing and deep learning algorithms used in scene text recognition [8]. We plan to generate semantic metadata like pedagogical objective of a book and run our tool on more heterogeneous sources.

Acknowledgements. This work is supported by *Development of National Digital Library of India as a National Knowledge Asset of the Nation* sponsored by Ministry of Human Resource Development, Government of India.

References

1. Constantin, A., Pettifer, S., Voronkov, A.: PDFX: fully-automated PDF-to-XML conversion of scientific literature. In: Proceedings of ACM Symposium on Document Engineering, pp. 177–180. ACM (2013)
2. Lopez, P.: GROBID: Combining automatic bibliographic data recognition and term extraction for scholarship publications. In: Agosti, M., Borbinha, J., Kapidakis, S., Papatheodorou, C., Tsakonas, G. (eds.) ECDL 2009. LNCS, vol. 5714, pp. 473–474. Springer, Heidelberg (2009). https://doi.org/10.1007/978-3-642-04346-8_62
3. Quoc, N.-H., Choi, W.-H.: A framework for recognition books on bookshelves. In: Huang, D.-S., Jo, K.-H., Lee, H.-H., Kang, H.-J., Bevilacqua, V. (eds.) ICIC 2009. LNCS, vol. 5754, pp. 386–395. Springer, Heidelberg (2009). https://doi.org/10.1007/978-3-642-04070-2_44
4. Sobottka, K., Kronenberg, H., Perroud, T., Bunke, H.: Text extraction from colored book and journal covers. Int. J. Doc. Anal. Recogn. 2(4), 163–176 (2000)
5. Tkaczyk, D., Collins, A., Sheridan, P., Beel, J.: Machine learning vs. rules and out-of-the-box vs. retrained: an evaluation of open-source bibliographic reference and citation parsers. In: Proceedings of the 18th ACM/IEEE on Joint Conference on Digital Libraries, pp. 99–108. ACM (2018)
6. Waltinger, U., Mehler, A., Lösch, M., Horstmann, W.: Hierarchical classification of OAI metadata using the DDC taxonomy. In: Bernardi, R., Chambers, S., Gottfried, B., Segond, F., Zaihrayeu, I. (eds.) AT4DL/NLP4DL -2009. LNCS, vol. 6699, pp. 29–40. Springer, Heidelberg (2011). https://doi.org/10.1007/978-3-642-23160-5_3
7. Wu, J., et al.: PDFMEF: a multi-entity knowledge extraction framework for scholarly documents and semantic search. In: Proceedings of the 8th International Conference on Knowledge Capture, p. 13. ACM (2015)
8 Yang, X., et al.: Smart library: identifying books on library shelves using supervised deep learning for scene text reading. In: Proceedings of the 17th ACM/IEEE Joint Conference on Digital Libraries, pp. 245–248. IEEE Press (2017)

Ownership Stamp Character Recognition System Based on Ancient Character Typeface

Kangying Li[1]($\boxtimes$), Biligsaikhan Batjargal[2], and Akira Maeda[3]

[1] Graduate School of Information Science and Engineering, Ritsumeikan
University, Kusatsu, Japan
gr0319ss@ed.ritsumei.ac.jp
[2] Kinugasa Research Organization, Ritsumeikan University, Kyoto, Japan
[3] College of Information Science and Engineering, Ritsumeikan University,
Kusatsu, Japan

Abstract. In the process of digital archive development of Asian ancient books, ownership stamps and the annotations should be retrievable to provide the origin and versions of the books and the important support of book collection culture. The development of ownership stamp image databases, the text in the ownership stamp, and the background description of the owner will not only narrow the gap between non-professionals and seal culture and art, but also enable people to know more about ownership stamps, which are types of cultural heritage. Meanwhile, it also provides a convenient comparison and reference tool for professional scholars. However, the variety of the written languages used on ownership stamps and the various layouts of the texts and patterns create difficulties for developing such a database. Most of the existing ownership stamp databases have manually created character illustrations for the entire content of the ownership stamp image, but usually no information for the location of the characters that appear in the images, which cause difficulties for non-professional scholars to understand the ancient characters and unknown character sculptural information. Through the usage of a font database, we propose an ancient character ownership stamp database retrieval support system, which will enable users to unscramble the characters of ownership stamps.

Keywords: Digital cultural heritage · Mean shift segmentation
Ancient character recognition of ownership stamps

1 Introduction

As a special information element of ancient books, ownership stamp (also called collectors' seal) contains a lot of important information of ancient books. Description about the contents and background of the collection is usually appeared in image databases. Such information includes the annotation of the seal texts, dynasty of the owner, name of the owner, seal script type, shape of the seal, etc. There are different functions of seals existed, such as, showing the ownership, proofing the legend, showing the identity of owners, showing the status, commanding the cherishing, clarifying the aspiration, verifying the versions, and making comments. For Asian countries where Chinese characters are used, it is not only essential to understand the

M. Dobreva et al. (Eds.): ICADL 2018, LNCS 11279, pp. 328–332, 2018.
https://doi.org/10.1007/978-3-030-04257-8_34

full content of an ancient seal, the understanding of every single character in it is an important matter to understand history and culture as well. We propose a notation recognition system for every single character in the ownership stamps, using the clustering algorithm and multi-feature extraction of ancient character typeface images.

2 Related Work

Fujitsu's seal recognition project [1] extracts Chinese library seals from the image pages of ancient documents, completes the missing stroke structure, and finally recognizes the complete library seal contents based on matching. We found that most of the existing researches are based on manually labeled databases with large amounts of data and focus on the recognition of the seals as whole. Due to the limited availability of labeled data, we propose a retrieval-based notation recognition system by using multi-feature analysis of ancient character typefaces. In the proposed method, single characters are extracted based on density feature clustering, and through the extraction of multiple features of the image and the calculation with the user input image, we recognize characters in the ancient ownership stamp images.

3 Proposed Method

The proposed method is divided into three steps: (1) character segmentation, (2) multi-feature extraction of ancient character typeface images, and (3) Character recognition by ranking the calculation results.

3.1 Character Segmentation

Different from the usual image binarization processing method, to highlight the spatial distribution characteristics of ownership stamps, k-means clustering heuristic is used in this study to do color quantization of the input image. First, we read the RGB value of the original image and set the k value to 2. Then we divide the result of color quantization into black and white values. Comparing to traditional methods, k-means based binarization method can retain more information of glyphs in the original image. The results will be described in the Sect. 4.

Due to the irregularity of the arrangement of characters in ownership stamps, we do not use the usual histogram watershed algorithm to determine and segment the single character. Because the Chinese characters' form and configuration have particular characteristics, i.e., structural stability in the center of gravity, and the gap between words, we consider the density of its spatial distribution characteristics. Kernel density estimation is used to analyze the pixel distribution characteristics in binary images. As shown in Fig. 1, in the representation of the three-dimensional image, each axis represents the horizontal and vertical coordinates of the image and the predicted values of its density characteristics respectively. The vertical axis of the three-dimensional coordinate diagram is density characteristics, and we can see that the ownership stamp images have definite distribution characteristics in the spatial distribution. Therefore, we chose the Mean Shift Clustering [2] method based on density to find the local maximum density points of pixel clusters as the center of gravity for clustering. Based on the results of cluster analysis, the text range of seal characters is predicted and processed.

Fig. 1. Character segmentation based on mean shift clustering

3.2 Multi-feature Extraction of Ancient Character Typeface Images

There are many variations in the shape of an ancient character, a slight change in the shape will result in a change in the calculation result of outline, skeleton feature, and corner feature. In the proposed method, we use the Generative Adversarial Network (GAN) to generate new data of character typeface from public seal script of Shirakawa font [3] and "說文解字True Type字型" [4]. The generated character data is trained as the training data of the VGG 19 [5] and pre-trained model is set as feature extractor to extract the output of pooling layer 3. We use Zhang-Suen thinning algorithm [6] to get the skeleton feature of the original typeface image and input both of original typeface image and their skeleton images to the extractor and obtain the pooling layer 3 feature. In addition, we also extract other features as shown in Table 1.

Table 1. Multi-feature extraction

Feature	Symbol	Method of extraction
Pooling layer 3 feature of original typeface image	*Pool3*	Pre-trained model
Pooling layer 3 feature of skeleton	*Pool3skeleton*	Pre-trained model
Corner feature of skeleton	*Harris_skeleton*	Harris corner detector
Count of corners	*Harris_count*	Harris corner detector
Density feature of skeleton	*Density_skeleton*	Kernel density estimation

3.3 Character Recognition by Ranking the Calculation Results

With the pooling layer 3 feature, we can get abstract character features, which can suppress the influence in the ranking results which are caused by shape changes of the same character. Using this feature, pruning operation is performed on the ranking. The result of the top 1,000 characters is used for the final ranking calculation. The ranking calculation method is shown in Fig. 2. The recognition target is also extracted by the method in Sect. 3.2 and the ranking is performed by calculating the Euclidean distance between the features stored in the database and target features. For features with different dimensions, we use hausdorff to calculate their distance. [w1, w2, w3, w4, w5] are the weights to be set for improving the search results. The initial setting is [1, 1, 1, 1, 1] and user interaction can be used to obtain the better results.

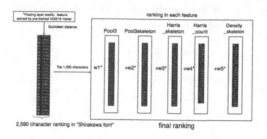

Fig. 2. Ranking calculation method experiments

Fifty randomly selected single characters in scanned images are used for the evaluation experiment. Evaluation of the proposed method is performed using the Mean Reciprocal Rank, and the result is 0.0566 when the weights are in initial setting.

In the Segmentation Evaluation Experiment, Results of the Proposed Method Are Shown in Table 2.

Table 2. The segmentation results

proposed method			

4 Conclusion and Future Work

In this paper, we propose a new method for recognizing characters in the scanned images of ownership stamps using ancient character typefaces. We expect to obtain a retrieval support system with good effectiveness after optimizing the proposed method through parameter adjustments.

References

1. Seal Retrieval Technique for Chinese Ancient Document Images, Fujitsu Research & Development Center Co. Ltd. http://www.fujitsu.com/cn/en/about/resources/news/press-releases/2016/frdc-0330.html. Accessed 12 May 2018
2. Comaniciu, D., Meer, P.: Mean shift analysis and applications. In: The Proceedings of the Seventh IEEE International Conference on Computer Vision. vol. 2. IEEE (1999)

3. Shirakawa Font. http://www.ritsumei.ac.jp/acd/re/k-rsc/sio/shirakawa/index.html. Accessed 1 June 2018
4. Master Ideographs Seeker for CNS 11643 Chinese Standard Interchange Code. http://www.cns11643.gov.tw/. Accessed 1 May 2018
5. Simonyan, K., Zisserman, A.: Very deep convolutional networks for large-scale image recognition. arXiv preprint arXiv:1409.1556 (2014)
6. Zhang, T.Y., Suen, C.Y.: A fast parallel algorithm for thinning digital patterns. Commun. ACM **27**(3), 236–239 (1984)

Use Cases and Digital Librarianship

Identifying Design Requirements of a User-Centered Research Data Management System

Maryam Bugaje⬤ and Gobinda Chowdhury(✉)⬤

Department of Computer and Information Sciences, Northumbria University,
Newcastle, UK
{maryam.bugaje,gobinda.chowdhury}@northumbria.ac.uk

Abstract. Research data repositories perform many useful functions, the key ones being the storage of research datasets, and making the same discoverable for potential reuse. Over the years, various criteria for assessing the user-centeredness of information systems have been developed and standards have gradually been improved. However, there has been less development in case of research data management (RDM) systems. By means of a combination of user-focused research methods viz. questionnaire surveys, face-to-face interviews, a systematic appraisal of existing services and a technical experiment, we have sought to understand the meaning of user-centeredness pertaining to research data repositories, and identify some key indicators of it. We have furthermore translated our findings into design requirements based on which we propose to develop and test a prototype of a user-centered RDM system. This paper reports on how we identified the design requirements that would make the RDM systems more user-centered.

Keywords: User-Centered design · Research data management
Information retrieval · Metadata · Research data repositories · Scientific data

1 Introduction

Research data repositories are an integral component of the RDM ecosystem, that combines all the essential functions of data management throughout the data lifecycle [1–4]. In addition to storing and retrieving data, and ensuring that it is discoverable and accessible, the burden of preservation and curation ultimately falls into the hands of repositories [3]. Recent data sharing mandates from research publishers, funding agencies, and governments have been the driving force behind the emergence of a host of research data repositories to meet the growing demand. However, many of which repositories are barely in a position to fulfill the comprehensive role of data disseminator and curator adequately enough to enable the realization of the benefits which were primary motivation of the mandates.

Research data repositories are necessarily end-user systems; the end-users being, among others (a) researchers in the roles of data producer and data consumer, (b) research funders who are keen to know the impact of their grants, (c) practitioners, (d) data scientists, and (e) other interested parties, including the general public. Making data publicly available, and making them discoverable and usable are different issues,

© Springer Nature Switzerland AG 2018
M. Dobreva et al. (Eds.): ICADL 2018, LNCS 11279, pp. 335–347, 2018.
https://doi.org/10.1007/978-3-030-04257-8_35

and in order to fully realize the benefits of data sharing [5–10], repositories must provide users with more than merely open access to research data. The importance of user-centeredness has generally been acknowledged as being central to the success of RDM systems [1, 11, 12], although as yet there aren't any clearly-defined criteria, established standards or guidelines for assessing specifically their usability or user-centeredness. Notwithstanding this lacuna, however, various efforts among institutions and research centers towards developing RDM products have resulted in user-needs studies prior to system design and made evident attempts to accommodate those needs [1, 13–15]. But, though notable, the designs of these systems still leave much room for improvement [16, 17].

In the next section we define the key concepts that form the foundation upon which we may proceed. Following this are the sections on methodology and requirements analyses of a user-centered RDM, in which we detail all the preliminary work which will go into, and culminate in, the system design section, where we present the conceptual design of the alpha version of a user-centered RDM system which we hope, in a future work, to develop into a prototype. Within the scope of this paper our research aims are to:

1. Gather sufficient practical information about researchers' data-seeking needs, practices, strategies and difficulties to enable us to make appropriate design choices as well as to identify areas for improvement;
2. Based on the above, prioritize user requirements and system features for a user-friendly RDM system; and
3. Determine resource requirements and the best allocation of the same for our system.

2 Background

Research Data Management is "the organization of data, from its entry to the research cycle through to the dissemination and archiving of valuable results" [18], and Research Data Management Systems are "the technical framework to collect, describe, and provide research data" [2]. Of the numerous problems and challenges facing RDM [5, 12, 19–21], our work focuses on those that can be mitigated through better engagement with the user and increased attentiveness to user needs in designing RDM systems. This being the case, we distinguish between simply RDM systems and specifically user-centered RDM systems; and, expanding upon our original definition of the former, we define the latter as in addition conforming in some degree to the formal guidelines set forth by research communities and authoritative bodies, such as the UK Research & Innovation Council (UKRI) [22], The Future of Research Communication and e-Scholarship (FORCE11) [23], and others [24] to improve the reuse potential and manageability of research data products. The guiding principles recommended by UKRI and FORCE11's FAIR principles are summarized in Table 1.

2.1   User-Centered Design

Data repository users can be identified in terms of their relationship to the system (i.e. primary users, e.g. researchers; secondary users, e.g. funding bodies; and tertiary users, e.g. search engines [25]) or the role(s) that they play in it (e.g. data creators, data consumers, and data administrators [26]). To be useful, the design of an RDM system must show due consideration to the needs of its potential users. For this, it is necessary to not only understand the different user types and groups but also to have a thorough appreciation of the tasks that each wish to accomplish through the system. In user-centered design, the interest of the end user is at the core of every design decision from the inception to the implementation of the system [26].

Research shows that users' information needs, and by inference, data needs, tend to be ambiguous, not definitely articulated [27], and often only recognized at sight [28]. Concerning this, it is worth noting that:

1. Users' knowledge of systems may range from very naive to highly skilled and sophisticated [28], and systems must be designed in such a way as to sufficiently enable the less sophisticated user to efficiently search for and find data; and
2. Users' data-seeking needs, as we observed from our face-to-face interviews with researchers, may go beyond a simplistic search for datasets on a single topic (e.g. data on climate change) and may entail more complex conditions such as associative relationships (e.g. climate change data related to ozone depletion) or comparative relationships (e.g. climate change data in which ozone depletion is compared with rise in sea levels) between multiple topics. There should be a matching capability in the system to enable the highly skilled user to satisfy his or her more complex data-seeking needs.

Data discovery is largely dependent upon good metadata [29] and although data creators are the primary providers of contextual metadata [8] and other complementary information about research data, they are not necessarily skilled in data management or knowledgeable as to its technicalities [8]. This being the case, it becomes the responsibility of the system to facilitate users (data creators) in the fulfilment of this important function to enhance the reuse potential of data [30].

Table 1. RDM guidelines by UKRI and FORCE11.

Principle	UKRI guidelines	FAIR principles
Findability (or discoverability)	✓	✓
Accessibility	✓	✓
Intelligibility	✓	
Assessability	✓	
Usability (or reusability)	✓	✓
Interoperability		✓

2.2 Aims of the System

Our system aims to at least partially comply with UKRI guidelines and the FAIR principles to address thereby some of the currently existing user-related issues of RDM systems hitherto alluded to, as well as others which will subsequently be considered in more detail in ensuing sections. We highlight our principal aims as follows:

1. To help data consumers (e.g. researchers, data scientists, practitioners) efficiently *discover* data, and provide them with necessary information to *access* and *use* the data;
2. To help data creators and proprietors expose their data effectively for *discovery;*
3. To add value to data by linking it with associated publications, data, or related or similar output and by enabling user annotation; and
4. To use system design & development best practices to enable the system to *interoperate* and future-proof it in the case of advancements in the field.

In the next section we describe our methodology and requirements-gathering process.

3 Methodology

Our design is the product of a variety of research methods, each addressing a specific part of the whole body of our research aims as set forth in Sect. 1, and each respectively reported in full in previously published (all except the one reporting on the face-to-face interviews, which is pending publication) research papers and conferences. Due to constraints of space which prevent our repeating the same in this paper, we refer the reader to the publications, listed below, for the full accounts:

1. Online questionnaire survey; addresses aims 1, 2 & 3, and is reported in [31]
2. Face-to-face interviews; address aims 1 & 2, and is reported in [32]
3. Market appraisal and review; addresses aim 1, and is reported in [17, 26]
4. A technical experiment comparing data retrieval (DR) with traditional information retrieval (IR); addresses aims 2 & 3, and is reported in [16]

Methods 1 and 2 above (questionnaire and interview) were conducted sequentially, the purpose of the latter being chiefly to probe further into and expand upon some of the findings and hints from the former. We briefly present each of the four in turn.

3.1 Online Questionnaire Survey

Data was collected via questionnaire surveys conducted at universities UK-wide between the summer and winter terms of the 2016/2017 session. The survey garnered a total of 201 (complete) responses from researchers at various stages in their academic careers. The questions asked were mainly with a view to understanding the following:

1. The type, volume, and variety of data used and created by researchers;
2. Researchers' common practices with respect to data storage;
3. Researchers' familiarity with standards, metadata, and their university data policy;

4. Requirements and opportunities for training & support;
5. Views, perceptions, and practices pertaining to data sharing and open access; and
6. Researchers' previous experiences on, and impressions about, using research data repositories.

Details of the survey and findings have been reported in [31].

3.2 Face-to-Face Interviews

We conducted semi-structured, face-to-face, interviews with 18 researchers; 6 each from the departments of History, Solar Physics, and Information Science at a British University. The disciplines were selected on the basis of the contrasting nature of their datasets with regards to size, conformity to metadata standards, methods of data collection/generation, and data formats among others [33]. The goal was to ensure diversity by studying representatives from two polar ends of the disciplinary spectrum (History and Solar Physics) with respect to data sharing practices and the use of technology [33], as well as a middle-ground (Information Science); with a view to learning the similarities that unify all, while exploring differences that make each unique. Key questions asked include amongst others the following:

1. Where and how do you obtain data for your research? Do you employ any strategy or have a standard workflow for this?
2. What are some of the problems you've faced before in finding, using, or accessing research data, if any?
3. What data repositories have you used before or do you currently use? What motivates you to use a particular repository rather than another?
4. Have you ever uploaded your own data in an online repository? Why or why not?
5. What are your thoughts on research data sharing and open access?
6. Do you or your research group follow any metadata formats for tagging research data? What are some of the issues you've faced in this regard, if any?

3.3 Market Appraisal and Review

To facilitate our review of research data repositories, we consulted the re3data.org directory to create the following non-mutually exclusive groups into which we organized the repositories: disciplinary, institutional, publisher-service, location-based, dedicated content-type, and commercial/general purpose repositories. For each group, we hand-picked a few representative examples, based on recommendation by Nature[1], for evaluation against the following performance yard-sticks:

1. *Use of metadata.* The degree to which metadata appears to be exploited to provide features for browsing, searching/querying, filtering and result presentation;
2. *Querying facility.* The level of expressiveness allowed in searching/querying the repository; and

---

[1] https://www.nature.com/sdata/policies/repositories.

3. *Result filtering.* The availability of options for filtering down search results, and the furthest granularity to which this is possible.

This study has been fully reported in [17].

3.4 A Technical Experiment Comparing DR with Traditional IR

We carried out a controlled experiment to demonstrate some fundamental differences between retrieval of data and text, and their corresponding implications on user interface design and on network and computing resource requirements. To do this, we consulted Wikipedia's broad classifications of academic disciplines and obtained 5 random keywords/phrases each of the domains of Arts & Humanities, Social Sciences, Natural Sciences, and Applied Sciences, the last of which we had represented by its sub-domain of Computer & Information Science. A search was conducted on each of the 20 total keywords/phrases for both data retrieval (using Dryad, UK Data Service, or DataOne) and text retrieval (using Thomson Reuters Web of Science database). The top 10 results of each search were noted for file size and file format(s). In computing file sizes, we considered for text retrieval (research publications) only full research papers; and for data retrieval (research datasets), both the dataset itself and any documentation(s) it comes with. Detailed findings and discussions may be found in [16, 17].

4 Study Findings and User Requirements Analyses

Key findings from our studies are summarized in Tables 2 (questionnaire & interview), 3 (market appraisal and review) and 4 (experiment comparing DR and IR) below (Tables 3 and 4).

Table 2. Summary of findings from questionnaire survey and interview.

Key findings
Incomplete documentation or its lack altogether often prevents datasets of interest from being reusable
Many users are unskilled information seekers and are unsure as to what search terms to use to find data
Researchers commonly follow non-standard, ad hoc methods for tagging or annotating their data with metadata
Tools for creating metadata are found to be too hard to use, and very few researchers have received any degree of formal training on metadata or data management
Data file sizes in the megabyte range are the most commonly used and produced, closely followed by files in the gigabyte range. File sizes in the terabyte range are rare in most disciplines
Google is frequently used for data search, though often with unsatisfactory results
Most researchers create new primary data rather than reuse existing data. The main reason(s) given for this is lack of knowledge about or access to existing data

(continued)

Table 2. (*continued*)

Key findings
The process of obtaining access to data may be particularly tedious in some disciplines (e.g. History)
There is a general reluctance among researchers to upload data online before the maximum number of papers have been published on it
Standard office documents (e.g. text, spreadsheets) are the most common file formats used and produced by researchers. Next are images, structured scientific and statistical data, and web-based data (e.g. social media data)
Many researchers felt that some way of visualizing datasets would be useful in helping them understand and decide on the usefulness of data
Researchers are generally reluctant to voluntarily spend long hours tagging data to upload online unless doing so is a requirement

Table 3. Summary of findings from market appraisal & review, with their corresponding implication(s) on user-experience

Key findings	Comments	Implications
Limited user interactivity	e.g. No feature(s) for previewing dataset content on the web browser before download. This unnecessarily increases the rate of download, making each session highly resource intensive	– Downloading data that ends up unused unduly strains network resources – Poor use of storage space – Renders download count unreliable as a measure of dataset relevance/usefulness/impact
Insufficient or unavailable metadata	The lack of use of standard metadata to sufficiently contextualize data for discovery [34, 35] & re-use [36] is a major challenge. Deficiency in metadata quality or quantity, along with the fact that using generic metadata for greater inclusivity directly translates into loss of nuanced features, represents a delicate problem	– Complex or precise queries cannot be supported – Loosely matching search results – Tedious manual browsing of results – Unproductive use of researchers' time – Threatens the discoverability and, consequently, reuse rate of research datasets
Quality of data questionable or not assured	Researchers tend to reuse the datasets of others whom they trust [37]. Many services do not have mechanisms to ensure the quality of user-uploaded datasets; nor are there any standard criteria for measuring the quality of research data	– Skepticism, which may stunt the rate of data reuse – Time which could be used more productively in active research spent on making inquiries about data

Table 4. Summary of findings from technical experiment comparing DR and IR, with resource implications of each.

Key findings	Implications
Text can be read online, while data often requires downloading prior to being "read" or used	More network (in terms of bandwidth) and storage resources are required for data retrieval
A single data item record may constitute several composite files (as many as 524 have been noted in this experiment)	A system, e.g. metadata schema, for efficiently identifying and linking associated files is imperative
Texts (research publications) often come as a single, self-sufficient file. Data is nearly always accompanied with separate documentation files	A system, e.g. metadata schema, for efficiently identifying and linking associated files is imperative
Unlike texts (research publications), the same dataset may come in many different file types or formats	This places additional burden on computing resources (e.g. more storage is required for the same dataset) and also human resources (e.g. in terms of data preservation/curation requirements)
The average retrieved file size of datasets is typically several times larger than that of text (research publication)	More network (in terms of bandwidth) and storage resources are required for data retrieval

4.1 User Requirements

We now proceed to extract from our findings that part of it which broadly or loosely spells out user requirements. For this, we adopt a structured approach by identifying the main themes around which the requirements are clustered, as shown in Table 5, and relating them to the UKRI guidelines and FAIR principles from Table 1 to which they contribute to conforming.

Table 5. Summary of user requirements and how they meet formal guidelines in the literature.

Broad theme	List of requirements	Guideline or principle
Search and discovery	Linking data to associated research publications and similar datasets	Findability
	Query expansion features to help users who are unsure of the precise search terms to use	Findability
	Optimizing repositories for search engines to index, for the benefit of those who use traditional search engines like Google for data search	Findability, interoperability
	Require the provision of some metadata with each uploaded dataset	Intelligibility, assessability, reusability
	Provide support for granular search, e.g. through enabling Boolean queries	Findability
	Use reliable methods for ranking research datasets based on different criteria useful to the user in making decisions	Assessability

(continued)

Table 5. (*continued*)

Broad theme	List of requirements	Guideline or principle
Access	Provide clear and full information on how to obtain access to data	Accessibility
User interface	Recognize and adequately cater to the different types of users and their roles (e.g. the typical researcher vs a research funding agent)	Findability
	Follow standards and best practices in designing and laying out the interface	Findability, interoperability
Other special features	Provide data visualization plugins	Intelligibility, assessability
	Provide features that allow some interaction with datasets on the web-browser before download, at least for commonly used file formats	Assessability
	Enable users to be able to make their data private or invisible to the general public during peer review (embargo period)	Accessibility
	Ensure there are clear statements about the relationship of each associated file(s) to the dataset in question	Intelligibility
	Offer automated or semi-automated methods for extracting or tagging metadata	Findability

5 Functional Requirements and Prototype Design

Focusing on the fourth aim of this study, the design proposed in this section was informed by the user requirements gathered from our studies and listed in Table 5. A simplified diagram of how the main components of our design are related and work together is given in Fig. 1 and explained in further detail in this section.

Persistent Identification. Our system will use a combination of Digital Object Identifiers (DOI) and the ORCID(s) of the data creator(s) as a means to uniquely identify data objects in the database.

Metadata. We collected the metadata elements of over 18 different data upload templates from institutional and non-institutional data repositories, as well as those recommended in the literature [38, 39]. From these, we selected those elements common across all templates (Table 6) for use in our proposed system. The uploading of disciplinary metadata will also be encouraged and supported where available.

Ontological Schema. Aside from the metadata schema, which describes the data object alone, we shall additionally use an RDF/XML ontological schema to establish the relationship between data objects to enhance discovery by linking and recommendation.

Searching Facility. Aside from supporting advanced search by variables culled from available metadata, dictionary look-up will be used for query expansion. All of the findability features identified in Table 5 will also be supported.

Table 6. Common metadata elements across all templates.

Mandatory elements	Optional elements
Title	Funder
Depositor name	Data license type (e.g. creative commons)
Data publisher	Date
Discipline	Keywords
	Data description
	Related publication URI (or URL)
	Publication title

Search results Ranking Facility. There will be options for users to rank returned search results by number of views or downloads and number of publications linked to it.

Search Results Filtering Facility. Users will be given the option to filter search results based on variables culled from available metadata

Test Collection. To test our prototype, we have built a small test collection consisting of over 200 datasets carefully described with at least the mandatory metadata elements specified in Table 6 above.

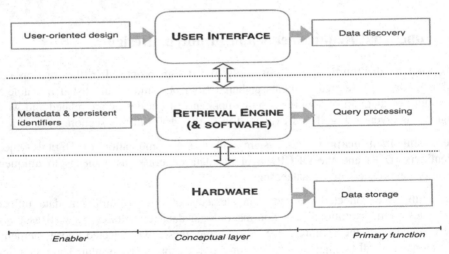

Fig. 1. A simplified conceptual diagram showing the workings of our system

6 Conclusion

The paper presents various thoughts and principles that went into the design of our user-oriented RDM system. It shows how the selection of our metadata elements [38, 39], and user requirements informing our design (Table 5), additionally comply with guidelines recommended in literature. Moreover, our metadata selection, being collated from the elements common to over 18 of the major institutional and non-institutional research data repositories, will enable interoperability. Some functionalities are more difficult to implement than others. However, we hope in a future work to demonstrate an actual prototype and present results from user evaluation studies to be conducted.

References

1. Arend, D., Lange, M., Chen, J., et al.: e! DAL - a framework to store, share and publish research data. BMC Bioinform. **15**(1), 214 (2014). https://doi.org/10.1186/1471-2105-15-214

2. Curdt, C., Hoffmeister, D.: Research data management services for a multidisciplinary, collaborative research project: design and implementation of the TR32DB project database. Program Electron. Libr. Inf. Syst. **49**(4), 494–512 (2015). https://doi.org/10.1108/prog-02-2015-0016

3. Cox, A., Pinfield, S.: Research data management and libraries: current activities and future priorities. J. Libr.

4. Amorim, R., Castro, J., da Silva, R.J., Ribeiro, C.: A comparison of research data management platforms: architecture, flexible metadata and interoperability. Univers. Access Inf. Soc. **16**(4), 851–862 (2016). https://doi.org/10.1007/s10209-016-0475-y

5. Patel, D.: Research data management: a conceptual framework. Libr. Rev. **65**(4/5), 226–241 (2016)

6. Perrino, T., et al.: Advancing Science Through Collaborative Data Sharing and Synthesis. Perspect. Psychol. Sci. **8**(4), 433–444 (2013)

7. The Royal Society: Science as an open enterprise (2012). https://royalsociety.org/~/media/policy/projects/sape/2012-06-20-saoe.pdf. Accessed 11 June 2018

8. Borgman, C.: The conundrum of sharing research data. SSRN Electron. J. (2011)

9. Costello, M.: Motivating online publication of data. Bioscience **59**(5), 418–427 (2009)

10. Faniel, I., Jacobsen, T.: Reusing scientific data: how earthquake engineering researchers assess the reusability of colleagues' data. Comput. Support. Coop. Work. (CSCW) **19**(3–4), 355–375 (2010)

11. Carlson, J.: Demystifying the data interview: developing a foundation for reference librarians to talk with researchers about their data. Ref. Serv. Rev. **40**(1), 7–23 (2012). https://doi.org/10.1108/00907321211203603

12. Mückschel, C., Nieschulze, J., Weist, C., Sloboda, B., Köhler, W.: Herausforderungen, Probleme und Lösungsansätze im Datenmanagement von Sonderforschungsbereichen. In: eZAI (elektronische Zeitschrift für Agrarinformatik), vol. 2, pp. 1–16 (2007)

13. Curdt, C., Hoffmeister, D., Waldhoff, G., Jekel, C., Bareth, G.: Scientific research data management for soil-vegetation-atmosphere data – the TR32DB. Int. J. Digit. Curation **7**(2), 68–80 (2012). https://doi.org/10.2218/ijdc.v7i2.208

14. bioCADDIE | biomedical and healthCAre Data Discovery and Indexing Ecosystem. https://biocaddie.org. Accessed 12 June 2018

15. Research Data Discovery Service: Laying the firm foundations for a Jisc UK Research Data Discovery Service. https://rdds.jiscinvolve.org/wp/. Accessed 12 June 2018

16. Bugaje, M., Chowdhury, G.: Is data retrieval different from text retrieval? An exploratory study. In: Choemprayong, S., Crestani, F., Cunningham, S.J. (eds.) ICADL 2017. LNCS, vol. 10647, pp. 97–103. Springer, Cham (2017). https://doi.org/10.1007/978-3-319-70232-2_8

17. Bugaje, M., Chowdhury, G.: Data retrieval = text retrieval? In: Chowdhury, G., McLeod, J., Gillet, V., Willett, P. (eds.) iConference 2018. LNCS, vol. 10766, pp. 253–262. Springer, Cham (2018). https://doi.org/10.1007/978-3-319-78105-1_29

18. Whyte, A., Tedds, J.: Making the case for research data management. Digital Curation Centre, dccacuk (2011). http://www.dcc.ac.uk/resources/briefing-papers/making-case-rdm. Accessed 12 June 2018

19. Santos, C., Blake, J., States, D.: Supplementary data need to be kept in public repositories. Nature **438**(7069), 738 (2005). https://doi.org/10.1038/438738a

20. Sallans, A., Lake, S.: Data management assessment and planning tools. In: Research Data Management: Practical Strategies for Information Professionals. pp. 87–107. Purdue University Press, West Lafayette (2014)

21. Dumontier, M., Gray, A., Marshall, M., et al.: The health care and life sciences community profile for dataset descriptions. PcerJ **4** (2016). https://doi.org/10.7717/peerj.2331

22. UK Research and Innovation: Concordat on Open Research Data (2016). https://www.ukri.org/files/legacy/documents/concordatonopenresearchdata-pdf/. Accessed 13 June 2018

23. Boeckhout, M., Zielhuis, G., Bredenoord, A.: The FAIR guiding principles for data stewardship: fair enough? Eur. J. Hum. Genet. **26**(7), 931–936 (2018). https://doi.org/10.1038/s41431-018-0160-0

24. Starr, J., Castro, E., Crosas, M., et al.: Achieving human and machine accessibility of cited data in scholarly publications. PeerJ Comput. Sci. **1**, e1 (2015). https://doi.org/10.7717/peerj-cs.1

25. Alsos, O.A., Svanæs, D.: Designing for the secondary user experience. In: Campos, P., Graham, N., Jorge, J., Nunes, N., Palanque, P., Winckler, M. (eds.) INTERACT 2011. LNCS, vol. 6949, pp. 84–91. Springer, Heidelberg (2011). https://doi.org/10.1007/978-3-642-23768-3_7

26. Bugaje, M., Chowdhury, G.: Towards a more user-centered design of research data management (RDM) systems [abstract]. In: Information: Interactions and Impact (i3), Aberdeen, 27–30 June 2017, pp. 53–55 (2017)

27. Taylor, R.: Question-negotiation and information seeking in libraries. Coll. Res. Libr. **76**(3), 251–267 (2015). https://doi.org/10.5860/crl.76.3.251

28. Morris, R.: Toward a user-centered information service. J. Am. Soc. Inf. Sci. **45**(1), 20–30 (1994). https://doi.org/10.1002/(sici)1097-4571(199401)45:1%3c20:aid-asi3%3e3.0.co;2-n

29. Willis, C., Greenberg, J., White, H.: Analysis and synthesis of metadata goals for scientific data. J. Am. Soc. Inf. Sci. Technol. **63**(8), 1505–1520 (2012). https://doi.org/10.1002/asi.22683

30. Van Noorden, R.: Data-sharing: everything on display. Nature **500**(7461), 243–245 (2013). https://doi.org/10.1038/nj7461-243a

31. Chowdhury, G., Walton, G., Bugaje, M.: Research data management: practices, skills and training needs of university researchers in the UK. In: Špiranec, S., Bartol, T., Stopar, K., Boh Podgornik, B. (eds.) 2017 Fifth European Conference on Information Literacy (ECIL), p. 30. Information Literacy Association (InLitAs), Saint-Malo (2017)

32. Bugaje, M., Chowdhury, G: Disciplinary contexts in research data management: a case-study of three disciplines (accepted contribution). In: Fifth European Conference on Information Literacy (ECIL), Finland (2018)

33. Borgman, C.: Big Data, Little Data, No Data, 1st edn. pp. 81–161. The MIT Press, Cambridge (2015)

34. Boru, D., Kliazovich, D., Granelli, F., Bouvry, P., Zomaya, A.Y.: Energy-efficient data replication in cloud computing datacenters. Clust. Comput. **18**(1), 385–402 (2015)

35. Chowdhury, G.G.: Sustainability of Scholarly Information. Facet Publishing, London (2014)

36. Weber, A., Piesche, C.: Requirements on long-term accessibility and preservation of research results with particular regard to their provenance. ISPRS Int. J. Geo-Inf. **5**, 49 (2016)

37. Research Information Network (RIN): To Share or not to Share: Publication and Quality Assurance of Research Data Outputs, p. 48 (2008). http://www.rin.ac.uk/system/files/attachments/To-share-data-outputs-report.pdf. Accessed 25 June 2018

38. Rumsey, S., Jefferies, N.: Challenges in building an institutional research data catalogue. Int. J. Digit. Curation **8**(2), 205–214 (2013). https://doi.org/10.2218/ijdc.v8i2.284

39. Weibel, S.: The Dublin Core: a simple content description model for electronic resources. Bull. Am. Soc. Inf. Sci. Technol. **24**(1), 9–11 (2005). https://doi.org/10.1002/bult.70

Going Beyond Technical Requirements: The Call for a More Interdisciplinary Curriculum for Educating Digital Librarians

Andrew Wertheimer[✉] and Noriko Asato

Library and Information Science Program, University of Hawai'i at Mānoa,
Honolulu, USA
{wertheim, asaton}@hawaii.edu

Abstract. The transformation of librarians to digital librarians is a revolutionary one in many ways. Information Schools have tried to transform our curricula to meet future needs by focusing on information architecture and metadata, but these are only part of the skills required. This paper explores a number of other academic disciplines, such as Law, Art, Publishing Studies, Museum Studies that should inform curricula for digital librarians. The paper concludes by calling for continued progress towards a more interdisciplinary professional degree.

Keywords: Digital libraries · Digital librarians · Interdisciplinarity
Professional education · Information competencies
Library and information science education

1 Introduction

Schools of Library and Information Science (LIS) or Information Schools (iSchools) in North America have made many strides in updating their graduate curricula to reflect the need of digital librarians in terms of transforming core knowledge. We can see an example of this in the change from teaching cataloging of print materials to teaching metadata for multimedia. They have also done a good job of expanding relevant technical skills, such as information architecture and digital preservation. However, there remain key gaps in the knowledge base required for digital library leaders who are creating their own digital libraries and digital archives with original content. This gap is more than simply a scattering of scanning standards and other technological practices, but rather points to a more "liberal arts" or interdisciplinary approach to the knowledge and skills that will be needed by future digital librarians.

This paper argues that the transformation from librarian to digital librarian has not been fully appreciated by iSchool faculty in terms of how disruptive it is to the required skills set. It was easy for faculty to initially become overwhelmed by the technological changes, but we must also realize and prepare to meet the challenges required to this radical transformation.

To visualize the disruption of digital libraries on LIS/iSchool skill sets, we should think about this from some distance, by looking at a subject like Collection Management.

M. Dobreva et al. (Eds.): ICADL 2018, LNCS 11279, pp. 348–355, 2018.
https://doi.org/10.1007/978-3-030-04257-8_36

Basically, the traditional model – dating back to Dewey's pioneering School of Library Economy – was that librarians used published reviews and other tools to select, and then purchase or subscribe to materials that were published by private publishers, distributors or government agencies. Librarians needed to simply use appropriate review sources to match published output to meet community needs. The fact that content was in digital form does not necessarily mean a change as long as one was still selecting e-books, streaming audio and video from commercial or government sources. This however is only a small portion of what is involved in Digital Libraries today, and especially in the future. Digital librarians/Digital Archivists are increasingly taking original content and sharing this online. Regardless whether content is born digital, or is digitized by the library, the fact that this is unpublished means librarians are now becoming publishers.

As publishers of original content, digital librarians can no longer simply use traditional tools to help guide selection of materials. They now need to know new domains of law, ethics, and marketing in order to select and promote appropriate materials. Like publishers, they need to be able to review materials using new sets of ethics. They may also need to be able to determine if information is factually correct, and determine if the author has the legal right to publish the content. They also need other skills to be able to edit, and present materials in a visually approachable way. They also may need skills to be able to control access and curate materials. Clearly, these skills which are quite different from the old skill set expected of librarians who only needed to select from existing published materials. As librarians publish original content, they now have legal, ethical and other expectations placed on them that go far beyond the questions of how to digitize and organize online content. This is even more important when it comes to collections that are culturally sensitive. New digital librarians need more cultural sensitivity and understanding in order to work with ethnic communities in order to cultural survival.

1.1   Review of the Literature: Emphasizing Position Descriptions

Studies on skills required by digital librarianship, such Shahbazi and Hedayati (2016), primarily looked at position descriptions in order to harvest lists of most relevant skills. As with most such studies, and there are indeed many using this approach, the reliance on position descriptions tends to highlight entry-level technological skills that are immediately required for uploading and maintaining digital collections. It is our yet untested theory that skills such as the ones we are highlighting (which can be seen as more cognitive skills, using Bloom's Cognitive Domain (1956) are harder to measure or describe on position descriptions, although they are foundational for professional development. Unfortunately, there is no published set of core competencies for digital librarians, which may be a reflection of the divide between the need for technical skills as well as a more nuanced set of skills that help digital librarians to make more executive or critical decisions in terms of questions like what should be digitized, what can be digitized, what curatorial decisions are involved, as well as questions about costs, impact, and ethics. This lack of agreed-upon minimum qualifications for digital librarians is an interesting contrast with many other library fields which developed position statements in response to Michael Gorman's efforts to establish a new ALA competency standard for librarians (Goodsett and Koziura 2016).

2 New Skills

This paper argues that in order for digital librarians to be more confident online publishers of original digital content, there are a number of courses or subject areas that should be added to curricular offerings for future digital librarians. We will review them below in alphabetical order of discipline. As we will discuss later, this list is more suggestive of what might be considered, rather than declaring this anything close to a more formal definite mandated curriculum for educating digital librarians.

2.1 Art

One subject that might not seem of immediate importance is art, although an affirmative response might be more forthcoming if one thinks about graphic design and digital libraries as essentially a form of visual communication. Many universities offer general courses for traditional and digital graphic design, including typography and layout. This competency should include not only the ability to make visually appealing design, for desktop or handheld device, but also how to make pages work for those with different visual and hearing abilities, including young people and the elderly. Logo creation or branding is often important when creating Digital Libraries. Another area that might be helpful is photography since it is easy to personalize a digital library with photographs of the community. These days anyone can take a photo with a smart phone, but this also means that our users now have higher expectations for quality compelling visual images.

2.2 Computer Science

Students focus mostly on courses and skills that relate to information architecture, but Computer Science (CS) or iSchool courses related to usability testing and Human Computer Interaction (HCI) would be highly relevant for digital librarians. CS courses in animation, social media might also be helpful in developing dynamic next generation portals. Many CS departments also introduce project management, which should be extremely helpful. They also need to know how teams collaborate, including best practices with collaborative software and how to successfully use outsourcing.

2.3 Digital Humanities

Digital librarians are often work on collaborative projects with faculty on Digital Humanities, Digital Social Sciences, or e-Science scholarship. Students can benefit greatly if they can work on such collaborations and also learn about how the information professions can best work with the various types of data. This would be a welcome paring with LIS/iSchool studies in Informatics/Bibliometrics/Webliometrics, especially for academic librarians who may be involved with open access repositories or scholarly publishing. Students interested in map librarianship or geographic information should take advanced courses in GIS. We see this as a growth area for academic and special librarians, as well as an LIS skill that can be applied beyond traditional libraries or digital libraries.

2.4 Education

One key reason that governments funded Digital Libraries was the promise to deliver primary sources to K-20 students. Funding for some digital library projects have included sample lesson plans for busy teachers so they can learn how to meaningfully incorporate these materials and assess student learning. Digital librarians understandably need some understanding of how student learning is assessed. Education schools also are excellent sources for basic pedagogical skills since more librarians at all levels are becoming increasingly involved with instruction.

2.5 Ethnic Studies

Many Digital Library Collections are on the experience of People of Color (POC) or Native People. Libraries are struggling to develop appropriate standards on how to work with such collections. The failure of the ALA to agree on a standard for dealing with traditional cultural expressions or (TCEs) shows the challenge for digital librarians to understand how POCs often have traditional culture taken out of context and then copyrighted by the entertainment industry, as was shown by Vaidhyanathan (2003). This need to be able to critically curate digital collections is especially important for those of us in the Pacific, as our oldest local collections have quite different provonances whether part of Indigenous oral narratives or early texts by missionaries and colonizers (Wareham 2002).

2.6 History of Science

Many universities offer interdisciplinary courses in the history of science. Science has always been the leading force in scholarly publishing, and much of the history of science develops around the history of scholarly publishing, including the development of scholarly societies, journals, presses, and important imprints. Beyond learning specifics about the sciences and scholarly publishing, students can also learn much by seeing how the development of printing changed the sciences and how both developments transformed society. In universities without History of Science offerings, students could equally benefit from an appropriate historiography course which introduces triangulating and critical approaches to primary and secondary data. History provides a useful sense of scale and critical distance for digital librarians when thinking about how digital libraries are changing scholarly publishing, libraries, and society today. This critical distance is of essence in the fast pace of technological change. Digital librarians need to be able to look at the long run and decide which projects are worthy of investment and which are simply fads that promise little return on investment. A historical understanding can be a great help in developing this attitude.

2.7 Law

Perhaps the most important skill digital librarians need is a deeper understanding of Intellectual Property Law. Digital librarians need to be able to understand what materials are in the public domain, and what may be still owned by others. This includes topics of works for hire, international agreements. In order to create binding agreements, students might also want to briefly explore another course focusing on contract law. Privacy is another important related area for digital librarians. In particular, digital librarians need to know what types of information are protected, such as medical, family, or student records. Another important core legal concept is intellectual freedom. The recent appointment(s) to the United States Supreme Court suggest that there will be major pendulum shifts in definitions of Intellectual Freedom. Librarians will probably need a stronger grounding in Constitutional and Case law in order to defend free speech in online collections. This will become even more so if our traditional intellectual freedom protections at the federal level shift to state and local laws, as once was the case, including the difficult question of community standards. If we return to such a legal framework, librarians and digital librarians will need to know much more than what is taught at most LIS/iSchools in terms of practical defenses of intellectual freedom. Tomorrow's graduates will need a stronger understanding of the basics of Constitutional and local case law to be able to defend free speech online.

2.8 Museum Studies

In today's world, museums, archives, and libraries are coming closer together, especially when it comes to digital collections. LIS/iSchool students should appreciate the differences between museums and libraries, such as how museums are more likely to track provenance and keep more detailed records on individual items than libraries (besides special collections), but there is much that LIS/iSchool students can learn about the skills involved with curating, and community engagement. Museum Studies courses may offer rich theoretical and critical angles on issues such as indigenous authorship, representation, and repatriation that are too infrequently considered in the LIS core. We should add that this paper does not mention Archival Studies, as this is considered core domain in LIS/iSchools.

2.9 Publishing Studies

Not all universities offer Publishing Studies, like Chicago or Columbia. Some schools offer an introductory course in their English Department. In either case, publishing courses can offer two very different sets of skills. Editing is an important skill in how one can shape a writer's text without changing the meaning. There is editing for language and also fact-checking. Both sets of skills will doubtlessly come in handy if the digital library will host journals, pre-prints, or curate exhibits. The other important set of skills relates to the acquisition, evaluation, and marketing of content. Digital librarians need to be able to use the same set of skills to create project budgets, project audience size, demand, and also be able to market projects. Digital librarians also need a fundamental understanding of the economics of scholarly publishing. This will become even more important as university libraries and university presses collaborate on projects like J-STOR, open access repositories, and create open access journals as alternatives to commercial journal publishers.

2.10 Other Disciplines/Other Courses

This paper is only scratching the surface in terms of relevant courses offered on campus. For example, a student who plans to work for the Library of Congress Digital Library might also benefit from more graduate level courses on American politics (Political Science) and Historiography (History). The point is that each graduate student will have her/his own trajectory of what makes a relevant course. An ideal way of allowing this to encourage students to explore, and then have a form that students can submit to their advisor with a rationale for the relevance of a course. Advisers should then negotiate with students, and encourage the student to try to have any research done in the course to find a way to relate it towards their LIS/iSchool career. One certainly could make a case for relevant coursework in Communications, Data Visualization, Psychology, Media Studies, Journalism, Women's Studies or any number of departments depending on actual course content in relevance to LIS/iSchool student learning objectives. Advisers will need to balance the desire to encourage each student's broad curiosity with a reflection that the LIS/iSchool degree is a professional one, so that our graduates should be able to meet many of the employers' basic needs. As an example, students often ask permission to take introductory level language courses for credit, but most LIS/iSchools usually reply that a language class would not count, although a graduate-level research methods or bibliography related to a language should count for credit.

3 Offering in the iSchool or Electives Beyond

These expanded skills are doubtlessly introduced to some extent in existing LIS/iSchool courses, but the difference is that instruction must be able to go on a much deeper level. For example, at the University of Hawai'i (UH) LIS Program we typically spend one day on Intellectual Property in our Foundations/Ethics course and a few more in Collection Management. This, of course, can only skim the surface in introducing a number of areas and resources that students are encouraged to investigate further either in their studies or in their professional lives.

The question facing LIS/iSchool faculty is if such content should be offered in the school or as electives or core courses in other units. A more interdisciplinary approach would be to encourage students to take such courses in other departments. For example, at UH, our Law School offers a graduate course on intellectual property. Students are encouraged to take such courses when they are advertised, cross-listed, and scheduled in a way that decreases conflict. The obvious advantage of such an approach is that experts in this area would offer courses. The challenge for LIS/iSchool students is that they might not have priority in enrollment; courses in other units, such as the Law School might also be more expensive. Students also might find some challenge if they don't have a basic understanding that would be shared by most law school students. Of course, some faculty encourage interdisciplinary courses by providing reference tools and allowing students to be in teams with matching knowledge/experience.

Another option would be to offer such advanced electives through a consortium, such as the Web-based Information Science Education consortium (WISE) of primarily North American iSchools, which allows schools to share a number of courses with advanced electives that might have low enrollment at any one school. As more schools cooperate in such endeavors, it allows them to be able to offer more unique electives and sharing of experts. One real advantage of this would be to encourage faculty members who are focused on advanced research on the area, but also who can create a course that is customized to the needs of LIS/iSchool students, such as starting from a more general introduction to law or including topics like creative commons, which are of more importance to LIS/iSchool students than to the typical law school student.

If schools want to consider allowing students to take courses either in other units or via other LIS/iSchools, faculty will need to consider the prevalent requirements, which limit the number of credits taken outside the School. Traditionally, ALA-accredited schools limited students to a maximum of 9 credits (3 courses) taken from either another accredited school or another department on campus. In schools that are funded by student credit hour, either option may have a negative impact, although this will allow for students to develop a more rigorous education that meets future needs.

4   Impact on Core Competency Statements and Accreditation

Beyond the aforementioned changes to LIS/iSchools, adopting such change has implications for the profession at large. It may be time to review, revise or replace ALA's 2009 Core Competencies Statements and reflect on how ALA Committee on Accreditation (COA) Standards (2015) help or hinder an interdisciplinary approach. The standards themselves seem to encourage interdisciplinarity:

> II.3 The curriculum provides the opportunity for students to construct coherent programs of study that allow individual needs, goals, and aspirations to be met within the context of program requirements established by the school and that will foster the attainment of student learning outcomes. The curriculum includes as appropriate cooperative degree programs, interdisciplinary coursework and research, experiential opportunities, and other similar activities. Course content and sequence relationships within the curriculum are evident.

However, more recent COA mandates emphasize the need for student learning metrics, which reflects the current culture of the imperative to provide assessment documentation in higher education. LIS/iSchools are becoming quite good about establishing metrics of student learning for their own courses, but it is somewhat harder to bring in courses from other academic units in this system. Of course, each discipline is creating their own metrics to document student learning, but it is not clear if other disciplines' metrics are sufficiently interoperable in the current reporting model.

5   Towards a Conclusion and the Need for More Research

We hope that this work in progress raises questions about the need for LIS/iSchool faculty to find alternative ways of measuring required skills for current and future digital librarians. It is our belief that LIS/iSchool faculty need to continue to do surveys with employers and other stakeholders to see if we are envisioning the correct types of skills that professionals will need in order to do well on the job both in the first year, and even more importantly, five or ten years after students graduated. Our belief is that many of the technical skills will have changed completely in that period, but the longest lasting set of skills will be the ones that reflect some of these philosophical, critical, and ethical skills that are offered by this wider and more interdisciplinary curriculum which helps professionals to think about the "why" rather than focusing on the "how to" kind of question.

There is value in examining how LIS/iSchools are giving students opportunities to take courses in other departments. Some of this is gathered in the annual ALISE and ALA surveys, but we see particular value of more research on courses specifically related to educating future digital librarians. Regardless whether students learn these skills in LIS/iSchools or as electives in other academic units will be key for them to be the places that will educate the next generation of digital librarians. As brick and mortar libraries place more and more investment on their digital libraries, it will be increasingly important to have qualified professionals who not only know the best way of scanning items, providing access, and creating a digital infrastructure, but also who can do the jobs once exclusive of museum curators, archivists, or publishers on making decisions about what information should be published and made available to the world. Such decisions need qualified professionals grounded in legal practice, ethics, research methods, who are able to make the most judicious decisions about what materials to publish. This clearly is the future of libraries. It is our opinion that LIS/iSchools will be able to educate professionals for this if they work towards such an expanded curriculum.

References

American Library Association: Committee on Accreditation: Standards for Accreditation of Master's Programs in Library and Information Studies, adopted 2 February 2015. http://www.ala.org/educationcareers/sites/ala.org educationcareers/files/content/standards/Standards_2015_adopted_02-02-15.pdf. Accessed 5 June 2018

Bloom, B.S., Engelhart, M.D., Furst, E.J., Hill, W.H., Krathwohl, D.R.: Taxonomy of Educational Objectives, Handbook I: The Cognitive Domain. David McKay Co., New York (1956)

Goodsett, M., Koziura, A.: Are Library Science programs preparing new librarians? Creating a sustainable and vibrant library community, vol. 125. Michael Schwartz Library Publications (2016). http://engagedscholarship.csuohio.edu/msl_facpub/125

Shahbazi, R., Hedayati, A.: Identifying digital librarian competencies according to the analysis of newly emerging IT-based LIS jobs in 2013. J. Acad. Libr. **42**, 542–550 (2016). https://doi.org/10.1016/j.acalib.2016.06.014

Vaidhyanathan, S.: Copyrights and Copywrongs: The Rise of Intellectual Property and How it Threatens Creativity. NYU Press, New York (2003)

Wareham, E.: From explorers to evangelists: archivists, recordkeeping, and remembering in the Pacific Islands. Arch. Sci. **2**, 187–207 (2002)

ETDs, Research Data and More: The Current Status at Nanyang Technological University Singapore

Schubert Foo$^{(\boxtimes)}$ ⓘ, Xue Zhang ⓘ, Yang Ruan, and Su Nee Goh ⓘ

Nanyang Technological University, Singapore, Singapore
sfoo@ntu.edu.sg

Abstract. Open access policies and mandates are advocated by many universities around the world to make scholarly data and outputs, including theses, dissertations, and research data freely available to the public. This paper presents the current status of open-access electronic theses and dissertations (ETDs), research data repositories and Research Management Information System (RIMS) at Nanyang Technological University (NTU), Singapore, and outlines future work to promote the deposit and sharing of research related outputs and information.

Keywords: ETD · Research data · Open access
Research Information Management System

1 Introduction

Open access facilitates scholarly communication freely, as a means to solve the problem of inaccessibility, primarily due to financial constraints [1]. Suber [2] characterizes the core concept of open access as (1) no "price barriers" (e.g. subscription fees); (2) no "permission barriers" (e.g. copyright and licensing restrictions); (3) "royalty-free literature" (i.e. scholarly works created for free by authors); and (4) "minimal use restrictions" (e.g. author attribution).

Open access publications are more often cited due to their higher availability and visibility. Moreover, the publication costs for open access are generally lower than that of the publications on both online and hard copy, and the processing time for publication is also shorter and accepted articles are rapidly published online compared to those of traditional journals [3]. Open access policies (mandates) are advocated by many universities around the world to make scholarly data and outputs, including theses, dissertations, and research data freely available to the public. However, the data and publications form only a small part of documents generated in the research life cycle. Many other forms of documents such as research proposals, meeting minutes, progress reports, study instruments, IRB approvals, and so on, are also important and form the total scope and trial of information generated in the research cycle. This paper first presents the current status of open-access electronic theses and dissertations (ETDs), research data repository and research information management system (RIMS) at Nanyang Technological University (NTU), Singapore. It subsequently outlines

M. Dobreva et al. (Eds.): ICADL 2018, LNCS 11279, pp. 356–361, 2018.
https://doi.org/10.1007/978-3-030-04257-8_37

future work to grow and extend this work to facilitate the preservation and sharing of research related documents and information.

2 Current Status Open-Access ETD and Research Data at NTU

DR-NTU (Digital Repository) is NTU's institutional repository (IR) that contains research publications, ETDs and other data generated by the faculty, researchers and students. In line with the growing worldwide trend to make research publications freely available on the Internet, NTU has implemented an open access policy on its research publication and research data with effect from 1 July 2011 [4, 5]. According to the policy, the full-text of higher degree theses (PhD and Masters by research only) would be made open access. These research students are required to submit the completed full-text digital version of their theses to NTU's Library via DR-NTU. Moreover, all NTU faculty and staff are also required to deposit their final research data used for their publications.

Due to the timing of platform (DSpace) introduction, ETDs were originally submitted to DR-NTU (Restricted Access) which basically restricts access to NTU staff and students. Following the introduction of DR-NTU (Open Access) in 2008, ETDs of PhD and Master of Engineering theses were gradually checked and transferred to the new platform twice a year. Figure 1 shows the current number and percentage of these open-access ETDs in DR-NTU. It is worth noting that currently the percentage of open-access ETDs, particularly for non-STEM theses, is very low. The main reason for excluding non-engineering Master's theses from the DR-NTU (Open Access) initially was primarily due to a concern of quality at that time. In view of the improved quality with a more stringent quality control process in the schools, as well as the introduction of academic plagiarism checkers like Turnitin, the risk of poor quality is now mitigated. As such, the total number of Open Access theses is expected to grow significantly as more existing restricted theses are transferred to open access, and as new theses are submitted directly into the open access platform.

The NTU Research Data Policy was launched in April 2016. It requires Principal Investigators (PIs) to submit a data management plan (DMP) for their research projects and for research data be made available on the IR for research data. The NTU research data repository DR-NTU (Data), based on a local installation built using the open-source Dataverse software developed by Harvard University, was launched in November 2017. In the first seven months following the launch, 257 dataverses, 239 datasets and 1,655 files have been added to the repository, with 1,165 downloads for the published datasets.

The common metadata used for ETDs and datasets include community (e.g. school/department, research center/project), author, title, date of issue and subject. The unique metadata for ETDs includes type (i.e. Master or PhD), abstract and full text; while for research datasets, the unique meta-data include dataset ID, description, keywords, dataset files, related publications, grant information, kind of data, software, depositor and deposit date.

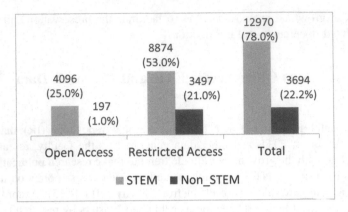

Fig. 1. Number of open vs. restricted access ETDs in NTU

As an ongoing part of the effort to better understand the research needs and practices of researchers in the university, NTU also participated in a 30-country international 'data literacy' survey [6] to understand the type of research data produced by NTU faculty and researchers, their collection and use of external research data, current research data storage avenues, data sharing concerns, and training needs for writing DMPs. The online survey for NTU was conducted over two months from December 2017 to January 2018. A total 643 responses were obtained of which 241 completed responses were used for data analysis. A snapshot of findings for NTU is elaborated below.

Figures 2 and 3 show the state of research data storage and sharing of research data by NTU researchers. It was found that only a small group of researchers were storing their data in the university's central servers or IRs. Most of the research data were stored in the researchers own devices, cloud or external repositories. This could be due lack of research data storage guidelines which leaves such storage issues at the discretion of the researchers. This situation is expected to improve over time with the recent launch of the institutional research data repository and on-going roadshows and workshops. Before the launch, there was no central platform for NTU research data to be made available for long-term archival and sharing. In terms of data sharing, the study found that majority of the researchers were mainly sharing data within their research teams. Only limited sharing is done with other researchers in the university and other institutions.

The study also elicited reasons of the researchers' concern for data sharing. Figure 4 shows that the 3 most cited concerns were attributed to those of (1) legal and ethical issues, (2) misuse of data, and (3) misinterpretation of data. NTU's advice to data depositors is for them to share their data responsibly and to provide as much metadata and data documentation as possible to facilitate proper reuse of their shared data.

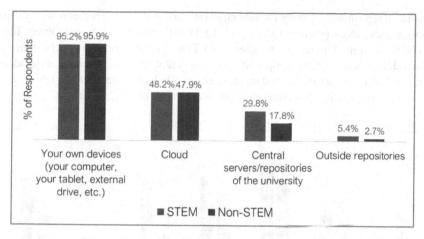

Fig. 2. Storage of research data by NTU researchers (multiple responses)

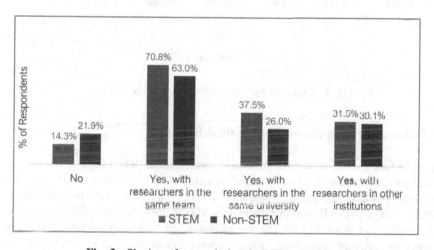

Fig. 3. Sharing of research data by NTU researchers

3   Initiatives to Promote Open Access ETDs and Research Data

NTU Library has been tasked with the responsibility, management and advocacy of DR-NTU and DR-NTU (Data). In this respect, a number of current initiatives have been undertaken to create awareness and educate researchers on the aspect of "data" in the research life cycle, and how research data needs to be properly planned, collected, processed, described, and eventually stored and curated in IRs to provide long term storage, access and re-use. Examples of activities to date have included organising regular workshops, seminars, roadshows and outreach events for researchers on managing, sharing and curating research data, and promoting the use of open access and institutional repositories. Others include engaging in collaborative projects with external collaborators/vendors (such as OATD.org, EBSCO), and use of Digital Object Identifiers (DOI) or equivalent unique handlers for ETDs to ensure long term persistence and discoverability. Such efforts are particularly important to be maintained, expanded or streamlined in future as research data management is being increasingly embraced by the research community, government departments and funding agencies [7].

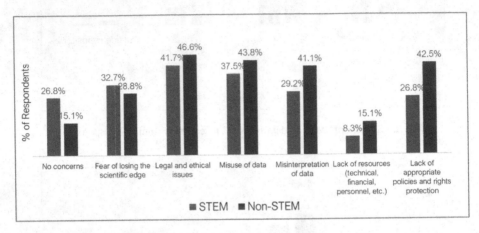

Fig. 4. Concerns for data sharing by NTU researchers

4   Future Developments and Consideration

Important functions of research information management (RIM) include registry of the institution's research outputs and facilitating external and internal assessments, internal reporting, publicly available researcher profiles and awards/grants management workflows [8]. NTU's Research Information Management System (RIMS) already has such functions in place. For the registry of institution's research outputs, NTU Library is presently actively 'recruiting' more paper publications and research data in its repositories. To expedite this work, there could be greater leverage on APIs or new ways, for example, ORCID to make it easier for research publications to be updated or deposited. Managing open access compliance is also gaining importance. More and more RIM (or CRIS) are providing such a function. This could be considered for NTU RIMS as well - specifically for checks against its papers and data repositories since the university has mandated research publications and data to be made available on open access. System built-in recording and tracking of such compliance checks would greatly reduce the current manual and tedious checks and trigger workflows. Another potential consideration would be the reporting of societal impact. Obtaining and reporting citation counts of publications are currently a pretty much manual and tedious process outside of NTU RIMS. Integrating such data into the RIMS publication lists would be very useful for annual appraisal and reporting purposes. Another potential new consideration, though possibly of less importance, could be to support the discovery of potential collaborators or expertise.

It is timely for NTU to review how it could leverage on its open access mandates, new research data repository, new potential APIs, ORCID, etc. to augment its research information management system, especially for RIM functions to include open access compliance checks and reporting societal impact. Specifically, to make DR-NTU an influential platform for collecting, preserving and promoting NTU's research outputs for open access, the planned future work includes optimization of the existing systems to improve user experience, increase open access percentage and discoverability of ETDs, research data and other publications There can also be more advocacy activities to further improve the awareness and usage of DR-NTU.

References

1. Ghosh, S.B., Kumar Das, A.: Open access and institutional repositories—a developing country perspective: a case study of India. IFLA J. **33**(3), 229–250 (2007)
2. Suber, P.: Open access overview - focusing on open access to peer-reviewed research articles and their preprints. https://legacy.earlham.edu/~peters/fos/overview.htm. Accessed 01 June 2018
3. PressAcademia: Advantages of Open Access. http://www.pressacademia.org/journals/rjbm/advantages-of-open-access. Accessed 07 June 2018
4. NTU (Nanyang Technological University). http://www.ntu.edu.sg/Library/Pages/open-access.aspx. Accessed 07 June 2018
5. NTU (Nanyang Technological University): NTU Research Data Policy. http://research.ntu.edu.sg/rieo/RI/Pages/Research-Data-Policies.aspx. Accessed 07 June 2018
6. Chowdhury, G., Walton, G. Kurbanoğlu,S., Unal, Y., Boustany, J.: Information practices for sustainability: information, data and environmental literacy In: The Fourth European Conference on Information Literacy (ECIL), Prague, 10–13 October 2016, p. 22 (2016)
7. Lee, D.J., Stvilia, B.: Practices of research data curation in institutional repositories: a qualitative view from repository staff. PLoS One **12**(3), 1–44 (2017)
8. Bryant, R., Castro, P., Clements, A.: Preliminary findings from the global survey of research information practices (2018). https://www.oclc.org/content/dam/research/themes/research-collections/Bryant_EARMA2018_Preliminary_findings_survey_RIM_practices.pdf. Accessed 25 June 2018

Author Index